Development Ethics

Nikos Astroulakis · Nikolaos Karagiannis

Development Ethics

Political Economy and Morality

palgrave
macmillan

Nikos Astroulakis
Economics
Tax and Customs Academy IAPR
and Hellenic Open University
Athens, Greece

Nikolaos Karagiannis
Economics
Winston-Salem State University
Winston-Salem, NC, USA

ISBN 978-3-031-75475-3 ISBN 978-3-031-75476-0 (eBook)
https://doi.org/10.1007/978-3-031-75476-0

This Palgrave Macmillan imprint is published by the registered company Springer Nature Switzerland AG
The registered company address is: Gewerbestrasse 11, 6330 Cham, Switzerland

Dedicated to
my mother Μαρία

— Nikos Astroulakis

my mother Σταυροστυλιανη

—Nikolaos Karagiannis

Contents

About the Authors

Nikos Astroulakis is an Economist at the Tax and Customs Academy of the Greek Independent Authority for Public Revenue, and an Adjunct Professor of Economics at the Hellenic Open University in Greece. His doctoral thesis and further research focus on Development Ethics within a Political Economy context. He has published 17 refereed journal articles and book chapters (in English, Greek, and Spanish). His paper "The Development Ethics Approach to International Development", published in the International Journal of Development Issues, was awarded by Emerald the Highly Commended Award Winner for Excellence 2012. He holds a Ph.D. in Economics from the University of Crete, Greece.

Nikolaos Karagiannis is Full Professor of Economics at Winston-Salem State University, North Carolina; a Research Scholar at the Global Institute for Sustainable Prosperity; an invited visiting scholar at the University of Cambridge, England; and the co-editor of *American Review of Political Economy*. He has published extensively in the areas of economic development, public sector economics, and macroeconomic policy analysis. He is the author, co-author, and co-editor of twenty-seven books, and has published 182 papers as refereed journal articles and book chapters and over 100 op-eds.

List of Tables

CHAPTER 1

Introduction

This book proposes a methodological framework for the holistic interpretation of the meta-ethical, normative-ethical, and applied-ethical principles that govern international development theory and policy. It also proposes a novel exploration of the study of development ethics as an important alternative approach to the dominant schools of thought of neoclassical economics and neoliberalism in international development. The idea of approaching the theme in this particular manner stems from the general perspective that the study of international development, despite the dominance of free-market economics, encompasses political, social, and ethical dilemmas. Broadly, as Fine (2004a, p. 96) observes, "[e]conomics as a discipline, in teaching, research and policy, is very poor at ethics." Relevant to this, development economics in line with neoclassical economics mainly operates by considering development as economic development, namely economic growth. Even if moral concerns are involved in the neoclassical economics theory and policy of international development, these issues are usually discussed or function in the ideologically neutral space of individual ethics. This means that ethical analysis is frequently reduced by neoclassical economists to the level of the moral preferences of the agents of the economy and the utilitarian tradition of outcome-based economic development. This can also be interpreted as an important component of an imperialism of economic

N. Astroulakis and N. Karagiannis, *Development Ethics*,
https://doi.org/10.1007/978-3-031-75476-0_1

positivism over the study of development economics and the theory and policy of international development.

In addition, the book shows that, in recent decades, neoclassical economics has performed as the intellectual defender of applied neoliberal policy in international development. More clearly, the hegemony of neoliberal policy in international development echoes the ascendancy of neoclassical economics in international development theory and policy, and vice versa. Thus, an appropriate exploration of international development should include the main aspects of neoclassical economics and neoliberalism at the levels of theory and policy.

The development ethicists' viewpoints regarding international development cannot be abstractedly positioned in the alleged ideologically and ethically neutral space of the conventional economic development theory and policy. Development ethics might need to shift its interest onto neoliberalism in the world reality of the twenty-first century. The present study contributes in this direction. We endeavour to integrate development ethics as an ethical alternative to neoclassical economics and neoliberal policy in international development, within the lines of heterodox economics, and political economy in particular.[1] In the tradition of Denis Goulet's development ethics, we accept that "[d]evelopment ethics is eclectic in its choice of subject matter but disciplined in its study of it" (Goulet, 1997, p. 1168). Therefore, the holistic-ethical investigation of international development introduces an eclectic way of approaching international development by incorporating the economy, politics, society, and related subjects. It also introduces a methodological approach to integrating these issues—the conjunction of political economy with moral philosophy.

In this opening chapter, we comprehensively address the fundamental issues that the book examines; necessary definitional explanations of the key words and terms; the research questions; the methodology used; and a prologue to the contents of the book.

[1] Although 'political economy' encompasses several major but quite different strands, our analysis emphasises realism and multi-disciplinarity, thereby stressing the importance of alternative heterodox and Post-Keynesian perspectives.

1 Conceptual Navigation for the Subject Matter of the Analysis

During the twentieth century, the study of development economics and international development gave rise to an interchange of ideas between economic development and other concepts, such as ethics. This interesting dialogue holds until now.[2] This book contributes to this dialogue in a specific manner. We deal with development ethics and international development from the perspective of political economy. In doing so, and without neglecting the existing reality in international development, we develop the process of our analysis based on the well-acknowledged methodological tools of moral philosophy and political economy.

Because of the perennial use of the terms 'ethics/ethical' and 'moral/morality', it is useful to offer an initial introductory observation about the use of these key terms from the beginning. In the study of philosophy (moral and political philosophy), the terms have somewhat subtle but different connotations. To be brief but precise, as van Staveren (2007, p. 21) notes, "[m]orality is about the actual beliefs or specific actions of individuals in terms of good and bad, whereas ethics is more general and concerns a reflection on the reasons for or against certain moral beliefs or actions." Nevertheless, in economics as a social science, including the subfield of economics and ethics, the terms 'ethics' and 'morality' are commonly used with similar meanings, as synonyms (Dutt and Wilber, 2010a, p. 4; Rowthorn, 1996, p. 15). In this book, the use of the terms is intermingled; however, we always keep in mind that 'ethics' has a broader meaning that underpins the whole spectrum of ethical actions (individual and social), while 'morality' better fits with individual beliefs and actions, as well as deontology and similar concepts.

Ethical analysis is penetrated by normative issues and value judgments. Thus, a few words of how normative issues and value judgments are elaborated by ethics and economics also seem necessary from the beginning. Normative issues are all personal or societal issues involving in their analytical investigation the "ought to be" or "should be" consideration. It includes an interplay of "what should happen in the economy, and how what is happening compares to this ideal" (Dutt and Wilber, 2010a, p. 17). In turn, value judgments are judgments that encapsulate

[2] See, for example, Arndt (1989) and Jomo and Reinert (eds.) (2005) for the history and evolution of development economics.

ethical beliefs, norms, and axioms as well as ideological postures and one's specific view of the world reality. What perhaps is equally important to mention at this point is that positive economic analysis is also entered by normative issues and value judgments in the realm of ethical analysis (see Chapter 3). To this, Hausman and McPherson (1993, p. 672) argue that "economists who refuse to 'dirty their hands' with ethical matters will not know what technical problems to investigate."

After these necessary observations, we turn to the conceptual navigation for the subject matter of the analysis. In positive neoclassical economics—the dominant intellectual concern within mainstream economics, in which economic phenomena can be adequately explained "using only certain mathematical-deductive forms of reasoning" (Lawson, 2006, p. 492; see also Dow, 2000, p. 158; Fine and Milonakis, 2009, p. 124)—international development has been chiefly perceived as a straightforward economic issue.[3] Mainstream economists, policy-makers, commentators, international organisations, and so on, have, in most cases, confronted the development problem within its global dimension in an instrumental and administrative manner. During the twentieth century, in particular, technological expansion, increased production, and the sense that people could overcome nature led many mainstream economists, government officials, and development planners to utilise an "engineering approach" to the concept of international development (Sen, 1987, p. 3). In this framework, international development was perceived as a measurable matter, as synonymous with economic growth (for instance, measuring variation in gross domestic product). Ethical inquiries into the concept of development were viewed mostly as an affair for philosophers and humanists rather than economists. To share an example regarding the debate within ethics and economics, Robbins (1945 [1932], p. 148) asserts that:

[3] "Positivism" as a philosophy of science pre-exists to "neoclassical economic positivism". In this book, we refer to neoclassical economic positivism as a specific version of positivism in economics and related areas; international development and development economics, in accordance with the historical ascendancy of neoclassical economics and the methods it uses.

> Unfortunately, it does not seem logically possible to associate the two studies in any form but mere juxtaposition. Economics deal with ascertainable facts; ethics with valuations and obligations. The two fields of enquiry are not on the same plane of discourse.

Robbins (1945 [1932]) expresses the view that perceives economics as a positive science that takes place after, or independently of, the elucidation of moral and ethical propositions.

Neoclassical economics usually confronts development as an end state of a Westernised type of development, and confronts development economics (in the form of economic growth theory and policy) as the means of achieving this kind of development. This mainstream perspective hides an economic, ideological, and ethical imperialism over the theory and policy of international development. Development is a predetermined notion. The means of achieving it are predetermined by the developed nations, international development institutions, and classes or groups of power in a similar way.

Almost half a century ago, Gunnar Myrdal posed the problem in the study of international development in its real-politics basis:

> The implication is that studies of the problem of underdeveloped countries are now too often undertaken with a view to the fortuitous and narrow political or strategic interests of one country or bloc, instead of with a view to the universal and timeless values that are our legacy from the Enlightenment. All sorts of studies are now justified by their contribution to the 'security' of the United States or Western countries (Myrdal, 1977 [1968], p. 6).

Myrdal's observations were written during the Cold War era; however, even in the period after the Cold War (1990 and beyond), the problem remains unresolved. Orthodox approaches to the study of international development, containing theory and policy, incorporate development within the interests of Western culture. A significant difference is that the strategic interests of the Western Bloc have been totally internationalised through the dominance of worldwide capitalism and the acceleration of market-based economic globalisation.

Historical analysis has shown that the orthodox economics approach—viewing development as growth—to international development cannot provide satisfactory answers to the development problems. International development has never delivered economic well-being to all nations and people in the world, as neoclassical theory often predicts. For instance, in the 1970s, Simon Kuznets (a Nobel Prize winner in economics) argued that a transformation of the economic, political, and social structure of developing and less-developed countries to the free-market economy would lead to advanced rates of economic growth (Kuznets, 1971). In the same direction, another Nobel Laureate, Milton Friedman (Friedman, 2002 [1962]), established the economic and ethical substratum of the idea that the more 'free market' an economy is, the greater the benefits of economic growth and freedom of choice for all nations and individuals. Despite these arguments, particularly after the 1970s, the applied international development policy reinforced the unequal distribution of wealth between the developed economies and groups of power and the developing world and poor people. Orthodox development economists and international development institutions have continually raised this issue over the years. They have also measured it. Nevertheless, they do not seem to have solved it. Contemporary worldwide realities prove that no considerable distance has been covered regarding ordinary problems such as water scarcity, famine, and bad sanitary conditions in the developing third world. At the same time, within developed nations, new problems have come to the fore, with massive consumption on the one side, and new, massive social groups below the poverty line on the other. Moreover, on an international scale, where development in terms of growth or industrial expansion has taken place (for instance in Brazil, China, and India), ecological destruction has been significant and social inequalities have been even more so. In the beginning of the twenty-first century, regional and personal inequalities were again at the centre of any international development discourse. For these and many other reasons, such as sovereignty conflicts, forced human migration, and resource exploitation, international development should be re-examined under considerations that arise from the ethical question of 'what is a good society?'

Over the last few decades, there has been growing interest in the study of economics and ethics. Because of the strong relevance of the discussion of economics and ethics to the study of international development and development ethics, we only mention seven selected book titles in the contemporary literature that examine the theme using a pluralistic and holistic manner within political economy and social studies. The books have been chosen chronologically. The first is *Economics and Ethics?*, edited by Groenewegen (1996). This edition comprises studies from an economist and philosopher's perspective against the background of a long utilitarian tradition in mainstream economics. The second is Vickers (1997) *Economics and Ethics: An Introduction to Theory, Institutions, and Policy*, which includes discourses on the topics of his title and focuses on the ethics–efficiency tensions that exist for both individual behaviour and societal fabrics. The third is *Ethics, Economics and Politics* by Little (2004). Little's book mainly focuses on the relation between economics and politics with moral philosophy. The fourth, *Ethics and the Market: Insights from Social Economics*, edited by Clary et al. (2006), is a collection of studies of the relation of ethical values with market functions in a social economics tradition. In the same direction, the fifth book, *Economics, Ethics and the Market* (Graafland, 2007), explores the ethical and methodological strategy of economics against ethical considerations of a mainstream economics, free-market perspective. The sixth is *The Economics of Ethics and the Ethics of Economics*, edited by Brennan and Eusepi (2009). In this book, the authors offer an interdisciplinary view on a variety of subjects in the fields of ethics, economics, and politics. The seventh, *Economics and Ethics: An Introduction* (Dutt and Wilber, 2010a), is an introductory book that navigates the reader to the interplay of moral philosophy and economics. Apart from the term 'ethics' in their titles, the common characteristic of the aforementioned literature is that the authors maintain a critical standpoint against the positive site of mainstream economics and the consideration of the value neutrality of economics as a 'natural' science.

Even though neoclassical economic positivism (both in theory and in practice) has largely followed the notion of value neutrality in the theoretical models and applied policy of international development, moral aspects never cease to influence and be influenced by development thinkers. In line with the social sciences (orthodox and heterodox), many scholars and development thinkers have admitted the perception that economic policy and economic efficiency lack ethics. This perception has gradually been established in works such as those by Boulding (1969), Arrow (1974), Hirsch (1976), Sen (1977; 1987), Buchanan (1985), Hirschman (1985), and Hausman and McPherson (1993). In addition, the ethical study of development mainly includes the discussion of the means and ends of development. In heterodoxy, there are those who advocate for the coexistence of ethical justifications and humanistic ideas within economics. For instance, Hardison and Myers (1964, p. 13) underline that there need be no conflict between economists and humanists: "The development of man for himself may still be considered the ultimate end, but economic progress can also be one of the principal means of attaining it." From the perspective of development ethics, Clark (2002a) also suggests a closer relationship between philosophers and social scientists in the field of development. He argues that, even though a great attempt has been made in this direction, further empirical work is needed in order for ethical considerations (such as what are a good life and a good society) to be adjusted to real development practices. Other influential studies in the social science perspective, within the context of an ethical justification of development, include those of Perroux (1950; 1955; 1981); Polanyi (2001 [1944]), Hirschman (1988 [1958]), Seer (1972), Griffin (1986), and Qizilbash (1996). There are also many other important studies that have considered moral issues in the fields of international development and economics in general. Some of them are mentioned in the context of the analysis, in relation to our topic.

In contemporary economic thought, development is broadly defined as economic growth plus social change. The United Nations, which speaks for worldwide economic and social development, is a strong supporter of this approach to development. Since the 1990s, the concept of a human development paradigm has been extensively accepted. According to Mahbub ul Haq, founder of the United Nations Human Development Report, "[t]he basic purpose of development is to enlarge people's choices ... The objective of development is to create an enabling environment for people to enjoy long, healthy, and creative lives."[4] In our times, as stated in this quote from the official representative of the United Nations, humanism is at the core of development discussions. In the same source, Amartya Sen, a Nobel Laureate in economics and a prominent development ethicist, states:

> Human development, as an approach, is concerned with what I take to be the basic development idea: namely, advancing the richness of human life, rather than the richness of the economy in which human beings live, which is only a part of it.

The contribution of Sen is crucial to the introduction of ethical justifications and a humanistic approach to social sciences, economics, development studies, and the field of development ethics (Sen, 1980; 1981; 1984; 1987; 1999). Sen is one of the central figures influencing the

[4] Human Development Reports: http://hdr.undp.org/en/humandev/.

equity issue within theories of justice. He also contributes to ethical affairs by perceiving the expansion of freedom as both the primary end and the principal means of development. In his influential book *On Ethics and Economics*, Sen (1987) draws a bridge between ethical matters and economic rationality. He advocates that the study of moral philosophy is inevitably necessary to the study of economics. Perhaps, Sen's most important contribution in this area lies in his critique of opulence and utility as providing appropriate meanings of development. Sen (1999) pays significant attention to the notion of "development as freedom" along with Nussbaum (2000), who also contributed to international development policy by inserting the concepts of functioning and a capability approach into international development. There is a vast discussion of Sen's literature on ethical development, as well as the issues that he highlighted for further research. Sen's contribution to the ethical study of economics and development also involves many aspects of the current development ethics discussion of international development that we are looking for in this study.

The purpose of this inquiry is to discover the principles, processes, and policy outlines that govern existing international development. To this end, the following examination involves essential thoughts and elements from the broad and pluralistic disciplines of political economy and moral philosophy. Moreover, this book critically presents and frequently stands up against the dominant viewpoints, objectives, and implied policies in contemporary international development. We argue that, in recent times, neoliberalism has been the dominant doctrine in international development, while the prevailing ideas, visions, and policies of neoliberalism in international development mainly correspond to the analytical tools of neoclassical economics (DeMartino, 2000; Lapavitsas, 2005; O'Hara, 2006; Chang, 2002; see also Saad-Filho and Johnston (eds.), 2005a; 2005b). When our analysis discusses the dominant economic theory and policy in international development, we mostly refer to neoclassical economics. Neoliberalism is supported by an alliance of schools of thought within economics by integrating, for instance, economists such as Frederick von Hayek from the Austrian school of thought, as well as many others. Nonetheless, this conceptual alliance has not always been obvious. With the aforementioned example in mind, one can safely surmise that von Hayek, to some extent, challenges neoclassical economic analysis from the angle of social liberal thinking (essays in Hayek, 1948;

Caldwell, 1988). In any case, we argue for a historically specific agreement of dominant economics on the neoliberal agenda. Following the economic and political changes of the 1970s, nationally and internationally, this agenda mainly involves the changing role of state policy and the free-market imperative. "The new terms of debate were set by neoliberal economists such as Milton Friedman, Friedrich von Hayek, George Stigler, James Buchanan, Gordon Tullock, Anne Krueger, Ian Little and Alan Peacock" (Chang, 2002, p. 540). What is important is that the analytical tools and theories of neoclassical economics remain the core intellectual background of neoliberal theory and policy in international development.

In this book, we deal with the dominant principles and tensions within economics and their interplay with the neoliberal doctrine in international development. Mainly for this reason, neoclassical economics, particularly in its dominant (positive) version, is the main objective of our critical view. Beyond the elucidation of the dominant perspectives of neoclassical economics and neoliberalism in the current appearance of international development, the development ethics alternative to those perspectives is analytically derived.

In short, development ethics is commonly defined as the ethical reflection on the means and ends of development on micro-social and macro-social levels of analysis. Ethical reflection can provide "a clearer understanding of the human condition, of the purposes of human activity, and of morally relevant facts central to decisions in political, social, economic and technological arenas" (Crocker, 2006, p. xxxii). Both neoclassical economics and development ethics are placed in an original analytical framework based on a moral philosophy and political economy approach.

Placing economic analysis in the tradition of political economy principally means and/or implies that economics belongs to the social sciences. Even though the social nature of economics in the context of political economy can be noticed in many different ways, political economy can be broadly seen as the study of people and society, including political and economic aspects, within a historically reliable method. In the initial page of their book *From Political Economy to Economics*, Milonakis and Fine (2009) propose that:

> The prime rationale underpinning this account is to put the case for political economy back on the agenda. This is done by treating economics as

> a social science once again. It involves transcending the boundaries of the social sciences through the reintroduction and full incorporation of the social and the historical into the main corpus of political economy, by drawing on the rich traditions of the past.

In this book, we put economics back on the agenda of political economy as a social science. In this light, the study of international development within the political economy context means (at least) that the economic, political, and social factors are embodied. Furthermore, we add the moral factor into the analysis. This analysis argues that economics in the political economy context has a moral dimension, which is required in the examination of international development.

One of the fundamental arguments of this book is that an adequate manner of studying the theme can be by using economics in the tradition of political economy and by addressing ethical questions in the discipline of moral philosophy. In this framework, we clearly argue that ethics alone does not adequately explain the world reality because the world reality overcomes ethical analysis. Primarily, the world reality results in historically reliable social interests. Ethical analysis is somehow subjected to them. For instance, Rawls (1951, p. 191) notes that:

> [W]e cannot determine the justness of a situation by examining it at a single moment. We must know what interests were in existence prior to its establishment and in what manner its present characteristics have been determined by human actions.

Even though the ethical study of human actions is necessary, it is not sufficient to understand the world reality if we see it apart from the broad social interests in existence. In our analysis, capitalism is the dominant worldwide economic system nowadays (Fukuyama, 1992). Thus, if one desires to analyse adequately the social reality in international development, it is essential to acknowledge the political economy concerns of the real world or, as Fine (2004a, p. 101) proposes, the "political economy of capitalism". On the other hand, we must never ignore that, in the tradition of (classical) political economy, "if we are going to wrestle with the ethical issues embedded in economics—both in theory and in policy—we must turn to philosophic ethics for help" (Wilber, 2004, p. 428). From the perspective of development ethics, Clark (2002a, p. 830) also suggests that "it is only through the synbook of scientific inquiry and philosophical reflection that we will uncover the central human values behind a more realistic and reliable development ethic." In this respect, the book investigates international development in the contexts of both political economy and moral philosophy.

In addressing the appropriate ethical questions in the investigation of international development, we accept the conceptual categorisation within the lines of moral philosophy. For moral philosophers, an ethical argument can be adequately analysed in a three-dimensional space: the meta-ethical, the normative-ethical, and the applied-ethical (Kagan, 1998, p. 2; Williams, 2006, p. 72; Frankena, 1951, p. 45). Accordingly, meta-ethics focuses on the ethical meaning and reasoning of the moral argument. Even more broadly, "[m]eta-theory occupies the debatable ground between philosophy and theory itself" (Hodgson, 2001, p. xiv). Normative ethics corresponds to the manner of how things should or ought to be; thus, it remarks on an ethical evaluation of the ethical argument. Finally, applied ethics refers to the ethical guidelines of the ethical argument as it functions in real-world situations. In this book, the ethical argument, which is being investigated, is based on inquiries into the conceptions of a good life and a good society in the holistic framework of international development. Taking into account the categorisation within moral philosophy, the research objectives and questions posed are as follows:

- *Meta-ethical level of analysis:* What is the nature of international development? This question reflects the vision with which each specific theoretical analysis views the end state of development. Moreover, meta-ethical analysis symbolises an image of a good society, based on ethical pre-beliefs, ideologies, axioms, values, theories, and the existing reality as a point of departure.
- *Normative-ethical level of analysis:* What should the relationship be between the means and the ends of international development? The discussion within normative-ethical responses is the way in which the end state of development, the particular vision of a good society, can be achieved. It constitutes a normative evaluation of the moral argument: a debate between the possible outcomes and instruments of a good society.
- *Applied-ethical level of analysis:* What form of applied ethics could be the most appropriate to policy in international development? Any attempt to formulate policy in international development confronts

practical and applied ethical issues. Applied ethics refers to those policy issues in any field of development: economy, politics, and society. The vision of a good society and the normative evaluation of how this vision can be achieved are shaped by applied ethics in specific policies.

To our knowledge, no such methodological exploration of international development has been attempted before. We do not claim that this book offers all answers or the only right ones; this inquiry is an attempt towards developing a novel paradigm for the ethical investigation of international development theory and policy from the perspective of moral philosophy and political economy. Students and scholars of economics and development studies, as well as the development ethics community, may find this approach useful. Policy-makers and development planners can also use this study to enhance their knowledge of the normative appraisal of international development, which this approach offers.

Regarding the use of the terms 'approach' and 'paradigm', in *The Structure of Scientific Revolutions*, Thomas Kuhn argues that "[t]hese I take to be universally recognized scientific achievements [paradigms] that for a time provide model problems and solutions to a community of practitioners" (Kuhn, 1970 [1962], p. viii). The Kuhnian perspective applies not only to mainstream but also to heterodox economics (Drakopoulos and Karayiannis, 2005).[5] In light of this, we claim that this inquiry is an effort towards developing a scientific paradigm. Thus, the term 'approach' is more often mentioned in the following discussion. Nevertheless, the use of both terms ('approach' and 'paradigm') refers to an initial but original attempt in the direction of analysing the world reality in a scientifically precise manner. In addition, as is well stated in the methodologies of social sciences and economics, whether orthodox or heterodox, what we label here as a scientific paradigm or approach is an effort to simplify the complexities of the reality (Dow, 2002; Blaug, 1992 [1980]). Referring to international development policy, Marangos (2009a, p. 200) points out that "[p]aradigms necessarily abstract from details so as to develop a framework to understand the complexities of the real world and attempt to reflect actual practices and economic processes."

[5] See also the special issue of the *Review of Radical Political Economy* in 1971, Vol. 3(2).

Equally important to the formulation of a scientific paradigm is the worldview, as well as the pre-existing value judgements in accordance with this worldview. Referring to this, Dutt and Wilber (2010a, p. 24) state that:

> A world view greatly influences the scientific paradigm out of which one works; value judgments are closely associated with the world view; theories must remain coherent with the world view; facts themselves are theory-laden; and therefore, the whole scientific venture is permeated by value judgments from the start.

Going even deeper, for the present analysis, value judgements are penetrated by ideological perspectives and interests. The ideological viewpoints and interests, as well as the political and historical heritage of each school of thought and economic theory, play a significant role in the formulation of a scientific paradigm within the lines of this theory. It is, to a large extent, the ideology and interests that influence the world views of a scientific paradigm within a specific school of thought. In such a manner, we might agree with the remark of Wilber (2004, p. 426):

> This world view shapes the interests of the scientist and determines the questions asked, the problems considered important, the answers deemed acceptable, the axioms of the theory, the choice of relevant facts, the hypotheses proposed to account for such facts, the criteria used to assess the fruitfulness of competing theories, the language in which results are to be formulated, and so on.

Nonetheless, there is a possible obstacle that can result in the generalisation of a scientific paradigm. There is always the danger for a general theory in action to "clumsily obscure all historical and geographical differences between different socio-economic systems" (Hodgson, 2001, p. 12). For instance, neoclassical economics interprets almost all socioeconomic issues as universal in place and ahistorical in time. As Myrdal (1977 [1968], p. 8) stresses, "[e]conomic theorists [implying dominant economics], more than other social scientists, have long been disposed to arrive at general propositions and then postulate them as valid for every time, place, and culture." However, because "[a] fundamentally different object of analysis may require a different theory" (Hodgson, 2001, p. 23), in the proposed analysis within the agenda of international development, neoclassical economics and development ethics do not, at all times, use a parallel examination of international development. Nevertheless, much effort has been made towards the formation of the responses of development ethics to neoclassical economics theory and policy regarding international development.

The original contribution to knowledge is the initial effort towards developing a paradigm of thinking and practice in international development issues without neglecting important factors, such as the existing reality of the ascendance of neoclassical economics and neoliberalism in international development theory and policy. Hence, the book provides an ethical evaluation of neoclassical economics and neoliberalism. Furthermore, it introduces the reader to the field of development ethics in a specific way. It is the first time since the 1960s and the foundation of development ethics for a book—in the field of development ethics—to seek to put together ethical reflection, application, and practice regarding ethical international development. Moreover, if we accept that contemporary international development is considered by neoclassical orthodoxy as a globalised market economy, and if we take seriously the evolution of neoliberalism in global affairs, markets, and societies, then we need to uncover the alleged value neutrality of orthodox economics by deepening our investigation into the ethical rules of neoclassical economics and neoliberalism. Thus, development ethics has to offer its alternative theoretical and policy proposals not abstractly but in response to the specific neoclassical economics theory and policy in international development.

The objective of the field of development ethics is the ethical study of development, locally, nationally, and internationally. Regarding this, Gasper (2008, p. 457) points out that "[d]evelopment ethics is an untidily bounded subject about untidy and often unpleasant realities." For development ethics, a central point of investigation would be the "untidy and often unpleasant realities" in international development, in a methodologically disciplined framework. Such a framework avoids, as far as possible and within the time available, the "untidily bounded" rhetoric within development ethics. From the literature on development ethics, there has not been a methodologically solid framework for the holistic-ethical investigation of international development. However, regarding its epistemological foundation, Goulet, the conceptual founder of development ethics, sees it as an intellectual field that belongs to the social sciences. Furthermore, development ethics accepts the principles of the interdisciplinarity in the choices of topics, in an eclectic manner. As Goulet (2006a, p. 64; 1992b, p. 140) mentions, for a development ethicist, theoretical writings are based on "the epistemological validation of value analysis and critique in the conduct of social science to arrive at a severely disciplined eclecticism." In the ethical study of international development, this severely disciplined eclecticism has not been clearly served by the existing literature on development ethics. In addition, sometimes, development ethicists act similarly to a number of pure philosophers who scrutinise the meaning of an ethical argument while abandoning the totality of the world reality. From our point of view, the dominance of neoclassical economics and neoliberalism, present in international development theory and policy, surrounds the existing reality.

The foundation of development ethics, like the foundations of other intellectual fields of study, appears to involve areas of consensus and controversy, which have been reviewed by development ethicists (Crocker, 1998; 2008; Goulet, 2006b; Gasper, 2008; Parfitt, 2012). For instance, Crocker (2008) underscores the sources of development ethics, the areas of agreement, and some controversies, mainly regarding the scope and the formulation of development ethics. In the words of Crocker (2008, p. 43), "no consensus exists on whether or how development ethics should extend beyond its central concern of assessing the development ends and means of poor, traditional, or nonindustrial societies." Nevertheless, apart from the rightful controversies among development ethicists regarding different aspects, there is an omission in the development ethics literature on the ethical discussion of a good society in the agenda of international development. We can find elements in the direction of the ethical argument of what comprises a good society in several works by development ethicists and, even more frequently, we can come across the issue of a good life and similar concepts (Dower, 1988; Crocker, 1991; 2008; Gasper, 2004; 2012; St. Clair, 2007). Nevertheless, to date, there has not been a precise methodological framework for the examination of the ethical argument of a good society in the holistic image of international development from the angle of development ethics.

The methodological framework suggested here is built in the tradition of social economics and heterodox political economy. In general, "[i]t [heterodoxy] is to be distinguished from the mainstream by its willingness to approach theory and method in a manner informed by available insights into the nature of social reality" (Lawson, p. 502; see also Lee, 2008, p. 27). In this book, this is mentioned as the 'political economy approach or context'. More precisely, a mutual belief within heterodoxy is that a good society cannot exist if deprived of the notion of the common good. In any school of thought within the tradition of heterodox political economy, a good society is the expression of specific notions of the common good. In heterodox political economy, the concept of the common good in a society is much more than a pecuniary issue.

We deliver two examples from the post-Keynesian and Marxian traditions. On the post-Keynesian side, Davidson and Davidson (1988, p. 3) point out that a good or civilised society, in the words of the authors, "provides the opportunity for all to earn a livelihood, while it encourages excellence in all endeavours that people undertake independent of the monetary rewards for such activities." Marxists usually find the meaning of a good society in a collective society. From a Marxist point of view, for example, Campbell (2012, pp. 28–29), mentioning the post-capitalist society of socialism as a necessary stage in the establishment of communism as the ideal type of end-state society (a good society), writes:

> Among the specifics that they [Marx and Engels] mention as characteristics of a near-term post-capitalist (socialist) society are a collective society, democratic decision-making, common ownership of the means of production, the end of money and markets and their replacement with democratic planning, individual labour carried out consciously as part of the total social labour, and an equal claim on the social product in accord with the time one contributes to social production.

In heterodox economics (including orientations by different school of thoughts within political economy), ethics and a good society are frequently approached within a market framework (Clary et al. (eds.), 2006a; 2006b). Nevertheless, a position that overlaps heterodoxy is that "the economic sphere is embedded within the larger social sphere, and 'the economy' and 'society' are not viewed as separate or at least separable spheres of life activity" (Clary et al., 2006, p. 1). Heterodox economists usually comment on the common good as an opposite concept to self-interest: "an effective and equitable economy cannot be built on calculated self-interest; significant decisions must be made for the common good" (Waters, 1988, p. 118). A good society is a social and ethical concept that is vastly based on the notion of the common good (Marangos (ed.), 2012; Dolfsma et al., 2005; Yeager, 2001; Lutz, 1999; Rothschild, 1993).

The present analysis of the ethical discussion of a good society is very near to Goulet's writings, particularly when he raises questions on "authentic development" (Goulet, 1975a; 1995; 1996; 2006a). Goulet's contribution to development ethics is essential to the foundation of the field (see Chapter 2). Almost the entire development ethics community acknowledges his role in building the foundation of development ethics as a distinctive field of knowledge among social studies, philosophy, and the humanities. In recent years, some reviews of the work and contribution of Goulet to development ethics have been offered by Drydyk (2013), Dutt and Wilber (2010b), Gasper and St. Clair (2010a, 2010b, [Ch. Introduction]), Gasper (2004; 2012), Crocker (2007), Dower (1998a; 1998b; 2010), and Parfitt (2012), among others. Astroulakis (2011; 2013a; 2013b) and Marangos and Astroulakis (2009; 2012) specify the ethical concept of a good society in the framework of international development from the angle of development ethics, and of Goulet in particular.

Consistent with Goulet's development ethics, in this book, a good society is identified as a question of values and the foundation—locally, nationally, and internationally—of a new, improved, and sustainable civilisation. On this note, Goulet (2006a, p. 176) states that "[d]evelopment is above all else a question of human values and attitudes, goals self-defined by societies, and criteria for determining what are tolerable costs to be borne, and by whom, in the course of change." The fundamentals of a good society are summed up in the good lives of people, social justice, and environmental consciousness. Ethics should be viewed not only as ends but also as 'the means of the means' (the ethics of means) of development in this regard. In a few words, any societal change ought to be challenged ethically at the level of means and ends.

The term 'good society' is, more or less, a synonym of the term 'development' as it is used in the development ethics literature and Goulet's writings. In the present analysis, we sometimes use the term 'ethical development', which refers to a good society as well. This clarification is made to distinguish between development ethics and the conventional approaches to development, essentially the neoclassical economics approaches of development as growth, as well as other mainstream approaches that confront development as 'economic plus social change' (e.g., the United Nations' approach). Referring to the conventional way of describing development, Goulet (2001, pp. 29–30) points out that "[t]he study of development was not a critical inquiry into societal value change, but a technical examination of how to mobilize resources efficiently and fashion institutional arrangements best suited to growth." Hence, in this book, the terms 'good society', 'development', and 'ethical development' are sometimes intermingled to specify the aim and process of development as mentioned above.

In addition, an important definitional inquiry is interwoven with the use of the term 'international development'. The term is employed in its broadest usage, within the context of political economy. International development is perceived as identical to 'global development': a term that has gained ground recently and involves the discussion of ethical issues in international development (see, for example, Soubbotina, 2004). There are two main reasons behind the decision to keep the 'old' term in this book. First, international development is based on a historical heritage—from colonialism to industrialisation and to modernism (and/or postmodernism). Sometimes, the terminology used embodies this historical background. Second, international development is closer to the subject matter of political economy (and international political economy), and it is within this topic that the present analysis takes place. In the context of political economy, international development can be seen as a concept that describes the theory and policy of related economic, political, and social issues.

In the development economics textbooks, the term 'international development' usually refers to specific geographical areas: mainly Africa, Latin America, and East Asia. This might have been useful in the twentieth-century examination of international development. However, since the last decades of the past century, the application of neoliberalism to developed and developing economies, the end of the Cold War in 1990, the collapse of the former bloc of planned economies and, finally, the emergence of economies such as China, India, and Brazil have moved the attention of the traditional theories in the study of international development towards more extensive views. In this globalised world economy, international development cannot adequately be investigated in strict geographical terms, as occurred in the past.

International development mainly portrays the process whereby national and international markets are combined into a single but complex whole. For many, this process is labelled 'globalisation'. In this book, we call it a globalised market economy, in order to emphasise the ascendency of the market mechanism to the global economy in the process of globalisation. However, international development is a historically dynamic term. From this point of view, international development describes a process in a specific global historical, geographical, and socioeconomic environment.

For example, the politics and economics of some of the Eastern European countries were different in the period of the Cold War. Economic and political conditions, as well as the sovereignty map, dramatically changed after the collapse of the Soviet Union and the decomposition of the former Yugoslavia in the 1990s. Consequently, in line with history, geography, and socioeconomic environments, the concept of international development does not refer to the developing or less-developed world only. It is not limited to the poor South—Latin American, Asian, and African countries—as is usually mentioned in the standard textbooks of international development theory.

By accommodating a broader conception of the term, in political economy, 'international development' (as can be determined from the adjective 'international') refers to developing countries as well as to transition economies (Central and Eastern Europe) and emerging economies (China, Brazil, and India)—among others (Bozyk, 2006). The Human Development Report (2013), *The Rise of the South: Human Progress in a Diverse World*, indicates the emergence of the global South in international development discussions. However, what perhaps is more crucial is the unequal distribution of global wealth among elites and non-elites. Regarding this, the authors of the report mention that

> Indeed, one can go further and state that there is a 'south' in the North and a 'north' in the South. Elites, whether from the North or the South, are increasingly global and connected, and they benefit the most from the enormous wealth generation over the past decade, in part due to accelerating globalization (Human Development Report, 2013, p. 2).

By accepting the examination of international development within the context of a globalised market economy, it means that the developed world is involved in at least two ways. First, since the middle of the 1970s, globalisation has followed the principles of neoliberalism, mostly derived from the advanced developed nations on both sides of the Atlantic Ocean: the United States and the United Kingdom. Second, the new conditions of globalisation, particularly since the worldwide economic and financial crisis of 2008, have affected unequally most of the people in the developed world.

One additional reason for approaching international development in the spectrum of the developing world and the developed world could be the persistence and, sometimes, the enhancement of worldwide economic dualism between developed and developing nations and societies. The international development problem of the global South is, so far, derived from the dominance of the global North. In addition, it is important to mention the role of international development institutions such as the World Bank, the World Trade Organization, and the International Monetary Fund, which all mainly specialise in the international development of the South while their headquarters are based in the North. Still, more importantly, they follow a specific set of neoliberal policies usually termed the 'Washington Consensus' (Fine et al. (eds.), 2003; Marangos, 2009b; Williamson (ed.), 1990a; 1990b). Indeed, the study of international development always entails conflicts and economic dualism between the North and the South, advanced and less-advanced economies, capital and work, elites and non-elites, rich and poor, and strong and vulnerable societies/people.

Therefore, international development involves the developed world and the developing world. For the aforementioned reasons, the view of the present analysis matches with perspectives of studies in the field of development ethics. This view is in agreement with Crocker's (2008, p. 43) statement that "restricting development ethics to 'developing' countries is defective" in many ways.

During the twentieth century, orthodox views related to development ethics have reduced the intersection between economics, politics, and philosophy. Neoclassical economics has become increasingly mathematical. But such a partial methodology has deprived our understanding of real-world issues. Furthermore, neoclassical economists largely ignore the role of the social character of economics and the contribution of moral philosophers and classical political economists to this topic. Bowels et al. (1999, p. 2) underline that the forefather (Leon Walras) of neoclassical economics,

> [I]n laying out the precepts of the then-young neoclassical paradigm, sharply distinguished his contributions from the social economics of the classical founders of the discipline and from his contemporaries in the German historical school and Marxian political economy. He sought a 'pure science' of economics as 'a relationship among things,' not 'people.'

As previously stated, Sen (1987) was vocal on the engineering perspective of mainstream economics towards any of the issues that it incorporates. However, the term not only refers to the manner in which mainstream economists incorporate economic phenomena as "logistic issues" and human behaviour as "being based on simple and easily characterizable motives" (Sen, 1987, p. 4) but also to the actual engineering tradition of neoclassical economics, mainly based on the work of Walras in the nineteenth century. Walras (1954 [1874]), and Jevons (1911 [1871]), among others, established the principles of marginalism and the general equilibrium theory in economics.

One basic connotation of neoclassical economics can be found by considering the prefix 'neo', which reflects the new stance or ideology of economics as a pure natural science that encompasses economic and social conditions in a marginalistic manner. This new approach to economic theory and policy—usually marked as the Marginal Revolution—has been characterised by the broad usage of the concept of marginal utility to explain economic and non-economic activities. Additionally, during the twentieth century, a transformation occurred in mainstream economics towards economic positivism. In respect of the philosophy of economic science (involving the history and methodology of economics), Terence Hutchison, a defender of logical positivism in economics, puts it clearly:

> The task of the economist is pure deduction from selected postulates of what we have called 'propositions of pure theory', that is, propositions devoid of all empirical factual content and concerned solely with terminology" (Hutchison, 1938, p. 53) … "Apart from pure Logic and Mathematics, scientific knowledge, explanation, and prognosis can only be based ultimately on empirical regularities (Hutchison, 1938, p. 163).

Based on such philosophical positions, some of the world-leading neoclassical economists have followed the root of economic positivism. In his well-known essay *The Methodology of Positive Economics*, Friedman (1953) stresses the importance of positivism to the formulation of the economic science. Accordingly, economics is a predictive science, but not at all explanatory. "Economists seek significant and usable predictions, not understanding or explanation" (Friedman, 1953, p. 7; see also Hausman, 1989, p. 120). Economic positivism accepts the sturdy posture that economy and society are ruled by general laws. Furthermore, economists, like other natural scientists, can discover those laws using the methods of 'pure' sciences, such as mathematics, to attain scientifically correct predictions. As Davidson and Davidson (1988, p. 58) remark,

> The 'hard science' claim of neoclassical economics recommends itself to the self-interest ideology of the powerful, for it rationalizes the existing distribution of income, wealth, and power as the natural outcome of some immutable law of nature.

Moreover, positivist analysis has influenced the methodologies of most of the social sciences, particularly in the second half of the twentieth century (Caldwell, 1994 [1982]; Fine and Milonakis, 2009).

The fields of development economics and international development have been similarly influenced by the aforementioned tendency. As Cross and Strachan (2001, p. 181) point out, "[s]ince the 1970s, a revival of 'classical'—that is neoclassical—nostrums about how economic systems work and how economic policy should be conducted has held sway over most of the economic world." In this book, we challenge the 'economic imperialism', based on neoclassical economic positivism, and support the social character of development economics and international development policy. One expression of neoclassical economic positivism in the international economy is monetarism. Monetarism—the policy doctrine of economic stabilisation through (nominal) interest rates, the supply of money, and inflation policy (mainly through the restriction of public spending and wages)—has prevailed in the macroeconomic level of international development policy in recent debates.

What is also important for our analysis is the ideology and ethics behind it. In *The Economic Theory and Ideology*, Fine (1980, p. 14) writes:

> The contribution to ideology of bourgeois economics[6] [neoclassical economics in our case], from the marginalism of the 1870s to the monetarism of the modern day might even be considered more significant than the role played by the theory in formulating policy.

In line with this statement, we argue that the transformation of economics from (classical) political economy to neoclassical economics and, soon after, to economic positivism raises ideological and ethical aspects that must be investigated. The field of development economics and the study of international development can also be better explained through their

[6] 'Bourgeois economics' is a Marxist term that refers to an economic ideology that focuses on the interest of the capitalists or, more broadly, the upper classes (bourgeoisie).

ideological and ethical examination without neglecting the economic aspects in the pluralistic heritage of political economy.

Relevant to this, we argue for a development ethics alternative to neoclassical economics because development ethics fits with the study of international development and its moral dimensions, while neoclassical economics is mainly harmonised with economic development theories and the applied neoliberal policy. Jomo (2005, pp. vi–viii), the editor of *The Pioneers of Development Economics: Great Economists on Development*, argues that, during the twentieth century,

> Development economics was first challenged [by neoclassical orthodoxy] and then overwhelmed by neoliberal dogma, which took the form of the 'Washington Consensus'... the recent 'new' development economics continues the intellectual offensive against a development economics tradition that constitutes an alternative to the Washington Consensus.

The 'new' or dominant development economics—the area within neoclassical economics that examines international development issues—mostly focuses on the materialistic nature of development. Economic growth, based on economic efficiency, guides international development policy. Economic rationalism in international development—the concept that nation-states and international institutions should increase their efficiency levels by leaving as much as possible of the decision-making up to the free market—is perhaps the foremost normative idea that is leading contemporary development policy (Pusey, 1991; Wright, 2003). This can also explain the belief of neoliberals in the benefits of the free market and the formulation of the applied development policy in the whole spectrum of international development. Development ethics, in the tradition of political economy, and 'old' development economics approach development and the concept of a good society not as issues of economic efficiency, in which there are winners and losers, but as the material and spiritual enhancement of all people and societies: the "human ascent", as Goulet often describes it (Goulet, 2006a, pp. 5–6).

2 The Description of Each Chapter

Because development ethics is a relatively new field within social studies and the humanities, an accurate and analytical view of the foundation of the field beyond its definition is needed. Therefore, Chapter 2 focuses on this topic. The chapter begins with the origins and identification of the field in relation to the theme of the book. Special consideration is given to the Aristotelian influence on development ethics, particularly the ethical incorporation of a good life and a good society, to which considerable attention has not been offered before in the development ethics literature. We also show that development ethics approaches the notion of a good society in a similar manner to Aristotle's *Nicomachean Ethics* and *Politics*. In this chapter, we review the underpinnings of Louis-Joseph Lebret and (his student) Denis Goulet's development ethics. In the 1940s, Lebret set the foundation for development ethics; Goulet, from the 1970s until his death in 2006, formulated the field of development ethics.

Then, we discuss the evolution of development ethics from Goulet's 1970s development ethics to the establishment of the International Development Ethics Association, in 1987, and beyond. In the introduction of the volume titled *New Directions in Development Ethics* and subtitled *Essays in Honor of Denis Goulet*, Dutt and Wilber (2010b, p. 1) maintain that "[t]he field [of development ethics] is a small one in terms of the number of people who have worked in it, but it is attracting a growing number of adherents both among academics and development practitioners from all over the world." Most of these adherents, whose work is related to our topic, are mentioned in the following chapters. Almost the entire development ethics community, individual positions aside, accepts Goulet's conceptual tradition of assessing development ethics as the ethical study of values in relation to local and international development. One of the main remarks of the analysis is that substantial work has been carried out in the areas of social justice, human rights, and basic needs, encapsulating Sen's idea of a capability approach in human development. Nevertheless, no attention has been paid to the holistic investigation of international development within a methodologically coherent framework.

Chapter 3 provides the analytical framework of the book. This analytical framework develops the study's techniques and processes: it is the *modus operandi* of the inquiry. In this part, we offer the book's basic elements of examining international development by combining the political economy tradition with its ethical orientations. Similarly, we open the discussion of how ethics is perceived in this effort. To this end, a distinction between 'individual ethics' and 'social ethics' is offered. One of the central ethical postures of the mainstream is that society is the sum of its individual agents (individuals, households, and business units);

thus, the sum of their individualistic preferences comprises the preferences of society as a whole. Likewise, ethical choices or actions are the subject matter of the ethical examinations of those individual agents. This belief implies that the market mechanism can work ethically if any of the agents that compose it act in an ethically correct way. Hence, in 'deontological ethics', an action is considered ethically good because of some attribute of the action itself.[7] In contrast, we maintain the position that society is more than the sum of individual preferences working smoothly in the market (Dugger, 1977). Social ethics refers to personal and social interactions, social norms, beliefs, and institutions in historical heritage.

Thus, the ethical questions posed should have objectives that relate to society as a whole, involving people's lives. In this manner, we put the research questions into the different categories of moral philosophy—meta-ethics, normative ethics, and applied ethics—from the perspective of social ethics. In this chapter, we also deploy the position that international development is viewed by neoclassical economics and its neoliberal counterparts as a globalised market economy. A key position is that neoliberalism is a political, economic, and ideological dogma with specific ethics; in other words, it constitutes an "ethic in itself" (Harvey, 2005, p. 3; see also DeMartino, 2000). Therefore, development ethics must not be addressed in an abstract and ideologically neutral framework but in relation to the dominant views of neoclassical economics and the existing reality. To this end, development ethics can be better explained (and can give a better interpretation of international development) within a political economy context in conjunction with moral philosophy.

In Chapter 4, we explore the meta-ethical basis of international development. Meta-ethical analysis of international development results in the vision for a better life and a good society according to the specific economic, ideological, and ethical postures of each theoretical analysis. Contemporary international development theory and policy are dominated by neoclassical economics. Therefore, we examine the meta-ethical orientation of neoclassical economics. In this respect, we mainly focus on the following concepts: 1. individual ethics and self-interest; 2. utilitarianism and utility maximisation; and 3. economic rationality, along with the notion of *homo economicus*. Social justice via ordinary people's

[7] Deontology mostly refers to the duties and obligations of the moral agents. Accordingly, 'deontological ethics' argues that at least some actions are morally obligatory regardless of their consequences for human welfare.

participation and the enhancement of capabilities are viewed in a subjective manner. Furthermore, the analysis develops the general meta-ethical view of contemporary international development as a globalised market economy, as well as the end state of development as economic well-being and consumer society in a Westernised mode. As Brown (2004, p. 212) argues, "[t]he notion of 'more is better' is a basic tenet of consumerism." We also point out that the "more is better" ethical position, along with outcome-based economic development, in the existing social and productive relationships leads international development to ecological destruction, resource exploitation, and highly unequal distribution of world wealth. To this unpleasantness, development ethics approaches the vision of a good society differently: it considers the good lives of all people in the world in the sense of human ascent. Finally, sustainability with the natural environment is considered as a component of a good society and international development.

In Chapter 5, the normative-ethical evaluation of international development is explored. Development is a process between means (institutions and policy instruments) and ends (objectives and outcomes). Normative-ethical analysis evaluates this relationship. We explain the reasons why even positive economics is penetrated by normative-ethical analysis. Furthermore, we address the position that the normative nature of neoclassical economics is principally represented by social choice theory and welfare economics. In turn, international development theory and policy are associated with the dominant normative-ethical dimension of neoclassical economics. With regard to this, our intention is to show that, either at the level of the ends or at the level of the means, international development is valued and ethically predetermined. The fundamental normative principles, which govern international development theory and policy, are interwoven with the welfarism of neoclassical economics (Hausman and MacPherson, 2006), economic rationalism, and neoliberal ideology. Development ethics deals *ex professo* with normative-ethical issues in development (Goulet, 1997, p. 1161; Crocker, 1991, p. 457; Gasper, 2004, pp. 18–19). In this part, we associate the development ethics normative assessment of the ends and means of international development with the preceding evaluation of neoclassical economics during the years of neoliberalism. As a result, we offer a clear view of the normative-ethical goals and strategies in international development as an alternative normative-ethical proposal to neoclassical economics and neoliberalism from the angle of development ethics.

In Chapter 6, the applied-ethical incorporation of international development is addressed. Applied ethics reflects the meta-ethical postures and normative-ethical evaluation of international development. Because of the individualistic nature of applied ethics, neoclassical economists frequently approach it in development (local, national, and international) as a form of business ethics. We challenge this mainstream stance in the analysis of applied ethics in international development. Also, in this part, applied ethics is positioned at the macro-social level of global ethics. In this light, we assume that free-market relations overlap with applied-ethical policy in contemporary international development. Thus, the leading applied-ethical structural factors in international development can be found: first, in the examination of free-market relations; second, in policies applied at the national level and the role of nation-state policy[8]; and third, in the rules, canons, and policies established by international development institutions. On the latter issue, the Washington Consensus policy in Latin America and internationally is examined as an applied-ethical example of the dominant international development institutions' policies in the developing world. Finally, in each of the levels mentioned before, we reveal the main policy theory elements of neoclassical economics and development ethics regarding international development.

The final chapter of the book, Chapter 7, is titled "Conclusion: Neoliberalism in International Development and the Comprehensive Development Ethics Alternative". The purpose of the concluding chapter is to clearly review the fundamental remarks of the analysis. One of the main tasks of the field of development ethics is to avoid the hindrance of ethical development by partial intellectual approaches. The application of development ethics to international development must ultimately contribute to this goal. In our analysis, we underline the methodological position that an alternative framework needs to be clearly specified. The particular results of the analysis of the ethical postures that overlap with international development are discussed, and specific alternative ethical viewpoints of development ethics in a political economy context are singled out. After the evaluation of the dominant perspectives (i.e., neoclassical economics and neoliberalism) in contemporary international

[8] Neither theorists nor practising policy-makers can ignore the vital and important role of state structures and institutions in achieving successful developmental outcomes. Experiences clearly show that developmental action can take place in diverse political and organizational settings.

development, a comprehensive framework for development ethics is offered.

To this end, it might be useful to put forth some specific comments. In the ethical study of international development, as in any other form of social science analysis, there are always limitations and simplifications. We could say that, because of the nature of the subject matter of this book—the involvement of ethics in (development) economics and international development theory and policy—the analysis is perhaps more intricate than that of other studies of political economy. However, we attempted to avoid many of the inadequacies that were pointed out in our analysis.

These difficulties are not only reflected in the meanings and context but also in the writing, terminology, and overall structure of the book. Therefore, a few more conceptual notes might be useful for the reader. First, the authors of the analysis come from a political economy background. As usual, the viewpoint and intellectual background of the scholar play a substantial role in the manner of analysis. For this reason, the incorporation of ethics and the terminology used have been mostly viewed from a political economy perspective, rather than from a moral philosophical perspective. Thus, the viewpoint is from economics to ethics, instead of from ethics to economics. Second, regarding the incorporation of development ethics, the literature review and bibliography strictly focus on those studies in, or closely related to the field of development ethics. Sometimes, political economy literature is quoted to identify specific issues, for instance, regarding cultural and environmental matters in relation to development ethics. Third, in terms of the macro-structure (the integrated book) and the micro-structure (the chapters), each chapter is notionally and structurally independent. At the same time, the book as a whole is robustly interrelated from a conceptual viewpoint. Fourth, the book, in terms of the development of its content, follows the "compromise model", as this approach sufficiently fits with the social sciences (Dunleavy, 2003, pp. 59–62). Accordingly, it focuses "on the material that readers 'need to know'" (Dunleavy, 2003, p. 61). In view of this, the literature review is distributed throughout the relevant chapters and contents when and where necessary, instead of being limited to one or two chapters at the beginning of the book. Fifth, the author-date style of referencing has been followed, while footnotes have been moderately used only when considered unavoidable.

References

Arndt, H. W. (1989). *Economic development: The history of an idea*. University of Chicago Press.

Arrow, K. J. (1974). *The limits of organization*. Norton.

Astroulakis, N. (2011). The development ethics approach to international development. *International Journal of Development Issues, 10*(3), 214–232.

Astroulakis, N. (2013a). Ethics and international development: The development ethics paradigm. *EAST-WEST Journal of Economics and Business, XVI*(1), 99–117.

Astroulakis, N. (2013b). Challenging conventional economics: An ethical development paradigm. *Revista Problemas del Desarrollo, 175*(44), 33–53.

Blaug, M. (1992 [1980]). *The methodology of economics or how economics explain*. Cambridge University Press.

Boulding, K. E. (1969). Economics as a moral science. *The American Economic Review, 59*(1), 1–12.

Bowels, S., Franzini, M., & Pagano, U. (1999). Introduction: Trespassing the boundaries of politics and economics. In S. Bowels, M. Franzini, & U. Pagano (Eds.), *The politics and economics of power* (pp. 2–8). Routledge.

Bozyk, P. (2006). *Globalization and the transformation of foreign economic policy*. Ashgate.

Brennan, G., & Eusepi, G. (Eds.). (2009). *The economics of ethics and the ethics of economics: Values, markets and the state*. Edward Elgar.

Brown, D. (2004). Conspicuous consumption, fashion and style in the global marketplace. In P. A. O'Hara (Ed.), *Global political economy and the wealth of nations: Performance, institutions, problems and policies* (pp. 208–221). Routledge.

Buchanan, A. (1985). *Ethics, efficiency, and the market*. Clarendon Press.

Caldwell, B. J. (1988). Hayek's transformation. *History of Political Economy, 20*(4), 513–541.

Caldwell, B. J. (1994 [1982]). *Beyond positivism: Economic methodology in the twentieth century* (Revised ed.). London: Routledge.

Campbell, A. (2012). Marx and Engels's vision of building a good society. In A. P. Society, & J. Marangos (Ed.). New York: Palgrave Macmillan.

Chang, H.-J. (2002). Breaking the mould: An institutionalist political economy alternative to the neoliberal theory of the market and the state. *Cambridge Journal of Economics, 26*(5), 539–559.

Clark, D. A. (2002). Development ethics: A research agenda. *International Journal of Social Economics, 29*(11), 830–848.

Clary, B. J., Dolfsma, W., & Figart, D. M. (2006). Introduction. In B. J. Clary, W. Dolfsma, & D. M. Figart (Eds.), *Ethics and the market: Insights from social economics* (pp. 1–8). Routledge.

Clary, B., Dolfsma, W., & Figart, D. (Eds.). (2006). *Ethics and the market: Insights from social economics*. Routledge.
Crocker, D. (1991). Toward development ethics. *World Development, 19*(5), 457–483.
Crocker, D. (1998). Development ethics. In C. Edward (Ed.), *Routledge encyclopedia of philosophy* (Vol. 3, pp. 39–44). Routledge.
Crocker, D. (2006). Foreword. In D. Goulet (Ed.), *Development ethics at work: Explorations—1960–2002* (pp. v–xxix). London: Routledge.
Crocker, D. (2007). Deliberative participation in local development. *Journal of Human Development, 8*(3), 431–455.
Crocker, D. (2008). *Ethics of global development*. Cambridge University Press.
Cross, R., & Strachan, D. (2001). Three pillars of conventional wisdom. *Review of Political Economy, 13*(2), 181–200.
Davidson, G., & Davidson, P. (1988). *Economics for a civilised society*. W.W. Norton & Company.
DeMartino, G. (2000). *Global economy, global justice: Theoretical and policy alternatives to neoliberalism*. Routledge.
Dolfsma, W., Finch, J., & McMaster, R. (2005). Market and society: (How) do they relate, and contribute to welfare? *Journal of Economic Issues, 39*(2), 347–356.
Dow, S. C. (2000). Prospects for the progress of heterodox economics. *Journal of the History of Economic Thought, 22*(2), 157–170.
Dow, S. C. (2002). *Economic methodology: An inquiry*. Oxford University Press.
Dower, N. (1988). *What is development? A philosopher's answer*. Centre for Development Studies Occasional Paper Series, 3. Glasgow: University of Glasgow.
Dower, N. (1998). *World ethics: The new agenda*. Edinburgh University Press.
Dower, N. (1998). Development ethics. In R. Chadwick (Ed.), *Encyclopedia of applied ethics* (pp. 755–766). Academic Press.
Dower, N. (2010). Development and the ethics of the means. In C. K. Wilber & A. K. Dutt (Eds.), *Development ethics new directions: Essays in honor of Denis Goulet* (pp. 29–37). University of Notre Dame.
Drakopoulos, S., & Karayiannis, A. (2005). A review of Kuhnian and Lakatosian "explanations" in economics. *History of Economic Ideas, XIII*(2), 51–73.
Drydyk, J. (2013). Development ethics and gender justice. *Éthique et économique/Ethics and Economics, 10*(2), 4–10.
Dugger, W. M. (1977). Social economics: One perspective. *Review of Social Economy, 35*(3), 299–310.
Dunleavy, P. (2003). *Authoring a Ph.D.: How to plan, draft, write and finish a doctoral thesis or dissertation*. Palgrave Macmillan.
Dutt, A. K., & Wilber, C. K. (2010). Introduction: Development ethics and development economics. In C. K. Wilber & A. K. Dutt (Eds.), *New directions*

in development ethics—Essays in Honor of Denis Goulet (pp. 1–26). University of Notre Dame Press.
Dutt, A. K., & Wilber, C. K. (2010). *Economics and ethics: An introduction*. Palgrave Macmillan.
Fine, B. (1980). *Economic theory and ideology*. Edward Arnold.
Fine, B. (2004). Economics and ethics: Amartya Sen as point of departure. *New School Economic Review, 1*(1), 95–103.
Fine, B., Lapavitsas, C., & Pincus, J. (Eds.). (2003). *Development policy in the twenty-first century: Beyond the post-Washington consensus*. Routledge.
Fine, B., & Milonakis, D. (2009). *From economics imperialism to Freakonomics: The shifting boundaries between economics and other social sciences economics as social theory*. Routledge.
Frankena, W. (1951). Moral philosophy at mid-century. *The Philosophical Review, 60*(1), 44–55.
Friedman, M. (1953). *Essays in positive economics*. Chicago University Press.
Friedman, M. (2002 [1962]). *Capitalism and freedom*. Chicago: University of Chicago Press.
Fukuyama, F. (1992). *The end of history and the last man*. New York: The Free Press: A Division of Macmillan, Inc.
Gasper, D. (2004). *The ethics of development*. Edinburgh University Press.
Gasper, D. (2008). Denis Goulet and the project of development ethics: Choices in methodology, focus and organization. *Journal of Human Development, 9*(3), 453–474.
Gasper, D. (2012). Development ethics—Why? What? How? A formulation of the field. *Journal of Global Ethics, 8*(1), 117–135.
Gasper, D., & St. Clair, A. L. (Eds.). (2010). *Development ethics*. London: Ashgate.
Gasper, D., & St. Clair, A. L. (2010). The field of development ethics—An introduction. In D. Gasper & A. L. St. Clair (Eds.), *Development ethics* (pp. 13–33). London: Ashgate.
Goulet, D. (1975). *The cruel choice: A new concept in the theory of development*. Atheneum.
Goulet, D. (1992). Ethics and development: A development ethicist at work. *Research and Explorations, 8*(2), 138–147.
Goulet, D. (1995). *Development ethics: A guide to theory and practice*. The Apex Press.
Goulet, D. (1996). Authentic development: Is it sustainable? In D. C. Pirages (Ed.), *Building sustainable societies: A blueprint for a post-industrial world* (pp. 189–205). Armonk, NY: M.E. Sharpe.
Goulet, D. (1997). Development ethics: A new discipline. *International Journal of Social Economics, 24*(11), 1160–1171.

Goulet, D. (2001). Ethical analysis in development economics. In A. K. Dutt & K. P. Jameson (Eds.), *Crossing the mainstream: Ethical and methodological issues in economics* (pp. 29–51). University of Notre Dame Press.

Goulet, D. (2006). *Development ethics at work: Explorations 1960–2002.* Routledge.

Goulet, D. (2006). Development ethics. In D. Clark (Ed.), *The Elgar companion to development studies* (pp. 115–120). Cheltenham: Edward Elgar Publishing.

Graafland, J. (2007). *Economics, ethics and the market: Introduction and applications*. Routledge.

Griffin, J. (1986). *Well-being; Its meaning, measurements and moral importance*. Oxford University Press.

Groenewegen, P. (Ed.). (1996). *Economics and ethics?* Routledge.

Hardison, F., & Myers, C. A. (1964). *Education, manpower, and economic growth*. McGraw-Hill.

Harvey, D. (2005). *A brief history of neoliberalism*. Oxford University Press.

Hausman, D. M. (1989). Economic methodology in a nutshell. *The Journal of Economic Perspectives, 3*(2), 115–127.

Hausman, D. M., & McPherson, M. S. (1993). Taking ethics seriously: Economics and contemporary moral philosophy. *Journal of Economic Literature, 31*(2), 671–731.

Hausman, D. M., & McPherson, M. S. (2006). *Economic analysis, moral philosophy, and public policy* (2nd ed.). Cambridge University Press.

Hayek, F. A. (1948). *Individualism and economic order*. University of Chicago.

Hirsch, F. (1976). *Social limits to growth*. Harvard University Press.

Hirschman, A. O. (1988 [1958]). *The strategy of economic development*. Boulder: Westview Press.

Hirschman, A. O. (1985). Against parsimony: Three easy ways of complicating some categories of economic discourse. *Economics and Philosophy, 1*(1), 7–21.

Hodgson, G. M. (2001). *How economics forgot history: The problem of historical specificity in social science*. Routledge.

Human Development Report. (2013). *The rise of the south: Human progress in a diverse world*. New York, NY: The United Nations Development Programme.

Hutchison, T. W. (1938). *The significance and basic postures of economic theory*. Macmillan.

Jevons, S. (1911 [1871]). *The theory of political economy*. London: Macmillan.

Jomo, K. S. (2005). Introduction. In K. S. Jomo (Ed.), *The pioneers of development economics: Great economists on development* (pp. 7–8). London: Zed Books.

Jomo, K. S., & Reinert, E. S. (Eds.). (2005). *Origins of development economics: How schools of economic thought addressed development*. Zed Books.

Kagan, S. (1998). *Normative ethics*. Westview Press.

Kuhn, T. S. (1970 [1962]). *The structure of scientific revolutions* (Second ed.). Chicago: The University of Chicago Press.
Kuznets, S. (1971). *Economic growth of nations: Total output and production structure*. Belknap Press of Harvard University Press.
Lapavitsas, C. (2005). Mainstream economics in the neoliberal era. In A. Saad-Filho & D. Johnston (Eds.), *Neoliberalism: A critical reader* (pp. 30–40). Pluto Press.
Lawson, T. (2006). The nature of heterodox economics. *Cambridge Journal of Economics, 30*(4), 483–505.
Lee, F. S. (2008). Heterodox economics. *The Long Term View, 7*(1), 23–30.
Little, I. (2004). *Ethics, economics, and politics*. Oxford University Press.
Lutz, M. A. (1999). *Economics for the common good*. Routledge.
Marangos, J. (2009a). What happened to the Washington consensus? The evolution of international development policy. *The Journal of Socio-Economics, 38*(1), 197–208.
Marangos, J. (2009b). The evolution of the term 'Washington consensus.' *Journal of Economic Surveys, 23*(2), 350–384.
Marangos, J., & Astroulakis, N. (2009). The institutional foundation of development ethics. *Journal of Economic Issues, XLIII*(2), 381–388.
Marangos, J., & Astroulakis, N. (2012). The development ethics perspective of a good society. In J. Marangos (Ed.), *Alternative perspectives of a good society* (pp. 79–98). Palgrave Macmillan.
Milonakis, D., & Fine, B. (2009). *From political economy to economics: Method, the social and the historical in the evolution of economic theory*. Routledge.
Myrdal, G. (1977 [1968]). *Asian drama: An inquiry into the poverty of nations*. London: Pelican books.
Nussbaum, M. (2000). *Women and human development: The capabilities approach*. Cambridge University Press.
O'Hara, P. A. (2006). *Growth and development in the global political economy: Social structures of accumulation and modes of regulation*. Routledge.
Parfitt, T. (2012). Development ethics: Means of the means? *Review of African Political Economy, 39*(134), 672–681.
Perroux, F. (1950). Economic space: Theory and applications. *The Quarterly Journal of Economics, 64*(1), 89–104.
Perroux, F. (1955). Note sur la notion de pôle de croissance. *Economie appliquée, 8*(1–2), 307–320.
Perroux, F. (1981). *Pour une philosophie du nouveau développement* (Vol. 4). Presses de l'UNESCO.
Polanyi, K. (2001 [1944]). *The great transformation*. Boston, MA: Beacon Press.
Pusey, M. (1991). *Economic rationalism in Canberra: A nation-building state changes its mind*. Cambridge University Press.

Qizilbash, M. (1996). Ethical development. *World Development, 24*(7), 1209–1221.
Rawls, J. (1951). Outline of a decision procedure for ethics. *The Philosophical Review, 60*(2), 177–197.
Robbins, L. (1945 [1932]). *An essay on the nature and significance of economic science* (second ed.). London: Macmillan.
Rothschild, K. W. (1993). *Ethics and economic theory: Ideas, models, dilemmas.* Edward Elgar.
Rowthorn, R. (1996). Ethics and economics: An economist's view. In P. Groenewegen (Ed.), *Economics and ethics?* (pp. 15–33). Routledge.
Saad-Filho, A., & Johnston, D. (2005). Introduction. In A. Saad-Filho & D. Johnston (Eds.), *Neoliberalism: A critical reader* (pp. 1–6). Pluto Press.
Saad-Filho, A., & Johnston, D. (Eds.). (2005). *Neoliberalism: A critical reader.* Pluto Press.
Seer, D. (1972). The meaning of development. *Journal of Development Studies, 8*(3), 21–36.
Sen, A. (1977). Rational fools: A critique of the behavioral foundations of economic theory. *Philosophy and Public Affairs, 6*(4), 317–344.
Sen, A. (1980). Description as choice. *Oxford Economic Paper, 32*(3), 353–369.
Sen, A. (1981). *Poverty and famines: An essay on entitlements and deprivation.* Oxford University Press.
Sen, A. (1984). *Resources, values and development.* Blackwell.
Sen, A. (1987). *On ethics and economics.* Blackwell.
Sen, A. (1999). *Development as freedom.* Oxford University Press.
Soubbotina, T. P. (2004). *Beyond economic growth: An introduction to sustainable development* (2nd ed.). Washington, DC: The World Bank.
St Clair, A. L. (2007). A methodologically pragmatist approach to development ethics. *Journal of Global Ethics, 3*(2), 143–164.
van Staveren, I. (2007). Beyond utilitarianism and deontology: Ethics in economics. *Review of Political Economy, 19*(1), 21–35.
Vickers, D. (1997). *Economics and ethics: An introduction to theory, institutions, and policy.* Greenwood Publishing Group.
Walras, L. (1954 [1874]). *Elements of pure economics.* London: George Allen and Unwin.
Waters, W. A. (1988). Social economics: A solidarist perspective. *Review of Social Economy, 46*(2), 113–143.
Wilber, C. K. (2004). Ethics and social economics: ASE presidential address, January 2004, San Diego, California. *Review of Social Economy, 62*(4), 425–439.
Williams, B. (2006). *Ethics and the limits of philosophy.* Routledge.
Williamson, J. (1990a). What Washington means by policy reform. In J. Williamson (Ed.), *Latin American adjustment: How much has happened?*

(Chapter 2). Washington, DC: Institute for International Economics. Republished online (November, 2002). http://www.iie.com/publications/papers/paper.cfm?researchid=486

Williamson, J. (Ed.). (1990b). *Latin American adjustment: How much has happened?* Institute for International Economics.

Wright, J. (2003). *The ethics of economic rationalism*. University of New South Wales.

Yeager, L. B. (2001). *Ethics as social science: The moral philosophy of social cooperation*. Edward Elgar.

CHAPTER 2

The Foundation of Development Ethics

1 Introduction

This chapter reviews the conceptual rise and the historical evolution of development ethics. Development ethics attempts to investigate the ethical study of development in a holistic and normative manner.[1] In the literature, development ethics is commonly defined as ethical reflection on the ends and means of local, national, and global development (Goulet, 1975a; 1995; 1997; 2006a; Dower, 1998b; 2010; Gasper and Truong, 2005; Gasper, 2006; 2012; Crocker, 1991; 1998). In this vein, Crocker (2008) employs the notion of development ethics as an explanatory device in exploring the mode of socioeconomic change in poor countries and regions. In particular, he stresses the significance of moral issues in accounting for the existence of global poverty and the alleged North–South division. The ethical analysis of development is not merely confined to the level of philosophical discourse but also offers "a space of analysis, evaluation and action regarding the trajectory of societies, with special reference to suffering, injustice and exclusion within societies and

[1] Regarding international development, the holistic and normative nature of development ethics is further discussed in Chapter 3. In recent times, development ethics has been accepted as a field of reflection, application, and practice for the ethical concept of development. Reflection refers to philosophical and theoretical debates, while application and practice refer to the ethical evaluation of development policy and practices (see Sect. 5 in this chapter).

N. Astroulakis and N. Karagiannis, *Development Ethics*,
https://doi.org/10.1007/978-3-031-75476-0_2

between societies at a global scale" (Gasper and Truong, 2005, pp. 373–374). To this end, development ethics combines tasks and methodological instruments from a variety of scientific fields, such as economics, political science, religious studies, anthropology, environmental studies, and ecology. Thus, it can be characterised as a multidisciplinary area of study or, as Gasper (2006, p. 1) states, an "interdisciplinary meeting place." As such, it encompasses the analysis of development with the numerous economic, political, cultural, institutional, ideological, and ethical aspects of individuals and societies. In the words of Goulet (1995, p. 27), "[t]he discipline of development ethics is the conceptual cement that binds together multiple diagnoses of problems with their policy implications through an explicit phenomenological study of values which lays bare the value costs of alternative courses of action." Furthermore, for Goulet (1997, p. 1168), "development ethics functions as a kind of 'disciplined eclecticism'... eclectic in its choice of subject matter but disciplined in its study of it." In turn, Dutt and Wilber (2010b, p. 14) state: "[d]evelopment ethics also has important implications for the methods of analysis and how one views the relation between analytical views of the economy and the real world". Concisely, the essence of development ethics refers to the effort of thrusting "debates over economic and social development into the arena of ethical values" (Goulet, 1975a, p. vii).

Development ethics has been formulated as a self-conscious field of study since the end of the 1960s, mainly by the pioneering work of Goulet. Thus, Goulet could be considered as the founder of development ethics in the form in which it appears today. Goulet's thinking has been directly influenced by the economic humanism of his teacher, Lebret. Lebret was a leading figure in the ethical study of the economy and the chief founder of the interdisciplinary research centre *Economy and Humanism*, which was founded in Marseille, France, in the 1940s. Goulet expands and elaborates on the ideas of his teacher to the analysis of development by studying and practising these ideas in relation to development agents. The ideas of both Lebret and Goulet on development ethics are viewed and analysed extensively in this chapter. Regarding the historical and notional evolution of development ethics, Goulet (1995; 1997; 2006a), going beyond his mentor, finds the origins of development ethics in the life and writings of the Indian social leader Mohandas Gandhi and of the Swedish development economist Gunnar Myrdal.

Recent studies of development ethics also refer to Lebret, Gandhi, and Myrdal as deep-rooted sources of development ethics (Crocker, 1998;

2008; Gasper, 2004; Gasper and St. Clair (eds.), 2010a, 2010b; Wilber and Dutt (eds.), 2010a, 2010b). However, according to the philosophical underpinning of development ethics and the concept of a good society, poor (or implicit) investigation has been carried out. To our knowledge, there has been limited research in the development ethics literature regarding the philosophical origins of the concept of a good society as a key concept in the determination of the meaning of development. Thus, regarding the philosophical origins of development ethics, an innovative application of Aristotle's philosophy to development ethics is introduced in this chapter.[2] This is done by exploring a closer and more explicit application of the moral and political philosophy ideas of Aristotle to the philosophical underpinning of development ethics and the concepts of a good life and a good society.[3]

Development ethics has been further expanded by a number of scholars, policy-makers, and practitioners (philosophers, social scientists, environmentalists, and religious theorists), usually called development ethicists. Development ethicists, along with the views of Denis Goulet, share the views of other development thinkers such as Paul Streeten and Amartya Sen. The expansion and significance of development ethics are demonstrated by the foundation of the International Development Ethics Association (IDEA) in 1984: an international organisation with the aim of promoting ethical debate within development. In more recent years, within and beyond the IDEA, development ethics has been utilised, as a self-conscious (in the manner of study) and interdisciplinary field (in the subjects of study), in international development and development studies, including (among others) development economics (Goulet, 1997; Wilber and Dutt (eds.), 2010a, 2010b; Gasper and St. Clair (eds.), 2010a, 2010b).[4] Nevertheless, its conceptual formulations and basic normative

[2] No one had written ethical treatises before Aristotle who followed Socrates and Plato in taking ethical virtues to be central to a well-lived life. In Aristotle's ethical writings, the systematic character of his discussion of moral themes was a remarkable innovation (Kraut, 2022). Christian and Kantian considerations of ethics developed much later.

[3] The ethical concepts of a good life and a good society are discussed as the key ethical arguments defining the meaning of development.

[4] The literature—utilised throughout the book—relies mainly on Anglophone writings, thus contributions in French, Spanish, and elsewhere may have been insufficiently acknowledged.

principles remain constant with the conceptual foundation of Goulet's development ethics.

Regarding the structure of the chapter, the second section briefly reviews the deeper origins of development ethics. The third section analyses the Aristotelian contribution to development ethics according to the notion of a good society. The fourth section investigates the rise of development ethics as an intellectual field of study based on the works of the pioneering development ethicists Lebret and Goulet. The fifth section analyses the constitutional principles of the IDEA and explains the contemporary state of development ethics. The sixth section concludes with the remarks of this chapter.

2 The Origins of Development Ethics

The approach of development ethics to investigating development in terms of social and ethical issues came to the forefront in the 1940s with Lebret and became known at the beginning of the 1970s through the writings of Goulet, particularly from his leading book *The Cruel Choice: A New Concept in The Theory of Development*, first published in 1971. Goulet (1968; 1975a; 1995; 1997; 2006a) identifies Louis-Joseph Lebret [1897–1966], Mohandas Gandhi [1869–1948], and the Nobel Laureate economist Gunnar Myrdal [1898–1987] as the forerunners of development ethics. In this study, we propose the Greek philosopher Aristotle [384 BC–322 BC] as the first historical founder of the philosophical underpinnings of development ethics in recognition of the notion of a good society.

For Goulet (1997, pp. 1161–1162), Gandhi is a theoretical and practical precursor of development ethics due to his endeavour of applying social planning and institutional reform to transforming Indian society. Gandhi's social planning theory and practices are based on the strong premise of equilibrium between human needs and wants. Gandhi, as quoted in Goulet (2006a, p. 192), argues that "there are enough goods in the poorest Indian village to meet the needs of all, but not enough goods in all of India to satisfy the greed of each one". Gandhi not only advocated but also attempted "the provision of basic needs over the multiplication of wants" (Goulet, 1997, p. 1162), which consists of one of the essential tasks of development ethics. Further, Gandhi integrates ethical development theory with applied social practices. According to Das (1979, p. 59), one of the main points of Gandhi's social planning theory is as follows:

"The coordination of the economic system... in terms of three types of planning processes: (a) the area development plans of local communities and clusters, (b) the marketing and reinvestment planning of the cooperative structure, and (c) centralized planning of large industries, the three processes being made to interact in a hierarchical indicative planning system of cluster/district/zone levels."

Gandhi's struggle against poverty, through economic and social planning, places him as one of the forerunners of development ethics.

Also, the writings of Gunnar Myrdal are equally important to development ethics. In his article *What Is Development?*, Myrdal (1974, pp. 729–730) states that:

"[B]y development I meant the movement upward of the entire social system... This social system encloses, besides the so-called economic factor, all noneconomic factors, including all sorts of consumption by various groups of people; consumption provided collectively; educational and health facilities and levels; the distribution of power to society; and more generally economic, social and political stratifications; broadly speaking institutions and attributes."

Furthermore, Myrdal investigates the methodological problem of objectivity in social research in connection with world economic dualism. In relation to objectivity, Myrdal holds a critical position on economic dualism between Western and non-Western societies. In Myrdal's (1969, p. 11) own words, "the use of Western theories, models, and concepts in the study of economic development in the South Asian countries... is a cause of bias seriously distorting that study". This statement indicates Myrdal's support for an alternative development pattern, with different means and goals to any development process. His viewpoints regarding of definition of development and worldwide economic dualism also place Myrdal in the forefront of development ethics.

To this end, even though development ethics is a new area of study, with direct forerunners (Lebret, Gandhi, and Myrdal) in the nineteenth and twentieth centuries, its origins regarding its perspective on a good life and a good society can be traced back to Ancient Greek philosophy and, in particular, to Aristotle's moral and political philosophy. Aristotle's contribution to the foundation of development ethics is merely mentioned in the writing of development ethicists (Goulet, 1997; 2006a; Clark, 2002a; Crocker, 2008; Dower, 2010), with no further endeavour to formulate a clear association of Aristotle's ethics and politics to development ethics. In our view, Aristotelian philosophy has significant weight in the foundation of development ethics.[5] Thus, the next section investigates the Aristotelian contribution to development ethics.

3 Aristotelian Philosophy and Development Ethics: What Is a Good Society?

Every school of thought relating to development theories follows a theoretical pattern of defining what the end state of development is (in the literature, this is called a good society). To our knowledge, there has been limited research in the development ethics literature regarding the philosophical origins of the concept of a good society. This section examines Aristotle's ethical and political theory, the philosophical basis regarding the notion of a good life, and how the Aristotelian vision of a good society influences the perspective of contemporary development ethics on a good society.[6]

Perhaps the key element of a good society is the ethical question of 'what is a good life?', which traces back to Ancient Greek philosophers and particularly to Aristotle's *Nicomachean Ethics* and *Politics*[7] (Aristotle, 1959 [1932]; Aristotle, 2000; Ross, 1995 [1923]). Sen (1987, p. 3) reminds us that:

[5] Aristotle wrote two ethical treatises: the ***Nicomachean Ethics*** and the ***Eudemian Ethics***. A third treatise, called the ***Magna Moralia*** (the "Big Ethics") is included in complete editions of Aristotle's works even though its authorship is disputed by some scholars. The notion of "ethics" can play an evaluative role and is not simply a description of someone's state of mind. Aristotle regards ***eudaimon***ia as a simple substitute for "living well" and his conclusion about the nature of happiness is in a sense uniquely his own (Kraut, 2022).

[6] Aristotle's analysis refers to a pre-capitalistic society, structured in a different socioeconomic model and productive relationships. Thus, our analysis relates the ethical aspects of the Aristotelian analysis to the ethical notion of good society in a philosophical level, keeping in mind the significant historical differences of the socioeconomic model of development. However, clear thinking about the best goals of human life and the proper way to put them into practice has not been a general achievement because the human psyche may or may not welcome the development of these insights.

[7] For Aristotle's *Nicomachean Ethics*, we used the version edited by Crisp (2000). For Aristotle's *Politics*, we used the version edited by Page et al. (1959). Here, they are cited as (Aristotle, 2000) and (Aristotle, 1959), respectively.

"Aristotle relates the subject of economics to human ends, referring to its concern with wealth" and that "economics relates ultimately to the study of ethics and that of politics, and this point of view is further developed in Aristotle's Politics".

In this vein, Clark (2002a, pp. 830–831) argues that, in ethical terms, "discussions of what makes a good life date back at least to Aristotle's Nicomachean ethics and the ancient Greek tradition". In this part, we investigate the contribution of the Aristotelian philosophy to development ethics. We show that, similar to the views of development ethicists, Aristotle's notion of politics encapsulates economic, social, cultural, and ethical aspects. It is also perceived as the means to achieve a good society.

3.1 Aristotle's Notion of a Good Life and the Concept of Eudaimonia

For Aristotle, the highest good of human life is '*eudaimonia*', which to some extent is synonymous with happiness. We argue that development ethicists adopt the Aristotelian concept of eudaimonia and advance it to the macro level of international development. "Man is by nature a political [social] animal" (Aristotle, 1959, p. 201). According to Ross (1995 [1923], p. 152), "[i]t has often been remarked that where Aristotle says man is a political animal we might prefer to say he is a social animal, needing his fellows in a variety of capacities and not merely as fellow citizens." Therefore, the way of achieving *eudaimonia* and a good life can only be accomplished via politics within an economic, social, and ethical base. Development ethics is consistent with the Aristotelian notion of politics as the means of accomplishing the aims of a good society. According to Aristotle's ethical philosophy, ethics examines and determines the rules of human behaviour within society. In his works *Nicomachean Ethics* and *Politics*, Aristotle postulates his view of human ethical behaviour, the stance of citizens on political affairs, and his proposal for a good society. Hence, Aristotle could be considered one of the pioneers in elaborating the concept of a good life within its political and social context.

Aristotle begins *Nicomachean Ethics* by posing the question of why humans act: "[e]very skill and every inquiry, and similarly every action and rational choice, is thought to aim at some good; and so the good has been aptly described as that at which everything aims" (Aristotle, 2000,

p. 3). Human behaviour consists of human actions based on the preferences of every individual. Thus, Aristotle examines humans' actions under the philosophical inquiry of 'what do people aim at when they act?' For Aristotle, any human action aims at a goal. In turn, there are two types of goals: 1. those that constitute ends in themselves, and 2. those that are means to achieving other goals. In many cases, both types of goals can occur simultaneously. For instance, exercising is an end in itself as well as the means for a healthy body. In that sense, human actions can be perceived as an inextricable matrix with successive aims.

In spite of this, a philosophical question that can be raised is whether there is any purpose in the entire course of actions. For Aristotle, the highest good, which all human actions should aim at, is that of *eudaimonia*. It is an end in itself: "happiness [*eudaimonia*], then, is obviously something complete and self-sufficient, in that it is the end of what is done" (Aristotle, 2000, p. 11). For Aristotle, *eudaimonia* consists in, and only in, virtuous activity: "[w]hat really matters for happiness [*eudaimonia*] are activities in accordance with virtue, and to the contrary of happiness [*eudaimonia*] the contrary kind of activities" (Aristotle, 2000, p. 17).

Regarding the modern use of the term '*eudaimonia*', it can be seen as synonymous to the term 'happiness'. However, a couple of alternative translations exist in the literature, for example 'flourishing', 'good living', and 'well-being'. Ross (1995 [1923], p. 122) points out that:

> "[T]he conventional translation of 'happiness' is unsuitable in the *Ethics*[8] for whereas 'happiness' means a state of feeling, differing from 'pleasure' only by its suggestion of permanence, depth, and serenity. Aristotle insists that "ευδαιμονία [*eudaimonia*] is a kind of activity; that it is not any kind of pleasure, though pleasure naturally accompanies it. The more non-committal translation 'well-being' is therefore better."

In the debate on the meaning of the term '*eudaimonia*', Crisp points out that Aristotle's use of the term could be "whatever makes a human life good for the person living it" (Aristotle, 2000, p. 206). An important issue in Aristotelian ethical thinking could be that a 'good life' is not only

[8] Aristotle investigates ethics mainly in his works *Nicomachean Ethics*, *Eudemian Ethics*, and *Great Ethics* (better known as *Magna Moralia*). The engagement with ethical matters is also distinctive in his work *Politics*.

discussed in an idealistic, mental context. In contrast to other Ancient Greek philosophical schools of that era, for example Epicureanism[9], Stoicism[10], and even Platoism, Aristotle inserts a notion of pragmatism into his philosophical thinking. Aristotle's *eudaimonia* can also be defined as "the state of having an objectively desirable human life" (Honderich, 1995, p. 252). Meanwhile, as Clark (2002a, p. 830) suggests:

> "The objective character of eudaimonia distinguishes it from the ancient philosophies of the Epicureans and Stoics, who saw the good in terms of mental tranquillity; and from modern concepts of utility, which are concerned with the achievement of a subjectively satisfactory life."

For Aristotle (2000), goods can be classified into three categories: (1) external goods; (2) goods of the soul; and (3) goods of the body. Aristotle argues that the aim (the end) of human action is found in goods related to the soul: "it [*eudaimonia*] was a certain kind of activity of the soul in accordance with virtue; and of the other goods, some are necessary conditions of happiness [*eudaimonia*], and others are naturally helpful and serve as useful means to it" (Aristotle, 2000, p. 16). Aristotle introduces a materialistic approach towards the goal of having a good life. As Aristotle (2000, p. 15) states, "[*eudaimonia*] obviously needs the presence of external goods as well, since it is impossible, or at least no easy matter, to perform noble actions without resources."

Aristotle incorporates the concept of a good life not only in his ethical work but also in his work concerning politics. In his view, politics is associated not only with the political but also with the social and ethical affairs of a state. The individual as a citizen is placed at the centre of the discussion of politics, and the state ('*polis*' in Greek) is placed at the centre of the discussion of ethics. In his work *Politics*, Aristotle describes a good life as a virtuous life of an individual who, at the same time, is a member of the state. In Aristotelian ethics, the good of the state (*polis*) in its totality is perceived as superior to the aim of a good life of any individual

[9] Epicureanism is the school of philosophy founded by Epicurus (341-270 BC). Epicurus is known for his contribution to hedonism. He taught that the point of all one's actions is to attain pleasure and avoid pain for oneself.

[10] Stoicism is a philosophical school founded by Zeno of Citium in the early third century BC. Stoic philosophy can be summarised by the belief that true happiness can be achieved by living according to nature.

separately. Therefore, Ross (1995 [1923], p. 120) accurately states that "Aristotle's ethics, no doubt, are social, and his politics are ethical."

For Aristotle, there are three reasons for the state's existence: first, to fulfil a human natural instinct; second, to satisfy a "common interest" of its citizens; and third, to protect its members (Aristotle, 1959). Aristotle believes that people establish societies not only because of need but also because of their political (social) nature; "even when men have no need of assistance from each other they nonetheless desire to live together" (Aristotle, 1959, p. 201). However, we must not overlook the fact that, for Aristotle, the state maximises the mutual welfare of its members and it is the means of achieving a good life: "[a]t the same time they [people] are also brought together by common interest, so far as each achieves a share of the good life" (Aristotle, 1959, p. 201). It is important to mention that in the Aristotelian view of a good life, the common interest is not only an economic matter; it also has a moral conception. Even though the road to *eudaimonia* and a good society demands material prosperity to a great extent, nevertheless, the virtuous lives of the members of the state are considered to be far more important.

3.2 *Aristotelian Influence on Development Ethics*

Development ethicists acknowledge the Aristotelian concept of politics as the means of achieving the end state of development conceived as a good society. As mentioned, in Aristotle's notion of politics, the aspects of ethical, social, and political affairs are entwined. For Aristotle, ethics determine not only the meaning of a good life, by identifying what is good and acceptable in human actions, but also the requirements of a virtuous life. At the same time, politics deals with norms and institutions (e.g. family, the education system, and the political system), as well as the actions that people and societies take to lead an organised and good way of life.

Development ethicists espouse Aristotle's notion of politics in its ethical and social form. By incorporating an Aristotelian vision of a good society into the development agenda, development ethicists do not analyse development in a merely economistic fashion of growth (i.e., GDP) and material consumption. On the contrary, they investigate development in broader terms to incorporate into the analysis the associated ethical, political, social, cultural, and environmental dimensions. In addition, the approach of development ethics to development maintains that politics is the means within a course of actions that lead to a good life and a good society. Thus, for both Aristotle and development ethicists, politics is the means to *eudaimonia* and to a good society. Moreover, for Aristotle, "the good life then is the chief aim of society, both collectively for all its members and individually" (Aristotle, 1959, p. 201). Accordingly, development ethics investigates the concept of a good society by taking into consideration the specific features of societies and individuals. In that sense, the approach of development ethics to a good society appears to have been strongly influenced by the Aristotelian perception of a good life.

Along with justice (in terms of equality of all people and nations in the world) and environmental conscience (in terms of individuals, nations, and international organisations), the concept of good lives for all humans is at the core of the discussion of a good society. Development ethicists, following the Aristotelian logic of an objective and realistic way of defining the term 'a good life', argue that economic growth and material consumption are necessary elements in a good life. In other words, the road to *eudaimonia* passes through material prosperity. Hence, they advocate the abundance of goods, in the sense that people need to have enough goods in order to achieve a good life.

However, the hyper-consumption manner of life in developed nations has distorted the way that a good life is perceived: 'having more' (material goods and wealth) leads to the impression of 'being more' (successful, attractive, and valuable) (Fromm, 1999; 2005). Development ethicists stand against this perception. In this vein, development ethics shares Aristotle's views that "the amount of property which is needed for a good life is not unlimited" and that "a man must have so much property as will enable him to live not only temperately but liberally; if the two are parted, liberality will combine with luxury; temperance will be associated with toil", concluding that "it should not be thought that the man who is to be happy will need many or great possessions, merely because it is not possible to be blessed without external goods" (Goulet, 2006a, p. 191).

For development ethicists, the abundance of goods must be investigated under a humanistic perspective, which attempts to specify how much is 'enough' in order for people to have a good life. "[T]he notion of 'having enough' is not devoid of objective sense. To have enough means to have what one needs in order to be and to be well" (Goulet, 2006a,

p. 29).[11] Even though there is no unique answer to the question 'what does one need in order to be and to be well?', it is widely acknowledged that underdevelopment (poverty, misery, diseases, mass famine, etc.) diminishes humanity. Thus, the concept of 'enough' should not only involve all the goods necessary to satisfy biological needs but also those goods that free part of the human energy towards a wider range of life aspects. In accordance with Aristotle, development ethicists point out that material prosperity, in the form of the concept of 'enough', should work as a means to the end state of development: *eudaimonia*. Thus, it is evident that development ethics adopts the Aristotelian vision of a good life, believing that *eudaimonia* is something beyond material consumption and pleasure. The true indicator of the road to *eudaimonia* is the qualitative enrichment of human beings in all relevant aspects of human life.

To summarise, we argue that Aristotle's ethical and political philosophy has significant influence on the foundation of development ethics. In this section, the Aristotelian vision of a good life and a good society has been presented. Both concepts appear to constitute the fundamental precursors and originators of the philosophical core of the view for a good society promoted by development ethics. Aristotle answers the philosophical question of 'what should be the aim of human actions?' by using the concept of *eudaimonia* within the confines of the state (*polis*). Aristotle's good society poses rules and norms and involves the concept of a good life in the micro-environment of the state, so that a good society can be conceived as a philosophical micro-model. Development ethics implicitly espouses *eudaimonia* as the end state of human actions and hence advances on this concept to the macro level of international development. Similar to development ethicists, Aristotle's ethical notion of politics, which encapsulates economic, social, cultural, and ethical aspects, is perceived as the means to achieving a good society. From this perspective, development ethicists accept and embody Aristotle's ethical notion of politics as the means to a good society.

[11] In this regard, all of the normal difficulties of ethical life remain, and they can be solved only by means of a detailed understanding of the particulars of each situation by utilising ethical virtues and developing and exercising practical wisdom (Kraut, 2022).

4 From Lebret's Economic Humanism to Goulet's Development Ethics

This section investigates the rise of development ethics through the works of the pioneering development ethicists Louis-Joseph Lebret and Denis Goulet. We can evidently argue that if Lebret can be seen as the direct precursor of development ethics, Goulet can be considered as the founder of development ethics in its contemporary form. The key idea, for both Lebret and Goulet, is the view of development as the question of values and the formation of a new civilisation (Goulet, 1995, p. 6). The section concentrates on the works of Lebret and Goulet for two main reasons. First, their work is noteworthy and well-recognised, even with some antinomies and critique, across the whole development ethics community. Second, they directly answer the questions 'what is the subject matter of development ethics?' and 'how should development ethics be formulated?' Lebret's basic ideas on development and human economy are analytically presented, as is the conceptual formulation of development ethics based on Goulet's writings.

4.1 Lebret and Economy and Humanism[12]

The direct precursor of development ethics is Lebret [1897–1966] and the philosophic and economic institute *Economy and Humanism*, of which Lebret was one of the main founders. As Goulet (2006a, p. 61) states, "Lebret stands as a giant in an infant discipline [development ethics]." Lebret was a social scientist and philosopher. He was a marine officer and, from 1923, a Dominican priest. In the following lines, the fundamentals of his work as determinants of the conceptual rise of development ethics are reviewed.

In 1941, Lebret (along with a group of economists, philosophers, labour activists, and maritime specialists) established an interdisciplinary research institute known as *Economy and Humanism* in Marseille, France. Essentially, *Economy and Humanism* constituted a social and philosophical movement aimed at elaborating the issues affecting human development, such as "institutions and systems, the myriad form of

[12] Lebret's writings are mostly in French. However, Lebret's writings are reviewed in English by Goulet. Thus, we refer to Goulet's last work (Goulet, 2006a), which overlaps the study of development ethics and Lebret's viewpoints.

social change, ideologies, competing pedagogies, economic sector, the dynamism whereby a populace may play a role in decisions affecting its own conditions" (Goulet, 2006a, p. 51). The main challenge for *Economy and Humanism* was to investigate critically the development problem in its multiple dimensions. In precise terms,

> Its goal was to examine critically the theoretical and political bases of competing economic systems, to create instruments for linking the analysis of small units with an understanding of national of worlds units, to discover how social change could be planned in cooperation with a populace and in harmony with its values and objectives, and to discover guidelines for intelligent action at all levels (Goulet, 2006a, p. 52).

In 1942, in the climate of the pre-Cold War era, a manifesto was published by the founders of *Economy and Humanism*. The manifesto claims to be against state socialism and the structural bankruptcy of liberalism. "Authority and a *distributive* economy do not necessarily mean static economy at national level. Nor do market and free economy necessarily mean an omnipresent market and the tyranny of price" (Goulet, 2006a, pp. 52–53). The proposals of the manifesto are to direct an economy towards being based on the needs and services of a human, rather than a profit economy. The manifesto is positioned against capitalism and centralised socialism. Regarding capitalism, the manifesto argues that the market system leads to hyper-consumption for a segment of society and gives the producers the ability to manipulate the desires of possible consumers. In the existing form of capitalism, there is no critical mechanism forming the basis for real human needs for all individuals and societies. A centralised socialist system, on the other hand, in its efforts to compete with capitalism, demotes "the importance of noneconomic values which do not collectivize existence, to the detriment of spiritual, artistic, and personal growth" (Goulet, 2006a, p. 58).

Beyond the criticisms of capitalism and centralised socialism, for Lebret, the concept of development has a multidimensional nature: "it [development] embraces economic, social, political, cultural, environmental, and spiritual components of human well-being" (Goulet, 2006a, p. 181). Lebret's views of ethical development are quoted as they have been codified by Goulet (2006a, p. 56):

- "Development is, above all, a task of forging new values and new civilizations in settings where most existing institutions contradict human aspirations.
- The only valid path is to seek optimum growth in terms of a population's values and in terms of resource limitations.
- Planning is futile unless it is a permanent association between decision makers at the summit and communities at the grassroots.
- Equity in the distribution of wealth and the achievement of dignity for all are priority targets of development efforts.
- Conflicts of interest can be solved only by eliminating privilege and launching a general pedagogy of austerity."

Based on the aforementioned principles, the main contribution of Lebret's economic humanism to development is concentrated on the fundamental problem of the unequal distribution of goods within and between societies. Lebret not only systematically investigates the human and societal needs and the role of development in accessing these needs in order to address the problem of inequality but also attempts to clarify what it incurs for social and human development. As Goulet (2006a, p. 57) underlines, "[Lebret] argued that satisfying an abundance of false needs at the expense of keeping multitudes in misery can never be authentic development", while "underdevelopment is a byproduct of the distorted achievements of those societies which incorrectly label themselves developed". For Lebret, ethical development ought to correspond to the spiritual and cultural origins of society. Needs should assist societal solidarity, resource sustainability, and the integral human necessity of all individuals and societies for a decent existence. According to Goulet (2006a, p. 57), Lebret codified three categories of needs:

- "Essential subsistence needs (food, clothing, housing, health care, and the like).
- Needs related to comfort and the facilities, which render life easier (transportation, leisure, labour-saving devices, pleasant surroundings, and so on).
- Needs related to human fulfilment or transcendence, whose satisfaction confers heightened value on human lives (cultural improvement, deeper spiritual life, enriching friendships, loving relationships, rewarding social intercourse, and so on). These may also be called

> 'enhancement goods'; they enhance human societies qualitatively and find their expression in cultural or spiritual achievement."

In brief, for Lebret, ethical development should be subordinate to the attainment of the aforementioned needs for all individuals and societies. The policy implications that one finds in Lebret's applied-ethical and development suggestions are harmonised with his presumptions of accepting these needs. For Lebret, development's ultimate goal can only be achieved when "all human beings in every society are entitled to enjoy the structural and institutional conditions which foster universal human ascent" (Goulet, 2006a, p. 58). Lebret frequently shares similar thoughts with Perroux (1950; 1955; 1981). In this light, development refers to the whole person and every person, and such development does not result from a pure accumulation of projects but from how these projects incorporate a local, regional, and global image of human development. For Lebret, "[t]he main criterion of value is not production or possessions, but the totality of qualitative human enrichment" (Goulet, 2006a, p. 60). Lebret's contribution evidently influenced the rise of development ethics. Lebret's concepts and policies on development are accurately accepted by almost all development ethics thinkers; however, the thinker most influenced by Lebret was his student Goulet.

4.2 Goulet's Development Ethics

Denis Goulet [1931–2006] was a social scientist and activist. As a student of Lebret, he was powerfully influenced by his mentor's life and ideas on the ethical view of the development problem. Goulet made Lebret's ethical concepts in development well known. Perhaps most importantly, he extended Lebret's notions to a distinctive field: development ethics. As Goulet's study of development ethics is largely affected by his teacher, his work can be considered as an expansion of Lebret's thoughts on ethical development. Thus, if Lebret can be considered as a direct precursor, Goulet can be labelled as the founder of development ethics as a self-conscious intellectual field.

His contribution is paramount and extensive (Goulet, 1971; 1975a; 1989; 1992a; 1995; 1996; 1997; 2006a). He offers an ethical analysis of development, by formulating general principles in almost all relevant aspects of development: technology, ecology and ethics, culture and tradition, the ethics of aid, the ethics of consumption, international issues, justice and globalisation, the role of religion, etc. In Goulet's work, the meaning of development is given by the phrase "human ascent", which encompasses "the ascent of all men in their integral humanity including the economic, biological, psychological, social, cultural, ideological, spiritual, mystical, and transcendental dimensions" (Goulet, 1971, pp. 206–207). From this angle, development is involved as "simultaneously and inextricably an economic and political matter, a social and cultural one, an issue of resource and environmental management, a question of civilization" (Goulet, 1995, p. 2).

In the ethical discussion of development, Goulet highlights a twofold ambiguity regarding the concept of development. First, he ascertains that development is used either descriptively or normatively. Second, he underlines the perception of development as the ends of any social change and the means in order to achieve those ends (Goulet, 1992a, p. 246). In the first case, he places the qualitative and moral elements together with the applied methods to forge a normative approach. In the second case, ethics in development is interpreted as the "means of means" or, as he argues, "ethics must somehow get inside the value dynamism of the instruments utilized by development agents and itself become 'a means of the means'" (Goulet, 1995, p. 25). Goulet proposes that, by interfering with political and economic matters (namely economic development and social change), ethical justifications should not only evaluate the ends of any particular course of social actions but also the means, economic choices, and technical methods, for instance, which have been used in order to attain those ends. In this way, ethics penetrate the value context and meaning of any social action. Ultimately, the whole development enterprise has to be critically subjected to ethical considerations. Thus, in response to the question of whether ethics is associated with the ends or means of human activity, Goulet (1997, p. 1165) suggests that "[e]thics is concerned both with ends and means of human action".

On this note, Goulet embarks on a discussion of how development ethics should be formulated by introducing an open dialogue on economic and social development, as well as its ethical reflections. In his most influential work, *The Cruel Choice: A New Concept in the Theory of Development*, first published in 1971, Goulet (1975a) poses the bedrocks of development ethics. The meaning of his work can be summarised in the effort of thrusting "debates over economic and social development into the arena of ethical values" (Goulet, 1975a, p. vii). The central ethical question that Goulet's development ethics investigates is 'what are the requirements of a good life and of a good society in the modern world?' In *The Cruel Choice*, Goulet (1975a, p. 60–95), for the first time, identifies three universally accepted ethical goals, namely: (i) life sustenance; (ii) esteem; and (iii) freedom. He also demonstrates three ethical strategies across the development effort of achieving the aforementioned goals. These strategies are: (1) universal solidarity; (2) the abundance of goods as a prerequisite to people's humaneness; and (3) the populace's representation in the matters of public interest and people's control over their destinies.[13]

Goulet bases his ethical study of development on two basic concepts: existence rationality and vulnerability. Both concepts overlap in his study of development ethics. Goulet's ethical analysis can be perceived as a theoretical ethical umbrella that involves the conceptual navigation of his development ethics.

4.2.1 Existence Rationality

For Goulet (1975a, p. 188), existence rationality is defined as "the process by which a society devises a conscious strategy for obtaining its goals, given its ability to process information and the constraints weighing upon it." Interpreting Goulet's words, existence rationality is considered as the system of meanings (customs, norms, beliefs, social attributes, etc.) within the economic, social, and political structure that exists in any society and determines the course of action undertaken to serve societal aims. More specifically, the system of meanings refers to how societies evaluate, employ, and apply particular strategies in order to assist what Goulet (1975a) sets as universal goals of development: life sustenance, esteem, and freedom.

In general, Goulet (1975a) accepts the taxonomy of societies as traditional, transitional, and modern. Each type has built an alternative system of meanings under a historical and social process. His argument is based on the premise that development should not be perceived as an alien body to the existing system of meaning of any societal type. If development is to be addressed, three conditions ought to be followed: "(a) new capacities for handling information must be generated; (b) vital resources hitherto not available must become exploitable; and (c) the alien rationality implicit in modernization must be re-interpreted in terms

[13] The ethical goals and strategies of development ethics are further discussed in Chapter 5.

of traditional existence rationalities"; Goulet (1975a, p. 189) calls this progress "expanded existence".

Further, Goulet (1971; 1975a; 1995) stresses the importance of the dynamic of value change in determining what is to be defined as 'development'. In his words, "'development' is above all a question of values" (Goulet, 1971, p. 205). The innovation and novel behaviour patterns that development brings up usually affect the value system of the society. A conventional approach to development—in terms of social scientists' study and practices—confronts values either as aids or as obstacles in attaining its goals. In other words, development goals are predetermined and values are used in a functional way by subordinating them. By contrast, Goulet's analysis looks into the dynamics of value change in each society and builds its paradigm on this idea. Societal value systems are threatened by changes, and social change is one of the main components of development. If we accept that development affects the values of society and vice versa, the concept of existence rationality should be investigated. The core value of existence rationality is to be concerned with the provision of those ingredients that ensure what any society defines as a good life. Thus, any change should be integrated into the principle of existence rationality or the system of meanings determined by each society.

4.2.2 Vulnerability

The second key component of Goulet's study of ethically founded development is vulnerability. It is mainly analysed within the dualism between developed and less-developed or underdeveloped (developing) societies and nations. "Vulnerability is exposure to forces one cannot control" (Goulet, 1975a, p. vii). For Goulet, vulnerability refers directly to underdeveloped conditions and indirectly to advanced developed conditions. It is better explained when we perceive vulnerability as an initial state. In developing societies, vulnerability implies barriers to meeting development goals. The dualism of the global economic system and international development—the North–South division of the world, developed and developing nations, rich and poor people and societies—largely explains the vulnerability of developing nations and poor societies. As economic history has shown, "the Industrial Revolution of Western capitalist economies not only accentuated the spread and aggravated the lag, but actually propelled industrial economies, on the one hand, and non-industrialized economies, on the other, into diverse paths"

(Goulet, 1975a, p. 39). More precisely, industrialisation in the developed world, in many cases, has been associated with the exploitation of resources, economic involvement, and political patronage in non-industrialised nations. Intervention from advanced to developing nations in the economic, social, and political environment makes developing countries vulnerable to being unable to discover and meet their development goals. Furthermore, vulnerability is a matter of power, as well as an ethical matter. It is a matter of power for the reason that societies that are less vulnerable have the advantage of asserting their own development aims, and such societies can also affect the meaning of the phrase 'a good life' based on their historical and societal needs.

4.3 The Conceptual Foundation of Goulet's Development Ethics

Turning now to the conceptual foundation of Goulet's development ethics, a general premise is that the study of development ethics can be forceful only if it takes place in the field of the social sciences, looking at applied policies and their ethical reflection (Goulet, 1995; 1996; 1997; 2006a). Almost all development ethicists agree with this premise. Goulet conceives the conceptual foundation of development ethics by answering the question 'what is development ethics?' In his words, "[t]he discipline of development ethics is the conceptual cement that binds together multiple diagnoses of the problem with their policy implications through an explicit phenomenological study of values which lays bare the value costs of alternative courses of action" (Goulet, 1995, p. 27). Further, development ethics should be formulated as "disciplined eclecticism": eclectic in its selection of subject matters and disciplined in its mode of studying them (Goulet, 1997, p. 1168). Accordingly, development ethics receives insight from the work of other intellectual fields, such as the social sciences and humanities, religious studies, and ecology. The elaboration of all these concerns and inceptions takes place under a wide ethical view in the discussion of development means and goals, quality of life, and respect for cultural diversity. Almost all Goulet's ethical thoughts permeate from the insight that development ethics ought to investigate development in light of fundamental philosophical queries on the meaning of a good life, the foundation of justice in society, and the human stance towards nature (Goulet, 1997, p. 1161). The study of development ethics attempts to discuss and codify the aforementioned philosophical inquires, borrowing scientific instruments from economists, political and religious researchers, anthropologists, environmental scientists, and others. More importantly, for Goulet, development ethics cannot only be described normatively but also practically. In his words, "to ethicists it is axiomatic that how development is pursued is just as important as what benefits are gained" (Goulet, 1997, p. 1168).

In sum, Goulet puts forth the concept of development and distinguishes it from the conventional notion of development—the way that dominant theories of development (e.g. development as economic growth) deal with the problem of development. Goulet endows the term 'development' with all those traits that development should entail in order to be human. For Goulet, development refers to the means and ends of human action or, in other words, to the vision of a better life and the way that this life can be accessed. In his words, "[d]evelopment is simultaneously the vision of a better life—a life materially richer, institutionally more 'modern', and technologically more efficient—and an array of means to achieve that vision" (Goulet, 2006a, p. 183). As previously mentioned, development ought to respond to longstanding philosophical inquiries concerning the meaning of a good life, the foundation of justice in society and within societies, and the stance of human individuals and societies towards nature. "Providing satisfactory conceptual and institutional answers to these three questions is what constitutes authentic development" (Goulet, 1996, p. 197; see also Goulet, 2006a, p. 150). Any concept of human fulfilment is highly relative and, as Goulet (1975a, pp. 96–108) points out, development can be examined as a dialectical process. Development goals are usually interactive, and no range exists among life sustenance, esteem, and freedom. The essential point is that development should not judge the aforementioned goals (as is conventionally the case), but these goals must become the criteria by which development itself must be judged (Goulet, 1995, p. 48). In this mode, grading a nation based on high economic growth does not mean that it has followed an ethical development pattern. Development cannot be achieved under the following circumstances: if massive consumption leads societies towards adopting an entirely material manner of living that emphasises the notion of 'have' instead of 'be'; if structural relations between nations and within them (among classes and individuals) are competitive and there is unequal distribution of development proceeds; if the exploitation of material resources leads to the destruction of ecological balance; and if technological advantages are used to abolish freedom.

As previously mentioned, development ethics relates to an ethical reflection on the ends and means of any developmental endeavour. Ethics is incorporated with "the value dynamisms of the instruments utilized by development agents", thus becoming a "means of the means" (Goulet, 1995, p. 25). Any instrumental action (an economic policy, for instance) should be tested under an ethical deliberation taking into account the aforementioned ethical considerations of life sustenance, esteem, and freedom. For all people and any society in the world, development ought to cover at least three aims that correspond to the aforementioned goals of development: (1) to pursue more and better life-sustaining goods for all human beings; (2) to create and improve the conditions that nurture the sense of esteem of individuals and societies; and (3) to release humans from all forms of servitude (to nature, to other people, to institutions, and to beliefs) (Goulet, 1995, pp. 47–48).

Goulet's development ethics renders for the social sciences and development economics a way to be critically aware of the moral content of choices. By the formulation of ethical strategies—the abundance of goods, universal solidarity, and participation—Goulet has shown an alternative road based on the normative principles of ethical development. Through this process, development ethics offers the ideal of hope, preserving hope "as the possibility of creating new possibilities" (Goulet, 1995, p. 28). At the end of the day, the essential task of development ethics is human ascent in all relevant aspects of life, and development should be perceived as the means and the end in this course of action.

Goulet's contribution can be identified in the unfolding, enrichment, and enhancement of development ethics. There is no doubt that there are alternative dimensions that someone can investigate as ethical considerations in the study of development. Although one critique of Goulet's work that it is as polymorphous as the nature of the study of ethics in development, an important consideration is that Goulet paved the way by bringing the study of ethics and value reflection to the concept of development.

5 The Contemporary Field of Development Ethics

In the tradition of Goulet, ethics penetrates almost all aspects of development. However, development ethics is not only a theoretical but also a practical manner of exploring development. As mentioned, Goulet postulates his principles by perceiving ethics in development "as the means of the means" (Goulet, 1995, pp. 24–27). With consideration to Goulet's positioning of ethics as the ends and means of development, almost all development ethicists accept the description of development ethics as the study of ethical reflection on the means and ends of local, national, and international development. By its definition and nature, development ethics is a pluralistic, interdisciplinary meeting place for social scientists (political scientists, economists, and psychologists), philosophers (moral and political), environmental scientists and ecologists, humanists, and practitioners of any kind to incorporate ethical issues and reflections into development. The interdisciplinary nature of development ethics motivated the creation of the International Development Ethics Association (IDEA). The IDEA was initiated in 1984, in Costa Rica. This section describes the constitutional principles of the IDEA and the evolution of development ethics from Goulet until the present. However, this does not imply that there are no contributory studies of development ethics beyond those of the IDEA. The IDEA's principal commitments are used as a theoretical pattern for reviewing contemporary aspects in the expanded interdisciplinary domain of development ethics. Additionally, the analysis that follows focuses on the development ethics studies that relate to the subject matter of this book: development economics and international development, rather than other crucial topics such as the ethical role of pedagogy or the ethics of aid in development, for instance.[14]

5.1 The International Development Ethics Association

According to its constitution, the IDEA is a unique international, cross-cultural, and interdisciplinary group of philosophers, development and environmental theorists, and practitioners. On that account, the

[14] Regarding the ethical task of pedagogy in development, see Gasper (2008) and Goulet (2006a, p. 22; 1995, pp. 5–9); for the ethics of aid, see Goulet (1995, [Chap. 12]), Goulet and Hudson (1971), and Dower (1998a, [Chap. 8]).

IDEA comprises a foundational umbrella where social scientists, philosophers, humanists, ecologists, technocrats, and practitioners with different origins, statuses, and backgrounds from all over the world discuss, discover, and act on crucial development issues. There are many prominent development ethicists (e.g. Crocker, Gasper, Clark, Dower, and Drydyk, to name just a few) who study development ethics in its contemporary form and accept the constitutional aims of the IDEA. According to its constitution, the aim of the IDEA is threefold[15]:

- "To apply ethical reflection to development goals and strategies and to relations between the 'North' and 'South'. Numerous groups are concerned with international development. Only IDEA, however, explicitly formulates and applies ethical principles to the theory and practice of global, national, and local development.
- To effect ethically sound development policies, institutions, and practices. In the light of reasonable ethical principles, IDEA is committed to bringing about improvements in development and environmental policies, institutions and projects.
- To promote solidarity, mutual support, and interchange among those development theorists and practitioners throughout the world who are seeking to implement ethically better development paradigms and strategies."

Accepting the aforementioned commitments, development ethicists involve ethical development in the levels of ethical value issues as Goulet theorised, in which ethical value issues are recognised as an important part of the development discourse. These issues are not peripheral or mere extras after the technical and economic analyses. Value issues ought to be at the very heart of all development thinking. For the IDEA, the discussion of value issues is concentrated on two key areas. The first is the careful defence of the basic normative theories (whether secular or religious) that justify a model of local, national, or global development. For example, such theories appeal to social justice, human rights, basic needs, and theological understandings of the human condition. The second is the application of values to decision-making, whether at the level of donor organisations or grassroots communities. There is a vast agenda on the

[15] Retrieved from the IDEA's website: http://www.development-ethics.org/.

ethics of means—both on how to realise the goals and what ethical limits must be observed in pursuing these goals. The aforementioned value issues can be taken up in a number of different but complementary ways. There are three main ways of incorporating ethical value issues within development ethics[16]:

- "Reflection: Philosophical thinking can clarify what development is; it can defend normative positions by critical and rational thinking about ethical alternatives; it can identify the complexities involved in the rational choice of means. Philosophical and theological reflection can provide a basic understanding of the human condition and of morally relevant facts.
- Application: the social scientist, technologist, economist, medial expert, or agriculturalist can integrate their expertise with properly articulated values to make their prescriptions and policies more ethically authoritative.
- Practice: the committed development worker or policy maker engaged with concrete problems can gain from more abstract thinking and at the same time keep such reflection firmly rooted in and informed by development practice."

As it seems, the IDEA's ethical guide to the nature of value issues and the way that these values issues are investigated maintains a close relationship with Goulet's stratum of development ethics. As Dutt and Wilber (2010b, p. 15) point out, "Denis Goulet himself contributed to all these levels of analysis, weaving them together in many of his contributions". In recent times, several studies of development have shared common or similar views with the IDEA and Goulet's development ethics thinking in studying current development situations. On this subject, Drydyk (2013, p. 4), in his presidential address during the nineteenth International Conference of the International Development Ethics Association (which took place in 2011), pointed out that "[t]here are many people who contribute to development ethics without saying so and without describing themselves as development ethicists". Some of these people are mentioned in the following section, which describes the evolution of development ethics from Goulet to the present.

[16] Retrieved from the IDEA's website: http://www.development-ethics.org/.

5.2 From Goulet to Recent Development Ethics

A couple of years after the publication of Goulet's *The Cruel Choice*, first published in 1971, American social scientist Berger (1974) published *Pyramids of Sacrifice*. Berger's book deals with the developing third world and specifically with the application of political ethics to social change. Moreover, he explores the incorporation of value neutrality in the fields of social sciences and development economics. In his words:

> No humanly acceptable discussion of the anguishing problems of the world's poverty can avoid ethical considerations. In addition, no political ethics worthy of the name can avoid the centrally important case of the Third World. It follows from these assumptions that this book is not primarily a scholarly work in the sense of 'value-free science' (Berger, 1974, p. vii).

Pyramids of Sacrifice was written during the Cold War era. In this regard, Berger (1974, p. xi) sums up his views on international development by beginning with the following postulation: "[t]he world today is divided into ideological camps. The adherents of each tell us with great assurance where we're at and what we should do about it. We should not believe any of them". This view is close to Goulet's beliefs about ethical development, regarding keeping an equal distance from two ideological camps. In addition, Goulet's development ethics has been influenced by Berger in various ways, particularly on how change affects development and vice versa. In 1975, Goulet himself wrote an article titled *Pyramids of Sacrifice: The High Price of Social Change* (Goulet, 1975b). In this article, Goulet debates some of Berger's views on ethical development. However, what is important is that "[l]ike Peter Berger in The Pyramids of Sacrifice, Goulet unmasks the abundant ways in which development agents—under the banner of doing good—can bring evil into the world" (Crocker, 2006, p. xxiv). In the years afterwards, Berger's (1987) writings on the structure of capitalism, cultural diversity, and globalisation enlarged the agenda of development ethics. Thus, recent development ethicists have identified Berger along with Lebret and Goulet as the contributors to development ethics as a self-conscious field (Gasper, 2004, p. 14).

Beyond social and economic change as the most important element of development, for development ethicists, the reflection of value issues in that change is also equally important. This reflection is a matter of the ends and means of any change. Regarding the discussion of the end and means of development, Dower (1988; 2010) was perhaps the first development ethicist after Goulet to explore systematically the idea of the ethics of means. For Dower, development ethics and Goulet's work opened the ethical debate between the ends and means of development. Until then, particularly in line with economic development, development had largely been accepted as an end state of economic growth. In turn, the means of development had been perceived as technical issues. "It has generally been agreed that economic growth is important, both in reducing the gap between rich and poor countries and in providing the basis for the reduction of extreme poverty" and "the main practical emphasis has been upon technical questions, about the means for generating growth" (Dower, 1988, p. 3). Dower stresses the normative essence of development by arguing the following: "if my analysis of development is at all correct, it will turn out that a major task for anyone thinking about development is a normative task: that of identifying and defending a set of values implicit in the model of development which is accepted" (Dower, 1988, p. 4). In the discussion of ethical values and the goals of development, Dower (2010, p. 31) poses two key ethical questions. First, 'is the goal being pursued one that ought to be pursued?' Second, 'are the actions being taken to realize the goal the right one?' He concludes that, "the pursuit of development ought always to be done ethically... because there is a certain kind of relationship between means and ends that make them ethically intertwined" (Dower, 2010, p. 35).

Paul Streeten's views on the means and ends of economic and human development are commonly discussed in the development ethics literature (Crocker, 2008, p. 36). According to Streeten (1994, p. 232), "[h]uman beings are both ends in themselves and means of production". Thus, beyond technical advances as a requirement of development, human development should assist people's capabilities. "This is not to say that technical analysis should be abandoned. Far from it. But we should never lose sight of the ultimate purpose of the exercise, to treat men and women as ends, to improve the human condition, to enlarge people's choices" (Streeten, 1994, p. 232). Since 1981, Streeten (along with Burki, ul Haq, Hicks, and Stewart) has argued that the "[f]irst, and most important, the basic needs concept is a reminder that the objective of the development effort is to provide all human beings with the *opportunity* for a full life. However a 'full life' is interpreted, the opportunity for achieving it presupposes meeting basic needs" (Streeten et al., 1981, p. 21, italics and quotation marks from the original). "Opportunity" is close in meaning to Sen's capability approach to international development (Sen, 1981; 1997; 1999). Streeten and Sen's studies of international development have led many development thinkers, practitioners, and policy-makers, as well as the United Nations Human Development Programme, in the direction of researching and indexing international development not only with economic but also humanitarian criteria.

Sen has also been acknowledged by the development ethics community and by Goulet himself as an exceptional contributor to the study of ethical development, not only because of his general involvement with issues concerning international development but mainly because of his attempt to formulate a normative conceptual relationship between ethics and economics. As well as adopting a normative approach, Sen (the same as Goulet) approaches development not only in a theoretical but also in an applied and practical mode. Goulet (2006a, p. 175) poses the problem thus: "within the economic discipline it was the value-free engineering stream of theory, methodology, and analysis which prevailed", in which Sen's contribution is crucial. For instance, Sen (1987) relates economics to the study of ethics by abolishing from economics the assumption of value neutrality. In his words;

> The methodology of so-called 'positive economics' has not only shunned normative analysis in economics, it has also had the effect of ignoring a variety of complex ethical considerations which affect actual human behavior and which, from the point of view of the economists studying such behavior, are primarily matters of it [development] (Sen, 1987, p. 7).

Moreover, Sen challenges the neoclassical notions of economic rationality and self-interest as the exclusive drivers of human behaviour. Sen (1987, p. 9) advises that "economics, as it has emerged, can be made more productive by paying greater and more explicit attention to the ethical considerations that shape human behaviour and judgement." The views of Sen and other development ethicists on ethics and economics have been influenced by Aristotelian moral and political philosophy[17]; thus, in many cases, Sen shares with Goulet (and vice versa) common ideas on the relationship between the means and the ends or, more broadly, on ethics and economics. To date, Sen's work has influenced the context

[17] An analytical view of the Aristotelian contribution to development ethics has been discussed in a former section of this chapter.

of current development ethics in various ways. In recent studies, development ethicists have analysed and strengthened Sen's agency-oriented view of development as a freedom and capability approach in the concept of global development (Crocker, 1991; 2008; Gasper, 2002; Clark, 2005). For several development thinkers (see, for example, Gasper and St. Clair (eds.), 2010a, 2010b; Haq and Ponzio (eds.), 2008), Sen is accepted as a kind of theoretical founder of the human development approach that led Mahbub ul Haq to establish the United Nations Development Programme's Human Development Report in 1994. "The leading theoretician here has been Amartya Sen, and the leading policy practitioner was Mahbub ul Haq, founder of the UNDP Human Development Reports (HDRs) and the human development movement in development analysis and advocacy" (Gasper and Truong, 2005, p. 375). Sen's capability approach has been enriched by recent development ethicists (Drydyk, 2010; Crocker, 1996; 2008; 2010; Clark, 2005; Gasper, 2002; 2004; 2007). Therefore, what is important is that contemporary studies of development ethics have embodied many of Sen's views into the theoretical and practical meaning of development.

One of the major topics in the development ethics discussion is poverty along with social justice, human rights, and basic needs. St. Clair's (2007) article, *A Methodologically Pragmatist Approach to Development Ethics* offers some ideas for reframing poverty as a global and moral problem. She argues that development ethics and global justice theories could help rethink alternative forms of globalisation. St. Clair (2007, p. 143) views development ethics "as a hybrid between a public moral-political philosophy and a public conception of social science". She also argues for methodological pragmatism in the nature of development ethics based on the contributions of Goulet and Sen. For Goulet (2006a, p. 19), "development ethics is useless unless it can be translated into public action". In turn, Sen's capability approach provides the applied or empirical basis of human development as it is adopted by the United Nations Development Programme. As St. Clair (2007, pp. 153–157) states, Sen's capability approach is methodologically pragmatist in the sense that "theoretical freedom is not the same as actual freedom for all"; St. Clair concludes by arguing that:

> [M]ethodologically, pragmatist development ethics is an offspring of Goulet's life and work, and a path forward in this interdisciplinary space includes to revisit, update and expand Goulet's insights in a way that

it may influence decisions of those who hold power (St. Clair, 2007, pp. 153–157).

Overall, St. Clair's approach agrees with Sen's and Goulet's contributions to applied and practical formations of development ethics.

At the level of application and practice and from the viewpoint of Goulet's formulation of the ethical goals and strategies of development, Jameson (2010) recognises the ethical goals of development (life sustenance, esteem, and freedom) as the ethical principles for macroeconomic development. In the words of Jameson (2010, p. 402), "he [Goulet] concluded that there are three ethically mandated goals for an economy, as gleaned from the human experience across countries and across time." Extending ethical strategies, Goulet's analysis of the abundance of goods can be perceived as an originator of new developments in happiness studies that suggest that overabundance does not even increase happiness, beyond a certain level of goods (see Dutt and Radcliff (eds.), 2009). More recently, Dutt and Wilber (2010b, p. 11) have observed that subjective well-being research has proven that "beyond a certain level of income and consumption, further increases do not add significantly, or not at all, to a person's happiness". The authors directly connect this approach to the development ethics strategy of the abundance of goods.

In turn, participation has been part of the advanced discussions of recent studies of development ethics. As participation is one of the focal points of development, recent development studies with the lines of development ethics have incorporated Goulet's ideas with new approaches. For instance, Crocker (2010) and Drydyk (2010) supplement Goulet's account of participation with Sen's ideas of participation and endowment in development, as well as in the concept of deliberative democracy. It is outside of the scope of this present section of the book to focus on these theories; however, in brief, this indicates the significance of Goulet's and Sen's development ethics ideas of participation as one of the major topics in the development ethics discourse.

Schwenke (2011) explores "the audacious" (in terms of philosophical and practical issues) agenda of development ethics. In his words (Schwenke, 2011, pp. 337–338), "development ethics can provide a basic understanding of the human condition and of morally relevant facts". Schwenke (2009) also provides a discussion of applied-ethical issues such as education, participation, and minorities' rights in the conceptual cadre of international development from the angle of development ethics. He discusses a variety of real experiences in the developing world (in Kenya, Uganda, and elsewhere), in accordance with the applied ethics theory and policy. In his final chapter, "Ethical Performance", he underlines the role of the public sector in human or ethical development. According to Schwenke (2009, p. 151), "[p]eople and institutions have the potential to perform to exceptionally high moral standards, to provide public services with honor and commitment, and to exemplify the ideals of dedicated public service". Schwenke's study of development ethics and international development is both theoretical and practical, while the field of development ethics is viewed as comprising both theory and applied policy. Very close to the beliefs of Goulet and other development ethicists (such as Crocker, Gasper, and Dower), Schwenke (2011, p. 338) remarks that "[t]he effectiveness of development ethics to shape and improve development itself still remains highly constrained by the troubling resistance of the development establishment to embrace it as a valued resource."

At the level of application, Enderle (1999; 2000; 2009) challenges business ethics from the angle of development ethics by introducing the concept of international business ethics and emphasising the roles of culture and values in business ethics. In this framework, ethics in a global business context is used in a broader sense, covering:

> [T]he whole 'economic domain of life' and thus dealing with the individual decision making of economic actors such as managers and employees, the shaping and conduct of economic organizations, business-related public policies, economic systems, and global economic and financial institutions alike (Enderle, 2000, p. 266).

What is important in the aforementioned works is that Enderle (1999; 2000; 2009) addresses the field of applied business ethics not only on a microeconomic level but also on a macroeconomic level, taking into consideration the international aspects of business ethics. Regarding application and practice, based on the aforementioned premise, Enderle (2009) proposes an ethically good manner of wealth creation to one of the emerging economies of the world China. "After all, business is about producing wealth, and ethics has to make sure that this is done properly" (Enderle, 2009, p. 290). In this regard, "properly" means that wealth creation considers more than financial capital by including physical, human, and social capital. "Wealth is not only private wealth but also encompasses public wealth, both influencing each other in multiple ways… Wealth is not merely material, but also has a spiritual side, which enables its creation to a truly human activity" (Enderle, 2009, p. 292). In the notes of this article, he states:

> I'm beginning to understand how important a proper concept of and a determined focus on wealth creation are precisely for addressing the issues of poverty and inequality between income and wealth. Furthermore, these vital problems cannot be dealt with in a purely technical and value-free manner. Culture and religion obviously matter, and their impact, for better or worse, needs to be investigated and evaluated (Enderle, 2009, p. 293).

In their paper *The Economy of Spirit*, Appleby and Bindenagel (2010) correlate religious aspects (as per Goulet and other development ethicists) with contemporary development issues as they are practically expressed by religious organisations. They draw upon the spiritual meanings of development in the sense of people and community solidarity. Appleby and Bindenagel (2010, p. 286) state that "the Western exaltation of the individual, conceptualized as an autonomous moral agent operating in an atomized society, further distorts the meaning and orientation of human person"; they argue that, based on the Catholic tradition, development ethics and "Goulet understood the community, not the individual to be the basic unit of society". At a practical level, Appleby and Bindenagel (2010) count a number of worldwide applications where religious-oriented organisations lift people out of poverty in various ways.

Beyond practical religious ethics, development ethicists have recently approached global poverty as a problem of ethics and social justice, highlighting the element of power in international development (Eskelinen, 2009; 2011). As the gap between development theory and practice is large, "I [Eskelinen] share the conviction of several philosophers concerned with 'development ethics' that the concept of development can be redefined" (Eskelinen, 2009, p. 81). Eskelinen (2009; 2011) mainly analyses the key development issues of poverty from the point of view of political philosophy following the beliefs of political realism. According to political realism, worldwide injustice conditions and the distribution of power among nations play significant roles in the incorporation of poverty. Regarding the applied terms of political realism, Eskelinen (2011) argues that even international institutions (the World Trade Organization, for instance) are just enough according to their constitutional aims, the major sources of injustice and poverty are rather the prevailing power relations of national governments.

We partly disagree with this particular position. Even though the role of a nation-state is still powerful in international development (Gilpin, 2001), strong conservative strains in the 1980s and 1990s within developed nation-states and dominant international development institutions have forced the international development pattern towards following the Washington Consensus policy applied in Latin America and elsewhere (Williamson (ed.), 1990a, 1990b; see also Marangos, 2009a; 2009b).

Stiglitz (1998; 1999; 2000a; 2000b; 2002a; 2002b; 2002c; Stiglitz et al., 2006; Serra and Stiglitz (eds.), 2008) argues for a new development paradigm in international development theory and policy, beyond the Washington Consensus. He argues that the policies of nation-states and international development institutions should be reinforced in line with the following general suggestion: "To be meaningful, the vision and actions must be set within a coherent framework, which requires setting priorities, encouraging partnership and taking into account the global and regional environment" (Stiglitz, 1998, p. 23). Stiglitz's views have been integrated into the agenda of development ethics (Crocker, 2006a). Beyond his critique of the applied policies and results of the Washington Consensus, Stiglitz (1998; 1999; 2000a) also argued for a Post-Washington Consensus policy in international development. In this respect, a good development policy rests on both the public sector and the private sector. Crocker (2006b, p. 42), in turn, acknowledges that "[d]evelopment ethicists, such as Stiglitz, enrich public discussion by challenging global citizens to improve development policies and global institutions so that globalization can be less of curse and more of a blessing."

Finally, in more recent development ethics literature, two selective edited volumes have incorporated development ethics as an interdisciplinary field of study. The first is *New Directions in Development Ethics: Essays in Honor of Denis Goulet*, edited by Wilber and Dutt (2010). The second is *Development Ethics*, edited by Gasper and St. Clair (2010a, 2010b). In the introductory chapter of the first volume, after an extended presentation of Goulet's life, work, and contribution, development ethics is placed in the field of development economics. The editors make a clear classification of the context, following IDEA codifications. "This discussion of the major themes of development ethics suggests that the subject involves various levels of analysis": those of reflection, application, and practice (Dutt and Wilber, 2010a, pp. 14–15). In the second volume, the editors accept development ethics as a broad, multidisciplinary field of debate. Gasper and St. Clair's (2010a, 2010b) book follows a holistic perspective on ethical development, including a variety of debates and concepts from well-established development thinkers such as Sen, Nussbaum, Oizilbath, Crocker, Stiglitz, the aforementioned editors, and Goulet, to name but a few of the contributors. In this edited volume, development ethics gives core attention to: the values proposed as constituting the meaning of human, societal, and/or global development; the evaluation of experience and alternatives; and the methods and methodologies of development (Gasper and St. Clair, 2010a, p. xv). In both editions, well-known and established development thinkers (some of whom have already been mentioned) challenge the debate on development issues on the pluralistic, multi-collective nature of development ethics. What is common is the presence of Goulet's leading conceptual formulation of development ethics as a self-conscious area of study in the interdisciplinary field of development.

Therefore, the concluding remark of this section is that the evolutionary study of development ethics has enriched the field with new insights, such as Sen's capability approach. However, it seems that the basic conceptual assumptions of development ethics remain based on Goulet's foundation. According to Gasper (2006, p. 2):

> Well before Sen, Haq and Nussbaum, he [Goulet] advocated that authentic development aims towards the realization of human capabilities in all spheres and that economic growth and technological modernity must be treated as, at best, potential means towards considered human values, not vice versa.

In the same vein, Dutt and Wilber (2010b, p. 12) argue that, "Goulet anticipated the writing of Sen and others on functioning and capabilities and on the fulfilment of basic needs by recognizing early on deprivations such as poor health, lack of education, and lack of self-respect." Hence, development ethics has recently been approached at the levels of reflection, application, and practice (see the IDEA's configuration of development ethics). Nevertheless, we can evidently argue that, even at the levels of application and practice, much work has been done by recent development ethicists; at the level of reflection/theory, development ethics is still based on Goulet's conceptual foundation.

6 Conclusion

The foundation of development ethics as a self-conscious field of study is mainly based on Goulet's life and work. The initiator of development ethics as an intellectual field, according to Goulet, is his teacher Lebret. Goulet shares with his teacher a common perspective on ethical development. For Goulet (2006a, p. 57), Lebret's main contribution to development ethics is his study of values and needs in development processes. Development is approached as a question of values, while needs should assist societal solidarity, resource sustainability, and the integral human need of all individuals and societies to a decent existence. Development ethics is based on these premises. Furthermore, Goulet extends the analysis of development ethics by investigating the relationship between the ends and the means of development. For Goulet, ethics penetrates almost all aspects of development. Thus, ethics inevitably becomes the means of the means. In turn, the concepts of existence rationality and vulnerability overlap almost all of Goulet's work on development ethics. Goulet's development ethics can be characterised as normative in the manner of analysis and as practical in the context. In view of this, Goulet suggests a bundle of ethical goals and ethical strategies that each society should espouse in order to enable its people to have good lives and to establish a good society.

Recent studies in the field of development ethics have incorporated development issues at the levels of reflection, application, and practice. The field of development ethics has been expanded, and new dimensions in the study of ethical development have been supported. The development ethics community has embraced the principles of Sen's capability approach and similar concerns. The contemporary areas of study within development ethics are centred on the emerging concepts of social justice, human rights, and basic needs. Moreover, world dualism and poverty relations have always been at the centre of the development ethics discussion.

Regarding the deeper origins of development ethics, after a brief review of Goulet's views on the precursors of development ethics (Lebret, Gandhi, and Myrdal), this chapter has analysed Aristotelian moral and political theory as the philosophical originator of development ethics.

According to the findings of the analysis, development ethics has been influenced by Aristotle's philosophy in the way that he evaluates the ends and means of development taking the notions of a good life and a good society into consideration.

To this end, we offer the following closing remarks regarding the foundation of development ethics. First, development ethics is a new interdisciplinary field within development studies, originating at the end of the 1960s. Second, the founding father of development ethics is Goulet, while contemporary development ethicists have enriched the field of development ethics, mainly with applied and practical work. Third, the deeper origins of development ethics can be found in the life and work of Gandhi, Myrdal, and Goulet's direct precursor Lebret, while the philosophical underpinning of development ethics can be traced back to Aristotelian moral and political philosophy.

References

Appleby, S., & Bindenagel, C. (2010). The economy of the spirit: Religion, ethics, and development in the thought of denis goulet and in contemporary practice. In C. K. Wilber & A. K. Dutt (Eds.), *New directions in development ethics: Essays in honor of Denis Goulet* (pp. 281–307). University of Notre Dame Press.

Aristotle. (1959 [1932]). *Aristotle politics*. (T. Page, E. Capps, W. Rouse, L. Post, E. Warmington, Eds., & H. Rackham, Trans.) London: William Heinemann Ltd.

Aristotle. (2000). *ARISTOTLE: Nicomachean ethics*. (R. Crisp, Ed., & R. Crisp, Trans.) Cambridge, UK: Cambridge University Press.

Berger, P. (1974). *Pyramids of sacrifice*. Basic Books.

Berger, P. (1987). *The capitalist revolution*. Aldershot: Wildwood House.

Clark, D. A. (2002). Development ethics: A research agenda. *International Journal of Social Economics, 29*(11), 830–848.

Clark, D. A. (2005). Sen's capability approach and the many spaces of human well-being. *The Journal of Development Studies, 41*(8), 1339–1368.

Crocker, D. (1991). Toward development ethics. *World Development, 19*(5), 457–483.

Crocker, D. (1996). Hunger, capability, and development. In W. Aiken & H. LaFollette (Eds.), *World hunger and morality* (2nd ed., pp. 211–230). Prentice Hall.

Crocker, D. (1998). Development ethics. In C. Edward (Ed.), *Routledge encyclopedia of philosophy* (Vol. 3, pp. 39–44). Routledge.

Crocker, D. (2006a). Foreword. In D. Goulet (Ed.), *Development ethics at work: Explorations—1960–2002* (pp. v–xxix). London: Routledge.

Crocker, D. (2006b). Development ethics, globalization, and Stiglitz. pp. 1–47. Working paper to appear in M. Krausz and D. Chottergee (Eds.), *Globalization, development, and democracy: Philosophical perspectives*. Retrieved from http://terpconnect.umd.edu/~dcrocker/Courses/Docs/PUAF698Q-Dev%20Ethics,%20Globalization%20and%20Stiglitz.pdf

Crocker, D. (2006c). Sen and deliberative democracy. In A. Kaufman (Ed.), *Capabilities equality: Basic issues and problems* (pp. 155–197). Routledge.

Crocker, D. (2008). *Ethics of global development*. Cambridge University Press.

Crocker, D. (2010). Participation in local development: Goulet and deliberative democracy. In C. K. Wilber & A. K. Dutt (Eds.), *New directions in development ethics: Essays in Honor of Denis Goulet* (pp. 308–332). Notre Dame University Press.

Das, A. (1979). *Foundations of gandhian economics*. St Martin's Press.

Dower, N. (1988). *What is development? A philosopher's answer*. Centre for Development Studies Occasional Paper Series, 3. Glasgow: University of Glasgow.

Dower, N. (1998). *World ethics: The new agenda*. Edinburgh University Press.

Dower, N. (1998). Development ethics. In R. Chadwick (Ed.), *Encyclopedia of applied ethics* (pp. 755–766). Academic Press.

Dower, N. (2010). Development and the ethics of the means. In C. K. Wilber & A. K. Dutt (Eds.), *Development ethics new directions: Essays in honor of Denis Goulet* (pp. 29–37). University of Notre Dame.

Drydyk, J. (2010). Participation, empowerment, and democracy: Three fickle friends. In C. K. Wilber & A. K. Dutt (Eds.), *New directions in development ethics: Essays in honor of Denis Goulet* (pp. 333–356). Notre Dame University Press.

Drydyk, J. (2013). Development ethics and gender justice. *Éthique et économique/Ethics and Economics, 10*(2), 4–10.

Dutt, A. K., & Radciliff, B. (Eds.). (2009). *Happiness, economics and politics: Towards a multi-disciplinary approach*. Edward Elgar.

Dutt, A. K., & Wilber, C. K. (2010). Introduction: Development ethics and development economics. In C. K. Wilber & A. K. Dutt (Eds.), *New directions in development ethics—Essays in Honor of Denis Goulet* (pp. 1–26). University of Notre Dame Press.

Dutt, A. K., & Wilber, C. K. (2010). *Economics and ethics: An introduction*. Palgrave Macmillan.

Enderle, G. (1999). An introduction to international business ethics. In G. Enderle (Ed.), *International business ethics: Challenges and approaches*. Notre Dame, IN: University of Notre Dame Press.

Enderle, G. (2000). Business ethics in the intercultural and global context: A conceptual framework. *Zeitschrift für Wirtschafts und Unternehmensethik (ZfWU)[Journal for Business, Economics & Ethics]*, *1*(3), 263–285.
Enderle, G. (2009). A rich concept of wealth creation beyond profit maximization and adding value. *Journal of Business Ethics, 84*(3), 281–295.
Eskelinen, T. (2009). *Putting global poverty in context: A philosophical essay on power, justice and economy*. University of Jyväskylä.
Eskelinen, T. (2011). Global basis structure and institutions: The WTO as a practical example. *Journal of Global Ethics, 7*(1), 47–58.
Fromm, E. (1999). *Man for himself*. Routledge.
Fromm, E. (2005). *To have or to be*. Continuum International Publishing Group.
Gasper, D. (2002). Is Sen's capability approach an adequate basis for considering human development? *Review of Political Economy, 14*(2), 435–461.
Gasper, D. (2004). *The ethics of development*. Edinburgh University Press.
Gasper, D. (2006). Introduction: Working in development ethics—A tribute to Denis Goulet. *Éthique et économique/Ethics and Economics, 4*(2), 1–24.
Gasper, D. (2007). What is the capability approach? Its core, rationale, partners and dangers. *The Journal of Socio-Economics, 36*(3), 335–359.
Gasper, D. (2008). Denis Goulet and the project of development ethics: Choices in methodology, focus and organization. *Journal of Human Development, 9*(3), 453–474.
Gasper, D. (2012). Development ethics—Why? What? How? A formulation of the field. *Journal of Global Ethics, 8*(1), 117–135.
Gasper, D., & St. Clair, A. L. (Eds.). (2010). *Development ethics*. London: Ashgate.
Gasper, D., & St. Clair, A. L. (2010). The field of development ethics—An introduction. In D. Gasper & A. L. St. Clair (Eds.), *Development ethics* (pp. 13–33). London: Ashgate.
Gasper, D., & Truong, T.-D. (2005). Deepening development ethics: From economism to human development to human security. *The European Journal of Development Research, 17*(3), 372–384.
Gilpin, R. (2001). *Global political economy: Understanding the international economic order*. Princeton University Press.
Goulet, D. (1968). Development for what? *Comparative Political Studies, 1*(2), 295–312.
Goulet, D. (1971). An ethical model for the study of values. *Harvard Educational Review, 41*(2), 205–227.
Goulet, D. (1975). *The cruel choice: A new concept in the theory of development*. Atheneum.
Goulet, D. (1975). Pyramids of sacrifice: The high price of social change. *Christianity and Crisis, 35*(16), 231–236.

Goulet, D. (1989). Participation in development: New avenues. *World Development, 17*(2), 165–178.
Goulet, D. (1992). Development indicators: A research problem, a policy problem. *The Journal of Socio-Economics, 21*(3), 245–260.
Goulet, D. (1995). *Development ethics: A guide to theory and practice.* The Apex Press.
Goulet, D. (1996). Authentic development: Is it sustainable? In D. C. Pirages (Ed.), *Building sustainable societies: A blueprint for a post-industrial world* (pp. 189–205). Armonk, NY: M.E. Sharpe.
Goulet, D. (1997). Development ethics: A new discipline. *International Journal of Social Economics, 24*(11), 1160–1171.
Goulet, D. (2006). *Development ethics at work: Explorations 1960–2002.* Routledge.
Goulet, D., & Hudson, M. (1971). *The myth of aid: The hidden agenda of the development reports.* IDOC.
Haq, K., & Ponzio, R. (Eds.). (2008). *Pioneering the human development revolution: An intellectual biography of Mahbub ul Haq.* Oxford University Press.
Honderich, T. (1995). *The Oxford companion to philosophy.* Oxford University Press.
Jameson, K. P. (2010). Ethics and contemporary macroeconomic policy. In C. K. Wilber & A. K. Dutt (Eds.), *New directions in development ethics: Essays in honor of Denis Goulet* (pp. 400–425). Notre Dame University Press.
Kraut, R. (2022). Aristotle's ethics. In E. N. Zalta and U. Nodelman (Eds.) *The Stanford encyclopedia of philosophy* (Fall). Stanford, CA: Stanford University. https://plato.stanford.edu/archives/fall2022/entries/aristotle-ethics/
Marangos, J. (2009a). What happened to the Washington consensus? The evolution of international development policy. *The Journal of Socio-Economics, 38*(1), 197–208.
Marangos, J. (2009b). The evolution of the term 'Washington consensus.' *Journal of Economic Surveys, 23*(2), 350–384.
Myrdal, G. (1969). *Objectivity in social research.* Pantheon Books.
Myrdal, G. (1974). What is development? *Journal of Economic Issues, III*(4), 729–736.
Perroux, F. (1950). Economic space: Theory and applications. *The Quarterly Journal of Economics, 64*(1), 89–104.
Perroux, F. (1955). Note sur la notion de pôle de croissance. *Economie appliquée, 8*(1–2), 307–320.
Perroux, F. (1981). *Pour une philosophie du nouveau développement* (Vol. 4). Presses de l'UNESCO.
Ross, D. (1995 [1923]). *ARISTOTLE* (Sixth ed.). Routledge.

Schwenke, C. (2009). *Reclaiming value in international development: The moral dimensions of development policy and practice in poor countries*. Praeger Publishers.

Schwenke, C. (2011). Development ethics: The audacious agenda. In R. S. Fortner & P. M. Fackler (Eds.), *The handbook of global communication and media ethics* (Vol. I–II, pp. 317–341). Oxford: Wiley-Blackwell.

Sen, A. (1981). *Poverty and famines: An essay on entitlements and deprivation*. Oxford University Press.

Sen, A. (1987). *On ethics and economics*. Blackwell.

Sen, A. (1997). *Resources, values, and development* (Expanded). Harvard University Press.

Sen, A. (1999). *Development as freedom*. Oxford University Press.

Serra, N., & Stiglitz, J. (Eds.). (2008). *The Washington consensus reconsidered*. Oxford University Press.

St Clair, A. L. (2007). A methodologically pragmatist approach to development ethics. *Journal of Global Ethics, 3*(2), 143–164.

Stiglitz, J. (1998). Towards a new paradigm for development: Strategies, policies and processes. In *9th Raúl Prebisch lecture, October 19* (pp. 1–33). Geneva: United Nations Conference on Trade and Development.

Stiglitz, J. (1999). More instruments and broader goals: Moving toward the post-Washington consensus. *Revista de Economia Politica, 19*(1), 94–120.

Stiglitz, J. (2000a). Unraveling the Washington consensus. *Multinational Monitor, 21*(4), 13–21.

Stiglitz, J. (2000b). Capital market liberalization, economic growth, and instability. *World Development, 28*(6), 1075–1086.

Stiglitz, J. (2002a). Information and the change in the paradigm in economics. *The American Economic Review, 92*(3), 460–501.

Stiglitz, J. (2002b). *Globalization and its discontents*. W. W. Norton.

Stiglitz, J. (2002c). Participation and development: Perspectives from the comprehensive development paradigm. *Review of Development Economics, 6*(2), 163–182.

Stiglitz, J., Ocampo, J. A., Spiegel, S., Ffrench-Davis, R., & Nayyar, D. (2006). *Stability with growth*. Oxford University Press.

Streeten, P. (1994). Human development: Means and ends. *The American Economic Review, 84*(2), 232–237.

Streeten, P., Burki, S. J., Haq, M. U., Hicks, N., & Stewart, F. (1981). *First things first: Meeting basic human needs in development countries*. New York: Oxford University Press (Published for the World Bank).

Wilber, C. K., & Dutt, A. K. (Eds.). (2010). *New directions in development ethics: Essays in honor of Denis Goulet*. University of Notre Dame.

Williamson, J. (1990a). What Washington means by policy reform. In J. Williamson (Ed.), *Latin American adjustment: How much has happened?*

(Chapter 2). Washington, DC: Institute for International Economics. Republished online (November, 2002). http://www.iie.com/publications/papers/paper.cfm?researchid=486

Williamson, J. (Ed.). (1990b). *Latin American adjustment: How much has happened?* Institute for International Economics.

CHAPTER 3

The Analytical Framework

1 Introduction

The purpose of this chapter is to offer a conceptual agenda for examining contemporary international development theory and policy in a political economy context through its ethical orientation, as well as to suggest a comprehensive ethical alternative. As the theme of the book indicates, this alternative is the development ethics approach to international development. Overall, the chapter aims to develop an ethical paradigm for studying international development theory and policy based on political economy and moral philosophy. By structuring a theoretical model of investigating current international development in ethical terms, a few fundamental methodological questions arise:

- How is ethics perceived?
- Why and how should international development be investigated in a political economy context in conjunction with moral philosophy?
- Which is the prevailing economic analysis that shapes contemporary international development?
- Why and how can development ethics be an ethical alternative to the dominant vision of contemporary international development?

The following parts of this chapter answer the aforementioned methodological issues, which comprise the analytical framework of the book.

N. Astroulakis and N. Karagiannis, *Development Ethics*,
https://doi.org/10.1007/978-3-031-75476-0_3

The study of international development and the global economy is dominated by neoclassical economic positivism (DeMartino, 2000; O'Hara, 2006). Neoclassical economics, in its positive form, is widely viewed as a value-free science (Alvey, 2000). According to Drakopoulos (1997, p. 286), "positive, value-free economics, in the sense of not relying on any particular set of value judgements or on any philosophical or psychological framework, is generally seen as ideal." It seems "ideal" due to the presumption of value neutrality, which implies objective and measurable outcomes to international development. In view of this, positive neoclassical economics accepts development as economic growth in a globalised open-market framework, where "[e]conomic growth is usually looked upon as the rate of change of real GDP (gross domestic product) (per capita), which is linked to growth in productivity, consumption and investment, government spending, and net exports" (O'Hara, 2006, p. xxii). Furthermore, for the vast majority of neoclassical economists, economic agents are presented as rational and self-interested. The market system is viewed as the mechanism that reflects economic rationality and the self-interested behaviour of economic agents. Built on the premises of marginalism, methodological individualism and economic rationality, neoclassical economics fails to incorporate into the analysis of international development any deeper reference to moral issues and value judgements. However, "even normal market transactions, where self-interest is most prevalent, have their own moral codes which are not observed simply out of fear of retribution" (Rowthorn, 1996, p. 31). The common failure of neoclassical economists to consider moral codes is a serious intellectual limitation. Similar critiques are offered by Atkinson (2009), Alvey (2000), DeMartino (2000), and Hausman and McPherson (1993). Based on this observation, the proposed analysis attempts to explore such moral omissions of neoclassical economics. Providing an ethical evaluation of neoclassical economic analysis, interwoven with international development theory and policy, is one of the main purposes of this book.

While the notion of ethics refers to the broad issues of how one should live or what is morally right and wrong (Dutt and Wilber, 2010a, p. 4), the political economy of ethical development constructs a theoretical framework whereby economic, political, and ethical issues come to the fore. In this vein, the notion of ethics not only applies at the level of the individual but also at the societal level, where the individuals interact. This calls for the idea of social ethics, which reflects, and is reflected by, individual and social interactions, personal and social values, and institutions. By referring to social interactions, social structure, and social change, social ethics adequately defines the meanings of the terms 'a good life' and 'a good society'.

To this effect, a holistic approach to the ethical aspects of international development, based on a normative type of analysis, is proposed. Specifically, the proposed analysis aims to identify the ethical aspects of contemporary international development and to offer a valid ethical alternative (development ethics) in a political economy context. The ethical argument that the analysis explores can be seen as the meanings and requirements of a good life and a good society in international development.

In terms of methodology, as moral philosophy suggests, there are three accepted levels of any ethical discourse: "metaethics, normative ethics, and applied ethics" (Kagan, 1998, p. 2). Meta-ethics examines the nature of an ethical argument. Normative ethics determines the moral course of actions towards achieving the ethical argument. Applied ethics inspects the policy implementation of the ethical argument in real-world situations. As the analysis in the subsequent sections indicates, a holistic-ethical investigation of international development has to respond to the meta-ethical, normative-ethical, and applied-ethical aspects of the ethical argument of a good life and a good society.

In this framework, the chapter investigates the ethical orientation of neoclassical economic analysis regarding contemporary international development. Furthermore, a methodological design towards developing a comprehensive development ethics paradigm for international development is suggested as an adequate ethical alternative to the neoclassical positivist vision of international development. In a political economy context, development ethics deals with the ethical challenges of international, economic, and social development in a holistic-ethical manner. Even though development ethics accepts that an economic growth pattern is necessary for international development, development ethics goes beyond economic growth and material well-being to determine ethical development as involving human ascent in all relevant fields of people's lives.

2 What Is Ethics?

The question that this section addresses is 'what is ethics?' or, differently, how ethics is perceived in this book.

2.1 *Ethics and Moral Philosophy: Religious and Political Aspects of Ethics*

Ethical assumptions and commitments penetrate almost all scientific fields; however, ethics as such (as an intellectual objective) is examined by moral philosophy. In the literature on philosophical studies, the terms 'ethics' and 'moral philosophy' (or 'ethical theory') are used interchangeably. In general, ethics attempts to answer the questions of how one should live, what is ethically good and bad, and what is right and wrong. In abstract terms, three concepts are central to the subject matter of ethics: 'good' (which refers to the ideal or the thing that is desired); 'right' (what is not wrong); and 'ought' (which refers to obligation, duty, or responsibility, both for the individual and for society) (Dutt and Wilber, 2010a, p. 4). On these issues, *in Principia Ethica*, Moore (1960 [1903], [§1:1]) suggests that:

> In the vast majority of cases, where we make statements involving any of the terms virtue, vice, duty, right, ought, good, bad, we are making ethical judgments; and if we wish to discuss their truth, we shall be discussing a point of Ethics.

In the proposed analysis, ethics is considered as the intellectual objective of moral philosophy. However, under the terms 'ethics' and 'moral philosophy', aspects of morality from religious and political philosophy are included. Usually, people's ethical views are shaped, to different degrees, by their religious and political views of morality. Thus, the proposed analysis of ethics holds a close connection between moral philosophy, on the one hand, and religious ethics and political philosophy, on the other.

The relationship between moral philosophy and religious ethics can be described as follows. Moral philosophy is the branch of philosophy that examines morality by using reasons and arguments regarding what is an ethically good way of living. In turn, religious ethics refers to what is good or bad in terms of religious beliefs. In many cases, religious beliefs and moral philosophy judgements are integrated, as people's religious and ethical views are frequently intermingled. Inevitably, personal beliefs (such as religious faith) penetrate into how people confront ethical values. Thus, moral philosophy and religious ethics are entwined in a historical process and they influence personal and societal beliefs, actions, and outcomes. For instance, Weber (2001 [1930]) explains the process of capitalism in Western societies as relying on the religious ethics of Protestantism.

The notion of ethics is also investigated in political philosophy. Ethics results in, and is influenced by, society and politics. Political philosophy's areas of study (such as social justice, civic rights, institutions, laws, and political authority) are at the core of the discussion of ethical justifications. In the Western ethical tradition, we have seen this clear influence since the times of Ancient Greece. For instance, Plato in *The Republic* and Aristotle in *Nicomachean Ethics* and *Politics* incorporate ethics and politics as a unified field of study. Regarding Aristotle's philosophy, Ross (1995 [1923], p. 120) suggests that "Aristotle's ethics, no doubt, are social, and his politics are ethical." In the philosophy literature, we can identify an epistemological dichotomy, at the level of causes and objectives, between moral philosophy and political philosophy. However, this book follows the broad premise that ethics influences and is influenced by societal and political factors, as people's political views result in human history, social reality, and the vision of a good life and a good society.

To this end, the institutions, norms, and social beliefs that have been erected in historical and societal heritage crystallise religious premises and political thoughts, which affect people's lives and ethical judgements. Related to the topic of the book, political economy and development ethics have in common some of their prominent origins through moral philosophy, religious ethics, and political philosophy. We can identify this influence in *The Wealth of Nations* (Smith, 1776), *Essays on the Principles of Population* (Malthus, 1798), *The Elements of Politics* (Sidgwick, 2005 [1897]), *The Protestant Ethics and the Spirit of Capitalism* (Weber, 2001 [1930]), and in Lebret's and Goulet's writings on development ethics. Hence, ethics refers directly to moral philosophy and indirectly to its links with religious and political aspects.

2.2 The Political Economy of Ethics: Individual Ethics Versus Social Ethics

The study of ethical international development incorporates economic, political, societal, and ethical issues into the analysis of international development under a historical perspective. Ethics is integrated into the subject matter of international development in a political economy context. The term 'political economy' is used in its broader definition as the study of politics and economics with consideration for the insights of ethics. As Sen (1987, p. 3) indicates, ethics is related to the study of economics and politics; thus, there is no scope "for dissociating the study of economics from that of ethics and political philosophy". Within the political economy context, the concepts of politics, society, and the economy are treated as a unified whole in a historical background. For the classical and founding moral philosophers and economists, such as Ricardo, Smith, Mill, Marx, Weber, Myrdal, Schumpeter, Veblen, and Keynes (to name some of those who characterise the different schools of thought within the political economy tradition), the discussion of the economy and development is determined to a large extent by ethical, ideological, and institutional parameters.

The political economy of ethics is considered as an alternative theoretical framework to mainstream positive economics, which is dominated by neoclassical economics. In neoclassical economics, "agents are entirely self-interested and unconstrained by moral considerations" (Rowthorn, 1996, p. 30). As such, it deprives development analysis of any conscious value/moral considerations. Therefore, it is necessary to define ethics in the political economy context in contrast to how ethics is perceived by positive neoclassical economics. This chapter considers individual ethics as the individualistic notion of ethics mainly accepted by positive neoclassical economics. By contrast, social ethics is perceived as the socially structured notion of ethics in a political economy context of analysis.

A key argument that overlaps the discussions is that neoclassical economics is falsely presented as a value-neutral science by not accepting value judgements within its methods. On the contrary, this chapter shows that there is a specific ethical evaluation in neoclassical economic analysis itself. To explain this better, in economic analysis and the world reality, values and facts are not always separate. Economic theory and policy are penetrated by ethical values, and normative and positive analyses coexist. In light of this, it is asserted that the economic theories or policies that appear to be positive are often based on specific value and ethical commitments. In neoclassical economics, as van Staveren (2007, p. 22) writes;

> This connection between facts and values becomes most visible in economic terms such as 'well-behaved utility functions' and 'robust model estimations', as well as in some theoretical notions such as 'freedom of choice', 'equilibrium', and efficiency as being 'optimal'.

In most cases, value judgements pre-exist positive economic analysis. This refers to the discussion of normative and positive analyses in economics. Hausman and MacPherson (1993) appraise this relationship between normative and positive aspects as the 'ought to be' and 'is' methodological dichotomy in economic theory and policy.

Neoclassical economics maintains that economic agents interact within an economy as self-interested, rational optimisers. "Rationality requires that preferences are complete, transitive and continuous and that choices are determined by preferences" (Graafland, 2007, p. 84). The hypothesis of *homo economicus*, or, in other words, the perception of people as rational and self-interested beings, assumes that people attempt to maximise their own utility, based on rational choices and individual preferences. This implies an individualistic-ethical determination of neoclassical economics. At the level of society, neoclassical social choice theory advances the aforementioned ideas to the level of the whole. In line with Arrow's (1951, p. 4) argument that "the social utility might be the sum of the individual utilities of their product", neoclassical social choice theory offers a framework for measuring people's interests and public decision-making. In this respect, ethics in the neoclassical form remains focused on the narrow argument that society is simply the sum of its individual agents. In typical neoclassical economic analysis, the individual agents that comprise the economy, and society in general, are individuals (or households) and organisations (business units, non-government sector, etc.). Their economic and societal preferences and choices mirror the preferences and choices of the economy and society as a whole.

However, this notion of ethics of neoclassical economics is problematic, as it reduces ethics to an individualistic level by its methodological individualism. Specifically, neoclassical economics employs an individualistic approach whereby ethics are assumed to hold between atomistic individual agents, which are the exclusive units of analysis. In neoclassical economics, ethics is applied only at an interpersonal level, hence depriving the analysis of any reference to the social structures and other issues (such as the elements of power and altruism) through which individual agents interact with one another. For positive neoclassical economics, society is described as the sum of individual agents interacting in a value-laden market under rational economic behaviour based on self-interest. This point of view comprises a type of ethics in itself.

In contrast to the views outlined above, ethics must be considered at a social level, as it is the social structural notion of ethics (social ethics) that lies behind ethics at an interpersonal level. In this conception, political economy analysis comes to the fore. Society is more than the sum of individual agents, and the economy is more than the sum of individualistic preferences. The vast majority of political economists would agree with Dugger's (1977, p. 299) posture that "society is more than a sum of disparate individuals interacting in markets. It is an evolving whole which can best be understood and improved as a whole". In response to this, ethics is perceived in its social aspect. Yeager (2001, p. 2), for instance, accepts ethics as a social science, where "[a]ll discussions of how people should behave, what policies governments should pursue, and what obligations citizens owe to their governments obviously involve ethics." Social ethics is more than the sum of the personal ethical standpoints of the individual parts of each society; social ethics refers to people's interactions and to social norms, beliefs, and institutions.

This does not mean that social ethics diminishes the influence of individual ethics on society and the economy. Instead, the analysis of ethics in the political economy context determines ethics with respect to moral philosophy, which to a large extent is based on individual aspects of ethics. Such aspects of individual ethics are concerned with motivation, intention, and consequence, as well as with questions such as what are good and bad actions of an individual (as an ethical agent). Social ethics embodies such aspects and refers to: people's social interactions; how society ought to be ethically structured; the meaning of a good life; and, finally, what a good society is. As Aristotle states, humans are social animals. People live in small or large communities/societies and interact with their micro- and macro-environments. Human behaviour takes place within a given ideological and ethical framework, which has specific values, beliefs, and worldviews. From the viewpoint of social ethics and social interaction, there are related topics that can be discussed. Such topics include theories of justice, the rules of ethics and social institutions, and the relation of ethics with development issues, including the discussion of ethics and economic analysis. This book accepts the assertion that ethics is the study of how people live (or ought to live) and interact in the society they have created.

Based on such analysis, a fundamental distinction can be made between individual and social ethics. To sum up, individual ethics offers a discussion of ethical values based on the concept of self-interest, mostly supported by neoclassical economics under the assumption that society is the sum of individual preferences. By contrast, social ethics, by taking into consideration individuals' personal ethical views, examines social interactions and confronts society as an interactive total or, in other words, as something more than the sum of individual preferences. Social ethics affects people's lives and views on how society ought to be structured. Furthermore, social ethics considers social norms, beliefs, and institutions in the context of historical heritage. As a result, social ethics analysis is suggested as an alternative framework. Hence, in the proposed analysis, ethics is perceived as social ethics.

2.3 The Level of Ethical Discourse in Moral Philosophy and Social Ethics

Moral philosophy investigates an ethical argument. From the perspective of social ethics, the ethical argument that needs to be investigated can be addressed as 'what are a good life and a good society?' As mentioned, in moral philosophy, there are three commonly accepted levels of ethical discourse: meta-ethics, normative ethics, and applied ethics (Kagan, 1998, p. 2).

2.3.1 Meta-Ethics

Meta-ethics can be defined as the branch of moral philosophy that explores, from a higher order, the nature of ethical views, assumptions, and commitments. It is an inquiry into ethical theories. Meta-ethical questions investigate the meaning of ethical claims and the structures and methods of ethical theories. Therefore, meta-ethics "concerned itself with the status of those claims: whether they could be knowledge, how they could be validated, whether they were (and in what sense) objective, and so on" (Williams, 2006, p. 72). In this framework, one can raise epistemological questions, such as 'what counts as the ethical truth?', or methodological questions pertaining to the justification of ethical commitments. Consequently, "schemes of morality" can be described as meta-ethical (Frankena, 1951, p. 45). In short, meta-ethical inquiry is concerned with the question 'what is the nature of the ethical arguments?' In terms of social ethics, if we accept that the ethical argument focuses on the issue of 'what are a good life and a good society?', then meta-ethics answers the question 'what are the subject matters of a good life and a good society?'.

2.3.2 *Normative Ethics*

Normative ethics responds to the discussion of 'how things should or ought to be'. Normative ethics can be described as an attempt to determine principles that can be used to articulate and justify ethical views, assumptions, and commitments within a broader framework of meta-ethical meanings. Whereas meta-ethical questions are of a higher order, normative issues are considered to be first-order or substantive questions. Normative ethics makes "substantive claims about what one should do, how one should live, what was [is] worthwhile, and so on" (Williams, 2006, p. 72). Regarding social ethics, the question can be posed as 'what should the relationship be between the means and the ends of attaining a good life and a good society?'

2.3.3 *Applied Ethics*

Applied ethics is the branch of moral philosophy that investigates ethical issues in private and public life in an applied manner. According to Kagan (1998, p. 3, emphasis in original), "[t]he attempt to apply the general principles of normative ethics to difficult or complex cases is itself an important part of moral philosophy. It is called *applied ethics*". In other words, applied ethics can be considered as the ethical examination of particular issues in private and public life that are matters of human life. Applied ethics responds to the question 'what are the applied policy implications in any area of private or public life?' Applied ethics aspires to solve real-world problems in the definition of meta-ethics and with the tools of normative ethics. Some examples of applied ethics are bioethics, business ethics, environmental ethics, and global ethics. If we put applied ethics into a question format from a social ethics perspective, it would be 'what are the ethical guidelines in any area of public or private life regarding the concepts of a good life and a good society?'

Table 1 Social ethics—levels of ethical discourse

	Ethical questions	*Social ethics*
Level of ethical discourse within moral philosophy		
Meta-ethics	What is the nature of the ethical argument?	What are the subject matters of a good life and a good society?
Normative ethics	How should things be or how should they ought to be?	What should the relationship be between the means and the ends of attaining a good life and a good society?
Applied ethics	What are the applied policy implications in any area of private or public life?	What are the ethical guidelines in any field of public or private life regarding the concepts of a good life and a good society?

2.3.4 Social Ethics: Levels of Ethical Discourse

It is clear that none of the aforementioned levels of ethical discourse can be characterised as independent. At the level of normative ethics, meta-ethical presumptions and justifications (of what is right or wrong, for instance) determine the normative nature of the adopted ethical principles. By contrast, at the level of applied ethics, normative endowments influence the ethical content of the applied policies. Hence, ethical views, statements, and actions can be interpreted under the three levels separately only as ethical interconnections between the different moral philosophy levels of ethical discourse.

Following the above determination of how ethics is perceived, the levels of ethical discourse are summarised in the following table. Additionally, how social ethics responds to the different levels of ethical discourse is presented in Table 1.

3 The Ethical Study of International Development

3.1 Methodological Considerations

A theoretical approach to investigating international development in a political economy context in conjunction with moral philosophy is suggested. Some important presumptions in the construction of a theoretical paradigm for the investigation of ethical international development need to be specified.

The study of international development is accepted as a dynamic and social process. International development reflects the conflict between different groups of interest within a society and among societies. It also reflects technological improvement and cultural change. Social interactions influence the laws that govern the world and determine the study of international development. These laws are social and dynamic. This indicates that international development cannot be a stationary field but is instead dynamic and social.

Regarding the use of the term 'paradigm', it can broadly be seen as referring to a philosophical or theoretical framework of any kind. In this book, the term refers to a scientific paradigm that could be seen as a philosophical and theoretical framework within which theories, laws, and generalisations, as well as the applications performed in support of them, are formulated. Meanwhile, within the epistemological perspectives of the social sciences, it is generally accepted that the complexity of the real world cannot be fully explained by scientific paradigms. In turn, the need of simplification of the complexity of the real world leads to the rise of scientific paradigms. Thus, a scientific paradigm usually depicts, in a simple manner, the process by which complex systems operate (Barratt-Brown, 1995, p. 1). Hence, in the social sciences, a paradigm is a theoretical framework based on simplifying assumptions and trying to codify and explain the laws that govern the real world. Moreover, a scientific paradigm for the ethical study of international development should be presented in a form that is open to potential refutation.

Overall, this chapter follows an alternative political economy pattern with ethical insights. As Barratt-Brown (1994, p. 20) argues,

> In political economy, words which are used in a certain accepted sense in economics may have to bear a rather different meaning. Thus, we may speak of models in political economy which are not the equilibrium models of economics but theories of hypotheses about political-economic relationships.

In this regard, terms in political economy are not always used in the manner that they are used in mainstream economics. For instance, to the question "is there 'a structure of scientific revolutions' in economics?", Coats' (1969) key remark is that the only paradigm in economics remains to the equilibrium theory based on the idea of market mechanism.[1] In our case, the term 'paradigm' in ethical international development within a political economy context does not imply equilibrium conditions as normally a model or a paradigm predicts in mainstream economics but to social and political-economic relationships under the purview of ethics.

Another important aspect of a social science paradigm is the relationship between objectivity, on the one hand, and subjectivity along with ideology, on the other. Different theoretical and ideological patterns reflect the real world in a different manner. "Thus, one's view of the nature of historical change—its structure, sequence and casual mechanism—will colour one's view of the permitted limits and permissible forms of generalizations" (Dobb, 1973, p. 22). To this end, Kuhn (1970, p. 15) states: "[h]istory suggests that the road to a firm research consensus is extraordinarily arduous." Subjectivity and ideology are at the centre of the discussion. The history of economic thought has shown that there is any kind of value neutrality in the adjective 'social' (social sciences, social economics, social reality, social ethics, etc.). This observation could stem from the fact that the prevailing ideology and the commonness of accepting social theories are a matter of the degree to which a scientific paradigm adequately reflects reality. As Hodgson (2001, p. xiii) argues, "[a] fundamentally different reality may require a different theory". Thus, based on the value pluralism of political economy, as an ethical and social science approach, the proposed ethical paradigm can be perceived as a synthesis of coherent traditions of scientific research and achievements that, for the time being, identify problems and adequate solutions.

The study of ethical international development follows a normative type of analysis. What we mean by normative type of analysis is that, even in the case of positive economic analysis (elaborating statistical data, for instance), normative judgements and presumptions are included. Normative analysis by its nature embodies value judgements and moral principles. For this reason, in normative economic analysis, "[n]ot only do moral principles bear on issues concerning evaluation and policy, but they also influence the question positive economists ask and the answers they find plausible" (Hausman and McPherson, 1993, p. 672).

Again, the issue of whether economics has moral neutrality comes to the fore. The question can be posed differently: 'is economics a positive

[1] See also Drakopolous and Karayiannis (2005), for a review of the explanations of the main paradigms in economics.

science or a social science?' If we accept, as we have done in this book, the social nature of economics, that leads directly to a normative type of analysis. In any case, even for those who accept the opposite (economics as a positive science), normative analysis and morality influence positive economic analysis at least in the ways that Hausman and McPherson (1993, p. 673) describe:

1. "The morality of economic agents influences their behavior and hence influences economic outcomes. Moreover, economists' own moral views may influence the morality and the behavior of others in both intended and unintended ways. Because economists are interested in the outcomes, they must be interested in morality.
2. Standard welfare economics rests on strong and contestable moral presuppositions. To assess and to develop welfare economics thus requires attention to morality.
3. The conclusions of economics must be linked to the moral commitments that drive public policy. To understand how economics bears on policy thus requires that one understand these moral commitments, which in turn requires attention to morality.
4. Positive and normative economics are frequently intermingled. To understand the moral relevance of positive economics requires an understanding of the moral principles that determine this relevance."

3.2 The Ethical Basis of International Development

Viewing international development in terms of moral philosophy and social ethics in the political economy approach, the preliminary ethical question that arises is 'what is the nature of a good life and a good society?' In other words, how are development and its final state (a good life and a good society) defined? The next step is defining the normative foundation of international development. Differently, what should societies and individuals be evaluated on in order to accomplish the end state of development, as it has been defined? This refers to the desired changes that lead to a good society and a good way of living. Finally, ethical analysis ought to investigate which forms of economic, political, and social matters in their ethical context are applied to any of the specific fields of the development enterprise. We call this three-dimensional approach to international development 'the ethical basis of international development', which is based on a political economy approach in conjunction with moral philosophy and its typical sub-categories of ethical discourse (meta-ethics, normative ethics, and applied ethics).

In accordance with the moral philosophical level of ethical discourse in respect of social ethics analysis, the questions that an ethical paradigm for exploring international development within the context of political economy ought to codify are as follows:

(i) **What is the nature of international development?** This question refers to the meta-ethical aspects of international development. More specifically, it answers the social ethics question of 'what are the subject matters of a good life and a good society?' within the concept of international development. The reply to this question determines (from a higher order) the desirable end state. From a political economy approach, "[a] view of a good society is concerned with the assessment of each economic and non-economic performance dimension in conjunction with the significance assigned to these performance dimensions" (Marangos, 2004, p. 32). A vision of a good society comprises a future image of the social reality; it is not the existing social reality. Even though the existing reality affects the vision of a good society through the appraisal of ethical judgements, a vision of a good society cannot be solely described by facts. In this light, a vision of a good society presupposes a normative rather than a positive type of analysis.

(ii) **What should the relationship be between the means and the ends of international development?** This question considers the normative-ethical aspects of international development. Normative-ethical questions imply an ethical inquiry of what the relationship should be between the means and the ends of attaining a good life and a good society. While the vision of a good life and a good society is a higher order meta-ethical issue, the relationship between the means and the ends of attaining this vision are considered first-order or substantive issues. Normative-ethical analysis corresponds to the normative principles that govern the process of developing a vision for international development. Thus, normative-ethical analysis cannot offer an abstract judgement of a good society; it should entail paying attention to the existing social reality and the desired changes to achieve the vision of a good society. Normative-ethical analysis provides a framework under which the aforementioned meta-ethical concerns of a good life and a good society should be evaluated and policy recommendations should be formulated.

(iii) **What form of applied ethics could be the most appropriate to policy in international development?** This question refers to applied-ethical aspects of international development. It reflects the applied-ethical issues, which consist of the private and public ethical guidelines for a good life and a good society. Applied ethics aims to solve real-world problems in the definition of meta-ethics and with the means of normative ethics. It is an applied guide for ethical decision-making and policy.

The incorporation of ethical questions comprises the ethical underpinnings of international development. However, such ethical questions do not have solid answers that can be derived from ethical analysis alone. The key argument is that the ethical responses affect and are affected by the social reality. Therefore, it is the mixture of economics, politics, ideological standpoints, and ethical justifications that identifies a more suitable response to the aforementioned ethical questions.

In the political economy context, ethical issues can be found within any of the schools of thought that one investigates. The pluralistic political economy tradition involves the recognition that, as well as the open-market structure of the global economy, other elements (such as ideology, power, policy, culture, institutions, values, and ethics) constitute the image of international development. The critical investigation of international development in relation to ethical questions in the course of the political economy tradition guides this novel ethical exploration of international development.

4 Contemporary International Development and Neoclassical Economics

Which is the prevailing economic theory that explains and shapes contemporary international development? This section attempts to answer this question. It presents some of the aspects of fundamental neoclassical economics and reveals a manner of evaluating the neoclassical economics vision of international development, referring to the meta-ethical, normative-ethical, and applied-ethical orientation of contemporary international development.

4.1 The Present Form of International Development

The dominant worldwide economic form in contemporary international development is an open-market structure in a globalised economy (Cohen, 2009; Rosser and Rosser, 2004; DeMartino, 2000; Radice, 2005; O'Hara, 2006). Historically, the liberalisation of the global market was accelerated after the end of the Cold War, in the late 1980s and the beginning of the 1990s, with the collapse of the Soviet Union, the decomposition of former Yugoslavia, and the transition to the market economy of the countries of the former socialist bloc. International development accepts the principles of a globalised market structure. Thus, the study of international development can be seen as a field involving the study of economic issues in a globalised economic environment. As Tomas (2000, p. 774) mentions, "[t]he current context of development is liberal capitalism as the dominant mode of social organization and the basis of globalization." In turn, mainstream neoclassical economics applies the usual positive approach to the study of globalisation and international development. In addition, world institutions and organisations such as the World Bank, the International Monetary Fund (IMF), and the World Trade Organization (WTO), in conjunction with the so-called Washington Consensus, accelerate and govern the contemporary globalised economy (Marangos, 2009a; 2009b). In this respect, DeMartino (2000, p. 3) points out that:

> [D]eveloping countries throughout the world have restructured their economies to reduce the scope of government intervention and to expand the significance of the domestic market. Governments have privatized publicly owned firms, established stock markets to facilitate the flow of private finance, deregulated banking, and dismantled programs which had provided public support for domestic industries.

In contemporary international development, the majority of developed and developing nations follow the above liberal prescriptions or neoliberal prescriptions in an open, globalised market environment. The assimilation of mainstream economic thinking into such ideas leads to the impression that "liberal capitalism is so dominant that there appears to be no question of wholesale social transformation in any other direction" (Tomas, 2000, p. 774). In both practice and theory, the dominant view of international development is as a globalised market economy in a free-market economics framework.

4.2 *Neoclassical Economics and Neoliberalism*

In this part, we describe the relationship of neoclassical economics with neoliberalism in the framework of contemporary international development as a globalised market economy. There are always alternative views on the terms and the relationship of them. At the level of economic methodology not at all times, the relationship of neoclassical economics and neoliberalism is profound. No rarely, neoclassical economists come up against neoliberal practices, as for instance in the case of new information economics. Nevertheless, in this study, we follow an explanatory pattern that derives from the general position that the dominant vision of contemporary international development and the global economy is expressed by neoclassical economics and neoliberalism. Thus, let us explain how this study functions the relationship of neoclassical economics and neoliberalism, as it is a crucial point to the overall discussion in the context of the present analysis; the incorporation of the holistic-ethical interpretation of international development theory and policy.

Particularly since the 1970s, the emergence of free-market dominance over economic and non-economic activities has been one of the main characteristics of contemporary international development. This feature of international development is commonly referred to by the term 'neoliberalism' (Chang, 2002; Chomsky, 1999; DeMartino, 2000; Fine, 2004b; Harvey, 2005; 2010; O'Hara, 2006; Dumenil and Levy; 2005). In Harvey's (2005, p. 2) words:

> Neoliberalism is in the first instance a theory of political economic practices that proposes that human well-being can best be advanced by liberating individual entrepreneurial freedoms and skills within an institutional framework characterized by strong private property rights, free markets, and free trade.

The adjectives 'private' and 'free' imply neither public intervention nor state intervention in the market functions. This refers to the dominant theories and policies of positive neoclassical economics, which work on the general premise that markets function efficiently without government intervention.

Nevertheless, not all neoclassical economists share the same views. For instance, new information economics calls for government intervention when markets fail due to asymmetric information. From the angle of new information economics, Stiglitz (2002, p. 483) points out that, without government intervention, the market equilibrium is not always efficient.

On the other hand, there is widespread critique from radical political economists that new information economics and similar concerns within neoclassical economics are interwoven with the newest perspectives of the relations between neoclassical economics, economics imperialism, and neoliberalism. For instance, Fine (2004b, p. 213) mentions that "[s]uch concerns have also reduced the appeal of neoliberalism, the idea that the world could and should be run as if a perfectly functioning set of markets with at most a light, facilitating touch by the state". He further argues that, at the same time, there has been "the emergence of a new and virulent strain of 'economics imperialism' based on market, especially informational, failure" (Fine, 2004b, p. 213).

This might also describe the movement away from the Washington Consensus and towards the Post-Washington Consensus policy in international development, in the general sense that less austerity and more institutional policy can diminish the 'bad' social policy results of neoliberal policies without challenging the core functions of the Washington Consensus policy, which is based on the privatisation of the economy and the ethics of free-market economics.

In this study, in using the term 'neoliberalism', we refer to the dominant theories and policies of positive neoclassical economics, based on the typical premise that markets function efficiently without government intervention, and the approaches that place free markets, strong private rights, and free trade at the centre of any discussions regarding economic and social change within economic globalisation. Nevertheless, while neoliberal policies challenge the idea of government intervention, in reality, they promote state power within their efforts to eliminate any established notion of a welfare state. "Under the ideological veil of nonintervention, neoliberalism involves extensive and invasive interventions in every area of social life" (Saad-Filho and Johnston, 2005a, 2005b, p. 4). We underline this apparent antinomy between the theory of neoclassical economics and the neoliberal applied policy in the formulation of existing international development. This occurs through the vanishing of any "obstacle", for example the influence of labour unions (Harvey, 2005, p. 168), in the functioning of the ideal type of market, whereas, "[i]n the neo-liberal framework, the ideal market is equated with the 'perfectly competitive market' of neoclassical economics" (Chang, 2002, p. 544). Albo et al. (2010, p. 28) consider the theme in its political economy context:

> Neoliberalism is not, in our view, about the extent of deregulation as opposed to regulation, or holding on tenaciously to this or that public policy component. Neoliberalism should be understood as a particular form of class rule and state power that intensifies competitive imperatives for both firms and workers, increases dependence on the market in daily life and reinforces the dominant hierarchies of the world market.

At the ethical level, the main difference between neoliberalism and classical liberalism can perhaps be seen in the beliefs regarding the significance of free markets. Neoliberals view the market as a good in itself: not as a means to other goals, for example individual liberty. In times of neoliberalism, individual liberty based on the ideology of self-interest is used as an ethical reason for promoting the commoditisation of everything and the influence of multinational and national corporations over individuals (Madjd-Sadjadi and Karagiannis, 2013, p. 13). Neoliberalism stresses the philosophy of universal corporatism and cedes economic and social life to extreme market functions, with either government intervention or non-government intervention. In this way, "the term neoliberalism suggests a system of principles that is both new and based on classical liberal ideas" (Chomsky, 1999, p. 19). As it seems, contemporary international development seeks to be involved in conspicuous and privatised consumption, shareholder value, global financing, and business profit. In this framework, the story that neoclassical economists and neoliberals tells us is that "this is the road to growth, development, happiness, and well-being" (O'Hara, 2006, p. xxi). Consequently, neoclassical economics is the intellectual defender of neoliberalism in international development, in line with Polavni's (2001 [1944], p. 60) observation that "[i]nstead of economy being embedded in social relations, social relations are embedded in the economic system".

Furthermore, in this study, we argue that neoliberalism in international development is historically specific. Since the 1970s, changes in the dominant political and economic agenda of how the economy can function have led to the rise of neoliberalism, both nationally and internationally. As Cross and Strachan (2001, p. 181) argue, the three pillars of the neoclassical–neoliberal conversional wisdom in international development are: "that free market solutions to economic problems are best; that price stability, i.e. zero inflation, is a good thing; and that financial institutions and capital flows are best deregulated." Neoliberal predominance might also be interpreted as "the by-product of a shift in the class relation of forces following the economic crisis of the early seventies" (Milios and Sotiropoulos, 2009, p. 5). Neoliberal policies of privatisation, open markets, and flexibility became dominant globally through the 1980s and beyond. This dominant form of neoliberalism, established in the 1980s in the United Kingdom and the United States, has become a prevailing policy dogma in international development, following the establishment of the Washington Consensus in the 1980s and 1990s.

4.3 Neoclassical Economics as a Neutral, Positive Science

Neoclassical economics presents itself in the form of a neutral, positive science like any natural science. In this vein, neoclassical economics does not take into account the impact of social ethics on international development. Additionally, neoclassical economists argue in favour of objectivity, based on the argument of the value neutrality of economics. Arguing for the value neutrality of economics, neoclassical economists frequently imply that economic analysis is an objective approach and should therefore be considered trustworthy.

During the twentieth century, economics took shape, largely as a positive science. The main representatives of this transformation are economists of the Chicago School of Economics and the Nobel Laureates Stigler, Friedman, and Becker, who are prominent representatives of economic positivism in the second half of the twentieth century. Alvey (1999; 2000), among others, examines the decline of economics during the twentieth century in terms of its ethical dimension. In more recent literature on political economy, Milonakis and Fine (2009) and Fine and Milonakis (2009) have indicated that economics has been established as a discrete academic discipline entailing reductionism that individualises, desocialises, and de-historicises economic analysis. They have also extensively discussed economic imperialism and the incursion of economic analysis into other social sciences.

In international development, within positive neoclassical economic analysis, the term 'development' has been synonymous with growth, which indicates mere material expansion that is measured solely in terms of gross domestic product (GDP). Positive neoclassical economics reduces the economic problem to that of achieving the efficient allocation of given resources across known competing ends (Steele, 2007, p. 90). Qualitative indicators and models are repeatedly used to measure the development problem, but they do not seem to solve it. Ethical inquiries into the concept of development are considered an intellectual task mostly for philosophers and humanists, rather than for economists. Regarding the debate between ethics and economics, Robbins (1945 [1932], p. 148) asserts that "economics deal with ascertainable facts; ethics with valuations and obligations. The two fields of enquiry are not on the same plane of discourse". Robbins' statement expresses the neoclassical tradition of perceiving economics as a positive science. For neoclassical economics, strict economic rationality and a positive methodology take centre stage in the analysis of development, banishing any social ethical consideration to theoretical inquiries.

4.4 *The Ethical Basis of Contemporary International Development*

Positive neoclassical economics sketches a neutral (in terms of values and ethics) image of international development, predominantly in the concept of open-market transactions, where "social good will be maximized by maximizing the reach and frequency of market transactions, and it seeks to bring all human action into the domain of the market" (Harvey, 2005, p. 3). However, there is an ethical deliberation in the market itself. The market is not a neutral device: it is a structure deliberately imposed to implement the goals of the dominant ideology and policy. Therefore, the market as a valued and ethical device can be ethically assessed (accepted or rejected) on that basis. Criticism of the market overlaps with a general critique of the dominant ideology and policy of liberalism and neoliberalism.

Therefore, in order to examine, define, and influence contemporary international development theory and policy, a comprehensive conceptual framework for international development and its ethical insights should be specified. Particularly, a specific typology that constitutes the ethical underpinnings of contemporary international development is suggested. It replies to the ethical questions as they are posed by moral philosophy from the perspective of social ethics. The responses to those ethical questions within contemporary international development as it is viewed by the dominant vision of neoclassical economics comprise the ethical basis of contemporary international development.

Within the concept of contemporary international development, the meta-ethical question is 'what is the nature of international development?' or, differently, 'what is the main aim or end state of international development within the dominant neoclassical theory?' Neoclassical economics interprets the objective of development to be the maximisation of economic well-being on an individualistic basis through the consumption of goods and services. Furthermore, the consumption model is based on the free market. In this model, the market has a significant position not only in the production or distribution of goods and services but in all human activities across people's lives. The meta-ethical basis of neoclassical economics is composed of an affluent society and economic well-being achieved through a free-market-oriented economy in which all or almost all human preferences and actions can be expressed in market transactions. At the core of the meta-ethical orientation of the neoclassical economic theory of international development is the pursuit of the consumption of goods and services.

Normative-ethical aspects of contemporary international development are expressed by the question 'what should the relationship be between the means and the ends of international development?', which is the neoclassical economics vision of a good life and a good society and how this vision could be achieved. In neoclassical theory, the maximisation of utility is achieved by increasing the production of goods and services. In other words, economic growth implies the material prosperity of individuals within society. In a globalised market environment, economic growth is oriented on the free market-oriented. The minimisation of state intervention in the economy is also important. By definition, a private market failure is accepted because it is better than a government failure; thus, a private hand is always preferable, even in the case of non-market goods and services (like social assistance). The normative basis of neoclassical economics is mainly based on economic growth under private market relations: a profit economy with a free-market structure.

Applied ethics responds to the question 'what form of applied ethics could be the most appropriate to policy in international development?' In neoclassical economics, applied ethics takes the form of individual ethics and business ethics. At the core of neoclassical microeconomic analysis are the individual and the business unit. In mainstream economics (including neoclassical synthesis), macroeconomic issues are usually explained with microeconomic tools (see Samuelson, 1947). According to Fine and Milonakis (2009, p. 5), "[a]ggregating over such optimising individuals allowed for Walrasian general equilibrium theory, and for this to serve as a prototype for the economy as a whole, albeit derived from microeconomic principles." Additionally, for positive neoclassical economists, the role of the state should be diminished. Society consists of business corporations and households and, therefore, can be mainly analysed with the tools of microeconomics. Considering ethics, neoclassical theories focus on the preferences of individual agents based on self-interest. Ethics in such theories is a mixture of deontological concerns and utilitarian ethics (van Staveren, 2007). For instance, business ethics is based on market-efficient outcomes and corporate responsibility. Again, the assumption is the same. The sum of individual agents (individuals and business units) equals the economy and society, and the choices on the basis of their preferences determine exclusively the analysis of applied ethics. In line with neoclassical economics, it is usually mentioned as business ethics.

Table 2 shows the responses of neoclassical economics to the particular ethical questions posed. The responses to the meta-ethical, normative-ethical, and applied-ethical questions as reflected by neoclassical economic analysis comprise an image of the ethical basis of contemporary international development.

5 The Development Ethics Alternative

Development ethics is proposed as an alternative to the ethical aspects of the dominant international development vision of neoclassical economic positivism. This part addresses the methodological issues of what the subject matter of the proposed development ethics paradigm is and how this ethical paradigm for international development should be theoretically formulated in a political economy context in conjunction with moral philosophy.

Table 2 The ethical basis of contemporary international development

Level of ethical discourse	*Ethical questions*	*Neoclassical economics*
Meta-ethics	What is the nature of international development?	An affluent society and economic well-being achieved through consumption
Normative ethics	What should the relationship be between the means and the ends of international development?	Economic growth and the accelerated production of goods and services under private market relations
Applied ethics	What form of applied ethics could be the most appropriate to policy in international development?	Individual ethics in the form of business ethics

5.1 *The Limitations of Development Ethics as an Alternative to International Development*

Development ethics, as per all other intellectual fields of study, offers areas of consensus and controversies (Crocker 1998; 2008; Clark; 2002a), as well as contradictions and constitutional gaps. Development ethics as a social science and a philosophical approach in the scholarly sense needs further exploration regarding the ethical study of international development.

As referred to in Chapter 2, the core elements of the conceptual formation of development ethics is based on the pioneering work of Goulet. In particular, almost all discussions on development ethics accept the foundational principles of Goulet's development ethics. However, searching the literature on development ethics, one can easily find that there appears to be lots of confusion on the approach of development ethics to international development. A methodological vacuum is apparent in the existing literature. Beyond the general premise that development ethics belongs to the social sciences because it evaluates applied policies while reflecting on ethical matters, one cannot find in the literature a comprehensive framework for studying and applying development ethics to international development. If we accept that neoliberalism mainly based on the analytical tools of neoclassical economics is the prevailing theory and policy in international development, then any alternative proposal within political economy has to respond adequately to the inappropriateness of the prevailing theoretical and policy settings in international development. Thus, a comprehensive alternative framework for the application of development ethics to international development is needed.

In terms of methodology, Goulet suggests that development ethics, as per other intellectual fields, ought to be investigated in a four-dimensional way. Accordingly, the study of development ethics should be systematic, cumulative, communicable, and testable (Goulet, 2006a, p. xxxii). Goulet seems to emphasise these attributes when he writes that "[d]evelopment ethics aspires to be faithful to these canons" (Goulet, 2006a, p. xxxii). However, Goulet's attributes remain elusive and largely vague, as he does not offer a systematic and precise analysis of these terms for international development. However, from the literature on development ethics, as well as from participating in the International Development Ethics Association (IDEA), we have not found a concrete and historically tested methodological framework through which development ethics can be evaluated in the systematic, cumulative, communicable, and testable manner that Goulet suggests. In addition, the IDEA's codification (reflection, application, and practice) of development ethics is a useful but abstract codification of the field.

Furthermore, unanimous consent over the definition and conceptualisation of development ethics is lacking. For instance, does it concern a new discipline, as Goulet (1997) states, or an interdisciplinary meeting place, as Gasper (2006) proposes? Criticism of development ethics notes a confused and complex frame and an unclear and arbitrary way of analysis. For instance, Gill (1973, p. 116), reviewing Goulet's development ethics book *The Cruel Choice*, emphasises that "[t]he problem with Goulet's analysis is not so much that it is wrong as that it is arbitrary". For the present study, development ethics cannot be thought out in a methodological vacuum concerning international development, as is characteristic of the existing literature. Thus, in order to make development ethics less arbitrary, it needs to be inserted into a comprehensive methodological framework for the ethical study of international development.

5.2 *The Political Economy of Development Ethics*

This chapter contributes in the direction discussed above. Ethics is positioned in a political economy context as social ethics. Ethical development in its global dimension (or ethical international development) is accepted as a field of study within political economy and moral philosophy. Put another way, political economy and moral philosophy are perceived as a unified field of study for the investigation of international development. Based on this presumption, we argue for a development ethics paradigm that fundamentally combines moral philosophy and political economy.

The proposed development ethics paradigm includes moral philosophy and political economy in a specific methodology by exploring and typifying international development in its ethical aspects. In this framework, moral philosophy poses the ethical questions, while political economy investigates the laws of political, economic, and social life and the relations between them within and among societies. Following our argument for combining the two fields (moral philosophy and political economy) in order to address international development, ethics provides us with 'the problem' through discussions of the philosophical dialectic of 'what is good and bad' and the corresponding value dimensions. At the same time, political economy gives us a framework that we can use to solve the problem, without compromising critical factors such as the economy, policy, ideology, and power. To use a development ethicist's argument, "the science [the political economy, in our case] describes and explains what is, was, and can be. To discern what ought to be is the task of ethics" (Crocker, 1991, p. 467). To this effect, this study attempts to encapsulate development ethics with all those attributes that make it an intellectual paradigm within the pluralistic boundaries of political economy and moral philosophy.

5.3 *Towards a Comprehensive Development Ethics Paradigm*

The proposed development ethics paradigm directly responds to the aforementioned ethical discourse on the meta-ethical, normative-ethical, and applied-ethical aspects of international development. A brief description of each of these levels in the context of development ethics follows.

Regarding the meta-ethical question of 'what is the nature of international development?', development ethics answers this in three ways. First, development is attained by all people achieving good lives. At the minimum, all people need all the goods necessary to cover their biological needs and to free part of their human energy so that they can enjoy good lives in the broader sense, including in the economic, biological, psychological, social, cultural, ideological, spiritual, mystical, and transcendental dimensions (Goulet, 1971, pp. 206–207). Leading a good life is perceived as 'being more' in terms of capability and functioning

(Sen, 1987). The development model based mainly on economic growth has distorted the way that a good life is perceived: 'having more' (material goods, wealth, etc.) leads to the notion of 'being more' (successful, attractive, valuable, etc.) (Fromm, 1999; 2005). Against this perception, development ethics talks about a good life in all aspects of human life; this is termed 'human ascent'. Second, development ethics advocates global justice in the form of non-elite nations or people participating in social planning and outcomes. The elements of power and vulnerability, in terms of between nations and within societies, are distinctive in this discussion. Third, ethical development evidently supports sustainability in terms of natural resources and humanity. Sustainability for development ethicists is an ethical and political matter. Technological advances give the means of attaining sustainability; the decision to attain sustainable development is a matter of ethics and politics.

According to the normative-ethical question of what the relationship should be between the means and the ends of international development, development ethics determines a normative set of ethical goals and strategies for attaining them. This study arranges and examines the ethical goals and strategies of international development from the viewpoint of development ethics (see also Astroulakis, 2011, pp. 224–228). Ethical goals can be codified into three categories with reference to attaining a good life: (i) life sustenance; (ii) esteem; and (iii) freedom. Life sustenance refers to the nurturing of life to maintain its fundamental elements. Esteem is a universally accepted value for the reason that all human beings in all societies feel the need for respect, dignity, honour, and recognition. Freedom is valued as a component of a good life in the sense that development ought to free humans from all servitudes (to others, to nature, to ignorance, to institutions, and to beliefs) in order to govern themselves and determine their own destinies. Ethical strategies, on the other hand, are normative judgements that provide the notional and practical framework through which ethical goals should be discussed and policy recommendations regarding these goals ought to be formulated. The ethical strategies are: (i) the abundance of goods; (ii) universal solidarity; and (iii) participation. The abundance of goods means that people need to have 'enough' goods to have good lives. In this regard, 'enough' should be, at the minimum, sufficient goods for the satisfaction of biological needs, in addition to freeing part of the human energy towards a wider range of life aspects, beyond satisfying first-order needs. Universal solidarity can be perceived as a philosophical issue: the need of all people for unity around their common fate. As Goulet (1995, p. 64) emphasises, "[a]ll philosophies and systems of thought postulate, at least implicitly, a common destiny for humans: the fate of one is the fate of all". Last but not least, for development ethicists, the participation of ordinary people and local societies in decision-making is one of the main points in addressing international development. Both normative-ethical goals and strategies are unswervingly derived from the meta-ethical orientation of development ethics.

Regarding applied ethics, development ethics investigates international development policies at the macro level while taking into consideration the micro traits of each society. In other words, development ethics, at a practical level, takes the form of global ethics (Crocker, 2008; Enderle, 1999; Goulet, 2006a; Gasper and St. Clair (eds.), 2010a, 2010b; Schwenke, 2009). Inevitably, the discussion of global ethics is long and the modelling of such ethics could be even more elongated. We will agree, at this point, with the statement of Crocker (2008, p.1) that "it [global development ethics] justifies, applies, and extends ethical reflection on development goals, policies, projects, and institutions from the local to the global level".

Furthermore, the concept of authentic development, as posed by Goulet (1996; 2006a), can also elucidate how development ethics perceives the applied-ethical discussion in international development. Authentic development refers, explicitly or implicitly, to the means and ends of human actions or, in other words, to the vision of a better life and the way that this life can be accessed. "Authentic development is a process of realizing material and social gains in a manner which enriches the lives of the people at large" (Goulet, 2006a, p. 161).

As previously mentioned, development ought to respond to meta-ethical inquiries concerning the meaning of a good life, the foundation of justice in society and within societies, and the stance of humans and societies towards nature. "Providing satisfactory conceptual and institutional answers to these three questions is what constitutes authentic development" (Goulet, 1996, p. 197). For development ethics, applied ethics (in each field of life) should correspond to the previously mentioned factors.

Constructing parallels between the moral philosophy sub-categories of meta-ethics, normative ethics, and applied ethics and the ethical questions that arise in each of them for international development constitutes the proposed development ethics paradigm for international development. Under the prism of the moral philosophy levels of ethical discourse, a

Table 3 The development ethics paradigm

Level of ethical discourse	*Ethical questions*	*Development ethics*
Meta-ethics	What is the nature of international development?	Authentic development: a good life, social justice, and sustainability with nature
Normative ethics	What should the relationship be between the means and the ends of international development?	Ethical goals and strategies in the concept of authentic development
Applied ethics	What form of applied ethics could be the most appropriate to policy in international development?	Global ethics in the concept of authentic development

specific typology of the ethical questions on international development and its development ethics responses is presented in Table 3.

6 Conclusion

The aim of this chapter has been to develop the analytical framework of the book. In turn, the main purpose is to investigate international development in ethical terms and to offer a comprehensive ethical alternative (to neoclassical economic positivism in international development) in a political economy context. This alternative, as mentioned, offers a development ethics paradigm in international development.

To assist the purpose of the book, it was necessary to investigate the ethical orientation of international development. Thus, a methodology for understanding international development under the prism of social ethics and the concerns of political economy has been established. As suggested, the economic, social, and political foundation of any developmental endeavour and the ethical reflection of this foundation on societies and individuals provide a better assessment of international development.

Neoclassical economics in its positive form carries the presumption of value neutrality in the study of international development. This chapter rejects this presumption, arguing that international development is a dynamic and social process. Additionally, economics as a social science is value and ethic specific. Thus, it is argued that neoclassical economics follows its own ethical pattern regarding international development. For neoclassical economics, society is the sum of individuals interacting in the market. Individuals' preferences and behaviour comprise the ethical image of a society. Within the concept of international development, neoclassical economics accepts ethics in the sense of individual and business ethics. Analysis within the political economy context, on the other hand, acknowledges ethics not only in its individual nature but also as social ethics in the sense of social interactions. Societal institutions, norms, and beliefs affect people's ethical views; in turn, people's ethical standpoints influence societal outcomes.

At the level of international development, what the study determines as ethical development is exactly the reflection of the economic, social, and political issues in the meta-ethical, normative-ethical, and applied-ethical aspects of social ethics. In this regard, a clear typology among the meta-ethical, normative-ethical, and applied-ethical questions to international development is offered.

The development ethics approach to international development has been selected as a crucial ethical alternative to mainstream perspectives of international development. As Clark (2002a, p. 830) observes, "[t]he cultivation of development ethics has the potential to produce a coherent account of human well-being for guiding development policy and thinking". The suggested development ethics paradigm espouses the investigation of international development from a wider perspective. By moving this investigation into a political economy context, it means that development ethics strongly accepts the nature of economics as an interdisciplinary field that bridges the social sciences and the humanities, taking into consideration the economic, political, cultural, institutional, ideological, and ethical aspects of society and individuals.

Based on political economy and moral philosophy, the notion of development has been redefined in this chapter. International development is perceived as many aspects together: "simultaneously and inextricably an economic and political matter, a social and cultural one, an issue of resource and environmental management, a question of civilization" (Goulet, 1995, p. 2). Thus, the general premise of this book is that the proposed development ethics paradigm as it is posed in international development within the political economy context can offer a useful ethical alternative to neoclassical economic positivism.

In the following three chapters of the book, extensive analyses of the ethical basis of contemporary international development and the development ethics alternative are presented.

References

Albo, G., Gindin, S., & Panitch, L. (2010). *In and out of crisis: The global financial meltdown and left alternatives*. PM Press.

Alvey, J. E. (1999). A short history of economics as a moral science. *Journal of Markets and Morality, 2*(1), 53–73.

Alvey, J. E. (2000). An introduction to economics as a moral science. *International Journal of Social Economics, 27*(12), 1231–1251.

Arrow, K. J. (1951). *Social choice and individual values*. Wiley.

Astroulakis, N. (2011). The development ethics approach to international development. *International Journal of Development Issues, 10*(3), 214–232.

Atkinson, A. B. (2009). Economics as a moral science. *Economica, 76*(s1), 791–804.

Barratt-Brown, M. (1994). *The economics of imperialism*. Penguin Books.

Barratt-Brown, M. (1995). *Models in political economy* (2nd ed.). Penguin Books.

Chang, H.-J. (2002). Breaking the mould: An institutionalist political economy alternative to the neoliberal theory of the market and the state. *Cambridge Journal of Economics, 26*(5), 539–559.

Chomsky, N. (1999). *Profit over people: Neoliberalism and global order*. Seven Story Press.

Clark, D. A. (2002). Development ethics: A research agenda. *International Journal of Social Economics, 29*(11), 830–848.

Coats, A. W. (1969). Is there a 'structure of scientific revolutions' in economics? *Kyklos, 22*(2), 289–296.

Cohen, S. I. (2009). *Economic systems analysis and policies: Explaining global differences, transitions and developments*. Palgrave Macmillan.

Crocker, D. (1991). Toward development ethics. *World Development, 19*(5), 457–483.

Crocker, D. (1998). Development ethics. In C. Edward (Ed.), *Routledge encyclopedia of philosophy* (Vol. 3, pp. 39–44). Routledge.

Crocker, D. (2008). *Ethics of global development*. Cambridge University Press.

Cross, R., & Strachan, D. (2001). Three pillars of conventional wisdom. *Review of Political Economy, 13*(2), 181–200.

DeMartino, G. (2000). *Global economy, global justice: Theoretical and policy alternatives to neoliberalism*. Routledge.

Dobb, M. (1973). *Theories of value and distribution since Adam Smith*. Cambridge University Press.

Drakopoulos, S. (1997). Origins and development of the trend towards value-free economics. *Journal of the History of Economic Thought, 19*(2), 286–300.

Drakopoulos, S., & Karayiannis, A. (2005). A review of Kuhnian and Lakatosian "explanations" in economics. *History of Economic Ideas, XIII*(2), 51–73.

Dugger, W. M. (1977). Social economics: One perspective. *Review of Social Economy, 35*(3), 299–310.

Duménil, G., & Levy, D. (2005). The neoliberal (counter-) revolution. In A. Saad-Filho & J. Johnston (Eds.), *Neoliberalism: A critical reader* (pp. 9–19). Pluto Press.
Dutt, A. K., & Wilber, C. K. (2010). Introduction: Development ethics and development economics. In C. K. Wilber & A. K. Dutt (Eds.), *New directions in development ethics—Essays in Honor of Denis Goulet* (pp. 1–26). University of Notre Dame Press.
Enderle, G. (1999). An introduction to international business ethics. In G. Enderle (Ed.), *International business ethics: Challenges and approaches*. Notre Dame, IN: University of Notre Dame Press.
Fine, B. (2004). Examining the ideas of globalisation and development critically: What role for political economy? *New Political Economy, 9*(2), 213–231.
Fine, B., & Milonakis, D. (2009). *From economics imperialism to Freakonomics: The shifting boundaries between economics and other social sciences economics as social theory*. Routledge.
Frankena, W. (1951). Moral philosophy at mid-century. *The Philosophical Review, 60*(1), 44–55.
Fromm, E. (1999). *Man for himself*. Routledge.
Fromm, E. (2005). *To have or to be*. Continuum International Publishing Group.
Gasper, D. (2006). Introduction: Working in development ethics—A tribute to Denis Goulet. *Éthique et économique/Ethics and Economics, 4*(2), 1–24.
Gasper, D., & St. Clair, A. L. (Eds.). (2010). *Development ethics*. London: Ashgate.
Gasper, D., & St. Clair, A. L. (2010). The field of development ethics—An introduction. In D. Gasper & A. L. St. Clair (Eds.), *Development ethics* (pp. 13–33). London: Ashgate.
Gill, R. T. (1973). Reviewed work(s): The cruel choice: A new concept in the theory of development by Denis Goulet. *Political Science Quarterly, 88*(1), 116–117.
Goulet, D. (1971). An ethical model for the study of values. *Harvard Educational Review, 41*(2), 205–227.
Goulet, D. (1995). *Development ethics: A guide to theory and practice*. The Apex Press.
Goulet, D. (1996). Authentic development: Is it sustainable? In D. C. Pirages (Ed.), *Building sustainable societies: A blueprint for a post-industrial world* (pp. 189–205). Armonk, NY: M.E. Sharpe.
Goulet, D. (1997). Development ethics: A new discipline. *International Journal of Social Economics, 24*(11), 1160–1171.
Goulet, D. (2006). *Development ethics at work: Explorations 1960–2002*. Routledge.
Graafland, J. (2007). *Economics, ethics and the market: Introduction and applications*. Routledge.

Harvey, D. (2005). *A brief history of neoliberalism*. Oxford University Press.

Harvey, D. (2010). *The enigma of capital, and the crises of capitalism*. Oxford University Press.

Hausman, D. M., & McPherson, M. S. (1993). Taking ethics seriously: Economics and contemporary moral philosophy. *Journal of Economic Literature, 31*(2), 671–731.

Hodgson, G. M. (2001). *How economics forgot history: The problem of historical specificity in social science*. Routledge.

Kagan, S. (1998). *Normative ethics*. Westview Press.

Kuhn, T. S. (1970 [1962]). *The structure of scientific revolutions* (Second ed.). Chicago: The University of Chicago Press.

Madjd-Sadjadi, Z., & Karagiannis, N. (2013). Why is neoliberalism dangerous? Criticism, alternative perspectives, and government policy implications. In N. Karagiannis, Z. Madjd-Sadjadi, & S. Sen (Eds.), *The US economy and neoliberalism: Alternative strategies and policies* (pp. 11–31). Routledge.

Malthus, T. R. (1798). *An essay on the principle of population*. London: J. Johnson.

Marangos, J. (2004). *Alternative economic models of transition*. Ashgate.

Marangos, J. (2009a). What happened to the Washington consensus? The evolution of international development policy. *The Journal of Socio-Economics, 38*(1), 197–208.

Marangos, J. (2009b). The evolution of the term 'Washington consensus.' *Journal of Economic Surveys, 23*(2), 350–384.

Milios, J., & Sotiropoulos, D. P. (2009). *Rethinking imperialism: A study of capitalist rule*. Palgrave Macmillan.

Milonakis, D., & Fine, B. (2009). *From political economy to economics: Method, the social and the historical in the evolution of economic theory*. Routledge.

Moore, G. E. (1960 [1903]). *Principia ethica (1903)*. Cambridge: Cambridge University Press.

O'Hara, P. A. (2006). *Growth and development in the global political economy: Social structures of accumulation and modes of regulation*. Routledge.

Polanyi, K. (2001 [1944]). *The great transformation*. Boston, MA: Beacon Press.

Radice, H. (2005). Neoliberal globalisation: Imperialism without empires? In A. Saad-Filho & D. Johnston (Eds.), *Neoliberalism: A critical reader* (pp. 91–98). Pluto Press.

Robbins, L. (1945 [1932]). *An essay on the nature and significance of economic science* (second ed.). London: Macmillan.

Ross, D. (1995 [1923]). *ARISTOTLE* (Sixth ed.). Routledge.

Rosser, B. J., & Rosser, M. V. (2004). *Comparative economics in a transforming world economy*. The MIT Press.

Rowthorn, R. (1996). Ethics and economics: An economist's view. In P. Groenewegen (Ed.), *Economics and ethics?* (pp. 15–33). Routledge.

Saad-Filho, A., & Johnston, D. (2005). Introduction. In A. Saad-Filho & D. Johnston (Eds.), *Neoliberalism: A critical reader* (pp. 1–6). Pluto Press.

Saad-Filho, A., & Johnston, D. (Eds.). (2005). *Neoliberalism: A critical reader*. Pluto Press.

Samuelson, P. (1947). *Foundations of economic analysis*. Harvard University.

Schwenke, C. (2009). *Reclaiming value in international development: The moral dimensions of development policy and practice in poor countries*. Praeger Publishers.

Sen, A. (1987). *On ethics and economics*. Blackwell.

Sidgwick, H. (2005 [1897]). The Elements of Politics. *Elibron classics edition first published in 1897 by Macmillan and Co. Limited, London*. Adamant Media Corporation.

Smith, A. (1776). *An inquiry into the nature and causes of the wealth of nation*. [E. Cannan, Ed. (1904), *2 vols*, London: Methuen]. Retrieved from ElecBook Classics, Book I–V.

Steele, G. R. (2007). *The economics of Friedrich Hayek*. Palgrave Macmillan.

Stiglitz, J. (2002). Information and the change in the paradigm in economics. *The American Economic Review, 92*(3), 460–501.

Tomas, A. (2000). Development as practice in a liberal capitalist world. *Journal of International Development, 12*(6), 773–787.

van Staveren, I. (2007). Beyond utilitarianism and deontology: Ethics in economics. *Review of Political Economy, 19*(1), 21–35.

Weber, M. (2001[1930]). *The protestant ethic and the spirit of capitalism*. (T. Parsons, Trans.) London and New York: Routledge.

Williams, B. (2006). *Ethics and the limits of philosophy*. Routledge.

Yeager, L. B. (2001). *Ethics as social science: The moral philosophy of social cooperation*. Edward Elgar.

CHAPTER 4

The Meta-Ethical Basis of International Development and the Development Ethics Alternative

1 Introduction

The aim of this chapter is to explore the meta-ethical aspects of international development in a political economy context and to reveal the development ethics meta-ethical alternative. Moral philosophers approach meta-ethics as the theory of the nature and truth conditions of moral judgement (Copp, 2007, p. 2; Geivett, 2005; Harman, 1977). According to moral philosophy, meta-ethical concerns should come prior to normative-ethical and applied-ethical analysis. As one moral philosopher argues, "[t]here is no use proceeding with either normative or applied moral philosophy without coming to certain definite conclusions about matters of metaethical concern" (Geivett, 2005, p. 994). If we accept that the moral judgement in international development is good lives for people and a good society in general, the meta-ethical question that arises is 'what is the ethical nature of a good life and a good society in international development?' The incorporation of initial and essential meta-ethical questions as mentioned above has a significant bearing on evaluating international development. It determines the end state of development: the vision of a good society. According to the beliefs of moral philosophers about the significance of meta-ethics, it is reasonable to assume that meta-ethical inquiries should come prior to normative-ethical and applied-ethical analysis in the examination of the

N. Astroulakis and N. Karagiannis, *Development Ethics*,
https://doi.org/10.1007/978-3-031-75476-0_4

ethical aspects of international development. Hence, the following analysis is based on the presumption that, in order to examine the ethical aspects of international development, the first step should be the analysis of the end state of development as addressed by the aforementioned meta-ethical question.

The analysis reveals, in a critical manner, the conceptual insights of the meta-ethical nature of neoclassical economics as the ethical background of the determination of the present form of international development. The analysis, then, turns to the scrutiny of international development as a globalised market economy under the influence of neoliberalism, which is scientifically sustained by neoclassical economics.[1] The meta-ethical vision of contemporary international development is also disclosed. Following this, the analysis goes on to investigate development ethics as an important alternative to the meta-ethical vision of a good society as posed by neoclassical economics. International development is redefined based on the meta-ethical concerns of development ethics within a political economy context. In the proposed development ethics approach within the political economy context, the meta-ethical vision of a good society is ethically determined beyond the neoclassical economics agenda of economic growth. Development ethics indicates an alternative vision of the meta-ethical aspects of international development, which is usually ignored in the heterodox economics literature.

To explore international development in meta-ethical terms within a political economy context, we need to identify what the prevailing form of contemporary international development is and which economic theory supports this form of international development. In order to identify better the prevailing form, the present analysis shows that international development is historically and ideologically determined. International development has followed a neoliberal pattern, particularly after the 1980s. The majority of the critical writings within political economy point to the general view that what has been described as neoliberalism in international development can be seen as a worldwide doctrine where all or almost all social and economic problems have a free-market solution (Harvey, 2005, p. 2; Howard and King, 2004, p. 40; Tsakalotos, 2004). Regarding the second issue (which economic theory supports

[1] Not all neoclassical economists are neoliberals. For a discussion of the relationship between neoclassical economics and economic neoliberalism in international development, see Chapter 3.

this prevailing form of contemporary international development), the view of international development as a globalised market economy in the shape of neoliberalism is scientifically sustained by a large part of neoclassical economics (O'Hara (ed.), 2004a, 2004b; DeMartino, 2000; Dutt, 2004a; 2004b). As DeMartino (2000, p. 4) points out that "[t]he most forceful and coherent defence of neoliberalism appears in mainstream economic theory, or 'neoclassical theory'."

With respect to mainstream economic theories, which view international development as a globalised market economy, there was an earlier methodological transformation in these theories. Since the second half of the twentieth century, mainstream economics, particularly in the lines of positive neoclassical economics, has appeared as a kind of natural science. As Friedman (1953, p. 4) argues, "positive economics is, or can be, an 'objective' science, in precisely the same sense as any of the physical sciences." Positive neoclassical economics has detached its analysis from ethical considerations. This detachment from ethical concerns was not a part of classical political economy. It first emerged during the Marginal Revolution of the 1870s and was further consolidated during the twentieth century, particularly in the second half (Alvey, 2000, p. 1231; Fine, 1980). Similar critiques of neoclassical economic positivism have been voiced by Cochran (1974), Galbraith (1991), Rothschild (1993), Weintraub (2002), Wilber (2004), Gassler (2007), Atkinson (2009), Milonakis and Fine (2009), and Fine and Milonakis (2009), to name just a few of the studies that have accepted economics as a social science. In Galbraith's (1991, p. 41) words, "it [economic positivism] assimilates economics to the hard sciences—physics, chemistry, biological sciences." According to Rothschild (1993, p. 16), "[t]he 'scientification' of economics... has led to a separation of economics from its ethical roots. The 'mainstream economics' of the twentieth century fully accepts this separation." The value-neutral stance of neoclassical economics is reflected in the positive analysis of all the social phenomena that the scientific paradigm of neoclassical economics investigates, as exemplified by what has been dubbed 'economics imperialism' (Fine and Milonakis, 2009). Economic positivism tries to analyse social and economic phenomena, just as biology includes the study of anatomy and physiology (Gassler, 2007, p. 112).

In this conceptual framework, neoclassical economics considers international development in a materialistic manner, as exemplified by the literature on economic growth and economic globalisation. The meta-ethical nature of international development, as it is defined by the question of 'what is the nature of a good society?', is based on the ethical view of a westernised consumerist society in a globalised market economy. In turn, the value-neutral analysis of economics liberates neoclassical economics from a wide range of alternative development patterns in international development. The experience of the Washington Consensus in Latin America during the 1980s is an example of the meta-ethical orientation of economic neoliberalism, scientifically based on the social and economic international development policies of neoclassical economics. The analysis shows that contemporary international development follows a neoliberal pattern of a globalised market economy based on the dominance of the economic positivism of neoclassical economics. Thus, the ethical insight of neoliberal policies in international development can be found in the neoclassical assessment of the value neutrality of economics as a positive science.

In contrast, for those accepting economics as a social science, value judgements are closely associated with the meta-ethical vision of international development policies. The meta-ethical aspects of a scientific paradigm and the moral judgement of a good society influence the scientific paradigm within which the scientist works. In turn, "value judgments are closely associated with the world view; theories must remain coherent with the world view; facts themselves are theory-laden; therefore, the whole scientific venture is permeated by value judgments from the start" (Wilber, 2004, p. 426). This can also be seen in the Schumpeterian notion of scientific process, in which "vision" means that "analytic effort is of necessity preceded by a preanalytic cognitive act that supplies the raw material for the analytic effort" (Schumpeter, 2006 [1954], p. 39). In this light, it is the meta-ethical vision of the scientific paradigm that shapes the meta-ethical vision of a good society:

> This world view [the meta-ethical vision of a good society] shapes the interests of the scientist and determines the questions asked, the problems considered important, the answers deemed acceptable, the axioms of the theory, the choice of relevant facts, the hypotheses proposed to account for such facts, the criteria used to assess the fruitfulness of competing theories, the language in which results are to be formulated, and so on (Wilber, 2004, p. 426).

Similar views regarding the normative manner in which a scientific paradigm investigates social phenomena, on the basis of a specific world-view of the social reality, have been accepted by various ethical and social perspectives in economics and political science, in both the heterodox and the orthodox traditions (see, for example, Boulding, 1969; Buchanan, 1985; Etzioni, 1987; Hausman and MacPherson, 1993; Little, 1995; Little, 2004; Vickers, 1997; Boyland and Gekker (eds.), 2009; Clary et al. (eds.), 2006a, 2006b; Groenewegen (ed.), 1996), as well as in the development ethics literature and in Sen's writings.[2]

In his ethical study of economics and development in *On Ethics and Economics*, Sen (1987) offers a concise introduction to the subject. He underlines the contrast between the self-consciously non-ethical character of positive neoclassical economics (which he terms 'modern economics') and the historical evolution of neoclassical economics largely as an offshoot of ethics. Sen (1987, pp. 2–5) precisely defines the dual relationship between ethics and economic efficiency. On the one hand, "there is the problem of human motivation related to the broadly ethical question 'How should one live?'"(Sen, 1987, p. 3). The second issue concerns efficiency and the judgement of social achievement: "[t]his 'ethics-related view of social achievement' cannot stop the evaluation short at some arbitrary point like satisfying 'efficiency'. The assessment has to be more fully ethical, and take a broader view of 'the good'" (Sen, 1987, p. 4). In his discussion of the meta-ethical orientation of neoclassical economics—the ends and the purposes of economics—Sen clearly points out that positive economics follows an engineering approach. The engineering approach is concerned primarily with logistic issues (rather than ultimate ends) and the ethical argument of how one should live or what a good society is. "The ends are taken as fairly straightforwardly given, and the object of the exercise is to find the appropriate means to serve them. Human behaviour is typically seen as being based on simple and easily characterizable motives" (Sen, 1987, p. 4).

Based on the above, the present analysis of the meta-ethical study of international development rejects the neoclassical positivist assessment of economics and development as a value-neutral science. Contemporary

[2] Sen's notion of the relationship between ethics and economics has influenced the development ethics literature. Furthermore, Sen's idea of the engineering nature of mainstream economics has been accepted and evaluated by development ethicists (Goulet, 1997; 2006a; Crocker, 2008).

international development follows a more historically specific and ideologically determined pattern than that of a globalised market economy through the dominant neoclassical theories of economic development. The end state of development, the vision of a good life and a good society, as the key ethical argument that constitutes the meta-ethical nature of international development, is largely affected by the dominant vision of economics in the presence of positive neoclassical economic analysis and neoliberalism. Neoliberals argue that economic growth and economic globalisation bring benefits to all nations and people. The openings of national economies to free trade and capital flows, along with the establishment of the economic system of competitive capitalism in developing economies, comprise the vision of neoliberal international development. However, as Dutt (2004b, p. xxv) says, even if this type of "globalization and neoliberalism bring[s] benefits to many, it may also promote uneven development, financial instability, corporate greed, environmental destruction, and ethnic tension". From our perspective, economic development in the form of economic growth as conceived by neoliberalism/neoclassical economics and economic well-being as defined in a consumerist way in terms of the Western type of material affluence have distorted the manner in which a good life and a good society are perceived. Nevertheless, for both proponents and opponents of an expansion of the scope of the market, there are important ethical and political economy issues that need to be engaged with and which are all too often ignored (Tsakalotos, 2004, p. 5). The following analysis investigates these ignored political and ethical issues in international development and in the context of a development ethics alternative to international development.

The meta-ethical approach of development ethics to international development is being reconsidered from the perspective of political economy. Development ethics as an alternative ethical paradigm to international development poses its critique of the conception of international development as a straightforward economic issue, as a subject of "identifying and quantifying the composition of economic growth packages" (Goulet, 2006a, p. 175). Development ethics complements Sen's position of the widespread "engineering" influence on economics, which observes that "within the economic discipline, it was the value-free 'engineering' stream of theory, methodology, and analysis which prevailed" (Goulet, 1997, p. 1160). Contrary to the neoclassical economics positivist vision of a good life and a good society, development ethics determines the meta-ethical meaning of development, the vision of a good society, within a three-dimensional approach. The first dimension is the relationship between the concept of a good life and the notion of human ascent; the second is the foundation of social justice in development; and the third is the position that humanity should adopt towards the natural environment (Goulet, 1975a; 1997; 2006a; Crocker, 2006, p. xvii-xviii; Gasper, 2012, p. 120). For development ethicists, "[e]thical judgments regarding the good life, the just society, and the quality of relations among people and with nature always serve, explicitly or implicitly, as operational criteria for development planners and researchers" (Goulet, 1997, p. 1161). In this respect, development ethics is presented as an alternative ethical paradigm *vis-à-vis* neoclassical economics positivism and the dominant vision of international development as a globalised market economy.

2 Neoclassical Economics and the Meta-Ethical Basis of Contemporary International Development

In this section, the meta-ethical nature of neoclassical economics and the meta-ethical aspects of contemporary international development are presented. Contemporary international development is viewed in an open-market economic framework, while the emergence of the global market in international development is supported by the dominant economic thinking.

2.1 The Meta-Ethical Nature of Neoclassical Economics

Neoclassical economics dominates the theoretical discourse on international development. Therefore, the revelation of the meta-ethical nature of neoclassical economics is of crucial importance to the investigation of the meta-ethical aspects of international development. What underlies a specific economic theory at the level of meta-ethics is its vision of a good life and a good society. This vision, implicitly or explicitly, is associated with distinct methodologies and a particular set of social values which, in turn, have implications for economic policy (Caporaso and Levine, 1993, p. 3; Marangos, 2004, p. 28). The meta-ethical nature of neoclassical economics reflects its beliefs and ideological standpoints regarding what constitutes a good life and a good society within the concept of international development. Hence, in order to evaluate further the meta-ethical nature of contemporary international development, we first need to discover the deeper ethical insights and the vision of neoclassical economics regarding what constitutes a good life and a good society or, in other words, the meta-ethical nature of neoclassical economics.

A good starting point for the discussion of the meta-ethical aspects of the dominant economic thinking in international development is the transition from classical political economy to neoclassical economics. The neoclassical economic paradigm has its historical roots in the marginalism of the 1870s (Fine, 1980, pp. 144–148). The acceptance of the principles of marginalism as the dominant method of analysis within economics reflects the passage from classical political economy to neoclassical economics. The application of the principles of marginalism through the deployment of the concept of *homo economicus*, which considers a rational, self-interested human being as making decisions at the margin, reshaped economics into a modern, positive science (Weintraub, 2002, p. 9). Moreover, the "engineering" nature of positive economics was also established during the transition from classical political economy to neoclassical economics (Sen, 1987, p. 4). Thus, this transition played an important role in the formation of the meta-ethical nature of the current dominant form of neoclassical economic positivism.

The transition from classical political economy to neoclassical economics brought about changes not only in economic theorising but also in economic methodology (Hausman, 1989, p. 117). For historians of economic thought, neoclassical economics was initiated by the theories of Jevons and Walras (Jevons, 1911 [1871]; Walras, 1954 [1874]). Jevons and Walras contributed to the creation of a new scientific paradigm in neoclassical economics in which the classical theories were found to be unsatisfactory and their replacement by neoclassical economics became imperative. Despite the wind of change in economics, "the first neoclassical economists were always under the spell of the classical economists" (Tsouflidis, 2010, p. 160). The efficient allocation of resources as the chief concern of economics came later on, mainly through the work of Robbins in the 1930s. In *An Essay on the Nature and Significance of Economic Science*, Robbins (1945 [1932]) defines economics as the study of the allocation of scarce resources among competing ends. In addition, neoclassical economics stipulates the efficiency of markets in achieving equilibrium in production and distribution. Through neoclassical economics:

> [T]he macro-dynamic view of the economy espoused by classical political economy gives way to static equilibrium analysis. The basic vehicle in this transformation, in addition to the exclusive use of the deductive method, was the concept of marginal utility, which became the keystone on which the whole neoclassical edifice has been erected (Milonakis and Fine, 2009, p. 97).

Neoclassical economics is based on several fundamental economic conceptions, such as economic rationality, economic efficiency and optimality, and marginal utility. All these conceptions are built around the foundational concept of *homo economicus* (the rational, optimising economic agent). Individuals are characterised by rational, maximising behaviour. In this neoclassical framework, prices are determined in a perfectly competitive market by supply and demand curves in equilibrium, without the use of market power or the presence of governmental discretionary power. In sum, according to Dutt and Wilber (2010a, p. 10), there are two ways to approach the nature of current neoclassical economics:

> One definition, which relates to the method, is that it analyzes the economy by examining the behavior of individual, self-interested, optimizing agents and how they interact with each other. The second is a narrower definition related to how the economy operates which, in addition to the assumption made in the first definition, assumes that the economic agents interact with each other in smoothly functioning markets in which all resources are being fully utilized and in which there are no distortions such as imperfect competition.

In other words, neoclassical economic theory is based on hypothesising free-market relations; perfect information and perfect competition; rational, maximising agents; and optimality. Based on these premises, neoclassical economic analysis tries to analyse the economic problems of international development. In this framework, three correlated and fundamental ethical issues overlap the discussion of the meta-ethical nature of neoclassical economics: 1. individual ethics and self-interest; 2. utilitarianism and utility maximisation; and 3. economic rationality, along with the notion of *homo economicus*.

2.1.1 Individual Ethics Based on Self-Interest

Neoclassical economics stresses the importance of individual actions in the determination of social phenomena. As Bowles (2004, p. 8) puts it, neoclassical economics "represent[s] economic behavior as the solution to a constrained optimization problem faced by a fully informed individual in a virtually institution-free environment". In this regard, society can be seen as the sum of individual preferences. The core idea of this perspective submits that what is good for an individual interacting with other individuals in the market, which is merely an extension of natural law, is also good for society. "Individuals as individuals are all that matters" (Cochran, 1974, p. 186). The individuals, in turn, are allowed, within defined limits, to follow their own values and convictions rather than somebody else's, and individuals should not be subject to coercion (Marangos, 2004, p. 45). From this perspective, neoclassical economics that is based on "the substantive version of the liberal position defends the market on the grounds that it fosters the development of the autonomous character, where that autonomy is seen as a component of the good life" (O'Neil, 1998, p. 33). Hence, in neoclassical economics, the meta-ethical nature of a good life may be better explained in the context of individual ethics and the notion of self-interest.

Regarding the neoclassical literature, the strong influence of the notion of self-interest in economics is mentioned by Edgeworth: "[t]he first principle of Economics is that every agent is actuated only by self-interest" (quoted in Hirshleifer, 1985, p. 54). In short, neoclassical economics assumes that society is no more and no less than the sum of the interests of the individual consumers, investors, workers, or employers interacting in the market. As Cochran (1974, p. 188) argues, "there was [is] no social organism with a life process of its own. There were [are] only individuals acting in their own self-interest." In this vein, the economy serves the individual preferences of consumers or investors; "therefore, public wants or needs must take second choice or whatever is left over" (Cochran, 1974, p. 188). The individual and his/her self-interested preferences are at the core of almost any ethical discussion within neoclassical economics.

The individualistic-ethical stance of neoclassical economics is mainly derived from the neoclassical usage of Adam Smith's notion of self-interest within the concept of the invisible hand, as referred to in *The Wealth of Nations* (1776). According to Smith (1776, p. 593):

> As every individual, therefore, endeavours as much as he can both to employ his capital in the support of domestic industry, and so to direct that industry that its produce may be of the greatest value; every individual necessarily labours to render the annual revenue of society as great

> as he can. He generally, indeed, neither intends to promote the public interest, nor knows how much he is promoting it... he intends only his own gain, and he is in this, as in many other cases, led by an invisible hand to promote an end which was no part of his intention.

In some cases, neoclassical economics reduces the notion of the invisible hand to the self-interested motives of individuals. "By adding the 'invisible hand' to individualism, conventional economics is able to argue that the well-being of everyone is served best when each individual single-mindedly pursues his/her own self-interest" (O'Boyle, 1994, p. 290). This notion provides an individualistic-ethical insight into the above quotation. In addition, as Bowles (2004, p. 26) points out, in Smith's argument, "individuals pursuing their self-interest will be 'led by an invisible hand' to implement socially desirable outcomes." Broadly, neoclassical economists in the tradition of Adam Smith and the liberal belief in *laissez-faire* argue that, by focusing on the self-interested behaviour of economic agents in a competitive free-market environment, common or public interest can be addressed. This line of argument has been subjected to intense criticism throughout the history of economic thought. For instance, in *The End of Laissez-faire* (1926), Keynes notes:

> Let us clear from the ground the metaphysical or general principles upon which, from time to time, *laissez-faire* has been founded. It is *not* true that individuals possess a prescriptive 'natural liberty' in their economic activities... The world is *not* so governed from above that private and social interest always coincide... It is *not* a correct deduction from the principles of economics that enlightened self-interest always operates in the public interest. Nor is it true that self-interest generally *is* enlightened; more often individuals acting separately to promote their own ends are too ignorant or too weak to attain even these. Experience does *not* show that individuals, when they make up a social unit, are always less clear-sighted than when they act separately (Keynes, 1972 [1926], pp. 287–288).

What Keynes clearly points out here is that there is no direct liaison between individualistic preferences and public interest. The meta-ethical nature of neoclassical economics based on the self-interested behaviour of economic agents acting in the free market does not necessarily promote the common or public good.

2.1.2 Utilitarianism and Utility Maximisation

The meta-ethical nature of neoclassical economics is also based on the ethical principles of utilitarianism. Following and building its theory on the principles of utilitarianism in the tradition of Jeremy Bentham [1748–1832] and John Stuart Mill [1806–1873] neoclassical economics is individualistic and outcome-based. Although there are philosophically rooted contradictions between Bentham's "hedonistic utilitarianism" and Mill's "ethical utilitarianism" (see Milonakis and Fine, 2009, pp. 28–29), what they have in common is an individualistically outcome-based form of utilitarianism (Dutt and Wilber, 2010a, pp. 43–45). In spite of this, for both Mill and Bentham, the common interest of the community is accepted as the sum of the interests of the members who comprise it. In Bentham's (2000 [1781], pp. 14–15) words;

> [B]y utility is meant that property in any object, whereby it tends to produce benefit, advantage, pleasure, good, or happiness... to prevent the happening of mischief, pain, evil, or unhappiness to the party whose interest is considered: if that party be the community in general, then the happiness of the community: if a particular individual, then the happiness of that individual.

Mill reformulates Bentham's principles and ideas on utility and suggests his particular popular form of ethical utilitarianism. As Mill (2004 [1879], p. 4) points out, "[a]ll action is for the sake of some end, and rules of action, it seems natural to suppose, must take their whole character and colour from the end to which they are subservient." However, while accepting the hedonism of Bentham and Epicurus, Mill adds an ethical manner of choosing among alternative pleasures. In this manner:

> [S]ome *kinds* of pleasure are more desirable and more valuable than others... Of two pleasures, if there be one to which all or almost all who have experience of both give a decided preference, irrespective of any feeling of moral obligation to prefer it, that is the more desirable pleasure (Mill (2004 [1879], p. 10, italics in the original).

We could argue that neoclassical economics follows Bentham and Mill's ethical utilitarianism, in the general way that ethical action is seen as bringing individuals a greater amount of utility. "It is therefore undoubtedly in the tradition of Utilitarianism to consider, above all, the consequences of general classes of acts" (Warnock, 2003, p. 11).

In the tradition of utilitarianism, ethics is mainly concerned with the results of an action. Consequently, the ethical worth of any action is evaluated by the outcomes. Moreover, as Sally (1998, p. 16) observes, "a certain breed of liberals cleaves to the doctrine of utility, undertaking a cost benefit calculation of individual utilities geared to 'maximising' social welfare." In this direction, neoclassical economics interprets almost all agent behaviour in terms of the optimising individual action in the narrow sense of utility maximisation. As Jevons (1911 [1871], p. 1) puts it, "[r]epeated reflection and inquiry has led me to the somewhat novel opinion, that value depends entirely upon utility." According to Milonakis and Fine's (2009, p. 70) interpretation;

> Value theory becomes a matter of productivity at the margin of whatever scarce resource contributes to output. And the location of the margin derives from demand, itself, the result of the utility maximisation of individuals, thereby forging a subjective theory of value.

Milonakis and Fine (2009, p. 98) conclude by arguing that, "the process of reducing subjectivity, and utility, to such narrow concerns is part and parcel of the making of the mainstream in its current form." What is noteworthy is that neoclassical economics accepts utilitarianism as an ethical background that better supports economic concepts such as utility maximisation. In turn, utility maximisation based on positive neoclassical economics involves almost all economic and social actions. In many cases, positive neoclassical economists extend the application of economic models based on the concept of utility maximisation to the study of "non-traditional areas (the very areas outlawed by Mill and others) such as the economics of crime, marriage, suicide, adoption, church attendance, and so on" (Alvey, 2000, p. 1245; see also Duhs, 1998; Fine and Milonakis, 2009). In addition, with the rise of neoclassical economic positivism, mainly (but not exclusively) promoted by economists of the Chicago School of Economics, the virtual nature of microeconomics came to the forefront within economics:

> This undoubtedly promoted the extension of Becker's economic approach to the other social sciences, but these and economists themselves remained dubious over the reduction of all economic and social behaviour to utility maximisation without due consideration of social and historical considerations (Fine and Milonakis, 2009, p. 52).

However, trying to obtain higher levels of self-interest utility is not the motivation for being good or doing good but merely a consequentialist ethical approach derived from the concepts of economic rationality and *homo economicus* (Dutt and Wilber, 2010a, p. 94).

2.1.3 Homo Economicus and Economic Rationality

Homo economicus is an ethical construction based on the concept of economic rationality. "Homo-economicus is one of the foundations of mainstream economics" (O'Boyle, 1994, p. 290). *Homo economicus* can be seen as a rational economic agent, characterised by self-interested goals and the rational choice of means to achieve those goals. As Posner (1977, p. 3) argues, economics "explores and tests the implications of assuming that man is a rational maximiser of his ends in life, his satisfactions—what we shall call his 'self-interest'." In turn, economic rationality, partly derived from research on human nature and evolutionary biology, is accepted as a notional mechanism that adequately interprets individuals' preferences and actions. "Rationality is an *instrumental* concept. In the light of one's goals (preferences), if the means chosen (actions) are appropriate the individual is rational; if not, irrational" (Hirshleifer, 1985, p. 59, brackets and italics in the original). Considering the concepts of *homo economicus* and economic rationality not only in an abstract theoretical sense but also in the dominant economic mechanism of the market, it seems that neoclassical economics responds to the general image of economics as a positive science that investigates individual or social outcomes in the value-neutral and ethically neutral economic environment of the market. Hirshleifer (1985, pp. 53–54) claims that "[o]ur [neoclassical economists'] heartland is an intellectual territory carved off by two narrowing conceptions: (1) of man as rational, self-interested decision-maker, and (2) of social interaction as typified by market exchange". Hirshleifer (1985, p. 54) remarks that the hypothesis of rational, self-interested agents (though admittedly inaccurate) has been proven to have great explanatory power in the areas where "we apply it", implying the domain of the market.

In the concepts of *homo economicus* and economic rationality, individuals appear as rational optimisers based on self-interested behaviour and represented by demand functions with exogenous preferences. Prices, in turn, are determined in a perfectly competitive market by supply and demand curves, in equilibrium, eliminating the element of market power (Bowles and Gintis, 2000, p. 1411). Indeed, in neoclassical economics, there is a widespread belief that individuals who behave in a rational manner will survive and those who do not will fail (North, 1990, p. 19).

However, the neoclassical view of individuals interacting in a value-laden market system in the form of *homo economicus*—the self-interested, rational, and utility-optimising agent—distorts the real-world actions and motivations of individuals. From new research on behavioural economics, it is now well-established that people do not simply act as self-interested optimisers. People have concerns for others, they follow norms, and they exhibit ethical values. These features of human nature affect how people behave, how they interact in specific institutional settings, and what outcomes occur in the market, in the economy, and in society as a whole. "Thus, ethical values can improve the working of markets and the economy as a whole in some cases, and they may result in unfavourable outcomes in some senses, and these features must be kept in mind for analysing the workings of the economy" (Dutt and Wilber, 2010a, p. 230). By providing the conception of individuals as *homo economicus*, neoclassical economics draws misleading and faulty implications not only at the level of individual behaviour but also in terms of how the economy functions because of people's interactions within society.

So far, the analysis has revealed the meta-ethical nature of neoclassical economics. The neoclassical premises of 1. individual ethics and self-interest; 2. utilitarianism and utility maximisation; and 3. economic rationality and the notion of *homo economicus* constitute the meta-ethical nature of neoclassical economics. These neoclassical premises can be seen as the ethical background for investigating the meta-ethical nature of international development.

2.2 International Development in a Globalised Market Economy

Since the 1970s, international development has taken the prevailing form of a globalised market economy based on the ascendency of neoliberalism as a specific market-based doctrine of economic and social policies in international development (DeMartino, 2000; Harvey, 2005; 2010; O'Hara, 2006). For economic neoliberalism, "the extension of market-based economic integration across all local, regional and national borders will provide humankind with the optimal means to achieve prosperity from now until eternity" (DeMartino, 2000, p. 1). Historically, the global dominance of neoliberal policies in international development was established during the time when Margaret Thatcher was Prime Minister of the United Kingdom [1979–1990] and Ronald Reagan was President of the United States [1981–1989]. As O'Hara (2006, p. 10) points out:

> [D]uring the 1980s, the Thatcher and Reagan revolution spread neoliberalism and globalization through the advanced nations—and later elsewhere—leading to attempts at greater privatization, reduced state spending, and reduced red tape and taxation (for the rich and corporations).

Referring to the neoliberal policies of Thatcher and Reagan, O'Hara (2006, p. 10) also notes that attempts were made at the international level to promote finance capital, advance the cause of free trade in the world economy, and decrease the power of labour. What happened in the following years is that "[t]hose who followed, like Clinton and Blair, could do little more than continue the good work of neoliberalization, whether they liked it or not" (Harvey, 2005, p. 63). For these reasons, in the 1980s, the time of Thatcher's governance in the United Kingdom and Reagan's presidency in the United States was a turning point in the economic history of international development.

The imperative of economic neoliberalism in international development can be seen in the role of the global market. Furthermore, neoliberalism:

> [L]egitimized the deregulation and global integration of financial markets; the more general drive to open up markets has provided capital, whether industrial, commercial or financial, with the means to seek out every nook and cranny where there's a profit to be made (Callinicos, 2009, p. 207).

Thus, the goal of neoliberalism as a market-based doctrine in international development is to promote the profits of capital in a globalised market environment. Besides, neoclassical theory as the scientific supporter of neoliberalism advocates that discretionary income and wealth redistribution policies should be eliminated in a global free-market economy. In turn, the market is assumed to be a neutral mechanism that promotes competitiveness. As Walras (1954 [1874], p. 84) argues:

> In fact, the whole world may be looked upon as a vast general market made up of diverse special markets where social wealth is bought and sold. Our task then is to discover the laws to which these purchases and sales tend to conform automatically. To this end, we shall suppose that the market is

> perfectly competitive, just as in pure mechanics we suppose, to start with, that machines are perfectly frictionless.

Furthermore, even in the presence of market failures, neoclassical economics does not imply government action; private solutions should be sought first. This is because, by definition, government failure results in worse outcomes than market failure; thus, markets are preferable, even if they are imperfect. In neoclassical economics, the relationship between private firms and consumers in the free market is at the centre of almost every discussion of a good life and a good society. State authority has no role, and it should not be allowed to act as a regulator where there is a market mechanism failure because private market solutions are more preferable or forthcoming (Bowles and Gintis, 2000; Marangos, 2004).

There is an apparent contradiction in the theory of neoclassical economics and the applied global policies of neoliberalism in international development. Although almost all neoclassical models and theories diminish state power and interventionism, in practice, neoliberalism recognises that political agencies, nation-states, or international institutions and organisations, can, and usually do, act as financiers, administrators, and regulators of markets in the direction of the extreme applied neoliberal economic and social policies as well as in the establishment of a competitive free-market environment. The Washington Consensus policy in Latin America can be viewed as an example of such interventionism in international development, as the neoliberal market policies of neoclassical economics have become the norm in virtually every Latin American nation (Cypher, 1998, p. 47; Gore, 2000; Serra and Stiglitz (eds.), 2008; Marangos, 2009a; 2009b).

Nevertheless, this apparent contradiction should not be seen as a disagreement between neoclassical theory and neoliberal practice. Actually, because neoclassical economics is outcome-based, what matters is the end state or the result of an economic policy. Therefore, in the effort to establish a globalised market economy in a private free-market framework, neoclassical policies in the form of neoliberalism accept that nation-states and international organisations, as the key policy agencies in international development, should act to promote this end. In this respect, "[n]eoliberalism recognizes that political agencies must frequently act as financiers, supervisors and regulators of markets and marketization" (Howard and King, 2004, p. 40).

With reference to international development, neoclassical theories of growth (such as Solow's (1956) exogenous growth model and its extensions and the free, open-trade, international structure based on Ricardo's law of comparative advantage and its neoclassical positivist expansions) constitute the neoclassical image of international development. Neoclassical theories of economic development assume, first, that the benefits of free trade will be shared between trade parties (nations and societies) in a mechanical way; secondly, they assume that the rate of economic growth is subject to the rate of savings in both national and international economies (Barratt-Brown, 1994, 1995, pp. 37–38). Moreover, accepting Schumpeterian ideas, neoclassical economics poses that free trade and competition are the source of innovation and the cause of economic growth (see, for example, Schumpeter, 2006 [1954]). In turn, the vital goal of the dominant neoclassical economic theories of development is to establish a process of sustained economic growth, in which "economic growth leads to increases in per capita income and wealth so, on average, the members of society are materially better off each year" (Little, 2003, p. 38). Neoclassical economics, then, claims that free trade and freely flexible exchange rates promote maximum efficiency and prosperity internationally (DeMartino, 2000; O'Hara, 2006). Since the 1940s (see, for example, Hicks 1939; 1959), neoclassical economists have argued that the main obstacles to international development are protectionism and hostility towards international capital. Competition in international development is desirable and "the more perfect it is the better the utilization of resources will be; monopolistic positions are either short-lived by their nature or caused by non-economic influences of political power groupings" (Barratt-Brown, 1994, 1995, p. 38). The conceptual idea is always the same: the free-market mechanism maximises economic growth and trade advantages through competitive forces. In this manner, economic growth in a global free-market framework leads to better outcomes for all international economies, societies, and individuals. In the neoclassical economics vision of international development, a globalised market economy has a significant position not only in the production or distribution of goods and services but in all human activities across people's lives (DeMartino, 2000; Harvey, 2005; 2010). To this end, free-market economists contend that this is the road towards a good society.

Neoclassical economics emphasises the need for a globalised market economy to satisfy nations' and people's wants through economic growth, without explaining adequately the relationship between the needs and the wants that must be satisfied in this way. For instance, Nussbaum (2003, p. 33) argues that economic growth is a bad indicator of life quality and human well-being. Neoclassical economics views the attainment of a good society as the end state of economic development; economic growth perceives international development as a globalised market economy.

2.3 Economic Well-Being and Consumerism in International Development

In neoclassical economics, a good life and a good society are viewed as an affluent life in a consumerist society. The meta-ethical neoclassical vision of international development is expressed by economic well-being through a global free-market economy in which all or almost all human preferences and actions can be expressed in market transactions. Also, in this vision, the benefits of the free market spread to all nations, societies, and people in the world. Hunter and Yates (2002, p. 330) point out that:

> "[T]he prism through which they [business executives and so on] see these positive benefits is the market itself, where the average person is regarded as a global consumer whose economic choices are expanding due to liberated, interconnected markets and whose social and political freedoms are expanding due to the democratization of information."

This quote reveals how neoliberals glorify a globalised market environment. The individual is a global consumer with social and political freedoms, under the assumption of perfect information or the "democratisation of information", in the words of Hunter and Yates (2002, p. 330).

At the meta-ethical level of analysis, economic growth in terms of wealth creation is perceived as an end state of international development. Wealth creation reflects an affluent material society in the presence of social and political freedom. For neoclassical economics, prosperity can be understood in terms of "an increased satisfaction of people's preferences and an enhanced ability of individuals to carry out whatever their own conception of the 'good' happens to be" (Tsakalotos, 2004, p. 5). Neoclassical economics interprets the objective of international development to be the maximisation of economic well-being on an individualistic basis through the consumption of goods and services. Human wants or preferences, according to neoclassical economics, are addressed through a market economy wherein the consumer is represented as a "commodity-acquiring, want-satisfying and utility-maximizing" agent (O'Boyle, 1994, p. 290). In this framework, economic well-being and consumerism are the fundamental ethical pillars of the neoclassical economics vision of a good life and a good society. As Brown (2004, p. 212) claims:

> It [consumerism] is a culture in itself. We talk about the consumer culture, the goods life, the idea of 'happiness-through-buying'. It is what essentially justifies and reproduces capitalism in the hearts and minds of its workers and businesses... Capitalism and today's global political economy tend, or at least try, to make everyone into a happy consumer. The notion of 'more is better' is a basic tenet of consumerism. What drives this system in many respects is the ready acceptance that the good life is the goods life.

In international development, however, the distribution of the outcomes of economic growth is not equally proportioned among nations and within nations and societies. Growth theories usually claim that economic development has increased the average income worldwide. For instance, Lucas (2000, p. 159) argues that "[t]he real income of an average person has more than doubled since World War II and the end of the European colonial age". This increase, however, in most cases, does not reflect an equal distribution of the benefits of economic growth between and within nations and societies.

However, economic growth has disproportionately benefited different nations of the world, with richer nations generally benefiting much more than poorer nations. "As a result, global income inequality has worsened dramatically since the early nineteenth century" (Firebauht, 2006, p. 6). In recent times, this situation has worsened. Empirical studies focusing on global economic growth and its benefits have shown that, during the last few decades, income inequality among nations has increased dramatically. For instance, Guillen (2001, p. 247) claims that "the evidence unambiguously indicates that there is today *more* inequality across countries than ten, twenty, fifty or even one hundred years ago." Hence, even though contemporary international development has increased the total outcome of economic growth, income, and (as a consequence) consumption via economic growth in a globalised market economy, the allocation of this outcome still remains unequally distributed between and within nations and societies.

Regarding the expansion of global income, consumerism, and the unequal distribution of both income and consumption, there are two related ethical issues: "the haves of the world are over consuming, that is, consuming too much", on the one hand, while "the have-nots of our world are consuming too little", on the other hand (Brown, 2004, p. 208). To expand statistically on the diversity in the distribution of consumption within international development, 86 per cent of all the world's goods and services are consumed by the richest 20 per cent of the world's consumers, while the poorest 20 per cent consume only 1.3 per cent of these goods and services (Rifkin, 2000, p. 231). This situation has not changed dramatically since the late 1990s. The dominant international development paradigm through economic growth does not adequately address such inequalities. However, viewing the global market as the imperative mechanism of international development focuses on the maximisation of gains, not the equal distribution of those gains between and within nations, societies, and people.

Moreover, the unequal distribution of the gains of economic growth has an environmental dimension. On the one hand, over-consumerism by developed nations and the rich classes leads to environmental crises. On the other hand, even in the case of poverty, poor nations over-use whatever resources they have in order to survive at the expense of environmental integrity. From this perspective, the environmental crises are caused both by material affluence and by poverty. Thus, the unequal distribution of goods and services not only results in distorted consumption but also in environmental instability (Brown, 2004; Okereke, 2008).

Evidently, the meta-ethical nature of international development as a globalised market economy is based on economic well-being and consumerism. The more people consume, the more economic growth is produced, and the more revenue, income, and profit the firms make. However, even the opponents of capitalism argue that there would be no production without consumption. Production and consumption are not problems in themselves. The manners of production and consumption, the distribution of what is being produced, and the relation of this distribution with the satisfaction of people's needs and wants call for the study of alternative ethical issues in international development.

3 The Development Ethics Meta-Ethical Alternative: A Good Life, Social Justice, and Sustainability in International Development

Development ethics offers an important alternative meta-ethical viewpoint of the ethical concerns of neoclassical economics and the dominant vision of international development as a globalised market economy. In this section, the international development meta-ethical concerns that have been described are contrasted with the development ethics meta-ethical notion of a good life, social justice, and sustainability. Development ethics comprises an alternative ethical paradigm regarding international development within a political economy context, which can be found useful in the investigation of the ethical aspects of international development in the direction of a good life and a good society.

The discussions among development ethics of the meta-ethical nature and notion of development itself take various forms and contain different methodologies (Goulet, 1975a; 2006a; Dower, 1998a; 1998b; Clark, 2002a; Crocker, 1991; 2008; Wilber and Dutt (eds.), 2010a, 2010b; Gasper, 2004; 2012; Gasper and St. Chair (eds.), 2010a, 2010b; Schwenke, 2011). In the development ethics literature, as the aforementioned edited volumes and monographs indicate, development ethicists, philosophers, and development thinkers (such as Sen, Nussbaum, Streeten, Griffin, Stiglitz, Pogge, Ramirez, Camacho, and Qizilbash, to name but a few) have made substantial contributions to the ethical discussion of development. Development ethics, as a pluralistic and interdisciplinary field, involves agreements as well as contradictions and controversies regarding the notion and methodologies of investigating ethical development.

At present, in the development ethics literature, there is no consensus regarding the meta-ethical nature of international development; in other of what constitutes a good life and good society in international development. One of the aims of the present analysis is to contribute in this direction. In this section, an attempt is made to define the meta-ethical nature of international development within the lines of development ethics in a political economy context, contrary to the dominant vision of neoclassical economic positivism. In this respect, development ethics is portrayed as the branch of political economy and moral philosophy that investigates the ethical consistency of the concepts of a good life and a good society within their local, national, and international dimensions. Development ethics is seen as an important ethical alternative to the neoclassical economics positivism in international development. In this section, we put forward the meta-ethical context of this approach.

Development ethics approaches the meta-ethical nature of international development in a substantially different manner than that of positive neoclassical economics. As Hodgson (2001, p. xiii) puts it, "a fundamentally different reality may require a different theory". In a similar fashion, the vision of a different reality—a good society—also requires a different theory.

Development ethics as an alternative ethical paradigm for international development incorporates the meta-ethical concepts of a good life and a good society in a substantially different manner. This different manner is not always antagonistic to market forces and the liberalisation agenda of classical political economists. For instance, development ethics accepts individuals' freedom of choice and economic growth (in the sense of material affluence that alleviates poverty) as two of the means of a good way of living. "Development was originally conceived as being equivalent to economic growth, modernization, or industrialization, but development ethics has brought a values[-based] focus to refine the concept and definition of development" (Schwenke, 2011, p. 321). In this vein, development ethics analysis is mostly based on an ethical definition of development: in other words, what the requirements of a good life and a good society are, as well as the ethical deliberation between the means and the ends of development. Furthermore, development ethics clearly stands against neoclassical economic positivism, global neoliberal policies, and the determination of international development solely as economic growth in a globalised market environment, focusing on the discussion of ethical values. In this manner, development ethics offers a supplementary ethical manner to approaching the meta-ethical aspects of international development beyond neoclassical economic positivism and neoliberal concerns and policies.

3.1 Development Ethics and the Meta-Ethical Notion of Development

Efforts were made to define precisely the essentials of the meta-ethical notion of development during a seminar titled *Ethical Issues in Development* that took place in Colombo, Sri Lanka, in 1986 (Goulet, 1996, pp. 197–198). It was agreed that any definition of development should take into account at least the following six conceptual propositions, which might reflect consensus on how development ethicists incorporate the idea of development: (1) an economic component, related to wealth, material life conditions (amenities), and their equal distribution among peoples; (2) a social ingredient, connected with social goods such as health, housing, education, employment, etc.; (3) a political dimension, in the sense of the protection of human rights and political freedom; (4) cultural elements, based on the idea that cultures cultivate people's identities and self-esteem; (5) ecological soundness, to promote a type of development that respects natural resources and forces for the restoration of the environment; and (6) a system of meaning, which refers to the manner in which a society perceives the beliefs, symbols, and values concerning the historical process and the meaning of life.

In other words, an ethical manner of viewing a good life and a good society ought to be assured in four areas of life: economic, political, social, and cultural (Goulet, 2006a, pp. 150–151):

> "Long-term economic viability depends on a use of resources which does not deplete them irreversibly. Political viability rests on creating for all members of society a stake in its survival: this cannot be achieved unless all enjoy freedom, inviolable personal rights, and believe that the political system within which they live pursues some common good and not mere particular interests. And if development is to be socially and culturally sustainable, the foundations of community and symbolic meaning systems must be protected. Otherwise, they will be steamrolled into oblivion under the pretext of submitting to the requirements of scientific and technological 'rationality'."

In the tradition of development ethics and of Goulet, the authors Dutt and Wilber (2010b, pp. 10–12) also offer a notional typology concerning the meta-ethical aspects of development in four dimensions. First, development should not only consider growth or the material well-being of the poor but should mainly focus on the ethical discussion of 'why one should care about the poor' and the issue of solidarity among individuals, societies, and nations. Second, environmental protection is important for both sustainability of the biological cycle and unity with future generations. Third, the evaluation of value change is important to any development effort. As the authors state, "modernization [implying economic and technological change] is not the goal if it is imposed from outside, especially if it destroys values that are of central importance to those who are experiencing development" (Dutt and Wilber, 2010b, p. 11). Fourth, development discussions should include a variety of themes on the means and ends of development and people's participation. As the authors put it, "development occurs only when people themselves decide what they mean by development" (Dutt and Wilber, 2010b, p. 11). The aforementioned codifications constitute a holistic-ethical image of development or the meta-ethical nature of development within development ethics in a political economy context. What follows is a specific analysis of the meta-ethical vision of development ethics with reference to international development.

At the level of international development, development ethics points out that "[t]he three main agents of economic globalization—multinational firms, international financial institutions, and a small number of powerful states—all employ globalization as a vehicle to promote market-based development" (Goulet, 2006a, p. 211). However, "what is often called 'development'[3]—economic growth, for instance—may be bad for people, communities and the environment" (Schwenke, 2011, pp. 318–319; see also Crocker, 2001). The consequences of development usually result in more blight for developing countries and vulnerable people. Therefore, the process of economic development in the developing world should be reconceived as beneficial change, usually specified as alleviating the poor's misery and the environmental degradation in developing countries. Challenging international development in the existing form of a globalised market economy, as proposed by positive neoclassical economics and neoliberalism, development ethics precisely defines that a good society is viewed not as economic growth in the narrow sense of the material expansion of well-being but as the qualitative enrichment of human beings in all relevant aspects of human life. Crocker (2006, p. xviii) argues that development ethics should not try to respond to such issues "in an authoritative way that ends debate in the way a referee ends controversy with the awarding of a penalty kick". Hence, he concludes by stating that development ethics "insists on the importance of the questions and the way they imply or presuppose issues about the good life, social justice, and a sustainable environment" (Crocker, 2006, p. xviii).

[3] When development ethicists refer to 'development', they imply the conventional notion of development as it is approached by the mainstream, implying economic growth, economic development, and market-based development.

Development ethics defines a good society as achieving three broad aims. First, a good society should at least cover people's material, cultural, and spiritual needs. Second, a good society ought to support adequately social justice and people's participation in decision-making. Third, a good society needs to ensure a worldwide ecological balance between environmental sustainability and humanity. In addition, for development ethics, within the concept of the ethical nature of a good society, any social construction and institution should service the aforementioned aims. However, as a response to the meta-ethical nature of international development, development ethics considers the micro-social environment as well as the macro-social environment, identifying the person as the smallest societal unit within intergovernmental surroundings. In view of this, development ethics directly responds to the aforementioned meta-ethical discourse in the following manner. Regarding the meta-ethical issue of what the subject matter of a good society is, development ethics provides three answers: a good life, social justice, and sustainability. The following sections investigate these three concepts.

3.2 A Good Life as Human Ascent

Are material prosperity and the consumption of goods essential meta-ethical aspects of a good life and a good society? Arguably, yes they are. However, the important point is that these are not the only essential aspects. The majority of development ethicists considers that economic growth is either central or at least necessary to a good life. However, the notion of a good life is culturally specific. As development ethicists argue, the Western concept of a good life (as material prosperity and consumption) may not be appropriate to all cultures and societies (Dower, 1998a; Goulet, 2006a; Schwenke, 2011). "No one ignores the importance of material ease and leisure in fostering culture and the good life" (Goulet, 2006a, p. 32). However, in many cases, the concept of material prosperity and the current model of consumption lead in the opposite direction: for many cultures, "the plenitude of good is not proliferation of goods" (Goulet, 2006a, p. 34).

For development ethics, the first dimension of achieving development[4] within the ethical concept of a good society is attained by achieving good lives for all persons and the whole person (Perroux, 1981, p. 32). As Goulet (1971, p. 206) states, "[a]uthentic development aims at a full realization of human capabilities". Human capabilities, later formulated as the capability approach, mainly by Sen (1987; 1997) and Nussbaum (2000), have an influential position in the conceptual meaning of a good life within development ethics. Development ethicists (Crocker, 1996; 2008; Clark, 2002a; 2006; Gasper, 2004, Ch. 7) have argued in favour of such approaches to the determination of a good life. As Crocker (2008, pp. 389–390) puts it:

> Applying a conception of the human as agent and of human well-being as a plurality of capabilities and functionings that humans have good reason to value, the capability development ethicist can inquire into the effects different kinds of globalization have on everyone's agency and capability for living lives that are – among other things – long, healthy, secure, socially engaged, and politically participatory.

So, what are the requirements or the ingredients of the full realisation of human capabilities that lead to a good life? For development ethics, at a minimum, all people should have access to all the goods they need to cover their basic biological needs and to free part of their human energy in order for it to be allocated to a wider range of life aspects, beyond covering first-order needs. Perhaps the most important aspect of achieving a good life is perceived as 'being more' instead of 'having more'. For development ethicists, "development deals with the pursuit of the good life, and that planners must somehow—implicitly or explicitly—decide whether plenitude of good is something other than proliferation of goods" (Goulet, 2006a, pp. 27–28). Development ethics pays particular attention to the aforementioned relationship between "goods" and "the good" (Goulet, 2006a, pp. 27–28).

Based on the insights of social psychologists such as Fromm (2005), development ethics argues that the development model—based mainly on the dominant theories of economic growth—has distorted the way that a

[4] In the development ethics literature, the terms 'development' and 'authentic development' (they are used interchangeably) express the development ethics vision of a good society.

good life is perceived, focusing on 'having more' (material goods, wealth, etc.). In most cases, this leads to the notion of 'being more' (successful, attractive, and valuable). A similar critique of the conventional economic growth pattern, the consumption model, and the materialistic manner of life is accepted by political economists such as Brown (2004) and O'Boyle (1994). For development ethics, 'being more' is not the case of 'having more' material affluence. People have material needs; however, covering these material needs through the consumption of goods and services does not mean that the people have a good way of living. A good life is accepted in its broader meaning, including economic, biological, psychological, social, cultural, ideological, spiritual, mystical, and transcendental dimensions (Goulet, 1971, pp. 206–207). Development ethics rejects the dominant influence of development solely as economic growth, which makes economic well-being and consumerism paramount in life (Crocker, 2006, p. xxii). Against this perception, development ethicists propose that a good life involves all aspects of human life or, in other words, what is termed 'human ascent':

> Men and women become makers of their own histories, personal and societal. They free themselves from every servitude imposed by nature or by oppressive systems, they achieve wisdom in their mastery over nature and over their own wants, they create new webs of solidarity based not on domination but on reciprocity among themselves, they archive a rich symbiosis between contemplation and transformation action, between efficiency and free expression. This total of development can perhaps best be expressed as the 'human ascent' – the ascent of all men in their integral humanity, including the economic, biological, psychological, social, cultural ideological, spiritual, mystical, and transcendental dimensions (Goulet, 1971, pp. 206–207).

In sum, development ethicists reject the notion of a good life as it is conventionally approached by neoclassical economics through material consumption (consumerism) and economic well-being. They propose that a good life be defined in terms of human capabilities. The good lives of people are a requirement for a good society. Thus, ethical development should identify what kind of good life and in which way a good life ought to be pursued. A good life is not only a quantified measurement of material consumption nor is it only a qualified amount of utility functions, as neoclassical positivist models usually describe. For development ethics, a good life covers the broader meaning of human ascent in all relevant aspects of human life.

3.3 Social Justice in International Development

Is a globalised market economy, following an economic growth pattern, a socially just economy? The response to this ethical question leads to the second ethical pillar of the development ethics meta-ethical aspect of international development. For development ethicists (Goulet, 1975a; 2006a; Crocker, 2008; Schwenke, 2011; Gasper, 2004), the foundation of social justice has a significant role in the determination of the concepts of a good life and a good society.

Development ethics accepts the critique of international development in the form of a globalised market economy as an unjust economy. "A market system, wholly uncorrected by institutions of justice, sharing, and solidarity, makes the strong stronger and the weak weaker... Markets as masters of society enrich the rich and pauperize the poor" (Ward, 1976, p. xii, cited in Goulet, 2006a, p. 179). The neoclassical models of economic growth usually depict inequality as unavoidable in the context of international development. These neoclassical models claim that economic growth (or, in other words, a 'greater economic pie') diminishes the gap between rich and poor nations and people. For instance, according to Kuznets's (1955) hypothesis, in the early stages of economic growth, income distribution worsens; by contrast, in later stages, it will improve. Even though Kuznets's hypothesis has been verified by some empirical studies, in general the hypothesis that economic growth can diminish inequality has historically failed in international development. As Max-Neef (1992, p. 51) puts it, "even with growth, the poor's share of the cake diminishes."

Generally, neoclassical growth theorists suppose that "the benefits of growth will either trickle down to poor people at a later time or, if they do not, corrective welfare measures can be adopted by political authorities to assure equity" (Goulet, 2006a, p. 148). Globalisation and economic growth offer gains. At the same time, in a globalised market environment, "economic policies and economic actions often generate winners and losers" (Rassekh and Speir, 2010, p. 33). In international development, in most cases, developed nations and rich people become richer and developing nations and poor people become poorer. Thus, the neoclassical claim that economic growth in a globalised market economy can, in a self-correcting way, reduce poverty and inequality is merely an illusion.

The redistribution of the gains of economic development is a crucial point of the ethical discussion of equity and social justice. This must guide global reform regarding international development. For development ethics, "[s]olidarity and social justice are especially pertinent to discussions of global reform" (Goulet, 2006a, p. 161). Such global reform means a new form of interdependence that leads to more solidarity and more social justice for all. For developing countries in particular, interdependence alone is not enough. In this new form of interdependence "new rules of reciprocity and of horizontal decision making must be established in realms of economics, ocean legislation, financial voting rights, and international resource bargaining" (Goulet, 2006a, p. 162). Along with national interdependence, "reciprocity or mutuality must lie at the heart of the relationship" between solidarity and social justice (Goulet, 2006a, p. 162).

Moreover, for development ethics, social justice takes the form of development for all, and it claims that there is no sound development without the just distribution of its benefits. In this discussion, effectual access to resources is perhaps more important than the upper-oriented redistribution of economic growth gains. As the point of access is of vital importance, "the poor must gain access to resources early in the decision-making process regarding the use of resources, and not merely as a corrective afterthought to vitiated distribution systems" (Goulet, 2006a, p. 166). This leads to the idea of "effective solidarity", which means that by "institutionalizing the principle that the world's wealth belongs to all its inhabitants, on the basis of priority needs, not on geographical accident or on differing technological abilities to extract or exploit resources that some groups enjoy over others" (Goulet, 2006a, p. 167).

Accordingly, ethical development should stand against the egalitarian perspectives that merely divide the world into the donors and the recipients of aid. For instance, the ethical responsibility for alleviating poverty-related suffering has to be discussed in terms of social justice, rather than in terms of charity (Eskelinen, 2009). "A new understanding of structural justice will need to state as its initial postulate that the rights of human societies and their members are founded on the requirements of integral development for all" (Goulet, 2006a, p. 167). Thus, social justice in the sense of effective solidarity and development for all is a prerequisite for the establishment of a good society. On this topic, Crocker (2008, p. 120) argues that:

> Both resources and access to them are necessary as means. But because people are diverse and diverse in different ways, the moral space in which justice is discussed must focus on the freely chosen conversion of accessed resources into valued ways of doing and being.

Therefore, what are these valued or ethical ways of 'doing and being' regarding social justice? Based on the premise that human values and aspirations are both individually and socially constructed, ethical development "should not be divorced from the hopes, expectations and aspirations of ordinary people" (Clark, 2002a, p. 833). In this way, development ethics advocates social justice in the form of non-elite nations and people participating in social planning and outcomes. In this respect, political and economic justice or equity should be put forward normatively by both policy-makers and ordinary people.

> For 'equity' is not only instrumentally valuable but is also good or right in itself. Rather than taking refuge in a doctrine of value neutrality or a narrow construal of their institutions' 'mandate' or 'comparative advantage,' policy professionals should debate with citizens on the merits of substantive concepts of justice as well as procedures for deciding this question (Crocker, 2008, p. 47).

The vast majority of development ethicists accept the general premise that the more ordinary people participate 'upstream' in decision-making, "the more fully people express their agency and the better the consequences with respect to social justice" (Crocker, 2006, p. xxiii).

Furthermore, in the discussion of 'doing' and 'being', many development ethicists and political economists make use of Sen's notion of equality, particularly regarding capability. The notion of capability essentially means that a person's good life does not depend only on the amount of commodities or resources that s/he owns; instead, it depends mostly on their capability to transform these commodities and resources into actions in the sense of the options of doing and being. Capability determines a person's ability to use the available resources in order to be free to choose a way of life that suits them based on their personal characteristics (age, gender, culture, religious beliefs, etc.) (Bertin and Sirver, 2006, pp. 198–199). For Clark (2006, p. 33), the capability approach has been adjusted to (among other things) focus on inequality, social justice, living standards, and rights and duties. Sen (1987, p. 59) himself argues that:

> The 'well-being aspect' is particularly important in assessing issues of distributive justice (including diagnosing economic injustice) and in evaluating the nature of the 'deal' that the person has in terms of personal advantage. The 'agency aspect' [based on the capability approach] takes a wider view of the person, including valuing the various things he or she would want to see happen, and the ability to form such objectives and to have them realized.

For Sen, then, the space of capabilities provides the most fruitful and ethically satisfactory way of looking at equality (Nussbaum, 2003, p. 35). In turn, "capabilities equality provides advocates of justice the world over with the right to judge practices and institutions in their own and others' cultures" (DeMartino, 2000, p. 26). More precisely:

> The notion of capabilities equality alerts us to the likelihood that differences in income will not be overcome through incentive mechanisms of the sort provided by the perfectly functioning free market. Inequalities in resource endowments and inequalities in capabilities are self-reinforcing, and so a system that ties reward to contribution is likely to induce deepening inequality over time. Public policy interventions are therefore needed to right the wrongs of inequality across the spectrum of functionings (DeMartino, 2000, p. 120).

To this, Crocker (2008, p. 390) adds that:

> Because agency and these valuable capabilities (or functioning) are the basis for human rights, social justice, and both individual and collective duties, a development ethic will also examine how a globalized world is a help or a hindrance as individuals and institutions fulfil their moral obligations to respect rights. The long-term goal of good and just development – whether national or global – must be to secure an adequate level of agency and morally basic capabilities for everyone in the world – regardless of nationality, ethnicity, religion, age, gender, or sexual preference.

The capability approach in general, and capability equality in particular, enclose development ethics ideas and practices in the discussion of social justice.

Moreover, in international development, social injustice encapsulates the notion of vulnerability as the limited access to social forces of change. Vulnerability is best expressed as the forces one cannot control (Goulet, 1975a, pp. 38–59; Camacho, 2010). In Goulet's (2006a, p. 45) words, "[e]ntire societies are vulnerable when they lack adequate defences against the social forces which propel them into the processes of change." The economic dualism in international development between developed and developing nations and societies explains to some extent the global injustice conditions. In most cases, the developed world has been associated with the exploitation of resources and economic, political, and cultural interventionism in the developing world. The resource exploitation and the interventionism of developed nations in the rest of the world make developing nations and societies vulnerable to these conditions and hence unable to determine their own development patterns. Thus, vulnerability is at the core of unjust development conditions in international development. Social justice should reflect such reasoning by alleviating the vulnerability of developing nations and societies. As Gasper and Truong (2005, p. 383) claim, "[v]ulnerability and capability are two sides of the coin of being human. The virtue of care connects the two, and must be fostered for democracy, solidarity and social justice to be possible."

In sum, development ethics argues for an ethical pattern to social justice. Social justice in international development is best expressed by the effective solidarity in the notion of development for all. At the core of the development ethics discussion for social justice is people's participation in decision-making. Furthermore, social justice not only concerns a lack of access to resources but also a lack of capabilities. Capability equality is part of the notion of 'doing and being' within the concept of social justice. Social justice is a fundamental element of a good life and a good society. Thus, any attempt towards just international development should eliminate the vulnerability of developing nations and societies. Given this, the globalised market economy is an unjust economy and, therefore, "economic justice needs to be nurtured and safeguarded by eternal vigilance and on-going corrective action" (Goulet, 2006a, p. 200).

3.4 Sustainability in International Development

The third ethical pillar of the development ethics meta-ethical aspect of international development is the sustainability of natural resources and the environment on a global scale, in addition to the relation of natural sustainability with humanity. In international development, the neoclassical positivist vision of development as economic growth in a globalised market with the dominance of economic well-being as material consumption is closely associated with the issue of environmental sustainability. From the angle of development ethics, Goulet (2006a, p. 151) puts the matter well:

> The ecological imperative is clear and cruel: nature must be saved or we humans will die. The single greatest threat to nature comes from 'development.' This same 'development' also perpetuates the underdevelopment of hundreds of millions of people. Therefore, the task of eliminating dehumanizing underdevelopment possesses the same urgency as the safeguard of nature. A comprehensive ethic of authentic development, of necessity, looks to sustainable resource use as well as equitable access to them. Along with this ethic, there is needed what Ignacy Sachs[5] calls an 'anthropological economics' that simultaneously serves human needs and manages nature with wisdom.

Usually, economic development regards environmental sustainability as a technical matter. A good example would be the estimation and reduction of greenhouse gas emissions. For development ethics, sustainability cannot be seen only as a method or a technical matter within the concept of development. Development ethics links sustainability with the notion of development itself. In this respect, the conventional notion of development as westernised economic growth is closely associated with the problem of ecological destruction. For development ethics, sustainability with nature is a holistic subject derived from the general notion of development.

Within political economy, it is generally accepted that exaggerated individualisation, on the one hand, and the structure of the global economy along with the emerging consumption model, on the other, are two of the basic causes of global environmental instability (Røpke, 1999, p. 410; Brennan, 2004, pp. 260–261). In this sense, sustainability means "moving away from the self-interested, consumer-oriented values that characterize the modern capitalist societies" (Brennan, 2004, p. 261). Regarding the structure of the global economy, worldwide economic dualism (the uneven development between developed and developing nations, between

[5] See Sachs (1984).

the North and the South) leads to the destruction of ecological capital. In recent years, "the increased desire for consumption goods in the developed core has further stressed the need to exploit natural resources in the underdeveloped periphery" (Brennan, 2004, p. 261; see also Carvalho, 2001; Muradian and Martinez-Alier, 2001).

Furthermore, the world's atmosphere and ecosystems (such as forests and oceans) cannot be adequately managed by a global market economy (Costanza, 1999; Bunyard, 2002). From the perspective of viewing international development as a globalised market economy, intergovernmental environmental protection institutions have, in many cases, been transformed into institutions that manage global resource allocation (such as in the United Nations *Convention on the Law of the Sea*). International environmental regimes now play vital roles in granting access to, and exercising control over, natural resources within international development. Okereke (2008, p. 5) argues that, in the presence of neoliberalism, environmental regimes are closely tied to the fact that institutions for global environmental governance have been transformed from their traditional role of the preservation of the worldwide natural environment into the preservation of natural resource allocation. In other words, "the distributive bargaining rather than environmental protection is the defining feature of international [environmental] regime efforts" (Okereke, 2008, p. 168).

However, global environmental policies reflect the dominant vision of sustainable development as a technical matter within the concept of economic development, where economic growth and market efficiency lead to environmental efficiency (Anderson and Lead, 1991; Bhagwati, 1993; Dobson, 1996; 1998; Petter, 1996). The concept of technocentric environmentalism—the notion that "the objective scientific 'experts' are those in whom trust should be placed when it comes to decision-making about the environment" (Petter, 1996, p. 37)—is deeper based on "the idea that we could buy our way to sustainability while producers of goods invented even more exotic ways of enabling us to do so" (Dobson, 1998, p. 488). Conventional approaches to sustainable development, particularly along the lines of neoclassical environmental positivism, usually depict the latter as a technical matter. In this and many other ways, given a particular path of development (as economic growth), environmental models of sustainable development reduce the scopes of their policies to the level of technical means. Thus, sustainable development is confronted as a value-neutral technical matter of reducing the rate of environmental destruction in a well-established development pattern: that of economic growth in a globalised market economy.

For development ethicists, environmental sustainability is not only a technical matter within the general concept of valued-laden economic development in a globalised market environment but is also part of the development concept itself. "The single greatest threat to nature—menacing irreversible destruction of its regenerative power—comes from 'development'" (Goulet, 1995, p. 119). In this respect, development ethics challenges the conventional notion of sustainable development as a technical part of economic development. Technical matters of environmental protection, even when they are useful, cannot lead international development to sustainability because of the inherent conditions (e.g., the manner of the production and consumption model, the notion of economic well-being, the extreme exploitation of resources, world dualism and the division between the North and the South, etc.).

The concept of environmental sustainability as development is ideological, value-based, and ethically determined. In this regard, for development ethicists, sustainability constitutes a political and ethical issue. Technical methods and means are subjected to ethics and politics. Therefore, a source of agreement among development ethicists is that, although technological advancement provides the means of attaining sustainability, the decision to attain sustainable development is a matter of ethics and politics.

As Brennan (2004, p. 261) argues, "the ideologies and institutional structures embedded in global free capital emphasize economic growth, social power, and control over the social and physical environment". For instance, the Kyoto Protocol of 1997 puts limits on the production of greenhouse gas emissions for the developed and developing nations that have signed the protocol. Nevertheless:

> These targets were arrived at through negotiations with government leaders, and they were not based on any general principles of fairness... This was necessary since under the prevailing conception of national sovereignty, countries cannot be bound to meet their targets unless they decide to sign the treaty that commits them to do so (Singer, 2002, p. 22).

As is apparent from this quote, the reduction of greenhouse gas emissions is more an agreement of power among sovereign nations than consensus on sustainable development in the sense of worldwide solidarity. Moreover, the Kyoto Protocol and similar agreements have not managed to solve the environmental problem.

For development ethicists, sustainable development is challenged under the premise that "development, as conventionally understood, requires continued economic growth, which may render sustainability impossible by further depleting non-renewable resources and polluting the biosphere" (Goulet, 1996, p. 190; see also Goulet, 2006a, p. 145). Furthermore, sustainable development in its international dimension is usually confronted by the presence of global politics and the element of power. Thus, "development ethics must enter into the formulation of environmental policy, and environmental ethics in the formulation of development policy" (Goulet, 1995, pp. 119–120).

Development ethicists and political economists commonly agree that sustainable development is closely linked to social and economic justice. Okereke (2008, p. 3) argues that "dominant approaches to environmental sustainability fail because they do not take sufficiently seriously the role of international equity or justice understood in more redistributive terms." Furthermore, in contrast to neoclassical economic positivism and the concept of wealth maximisation or economic growth in any economic development decision, sustainability should entail a kind of intergenerational justice:

> A just society is one that not only ensures equality among its present members, but that also conducts itself in a manner that ensures the capabilities achievements of those who will follow. Institutions must ensure that the physical environment is not ransacked in pursuit of maximum wealth or utility (DeMartino, 2000, p. 144).

From the perspective of development ethics, Goulet (1995, p. 119) claims that "[t]he only antidote to pseudo-development is a working ethic... Such an ethic joins the two normative streams, linking the concern for environmental responsibility with the drive for universal economic justice."

In this framework, development ethics accepts environmental sustainability in a holistic manner, similar to the Aristotelian notion of the 'philosophy of nature'. In this view, nature is everywhere; consequently, ecology looks at the whole picture: "the totality of relations" (Goulet,

2006a, p. 152). These relations are derived from the spheres of the environment, demography, resource systems, and technology:

> [Ecology's] special contribution to human knowledge is to draw a coherent portrait of how these four realms interact in patterns of vital interdependence. Ecological wisdom is the search for optimal modes and scales in which human populations are to apply technology to resource use within their environments. Both as an intellectual discipline and as a practical concern, ecology presupposes some philosophy of nature (Goulet, 2006a, p. 152).

According to the philosophy of nature, humans and the environment are considered as a unified whole:

> Nature is diminished when its human members are kept 'underdeveloped.' Conversely, humans cannot become truly 'developed' if they violate their supportive nature… The only authentic form of development is that which is conducted in the mode of solidarity, binding all persons and communities to each other and to the planet they inhabit (Goulet, 2006a, p. 154).

Thus, ethical development should clearly support sustainability with natural resources and humanity. Sustainability with nature and humanity ought to underline the idea of development as the ultimate ends and means. Development ethics approaches the notions of a good life and a good society through a concept of ethical development that includes sustainability with nature as a vital part of human existence.

4 Conclusion

The preceding analysis has investigated the meta-ethical basis of international development. The meta-ethical questions explored include such questions as 'what is the vision of a good life and a good society in international development?' The analysis is based on the key argument that international development is ideologically and historically determined. As has been shown, the contemporary form of international development is scientifically dominated by neoclassical economics positivism and neoliberal ideology.

Since the 1980s, international development has followed the pattern of neoliberalism under the political regimes of Thatcher in the United

Kingdom and Reagan in the United States. Since then, neoliberalism as the dominant paradigm in international development has been applied in the rest of the world. In this framework, international development takes the shape of a globalised market economy. As mentioned, neoclassical economics scientifically assists neoliberal ideologies and policies in contemporary international development. This is the result of an early transformation in economics. Since the Marginal Revolution, and especially since the middle of the last century, economics has gradually been transformed from a social science into a positive science. This transformation includes not only a change in the theory but also in the methodology of economics. This transformation first took shape in the writings of Jevons and Walras. In the transition from classical political economy to neoclassical economics, a critical role was played by the notion of *homo economicus* (which states that individuals are characterised by rational, maximising behaviour) and the notion of equilibrium (which states that prices are determined in a perfectly competitive market by supply and demand, without or with very limited governmental discretionary power). Along with the narrow concept of marginal utility, perhaps of equal importance to the transformation was the deduction of macroeconomic issues in static equilibrium analysis (Milonakis and Fine, 2009, p. 97). Under what Sen has called the 'engineering approach', positive neoclassical economics appears as neutral in terms of ethics and values. The present analysis, however, has rejected this assumption of the neutrality of positive neoclassical economics. It has been shown that neoclassical economics follows its own ethical pattern. It is permeated with a particular ethical viewpoint. Therefore, "[r]ecognizing this will facilitate the creation of a better economic theory and the construction of wiser economic policies" (Wilber, 2004, p. 425).

The present analysis has contributed in this direction. The meta-ethical nature of neoclassical economics is mainly derived from individual ethics on the basis of self-interest, utilitarianism, and economic rationality associated with the notion of *homo economicus*. Our analysis has shown that these concepts represent the meta-ethical nature of neoclassical economics. The meta-ethical views of neoclassical economics shape the basis of the meta-ethical nature of contemporary international development as a globalised market economy. The meta-ethical argument of a good society and a good life is perceived by neoclassical economics and neoliberal ideology as economic growth, in the Western sense of economic well-being and consumerism. The consumption model is based on self-interested, individualistic preferences in a free-market environment. For dominant theories of economic development, economic growth under open, free-market conditions leads to the maximisation of development gains. At the core of the meta-ethical notions of a good life and a good society is the element of the consumption of goods and services. As Brown (2004, p. 212) states, consumerism is a culture in itself. It has been argued that the prevailing consumption and economic development models, in terms of the expansion of gross domestic product (GDP), have distorted the way in which a good life and a good society are perceived. The unequal distribution of the gains of economic growth, the dualism of the world economy, the division between poor and rich nations and classes, the ecological imbalance, and the exploitation of resources are some of the consequences in international development.

An alternative perspective to the neoclassical vision of the meta-ethical nature of international development has been proposed through the investigation of development ethics within a political economy context. Development ethics within the context of political economy can be depicted as the ethical deliberation of local, national, and international development. The notion of development is normatively defined. For both development ethicists and political economists, the concept of development represents an interdisciplinary field. In this regard, a good life, social justice, and sustainability are the ingredients of a good international society. For development ethicists, a good life involves human ascent. Development should assist not only all persons but also the whole person (Perroux, 1981, p. 32). Moreover, a good life cannot only be derived from the material consumption of goods and services, as in the conventional Westernised consumption model. Accepting Sen's capability approach, development ethics uses the notion of 'being more' in a functioning and capability manner. Broadly speaking, for development ethics, a good life should lead to the human ascent of people.

The second ethical pillar of the development ethics meta-ethical vision of international development is that of social justice. Social justice is a prerequisite for a good society. The concept of social justice includes access to resources, the participation of ordinary people in decision-making, and the capability equality of people. In addition, effective solidarity, in the general notion of development for all, overlaps with the development ethics notion of social justice in international development. Reducing the vulnerability (the conditions that one cannot control) of poor nations and societies could lead to a more equal world.

Development ethics accepts sustainability with nature and humanity as the core element of development itself. An important issue is that natural sustainability and humanity are perceived as an involving whole. The conventional model of economic development is problematic for both nature and people. Sustainable development is not simply a technical matter: it is an ethical and political decision. Therefore, social justice, in turn, affects sustainability because there can be no sustainable development in an unjust economic environment.

In sum, the basic task of this chapter has been to bring to the fore the aforementioned discussion of the meta-ethical basis of international development and the development ethics alternative.

References

Alvey, J. E. (2000). An introduction to economics as a moral science. *International Journal of Social Economics, 27*(12), 1231–1251.

Anderson, T. L., & Leal, D. R. (1991). *Free market environmentalism*. Westview Press.

Atkinson, A. B. (2009). Economics as a moral science. *Economica, 76*(s1), 791–804.

Barratt-Brown, M. (1994). *The economics of imperialism*. Penguin Books.

Barratt-Brown, M. (1995). *Models in political economy* (2nd ed.). Penguin Books.

Bentham, J. (2000 [1781]). *An introduction to the principles of morals and legislation*. Kitchener: Batoche Books.

Bertin, A. L., & Sirven, N. (2006). Social capital and the capability approach: A social economic theory. In B. J. Clary, W. Dolfsma, & D. M. Figart (Eds.), *Ethics and the market: Insights from social economics* (pp. 191–203). Routledge.

Bhagwati, J. (1993). The case of free trade. *Scientific American, 269*(November), 42–49.

Boulding, K. E. (1969). Economics as a moral science. *The American Economic Review, 59*(1), 1–12.

Bowles, S. (2004). *Microeconomics: Behavior, institutions, and evolution*. Princeton University Press.

Bowles, S., & Gintis, H. (2000). Walrasian economics in retrospect. *Quarterly Journal of Economics, 115*(4), 1411–1439.

Boylan, T., & Gekker, R. (Eds.). (2009). *Economics, rational choice and normative philosophy*. Routledge.

Brennan, A. J. (2004). Environmental problems of the world: Global warming and biodiversity. In P. A. O'Hara (Ed.), *Global political economy and the wealth of nations: Performance, institutions, problems and policies* (pp. 245–266). Routledge.

Brown, D. (2004). Conspicuous consumption, fashion and style in the global marketplace. In P. A. O'Hara (Ed.), *Global political economy and the wealth of nations: Performance, institutions, problems and policies* (pp. 208–221). Routledge.

Buchanan, A. (1985). *Ethics, efficiency, and the market*. Clarendon Press.

Bunyard, P. (2002). Deforest the Amazon—Destroy the world. *The Ecologist, 32*(6), 32–33.

Callinicos, A. (2009). *Imperialism and global economy*. Polity Press.

Camacho, L. (2010). Goulet on vulnerability as a key concept in development ethics. In C. K. Wilber & A. K. Dutt (Eds.), *New directions in development ethics: Essays in honor of Denis Goulet* (pp. 142–154). Notre Dame University.

Caporaso, A., & Levine, D. P. (1993). *Theories of political economy*. Cambridge University Press.

Carvalho, G. (2001). Sustainable development: Is it achievable within the existing international political economy context? *Sustainable Development, 9*(2), 61–73.

Clark, D. A. (2002). Development ethics: A research agenda. *International Journal of Social Economics, 29*(11), 830–848.

Clark, D. A. (2006). Capability approach. In D. A. Clark (Ed.), *The Elgar companion to development studies* (pp. 32–45). Edward Elgar.

Clary, B. J., Dolfsma, W., & Figart, D. M. (2006). Introduction. In B. J. Clary, W. Dolfsma, & D. M. Figart (Eds.), *Ethics and the market: Insights from social economics* (pp. 1–8). Routledge.

Clary, B., Dolfsma, W., & Figart, D. (Eds.). (2006). *Ethics and the market: Insights from social economics*. Routledge.

Cochran, K. P. (1974). Economics as a moral science. *Review of Social Economy, 32*(2), 186–195.

Copp, D. (2007). *Morality in a natural world: Selected essays in metaethics*. Cambridge University Press.

Costanza, R. (1999). The ecological, economic, and social importance of the oceans. *Ecological Economics, 31*(2), 199–213.

Crocker, D. (2001). Globalization and human development: Ethical approaches. In E. Malinvaud, & L. Sabourin (Eds.), *Globalization ethical and institutional concerns, proceedings of the seventh plenary session of the pontifical academy of social sciences, 25–28 April 2001*. Vatican City: The Pontifical Academy of Social Sciences.

Crocker, D. (1991). Toward development ethics. *World Development, 19*(5), 457–483.

Crocker, D. (1996). Hunger, capability, and development. In W. Aiken & H. LaFollette (Eds.), *World hunger and morality* (2nd ed., pp. 211–230). Prentice Hall.
Crocker, D. (2006). Sen and deliberative democracy. In A. Kaufman (Ed.), *Capabilities equality: Basic issues and problems* (pp. 155–197). Routledge.
Crocker, D. (2008). *Ethics of global development*. Cambridge University Press.
Cypher, J. M. (1998). The slow death of the Washington consensus on Latin America. *Latin American Perspectives, 25*(6), 47–51.
DeMartino, G. (2000). *Global economy, global justice: Theoretical and policy alternatives to neoliberalism*. Routledge.
Dobson, A. (1996). Environment sustainabilities: An analysis and a typology. *Environmental Politics, 5*(3), 401–428.
Dobson, A. (1998). *Justice and the environment: Conceptions of environmental sustainability and dimensions of social justice*. Oxford University Press.
Dower, N. (1998). *World ethics: The new agenda*. Edinburgh University Press.
Dower, N. (1998). Development ethics. In R. Chadwick (Ed.), *Encyclopedia of applied ethics* (pp. 755–766). Academic Press.
Dutt, A. K. (2004). Uneven development, convergence and north-south Interaction. In P. A. O'Hara (Ed.), *Global political economy and the wealth of nations: Performance, institutions, problems and policies* (pp. 63–83). Routledge.
Dutt, A. K. (2004). Foreword. In P. A. O'Hara (Ed.), *Global political economy and the wealth of nations: Performance, institutions, problems*. London: Routledge.
Dutt, A. K., & Wilber, C. K. (2010). Introduction: Development ethics and development economics. In C. K. Wilber & A. K. Dutt (Eds.), *New directions in development ethics—Essays in Honor of Denis Goulet* (pp. 1–26). University of Notre Dame Press.
Dutt, A. K., & Wilber, C. K. (2010). *Economics and ethics: An introduction*. Palgrave Macmillan.
Eskelinen, T. (2009). *Putting global poverty in context: A philosophical essay on power, justice and economy*. University of Jyväskylä.
Etzioni, A. (1987). Toward a Kantian socio-economics. *Review of Social Economics, 45*(1), 37–47.
Fine, B. (1980). *Economic theory and ideology*. Edward Arnold.
Fine, B., & Milonakis, D. (2009). *From economics imperialism to Freakonomics: The shifting boundaries between economics and other social sciences economics as social theory*. Routledge.
Firebauht, G. (2006). *The new geography of global income inequality*. Harvard University Press.
Friedman, M. (1953). *Essays in positive economics*. Chicago University Press.
Fromm, E. (2005). *To have or to be*. Continuum International Publishing Group.

Galbraith, J. K. (1991). Economics in the century ahead. *The Economic Journal, 101*(404), 41–46.

Gasper, D. (2004). *The ethics of development*. Edinburgh University Press.

Gasper, D. (2012). Development ethics—Why? What? How? A formulation of the field. *Journal of Global Ethics, 8*(1), 117–135.

Gasper, D., & St. Clair, A. L. (Eds.). (2010). *Development ethics*. London: Ashgate.

Gasper, D., & St. Clair, A. L. (2010). The field of development ethics—An introduction. In D. Gasper & A. L. St. Clair (Eds.), *Development ethics* (pp. 13–33). London: Ashgate.

Gasper, D., & Truong, T.-D. (2005). Deepening development ethics: From economism to human development to human security. *The European Journal of Development Research, 17*(3), 372–384.

Gassler, R. S. (2007). Political and social economics: Beyond orthodoxy and heterodoxy. *Forum for Social Economics, 36*(2), 109–125.

Geivett, D. R. (2005). Metaethics. In K. J. Roth (Ed.), *Ethic-encyclopedias* (pp. 943–944). Salem Press.

Gore, C. (2000). The rise and fall of the Washington consensus as a paradigm for developing countries. *World Development, 28*(5), 789–804.

Goulet, D. (1971). An ethical model for the study of values. *Harvard Educational Review, 41*(2), 205–227.

Goulet, D. (1975). *The cruel choice: A new concept in the theory of development*. Atheneum.

Goulet, D. (1995). *Development ethics: A guide to theory and practice*. The Apex Press.

Goulet, D. (1996). Authentic development: Is it sustainable? In D. C. Pirages (Ed.), *Building sustainable societies: A blueprint for a post-industrial world* (pp. 189–205). Armonk, NY: M.E. Sharpe.

Goulet, D. (1997). Development ethics: A new discipline. *International Journal of Social Economics, 24*(11), 1160–1171.

Goulet, D. (2006). *Development ethics at work: Explorations 1960–2002*. Routledge.

Groenewegen, P. (Ed.). (1996). *Economics and ethics?* Routledge.

Guillén, M. F. (2001). Is globalization civilizing, destructive, or feeble? A critique of five key debates in the social science literature. *Annual Review of Sociology, 27*, 235–260.

Harman, G. (1977). *The nature of morality: An introduction to ethics*. Oxford University Press.

Harvey, D. (2005). *A brief history of neoliberalism*. Oxford University Press.

Harvey, D. (2010). *The enigma of capital, and the crises of capitalism*. Oxford University Press.

Hausman, D. M. (1989). Economic methodology in a nutshell. *The Journal of Economic Perspectives, 3*(2), 115–127.
Hausman, D. M., & McPherson, M. S. (1993). Taking ethics seriously: Economics and contemporary moral philosophy. *Journal of Economic Literature, 31*(2), 671–731.
Hicks, J. (1939). *Value and capital*. Oxford University Press.
Hicks, J. (1959). *Essays in world economy*. Oxford University Press.
Hirshleifer, J. (1985). The expanding domain of economics. *The American Economic Review, 75*(6), 53–68.
Hodgson, G. M. (2001). *How economics forgot history: The problem of historical specificity in social science*. Routledge.
Howard, M. C., & King, J. E. (2004). The rise of neo-liberalism in advanced capitalist economies: Towards a materialist explanation. In P. Arestis & M. Sawyer (Eds.), *The rise of the market: Critical essays on the political economy of neo-liberalism* (pp. 38–73). Edward Elgar.
Hunter, J. D., & Yates, J. (2002). In the vanguard of globalization. In P. L. Berger & S. P. Huntington (Eds.), *Many globalizations: Cultural diversity in the contemporary world* (pp. 323–357). Oxford University Press.
Jevons, S. (1911 [1871]). *The theory of political economy*. London: Macmillan.
Keynes, J. M. (1972 [1926]). The end of laissez-faire [1926]. In D. Moggridge (Ed.), *The collected writings of John Maynard Keynes* (Vol. 9). London: Macmillan.
Kuznets, S. (1955). Economic growth and income inequality. *The American Economic Review, 45*(1), 1–28.
Little, D. (1995). *On the reliability of economic models: Essays in the philosophy of economics*. Kluwer Academic Publishers.
Little, D. (2003). *The paradox of wealth and poverty*. Westview Press.
Little, I. (2004). *Ethics, economics, and politics*. Oxford University Press.
Lucas, R. E. (2000). Some macroeconomics for the 21st century. *Journal of Economic Perspectives, 14*(1), 159–168.
Marangos, J. (2004). *Alternative economic models of transition*. Ashgate.
Marangos, J. (2009a). What happened to the Washington consensus? The evolution of international development policy. *The Journal of Socio-Economics, 38*(1), 197–208.
Marangos, J. (2009b). The evolution of the term 'Washington consensus.' *Journal of Economic Surveys, 23*(2), 350–384.
Max-Neef, M. A. (1992). *From the outside looking in: Experiences in 'Barefoot Economics.'* London: Zed Books.
Mill, J. S. (2004 [1879]). Utilitarianism by John Stuart Mill. (Reprinted from FRASER'S MAGAZINE (Seventh Ed.) London Longmans, Green,

and Co.[1879]). A Penn state electronic classics series publication: Pennsylvania State University. http://www2.hn.psu.edu/faculty/jmanis/jsmill/Utilitarianism.pdf

Milonakis, D., & Fine, B. (2009). *From political economy to economics: Method, the social and the historical in the evolution of economic theory*. Routledge.

Muradian, R., & Martinez-Alier, J. (2001). Trade and the environment: From a 'Southern' perspective. *Ecological Economics, 36*(2), 281–297.

North, D. C. (1990). *Institutions, institutional change and economic performance*. Cambridge University Press.

Nussbaum, M. (2000). *Women and human development: The capabilities approach*. Cambridge University Press.

Nussbaum, M. (2003). Capabilities as fundamental entitlements: Sen and social justice. *Feminist Economics, 9*(2–3), 33–60.

O'Neil, J. (1998). *The market: Ethics, knowledge and politics*. Routledge.

O'Boyle, E. J. (1994). Homo socio-economicus: Foundational to social economics and the social economy. *Review of Social Economy, 52*(3), 286–313.

O'Hara, P. A. (Ed.). (2004). *Global political economy and the wealth of nations: Performance, institutions, problems and policies*. Routledge.

O'Hara, P. A. (2004). Viability of national government policies in a global political economy. In P. A. O'Hara (Ed.), *Global political economy and the wealth of nations performance, institutions, problems and policies* (pp. 327–346). Routledge.

O'Hara, P. A. (2006). *Growth and development in the global political economy: Social structures of accumulation and modes of regulation*. Routledge.

Okereke, C. (2008). *Global justice and neoliberal environmental governance*. Routledge.

Perroux, F. (1981). *Pour une philosophie du nouveau développement* (Vol. 4). Presses de l'UNESCO.

Petter, D. (1996). *Modern environmentalism: An introduction*. London: Routledge.

Posner, R. A. (1977). *The economic analysis of law* (2nd ed.). Little, Brown and Co.

Rassekh, F., & Speir, J. (2010). Can economic globalization lead to a more just society? *Journal of Global Ethics, 6*(1), 27–43.

Rifkin, J. (2000). *The age of access*. Tarcher/Putnam.

Robbins, L. (1945 [1932]). *An essay on the nature and significance of economic science* (second ed.). London: Macmillan.

Røpke, I. (1999). The dynamics of willingness to consume. *Ecological Economics, 28*(3), 399–420.

Rothschild, K. W. (1993). *Ethics and economic theory: Ideas, models, dilemmas*. Edward Elgar.

Sachs, I. (1984). *Dıvelopper, les Champs de Planification*. Universitı Coopırative.

Sally, R. (1998). *Classical liberalism and international economic order: Studies in theory and intellectual history*. Routledge.

Schumpeter, S. A. (2006 [1954]). *History of economic analysis. Edited from manuscript by E.B. Schumpeter, with an introduction by M. Perlman*. Taylor & Francis e-Library, Routledge. (First published in Great Britain in 1954 by Allen & Unwin (Publishers) Ltd.)

Schwenke, C. (2011). Development ethics: The audacious agenda. In R. S. Fortner & P. M. Fackler (Eds.), *The handbook of global communication and media ethics* (Vol. I–II, pp. 317–341). Oxford: Wiley-Blackwell.

Sen, A. (1987). *On ethics and economics*. Blackwell.

Sen, A. (1997). *Resources, values, and development* (Expanded). Harvard University Press.

Serra, N., & Stiglitz, J. (Eds.). (2008). *The Washington consensus reconsidered*. Oxford University Press.

Singer, P. (2002). *One world: The ethics of globalization*. Yale University Press.

Smith, A. (1776). *An inquiry into the nature and causes of the wealth of nation*. [E. Cannan, Ed. (1904), *2 vols*, London: Methuen]. Retrieved from ElecBook Classics, Book I–V.

Solow, R. M. (1956). A contribution to the theory of economic growth. *The Quarterly Journal of Economics, 70*(1), 65–94.

Tsakalotos, E. (2004). Social norms and endogenous preferences: The political economy of market expansion. In P. Arestis & M. Sawyer (Eds.), *The rise of the market: Critical essays on the political economy of neo-liberalism* (pp. 5–37). Edward Elgar.

Tsoulfidis, L. (2010). *Competing schools of economic thought*. Springer.

Vickers, D. (1997). *Economics and ethics: An introduction to theory, institutions, and policy*. Greenwood Publishing Group.

Walras, L. (1954 [1874]). *Elements of pure economics*. London: George Allen and Unwin.

Ward, B. (1976). Foreword. In M. U. Haq (Ed.), *The poverty curtain, choice for the third world*. New York: Columbia University Press.

Warnock, M. (2003). Introduction. In M. Warnock (Ed.), *Utilitarianism and on liberty (including Mill's 'Essay on Bentham' and selections from the writings of Jeremy Bentham and John Austin)* (2nd ed., pp. 1–16). Blackwell Publishing.

Weintraub, E. R. (2002). *How economics became a mathematical science*. Duke University Press.

Wilber, C. K. (2004). Ethics and social economics: ASE presidential address, January 2004, San Diego, California. *Review of Social Economy, 62*(4), 425–439.

CHAPTER 5

The Normative-Ethical Basis of International Development and the Development Ethics Alternative

1 Introduction

In the preceding chapter, the meta-ethical aspects of international development have been discussed. As mentioned, the present form of international development as a globalised market economy is sustained by neoclassical economic analysis. Neoclassical positivism perceives economics as a positive science that is free of values and ideologies. This is associated with the view that economics is an "objective" science (Friedman, 1953, p. 4). This perception has been rejected in the present study. Even for those who accept economics as a neutral, positive science, normative evaluations are not avoided because even positive economic analysis incorporates (out of necessity) normative judgements and presumptions (Hausman and MacPherson, 1993, p. 672; Dutt and Wilber, 2010a, pp. 30–31). If normative values permeate positive economics, they *a fortiori* permeate normative and economic policy (Dutt and Wilber, 2010a, p. 30). Based on these fundamental observations, we argue that the meta-ethical concepts advanced in the previous chapter are reflected in the normative-ethical analysis that follows. As moral philosophers affirm, meta-ethics and normative ethics are far from being independent of one another. Meta-ethical views are included in the normative-ethical analysis; thus, "differences in meta-ethics entail differences in normative ethics" (Gewirth, 1960, p. 204). Putting it in the context of the present study, normative-ethical analysis provides

N. Astroulakis and N. Karagiannis, *Development Ethics*,
https://doi.org/10.1007/978-3-031-75476-0_5

the notional framework under which the discussed meta-ethical concerns of a good life and a good society should be evaluated in international development.

The present chapter explores the normative-ethical aspects of international development or, in other words, what should the relationship be between the means and the ends in international development. While the vision of a good life and a good society is a meta-ethical issue, the relationship between the means and the ends of achieving this vision is considered a normative-ethical issue. Normative analysis is described by the general concern of 'how things should or ought to be', which implies the evaluation of alternative potential actions or choices. Normative ethics in economics deals with the ethical content of decisions and actions, the actual economic choices, and the grounds of relevant evaluative judgements (Vickers, 1997, p. 51). The exploration of the dominant normative-ethical principles and values that govern neoclassical economic analysis is necessary due to their reflection on the normative-ethical basis of international development theory and policy. Thus, in order to examine the normative-ethical basis of international development, the key normative elements of the neoclassical economic analysis should be specified. To be more precise, the normative manner in which neoclassical economic analysis evaluates the judgements within the issue of development is reflected in the relationship between the procedures and the outcomes—the means and the ends—of international development. At the level of economic analysis:

> [N]ormative economics is concerned with whether one economic state of affairs is better or worse than another, and hence with the question whether one action or measure, one policy or institutional framework, is better than another in the light of its probable consequences (Little, 2004, p. ix).

In this regard, the normative-ethical nature of neoclassical economics is better expressed using social choice theory and the broader field of welfare economics (Arrow, 1951; Arrow et al. (eds.), 2002 [Vols. 1 and 2]; Feldman and Serrano, 2006; Samuelson, 1947). However, in neoclassical welfare economics, one can come across different and sometimes contradictory approaches (Buchanan, 1959). In any case, "[w]herever economic activity, directly or indirectly, affects the social order, we are in the realm of welfare economics" (Gintis, 1972, p. 574).

In this chapter, the dominant form of the normative principles and values of neoclassical economics is analysed. The dominant normative neoclassical approach in welfare economics is criticised using the term 'welfarism' (Hausman and MacPherson, 1993; 2006; Sen, 1977). "Neoclassical theory's commitment to welfarism is tied to a notion of maximization—the maximum quantity of goods yields maximum satisfaction and, hence, maximum social welfare" (DeMartino, 2000, p. 144). Furthermore, international development is normatively assessed using the principles of economic rationalism and neoliberal ideology. In what follows, the normative-ethical nature of neoclassical economic analysis, of the term 'welfarism' and the normative implications of welfarism, and of economic rationalism and neoliberal ideology in international development are further explored. Following this, the specific relationship between the means and the ends in international development is determined. Neoclassical economics in the tradition of utilitarianism evaluates international development in terms of predetermined outcomes. Moreover, neoclassical economics uses specific normative means in order to achieve these outcomes. In international development, as Wilber (2010, p. 157) mentions, "[t]he resulting advice is well-represented in the free market focus of the Washington Consensus and its successors." The Washington Consensus as a neoliberal manifesto in international development is evaluated in terms of its normative-ethical aspects as an example of the contemporary normative-ethical basis of international development. The relationship between the ends and the means in international development and the ethical evaluation of this relationship within the contexts of neoclassical welfarism, economic rationalism, and neoliberal ideology comprise the normative-ethical basis of contemporary international development theory in general and the Washington Consensus in particular.

Moreover, the normative-ethical nature of development ethics in relation to international development theory is analysed. Development ethics offers an alternative to the neoclassical normative-ethical evaluation of international development. For development ethicists, development is commonly accepted as the normative study of ethical values. Beyond its applied and practical character, development ethics as a field can be perceived as an attempt to trust normative debates about economic and social development in the sphere of ethical values (Goulet, 1975a, pp. 331–334). Such debates involve the normative-ethical discussion of value change and ethical rationality. In addition, development ethics proffers a completely different approach to the normative-ethical evaluation of international development theory. The means, institutions, and policy instruments, as well as the ends (the outcomes) of international development, are subjected to normative-ethical discussion. Accordingly, ethics is perceived as 'the means of the means' of development. Any economic or social change, which economic development usually brings to people and societies, ought to be evaluated at the level of ethics. In a critical and ethical manner, development is dealt with as a means to achieving profound and universal human values: those of freedom, esteem, and well-being for all people and societies. The present analysis specifies the universal human values of development ethics as normative-ethical goals. Furthermore, a set of normative-ethical strategies in the direction of bringing about a good society are analysed. The discussion of the ethical values, value change, rationality, and the normative-ethical goals and strategies that development ethics involves represents an alternative normative-ethical proposal to neoclassical welfarism, economic rationalism, and neoliberalism in the ethical investigation of international development.

2 Neoclassical Economics and the Normative-Ethical Basis of Contemporary International Development

2.1 *The Normative-Ethical Nature of Neoclassical Economics*

In arguing for the normative-ethical nature of neoclassical economics, we mean that neoclassical economics promotes a series of normative-ethical principles and values that are generally acknowledged in the policy-making within the international political and economic community, which comprises international development institutions (e.g., the World Bank, the World Trade Organization, and the International Monetary Fund) and international and national economic policy makers. In other words, the neoclassical normative-ethical principles and values are globally accepted by the economic and political elites in the normative formulation of the notion of development. In this respect, these principles and values noticeably determine the applied policies, institutions, and outcomes in international development and influence the normative-ethical basis of contemporary international development.

As mentioned, the normative nature of neoclassical economics is mainly invoked in welfare economics and social choice theory. In a broad, definitional approach to these terms, in the introduction of the first volume of *The Handbook of Social Choice Theory and Welfare*, Suzumura (2002, p. 1) defines social choice theory and welfare economics as follows:

> Social choice theory is concerned with the evaluation of alternative methods of collective decision-making, as well as with the logical foundations of welfare economics. In turn, welfare economics is concerned with the critical scrutiny of the performance of actual and/or imaginary economic systems, as well as with the critique, design and implementation of alternative economic policies.

In this general framework, normative economic analysis evaluates and scrutinises reality and the vision of this reality, as the authors have claimed. Thus, it can be argued that social choice theory and welfare economics within the neoclassical framework correspond to the normative-ethical nature of dominant economics.

Welfare theory within the neoclassical framework presupposes a utilitarian ethical tradition (Atkinson, 2009; DeMartino, 2000; Hausman and McPherson, 1993; 2006; Suzumura, 2002; Buchanan, 1959).[1] The utilitarian ethical tradition in economics permeates the works of Mill, Marshall, Edgeworth, and Sidgwick, and "it served as a natural basis for the synthesis of this tradition in the hands of Arthur Cecil Pigou in the early twentieth century" (Suzumura, 2002, p. 6). Pigou's (1920) *The Economics of Welfare* represents the foundation of what is commonly called 'old' welfare economics. Formally, neoclassical economic analysis is mainly based on the Pareto principle (Pareto, 1927), usually referred to as 'new' welfare economics. As Suzumura (2002, p. 7) mentions, "Pareto efficient resource allocation became the central exercise in this phase of the 'new' welfare economics, which may be duly represented by John Hicks." Nevertheless, in both old and new welfare economics, the analytical framework is individualistic in the way that all social phenomena have to be explained solely in terms of individual behaviour. Furthermore, old

[1] Utilitarianism is a theory stating that ethical decisions should be based on the expected outcome or consequences of those decisions. Thus, it is labelled as the best-known variety of consequentialism. Furthermore, according to the hedonic form of utilitarianism, "an action or policy is right if it results in no less happiness or no less preference satisfaction than any alternative" (Hausman and MacPherson, 2006, p. 313). See also Chapter 4.

and new welfare economics accept, at different levels and in different manners, the utilitarian ethical tradition.

On this ethical foundation, perhaps the fundamental principle of utilitarianism is that it accepts as useful whatever maximises the 'good' in terms of the outcomes. In other words, the underlying normative-ethical principle of neoclassical economics, based on the tradition of utilitarianism, is that the ethical quality of an action, a decision, or a policy is determined solely by its outcome. In this respect, "[a] utilitarian is a consequentialist who says that what is good is individual 'welfare' or 'well-being'" (Hausman and McPherson, 2006, p. 99).

What is more, neoclassical economists usually evaluate economic decisions and actions in terms of their welfare consequences at an individualistic level, as identified by rational behavioural and individual preferences. Typically, economists focus on only one of the many evaluative questions that could be asked about economic institutions, policies, and outcomes: "'How well do they satisfy preferences?'" (Hausman and McPherson, 2006, p. 97). These preferences are mainly formed based on rational behaviour. "Rational behavior proceeds in terms of decision criteria inherent in the formulated objective functions and in satisfaction of what are generally a well-defined set of axioms of choice or action" (Vickers, 1997, p. 3). What is important is that this set of axioms of choice or action is formulated in a utilitarianism ethical framework, in which "[p]rominent among the formative influences on economics was the commitment that the subject made to varying forms of utilitarianism" (Vickers, 1997, p. 8). Therefore, neoclassical economics measures human welfare in terms of utility.

Based on the utilitarian ethical tradition, neoclassical economics proceeds based on the assumption that the sum of the utility of individuals represents the overall utility of society. However, "[i]n any normative investigation, rationality plays an important role and this suggests that both social and individual preferences should satisfy the expected-utility hypothesis" (Blackorby et al., 2002, p. 543; see also von Neumann and Morgenstern, 1947). In relation to this, social choice theory is mainly about social preferences and how they might be formed (Feldman and Serrano, 2006). Thus, social choice theory offers answers to how political and economic decisions are taken by individuals in the framework of a capitalist democracy. In the words of one of the founders of social choice theory (Arrow, 1951, p. 1), "[i]n a capitalist democracy there are essentially two methods by which social choices can be made: voting, typically used to make 'political' decisions, and the market mechanism, typically used to make 'economic' decisions." Consequently, it can be argued that the normative-ethical nature of neoclassical economics as it is reflected in welfare economics and social choice theory in the tradition of utilitarianism is based on outcomes, as implemented by rational behaviour and the individual preferences evaluated through the market mechanism.

In neoclassical economics, the imperative normative-ethical device in the evaluation of economic policies and outcomes is the market mechanism. In the normative analysis of welfare economics, neoclassical economics evaluates the market mechanism itself. For Feldman and Serrano (2006), "[w]elfare economics is mainly about whether the market mechanism is good or bad" (p. xi) ... "the normative idea here is that a competitive economy is 'good', in the sense that it produces an optimal outcome" (p. 5). Hence, a good market mechanism maximises individual and social utility in the framework of a competitive economy. Based on this normative idea, neoclassical welfare economics evaluates social utility as the sum of the utility of the individuals that comprise the particular society. In addition to this, individual utility is measured by the indifference curves drawn based on rational, individual preferences and the ethical idea that individuals act in an economy and market as *homo economicus*.

Neoclassical welfare economics considers that the observant economist is able to "read" individual preference functions (Buchanan, 1959, p. 126). However, as neoclassical economists commonly assume:

> The first fundamental assumption that we make about people is that they know what they like: they know their preferences among the set of things. If a person is given a choice between *x* and *y*, he can say (one and only one sentence is true): 1. He prefers *x* to *y*. 2. He prefers *y* to *x*. 3. He is indifferent between the two (Feldman and Serrano, 2006, p. 11).

This simple theoretical model describes the realm of the dominant normative-ethical nature of welfare economics. Based on the assumption of economic rationality, in the sense that people know their preferences among a set of things, the dominant form of welfare economics (new welfare economics) is expressed by the Pareto principle. More precisely, at the level of normative-ethical analysis, neoclassical economics evaluates outcomes in accordance with individuals' welfare. "'Social welfare' means the aggregate of 'individual welfares' of all members of society" (Gintis,

1972, p. 574). In this way, the problem of social welfare is reduced by neoclassical economists to the problem of aggregating individual welfare. Principally, individual welfare is based on Pareto optimality, according to which the effect of a change from one social state to another can be judged as socially good if at least one individual is made better off without making anybody else worse off (Pareto, 1927). In this respect, for the economy as the sum of its individuals, a situation, a state of affairs, or an allocation in an economy is Pareto optimal if there is no alternative available that makes some individuals better off and no one worse off (Feldman and Serrano, 2006).

Nevertheless, normative neoclassical economics does give an answer to one fundamental normative-ethical question 'who should make choices?' The answer can be found in Feldman and Serrano's (2006, p. 4) words:

> The most important results in welfare economics indicate that competitive market mechanisms are good in the sense that they are Pareto optimal. The most important results in social choice theory are connected with attempts to answer this general question: When is A socially better than B?

It is generally accepted that the leading normative position among neoclassical economists regarding development is that free-market choices, despite their imperfections, are always preferable to government interventions. The Pareto criterion provides the moral basis of the defence of the market, while "[w]elfare theory has based important theorems on this principle that explain why economists defend the ideal of the perfect competitive market" (Graafland, 2007, p. 31). Neoclassical economics responds to the normative question of 'who should make choices?' by arguing that most choices ought to remain with the individual in a market mechanism without government interference (Hodgson, 1999, p. 73). Accordingly, free-market choices result in a competitive economy as a system of profit-maximising firms and rational or utility-maximising individuals. Normative neoclassical economics links competition to optimality. Social choice theory, in turn, draws upon the idea of whether a voting mechanism can improve upon the results of a free-market economy.

In addition, both welfare economics and social choice theory restrict the scope of their analysis to individual ethics in the tradition of utilitarianism and the context of methodological individualism. Methodological individualism can be seen as an ethical doctrine in which social conditions are explicated at an individualistic-ethical level, on the premise that "social phenomena must be explained by showing how they result from individual actions, which in turn must be explained through reference to the intentional states that motivate the individual actors". Accordingly, for Hodgson (1999, p. 69), "at the root of their [neoclassical economists'] utopia is the idea that the individual is generally the best judge of his or her own welfare". At the normative-ethical level, neoclassical economics reduces the scope of its analysis to the level of individuals' behaviour in relation to the scarcity of the means in the economy. As Robbins (1945, p. 15) states, "[h]ere, then, is the unity of subject of Economic Science, the forms assumed by human behaviour in disposing of scarce means." Based on the hypothesis of scarce means, "it [economics] was to concern itself with questions involving scarcity, hence becoming the science of choice" (Fine and Milonakis, 2009, p. 4). Broadly speaking, neoclassical economists explore welfare economics with concepts such as Pareto efficiency (or optimality), marginal utility, and market equilibrium. This has been the case ever since the Marginal Revolution of the 1870s[2] (Hodgson, 2001; Milonakis and Fine, 2009; Fine and Milonakis, 2009). According to Milonakis and Fine (2009, p. 5):

> It [marginalist economics] has strengthened its commitment to falsifiability (or to close consistency with empirical evidence through statistical methods), to axiomatic deduction from abstract assumptions, to methodological individualism of a special type (utility maximisation), and to equilibrium (and efficiency) as an organising concept.

In this normative-ethical framework, neoclassical economic analysis applies marginalist principles to all of the problems under investigation, based on the ethical background of utilitarianism and methodological individualism. "The economy is made up of an aggregation of individual agents, all of whom maximise utility, even if some do so indirectly through profit maximisation" (Fine, 2003, p. 6).

This type or normative analysis is usually called 'welfarism': a term coined by Sen in the 1970s (see Sen, 1979a; 1979b; 1987). In more recent literature, Gravel and Moyes (2013, p. 529), referring to Sen's definition of the term, have accepted welfarism as a normative approach

[2] See also Chapter 4.

that ranks social states on the basis of the distribution of welfare levels achieved by the individuals in those states. Hausman and McPherson (2006, p. 218) perceive welfarism as "restricting the inputs to social welfare functions to information about individual preferences", in which the function of social welfare is perceived as any ranking of social states (Burk, 1938; Samuelson, 1947). In a similar fashion, for DeMartino (2000, p. 44), welfarism is defined as the assessment of economic outcomes that is derived exclusively from the subjective states of those affected by the outcomes. In such a manner, it is assumed that each individual is able to evaluate his/her own conditions under alternative economic outcomes. Finally, in Sen's (1979a, p. 464) words, welfarism is defined as "the principle that the goodness of a state of affairs depends ultimately on the set of individual utilities in that state, and—more demandingly—can be seen as an increasing function of that set."

Taking into account all of the aforementioned approaches, neoclassical welfare economics can be described as the evaluation of economic outcomes in terms of their impact on individual welfare. This argument is criticised by welfarism. In turn, welfarism denotes a normative-ethical methodology that uses individual welfare as the basis for judging the overall welfare state of a society. In this respect, "[w]elfarism is the view that the only things of intrinsic value for ethical calculation and evaluation of states of affairs are individual utilities" (Sen, 1987, p. 40). Consequently, normative neoclassical economics proposes a strictly individualistic-ethical way of approaching an economy. This normative-ethical approach of neoclassical economics is reflected at the level of international development institutions, policies, and outcomes, as well as in the relationship between the means and the ends of development.

2.2 *Neoclassical Economics and the Normative-Ethical Relationship between the Means and the Ends in Contemporary International Development*

Welfarism (or, in other words, the normative-ethical approach of neoclassical economics) is expressed in the present form of international development at the level of the evaluation of institutions, policies, and outcomes. Without the criterion of welfarism, neoclassical economists would have little basis for defending free trade and the competitive market economy (DeMartino, 2000, p. x). As mentioned, society is viewed as the sum of its individuals or, rather, the sum of their individual preferences. Neoclassical welfarism does not claim generality. "Rather, it claims validity within its own realm of application—that is, in considering those aspects of welfare that involve marshalling scarce resources toward the satisfaction of competing ends" (Gintis, 1972, p. 577). As Archibald (1959, p. 327) argues, "[s]o long as we are enquiring into the relationship between ends and scarce means, our enquiry is positive." In the ethical tradition of utilitarianism, international development is evaluated at the level of the ends (outcomes). The ends, the means, and the framework for judging international development are predetermined by the normative-ethical nature of neoclassical economics. This normative nature reflects a particular normative-ethical relationship between the ends (the outcomes) and the means (the policies) in international development theory.

Derived from social choice theory and welfare economics (in the form of welfarism as the leading normative-ethical background in international development), neoclassical economics determines the normative relationship between the means and the ends of international development in a specific manner. The ends of international development as they have been previously described (see Chapter 4) are economic growth and a consumerist society defined in terms of Westernised material affluence. Succinctly, for neoclassical economics, the ends of international development are economic growth in the sense of wealth creation, economic well-being, and the establishment of a Western-type consumerist society. The means of achieving these ends are both social and economic change in the direction of a globalised market economy. A globalised market economy can also be perceived as the framework that determines the means for achieving a good society in line with the neoclassical model of international development. The normative-ethical basis of contemporary international development evaluates the ends and means of development in the current framework of a globalised market economy.

This framework of a globalised market economy is normatively assessed by neoclassical economics, in which the meta-ethical image of a good society is economic growth. However, the principles that govern economic growth are not only ends in themselves; they also describe the adequate and predetermined means of achieving a good society. Based on utilitarianism, neoclassical economics argues in favour of the aggregative principle that the greatest good of a society is evaluated by the greatest economic outcome. Thus, "those actions or policies that result in an increase in the level of gross domestic product are automatically, and for that reason, desirable" (Vickers, 1997, p. 54). The importance of a globalised market economy as the imperative apparatus that verifies the status of international development determines the means (the institutions and policies) of international development.

It is worth mentioning that the normative-ethical nature of neoclassical economics at the level of international development evaluates existing institutions and policies within a framework that is predetermined, value laden, and ethically laden, which is itself within a specific globalised market structure. In this predetermined value-neutral framework, normative neoclassical economics evaluates the ends and means of international development (the relationship between the outcomes and the policies) in terms of economic efficiency. However, economic efficiency in the sense of maximising an outcome from the use of scarce resources is meaningless as it lacks a value scale against which various possible outcomes can be measured (Buchanan, 1959, p. 126). Hence, the predetermined premise of the value neutrality and the ethical neutrality of economics represents an obstacle to its normative-ethical analysis. Normative economics in the form of new welfare economics does not depend on value judgements. New welfare economics, in the Paretian sense (where all criteria involving interpersonal comparisons of utility are avoided), evaluates the criterion of achieving a goal: not the ethical or value judgements of the goal itself. "The argument is, first, that the theorems of the new welfare economics need not be prefaced by judgments of value and, second, that attempts to base the new welfare economics on judgments of value only cause unnecessary difficulty and confusion" (Archibald, 1959, p. 316).

Another important normative concern that determines the normative-ethical basis of international development and the relationship between the means and the ends of international development is that of economic rationalism. The ethical background of economic rationalism is economic rationality. This has been previously discussed (see Chapter 4) as one of the main ethical insights of neoclassical economics. The analysis mainly involves the discussion of economic rationality at an individualistic level or the discussion of the rational behaviour of the economic agents. In normative-ethical analysis, economic rationalism is positioned on the grounds of the normative-ethical evaluation of the economic institutions, policies, and outcomes of international development. Based on the preceding analysis of economic rationality as one of the major ethical insights of neoclassical economics, the present discussion advances the concept of the normative evaluation of international development. The term 'economic rationalism' as presented here was first used by Pusey (1991) in his monograph *Economic Rationalism in Canberra*. For Pusey, economic rationalism has been approached as a normative economic dogma with policy implications. In his words:

> The central agencies at the top level represent a new and minimalist laissez-faire state set in norms that come from a dominating neoclassical economic rationalism that is anti-statist, anti-union, and either asocial or anti-social in its basic orientations to policy (Pusey, 1991, p. 6).

The main normative idea of economic rationalism in international development is that national states and international institutions should increase efficiency by leaving as much as possible up to the free market. This normative idea of economic rationalism is assisted by the argument for increasing the efficiency of an economy and, as a consequence, maximising the total wealth in the sense of economic growth.

Economic rationalism can be analysed in its normative, economic, and ethical aspects. From an economic point of view, economic rationalism (by maximising efficiency) minimises the expenditure required to obtain an end product. Also, it maximises the output of the desired end product (Wright, 2003, p. 3). From the perspective of ethics, the focus is on the manner and the consequences of increasing efficiency for people and societies. This includes the normative-ethical discussion of social justice, the equal distribution of products, the labour conditions, the environment, and similar concepts. Importantly, based on the principles of economic rationalism and the normative concept of the maximisation of efficiency, the defenders of free-market economics in international development emphasise its significance in maintaining and increasing the efficient production of wealth nationally and internationally by minimising government expenditures for wages and the social welfare state. In this regard, economic rationalism approximates the normative principles of economic neoliberalism. Nevertheless, "[t]he economic rationalist will emphasise efficiency, the neo-liberal, freedom" (Wright, 2003, p. 18). In any case, economic rationalism and neoliberalism coexist; while the former is a normative economic dogma with policy implications, the latter is an ideological posture in international development.

In achieving the ends of international development, neoclassical economic analysis explores economic growth theories.[3] Referring to international development, most of these theories associate economic growth with the amount of savings that lead to investment and economic development at a national or international level. For instance, the long-run Solow–Swan growth model predicts such a relationship (Solow, 1956; 1957; Swan, 1956). Nevertheless, neoclassical economists may disagree on how best to increase the level of investment and improve resource allocations, although they agree that these are the fundamental means of economic growth (Stiglitz, 2002a, p. 164). It is not within the scope of the present analysis to review neoclassical growth theories. What we focus on are the normative-ethical ingredients of economic growth: the means by which the end state of international development (a good society) is achieved. In accordance with the means of contemporary international development, both 'traditional' concepts (such as population growth, productivity, technological progress, and capital accumulation) and 'new' concepts (such as open international trade, free capital flows, and structural reforms) are some of the central ingredients of the neoclassical growth theories of development that portray economic and social change[4] in international development. In short, the ideology of *laissez-faire* economics and neoliberalism best describes the normative means for achieving economic growth and change in international development. In other words, the means of economic and social change are subjected to free-market economics and neoliberal ideology. In this regard, for neoclassical economists, "[g]lobal social welfare is enhanced by the unfolding of the processes of market competition which induce rising efficiency, lower costs, and increasing standards of living—at home and abroad" (DeMartino, 2000, p. 182).

[3] Economic growth theories refer to the instrumental use of the means for achieving the end goal of economic growth.

[4] Development is commonly defined as social and economic change (e.g., in the approach of the United Nations). In the context of our analysis here, development refers to economic development. However, the economy, politics, and society are accepted in the present analysis as a unified whole. Thus, economic change implies changes in politics and society.

2.3 A Normative-Ethical Evaluation of the Washington Consensus

This section contributes to a normative-ethical evaluation of the Washington Consensus as the dominant policy in international development under the premises of normative neoclassical economics, economic rationalism, and neoliberal ideology. The Washington Consensus comprises a set of policy instruments with applied implications in international development. Thus, in the development economics literature, the policy reforms for international development proposed by the Washington Consensus are usually approached from a positivistic and technocratic perspective. Nevertheless, even as a policy framework, the Washington Consensus is valued and ethically determined. Thus, before it is investigated further, it is necessary to provide a normative-ethical evaluation of the Washington Consensus.

Historically, during the 1980s and 1990s, many developing countries in Latin America and East Asia and the transitional economies of Eastern and Central Europe adopted free trade, privatisation, and structural reforms in the direction of economic rationalism and neoliberalism. It was during the debt crisis of the 1980s that many countries, often under the guidance of and with the conditional financial support of the IMF in particular, attempted thorough structural reforms featuring far greater openness to trade and capital flows (Little, 2004, p. 118). In the development economics literature, the above policies are usually referred to by the term 'Washington Consensus', which is used in various ways. A conventional manner of holistically approaching the term is to view it as a strategy for accelerating economic growth in developing economies by enhancing the power of the free market (Arrébola-Rodríguez, 2011, p. 20). It is useful, however, to mention that similar neoliberal reforms have taken place in developed capitalist economies too. As Fine (2003, p. 3) argues:

> The Washington consensus had emerged in the early 1980s as the neoliberal counterpart for developing economies to the Reaganism and Thatcherism that had been prescribed for developed economies—an ideology of reliance upon market forces and of the reduction of state interventionism and expenditure to a minimum.

In this light, the Washington Consensus is conceived both as the specific policies in Latin America, as the 'godfather' of the term (Williamson (ed.), 1990; Williamson, 1990a; 1990b; 1993) uses it, and as a synonym of the neoliberal policies in international development (Marangos, 2009a). The evolution of the term and its implications for international development and development economics have been reviewed by Marangos (2007; 2008; 2009a; 2009b), Stiglitz (2002a), Serra and Stiglitz (eds.) (2008), Fine et al. (eds.) (2003), Gore (2000), Cypher (1998), Stewart (1997), Williamson (2000), and Kaczynski and Williamson (eds.) (2003), among others. In all these studies, even if not totally uncontroversially, the Washington Consensus has been accepted as a framework or guide for policy reforms in international development.

The Washington Consensus is viewed as a "neoliberal manifesto" (Marangos, 2009a, p. 197) for policy reforms in international development. The Washington Consensus is proclaimed as a positive policy guide, as "Williamson avoided any direct equity concerns and redistributive policies in formulating the consensus since Washington, at the time, was not interested in equity" (Marangos, 2009a, p. 198). However, beyond its positive nature as a policy guide, the Washington Consensus can be regarded as a normative assessment of specific policy reforms. As mentioned in the preceding analysis, it is in the normative-ethical nature of neoclassical economic analysis to avoid valued and ethical evaluations of recommended institutions and policies. In contrast to the suggested positive and value-neutral view of the Washington Consensus policy, for our purposes, the Washington Consensus is viewed as a normative neoliberal manifesto for policy reforms in international development. More precisely, it is approached as a normative issue because it poses the norms and principles for the policy reforms. Also, it is approached as neoliberal because the policy reforms suggested are based on economic rationalism (the increase of economic efficiency), free-market economics, and a 'free' political structure.

The Washington Consensus policy reforms are consistent with the normative-ethical nature of neoclassical economics. As mentioned already, welfare economics is concerned with the critique, design, and implementation of specific economic policies. For instance, Marangos (2007) observes that the application of the Washington Consensus as a neoliberal manifesto was consistent with neoclassical analysis and neoliberal policy in transitional economies. In the case of the transition from a centrally administered economy to a market-based economy, the process was reflected by a substantial reduction in output, increased unemployment, hyperinflation, corruption, and illegal activities. "It is alleged and being established as common knowledge that these results were due to the implementation of the orthodox policies inspired by the Washington Consensus" (Marangos, 2007, p. 33), in the form of neoclassical economic analysis and neoliberal policy.

Going back to the initial use of the term in November 1989, at a conference organised by the Institute for International Economics, Williamson (1990a; 1990b, pp. 9–34) outlined ten policy reforms for structural adjustment in Latin America. These policy instruments are typified around ten policies: 1. fiscal discipline; 2. reordering public expenditure priorities; 3. tax reform; 4. liberalising interest rates; 5. a competitive exchange rate; 6. trade liberalisation; 7. the liberalisation of inward foreign direct investment; 8. privatisation; 9. deregulation; and 10. property rights. The economic policies that the Washington Consensus urges the rest of the world to apply are described as "prudent macroeconomic policies, outward orientation, and free-market capitalism" by Williamson (1990a) and portrayed as "the conventional wisdom on the day" (Williamson, 1993, p. 1329).

At the level of ethical analysis, the proposed Washington Consensus policy instruments determine the normative-ethical relationship between the ends and means of the specific policy, on the one hand, and the outcomes for international development, on the other. Williamson (1990a) characterises the ten axes of the initial Washington Consensus as policy instruments, not as objectives and outcomes. "The 10 topics around which the paper is organized deal with policy instruments rather than objectives or outcomes" (Williamson, 1990a). This implies the neutral stance (in terms of values and ethics) of the Washington Consensus policy instruments. Furthermore, defining any sort of normative relationship between the means and the ends of the Washington Consensus is avoided. In the same paper, however, referring to the ethically neutral and value-neutral stance of the suggested policy instruments, it is clearly stated that "the standard economic objectives of growth, low inflation, a viable balance of payments, and an equitable income distribution should determine the disposition of such policy instruments" (Williamson, 1990a). These policy instruments are perceived as means to specific ends (objectives and outcomes). Thus, beyond their positive nature as recommended applied policies in international development, the Washington Consensus policy instruments can be seen as normative means that have been chosen from among alternative options, economic theories and policies, based solely on neoclassical economic analysis, economic rationalism, and neoliberal ideology. To assist the argument better, in the aforementioned quotation, Williamson precisely defines the objectives of the policy instruments of the Washington Consensus as economic growth, low inflation, and a viable balance of payments (the economic objectives), along with equitable income distribution (the social objective). Moreover, he identifies the relationship between the normative objectives (the goals) and the policy instruments (the means) of achieving such objectives. This normative-ethical relationship can be seen in the Washington Consensus as it is a neoliberal manifesto in the tradition of utilitarianism. As a neoliberal manifesto, the Washington Consensus focuses on the ends (the objectives) and the fact that the means (the policy instruments) "should determine", in Williamson's (1990a) words, the aforementioned objectives, which are proposed as neutral in terms of values and ethics.

In addition, both the ends and the means of the Washington Consensus are inspired by international financial institutions (the International Monetary Fund and the World Bank), the US Executive Branch, the Federal Reserve Board, the Inter-American Development Bank, those members of Congress interested in Latin America, and the think tanks concerned with economic policy, all based in Washington. "They are economic policy instruments that I [Williamson] perceive 'Washington' to think important, as well as on which some consensus exists" (Williamson, 1990a). This provides our analysis with additional evidence: the Washington Consensus policy normatively assists the ethical basis of international development as economically and culturally oriented by a Westernised form of economic development under specific means (the policy instruments). Moreover, this implies an economic and ethically imperialistic expansion of the dominant concepts of neoclassical economics, economic rationalism, and neoliberal ideology into international development. The neoliberal ideology is defined in a specific manner, with specific means in the neoliberal principle of "one-size-fits all" (Stiglitz, 2002a, p. 141). These means are derived apart from the nations and the people that are supposed to be the recipients of the results of economic development. In Williamson's (1990a) words, the Washington Consensus "aims to set out what would be regarded in Washington as constituting a desirable set of economic policy reforms."

Based on the preceding analysis, the Washington Consensus policy reforms have been evaluated not at the level of applied policy instruments but on the normative-ethical grounds of the choice of these specific policy instruments as the appropriate, prearranged means of achieving predetermined goals. The normative-ethical relationship between the means and the goals of the Washington Consensus is dependent on the neoclassical vision of a good society as economic development, namely economic growth, in a free-market, capitalist environment, and a globalised market economy.

3 The Development Ethics Normative-Ethical Alternative to International Development

The normative-ethical principles of neoclassical welfarism, economic rationalism, and neoliberal ideology consider international development as a globalised market economy. In this framework, the imperialism of the market-liberal model of values and institutions, which has been enforced internationally, is profound (Gasper, 2004, p. 194; Slim, 1995). The means and ends of international development are predetermined by ethics and values. "Modern economics stresses rational calculation, the baser material objectives, and scientific neutrality on moral issues" (Alvey, 2000, p. 1232). Thus, the relationship between the means and the ends in international development is accepted as value laden, although "neoclassical theory is self-consciously silent with respect to value judgements" (DeMartino, 2000, p. 42). A similar assessment of neoclassical economics can be found in many studies in the broad field of economics and ethics (Sen, 1987, p. 40; Galbraith, 1991, p. 124; Drakopoulos, 1997, p. 286; Hausman and MacPherson, 1993) and in the development ethics literature (Wilber, 2010; Gasper, 2004; Dower; 1998a; 1998b). As Goulet (1989, p. 154) argues, "[p]ositivists suffer from an overdose of success in description and analysis, resulting in the atrophy of their ability of engage in normative and evaluative inquiry."

Development ethics in the political economy context introduces an alternative perspective to the normative-ethical determination of the relationship between the means and the ends in international development, beyond the dominant perceptions of neoclassical welfarism, economic rationalism, and neoliberalism. Even though many development ethicists accept a liberal logic, their normative stance responds to the claim that "liberal logic suggests that people should be able to choose against liberalism" (Gasper, 2004, p. 196) and neoliberalism, just as the present analysis does. In this respect, the means (the institutions and policies) and the ends (the outcomes) of international development are not conceived as ethically laden and value laden or predetermined. Both the means and the ends are subject to ethics and values. In the normative-ethical investigation of the means and ends of development, the value change that development typically brings to people and societies, the ethical evaluation of rationality, and a set of universal normative-ethical goals and strategies in international development comprise the leading ideas in the development ethics normative-ethical discourse regarding a good life and a good society in international development. However, as in the case of neoclassical economics, it is impossible for the present analysis to cover all the ideas and specific debates in the development ethics normative-ethical discourse, not only because of limited space but mostly because of the pluralistic and interdisciplinary character of development ethics. Hence, the present analysis highlights the basic ideas of normative-ethical development ethics in the methodological framework of the present thesis, which encloses development ethics in a political economy context.

3.1 The Normative-Ethical Nature of Development Ethics

Development ethics is perceived as the ethical reflection of the ends and means of any purposeful socioeconomic activity towards development and the achievement of a good society on a local, national, and global scale. Development ethicists pose normative-ethical questions about not only 'what' ethical development should be achieved but also 'why' and 'how' (Gasper, 2012). Hence, development ethics can be perceived as the field that deals *ex professo* with such normative issues (Goulet, 1997, p. 1161).

At the normative-ethical level of analysis, the term 'development' is perceived as the change that connects the means and the ends of a good society. In addition, in the conventional language of mainstream development economics, 'development' is either descriptive or normative. It is used descriptively when listing a nation's GDP growth rate, trade balance, savings or investments, and similar macroeconomic statistics, while it is accepted as normative when it refers to Westernised modernisation by decrying the economic growth theory's failure to produce human development. "These twin ambiguities are unavoidable, for development is simultaneously a goal and a means thereto, and a label of what is as well as a pointer to what ought to be" (Goulet, 1989, p. 152; see also Goulet, 1968). Accordingly, one of the main subject matters of development ethics is the ethical reflection of alternative means and ends, in which ethical reflection can be defined as normative assessments by critical thinking about ethical replacements:

> Philosophical [ethical] reflection can clarify what the goals of development are; it can defend normative positions by critical and rational thinking about ethical alternatives; it can help to sort out the complexities involved in the rational choice of means (Crocker, 2006, p. xxxiii).

In this regard, development ethics offers a normative-ethical concern for good international development.

Development ethics investigates the normative-ethical role of ethical values and value change in international development. In the conventional realm of international relations, ethical values are commonly perceived as the projection of interests; thus, value change moves in the direction of a globalised market economy. From the angle of development ethics, it is argued that "the ideology of 'development' as economic growth through free markets, preached as universal values for all, may seem to many in the South as a way of promoting the values important to the leading players in the global market" (Dower, 1998a, p. 32). Thus, development ethicists stress the importance of the dynamic of value change in determining what, why, and how the normative-ethical relationship between the means and the ends of a good life and a good society should be defined.

For instance, the innovation and novel behaviour patterns that economic development brings about usually embrace the value and cultural systems of society. Referring to international development, a globalised market economy could not exist without the creative cultural process of continual innovation, capital or investment accumulation, competition and growth, all operating incessantly over time across many continents, nations, and societies (O'Hara, 2006, p. 34). This encompasses the idea of the dynamics of value change. Development ethics looks into the dynamics of value change in each society and builds its paradigm based on this idea. For development ethicists, innovation and novel behaviour patterns can be useful only if they can be adjusted to the value change and the meaning of a good life that every society espouses.

Institutional changes and the role of technological modernisation are fundamental issues in the discussion of value change. There is a debate founded on the argument that "while technology has universal adaptability, institutions are culture specific" (Street, 2001, p. 1861). Development ethicists stress that "[m]ore important than the rapidity with which modern forces or images impinge upon traditional cultures… are the social structures and contexts within which changes are proposed or imposed" (Goulet, 2006a, p. 136). It is certain that both the economic and the non-economic impacts of large-scale institutional change destroy the ethical basis of society, resulting in "maximal dislocation" of the institutional fabric of society. On this note, Marangos and Astroulakis (2009, p. 386) argue that:

> [T]here is a conflict between the emerging technology and the social institutions and the ethical perspectives that have a propensity to preserve existing power relations that restrain further technical progress and development. The forces inhibiting social progress and economic development are rooted in institutional-ceremonial cultures and patterns of behaviour that can actually be obstructive in achieving a good society.

To enhance our understanding of the importance of value change in the normative-ethical basis of international development, we first need to identify that there is cultural diversity among different types of societies within international development. Development ethics accepts the taxonomy of societies not only as developed and developing (which implies economic dualism in international development) but also as traditional, transitional, and modern, which entails cultural diversity (Goulet, 1975a, p. 188). Each of these societies has built an alternative system of meanings and a cultural identity, which are determined by a set of values, beliefs, norms, institutions, habits, and human relations, through a historical and social process. In turn, change is one of the main components of development. However, "[w]hen innovations are proposed or imposed on them, traditional societies receive stimuli to change which challenge their normative values" (Goulet, 2001, p. 34).[5] For development ethicists, any desirable social or economic change should subordinate and be subordinated by the system of meaning (beliefs, norms, attitudes, institutions, etc.) that each society (traditional, transitional, or modern) has adopted.

A central point in this discussion is the normative-ethical assessment of value change. For development ethicists, ethics plays a normative role. "What is meant by the normative role of ethics is that rulers may exercise political power constructively with a view to implementing desired values"

[5] See also Knoedler (1997), 'Veblen and technical efficiency'.

(Goulet, 2006a, p. 22). The normative-ethical evaluation of value change designates the normative strategies employed by all societies to process information and to make practical choices designed to assure their survival and satisfy their needs for esteem and freedom. These strategies may vary widely, and they are conditioned by numerous constraints. However, ethics as a normative device is central to the development ethics claim that certain universal goals are common to traditional, transitional, and modern societies alike. According to the development ethics normative-ethical approach for a good society, value change should be in accordance with the system of meanings that exists in any society and determines the course of action undertaken to serve societal aims. More specifically, the normative-ethical assessment of value change addresses how societies evaluate, employ, and apply particular strategies in order to assist the universal normative-ethical goals of a good society: those of life sustenance, esteem, and freedom (Goulet, 1975a; 1975b, viii). Thus, development change should not be perceived as alien to the system of meaning of each society. So, how should development change be perceived?

If a good society is to be established, three basic normative-ethical conditions ought to be satisfied: "(a) new capacities for handling information must be generated; (b) vital resources hitherto not available must become exploitable; and (c) the alien rationality implicit in modernization must be re-interpreted in terms of traditional existence rationalities" (Goulet, 1975a, p. 189). The core value in the discussion of development change is the provision of those inputs that ensure what any society normatively defines as a good life. Thus, any change should be integrated into the system of meanings determined by each society and the aforementioned basic conditions of change. In light of this, the acceptance or rejection of any development change depends mainly on the normative-ethical manner in which change is evaluated, as the "development planning cannot be simply a matter of applying causal knowledge" (Dower, 1988, p. 21).

To investigate further the normative-ethical manner in which development change should be perceived, development ethicists, and Goulet in particular, have opened a dialogue on a triple rationality in decision-making: technological, political, and ethical rationality. Goulet (1986), in his article *Three Rationalities in Development Decision-Making*, illustrates the normative working of a triple rationality. In this context, the term 'rationality' is defined as "any mode of thinking, universe or cognitive assumptions, and methodological procedures or body of criteria for establishing truth and validity" (Goulet, 1986, p. 301). Thus, instead of economic rationality and economic rationalism as causal knowledge in neoclassical economics, development ethics describes a triple rationality according to which the normative-ethical meaning of a good society should be incorporated for the elimination of institutional, political, and technological inertia. First, technological rationality refers to the application of scientific knowledge to any problem-solving or otherwise to the 'hard logic' of accessing aims. "Technological rationality thus obeys a hard logic guided by a calculus of efficiency in the assessment of time or the utility of any object [material, institutional, or human]" (Goulet, 1986, p. 302). Second, political rationality consists of the rules of decision-making. The aim of politicians, policy makers, and persons or groups with power (political, economic, and cultural) is to maintain their roles in the decision-making process. In Goulet's (1986, p. 302) words, "their veritable goal is to preserve certain institutions and rules of the [decision-making] game, or their special power position within those institutions." Third, ethical rationality represents the holistic perspectives that people have about the world around them or the different systems of meanings (beliefs, norms, attitudes, institutions, etc.) that any society has adopted. Ethical rationality refers to a moral evaluation about what is good and bad, right and wrong, fair and unfair. In the field of decision-making, ordinary people must accept or reject political or technical decisions based on an ethical evaluation of their needs and wants and the common interest of society. Any social or economic change has to be ethically rational. Thus, "it [ethical rationality] is the spirit which relativizes the goals pursued by other rationalities" (Goulet, 1986, p. 303).

In this way, development ethics adds the element of value change and the discussion of rationality to the normative-ethical analysis of international development. The discussion of development change, values, and rationality overlaps with the normative-ethical nature of development ethics. For development ethicists:

> The normative dimensions of the decisions as to what we or others ought to do (or ought to have done) in response to poverty, exclusion, marginalization, and urgent need warrant our careful thought and evaluation: factually, conceptually, and ethically (Schwenke, 2011, p. 320).

At the level of international development, the normative-ethical foundation of a good life and a good society incorporates ethical analysis based on the aforementioned premises.

3.2 Development Ethics and the Relationship Between the Means and the Ends in International Development

Along with the discussion of value change and rationality, development ethics has opened the normative-ethical dialogue on the means and the ends of development. "Moral reflection on the ends and means of 'development,' where 'development' most generically means beneficial societal change, is one important effort" (Crocker, 2008, p. 1). Development ethics provides an answer to the fundamental normative-ethical question 'should ethics be concerned with the ends or the means of development?' Following the general premises that ethics should be concerned with both the ends and the means of development (local, national, and international) and that the ethical concept of a good society should refer both to the means and the ends of international development (or, in other words, to the vision of a better life and the way that this life can be accessed), development ethics specifies that ethics should be perceived as the 'means of the means' of development. On the issue of how ethics is interwoven with the means and the ends of development, Goulet (1975a, p. 116) claims that ethics in development "must become a 'means of the means': a transfiguration of means into something more than purely technical, social, or political instruments." In this light, a leading idea in the normative-ethical discussion of the relationship between the ends and the means of development is the presence of ethics as the means of the means. Recent reviews on the development ethics idea consider ethics as the means of the means of development, and the crucial implications of such relationships between the means and the ends of development are offered by Goulet (2006a), Gasper (2004; 2012), Parfitt (2012), Crocker (2008), Dower (1988; 2005; 2010), Dutt and Wilber (2010a), Wilber (2010), Marangos and Astroulakis (2012), Astroulakis (2013a; 2013b; 2011), and Schwenke (2011).

This discussion has led to the formulation of a new field in development studies, with implications for the humanities and social studies, as well as for development economics and the study of international development and the ethics of the means. The core idea of the ethics of the means is based on the Aristotelian ethical tradition that "[e]very skill and every inquiry, and similarly every action and rational choice, is thought to aim at some good; and so the good has been aptly described as that at which everything aims" (Aristotle, 2000, p. 3). Development ethics has been inspired by Aristotelian ethics (Chapter 2; Marangos and Astroulakis, 2012). Regarding development, development ethicists underline a few important normative-ethical questions in the tradition of Aristotelian ethics and the formulation of the field of the ethics of the means. "First, is the goal being pursued one that ought to be pursued? Second, are the actions being taken to realize the goals the right ones?" (Dower, 2010, p. 31). The responses to these normative-ethical questions initiate the discussion of the means and the ends of international development.

For development ethicists, ethics ought to penetrate into every corner of the dialogue on international development, in terms of not only the ends (as in the case of neoclassical economics in the tradition of utilitarianism) but also the means of development. Thus, ethics should be recognised as the means of the means. "There is a morality of the means, since means are not, or rather ought not to be regarded as, technically efficient ways of producing results and nothing more" (Dower, 1988, p. 7). For example, in the process of decision-making, mainstream policy makers usually want to know what ethical commitments, if any, are aids or obstacles to development. Thus, "[t]hey use moral values instrumentally when trying to instil them as factors to bring about some model of development" (Crocker, 2008, p. 92). This is not a case of perceiving ethics as the means of the means in international development. "Development ethics asks what should be the ends and morally acceptable means of development rather than merely how societies mobilize values to reach some given conception of development" (Crocker, 2008, p. 92). This implies that the whole development enterprise has to be critically subjected to ethical issues concerning not only the end state of development but also the means of attaining it. Thus:

> [N]ormative strategies [as normative-ethical means] elaborated by ethicians should not be regarded by developers as mere velleities born of moral passion over the indignities wrought on mankind's poor by heartless wielders of power. They ought rather to be seen as frontiers of new political possibilities (Goulet, 2006a, p. 21).

Mainstream development economists confront development as economic growth based on competition, trade policy, and technological modernisation. They also accept that economic development (in terms of growth, capital accumulation, technological change, the structural transformation of the economy, and the modernisation of social, cultural, and political institutions necessary to facilitate economic development (Clark, 2002a, p. 831) brings changes to social life. For development ethics, both economic growth and social change (including technological modernisation) "must be treated as means relative to the larger human values" (Goulet, 2006a, p. 64), where the "larger human values" include human freedom, social justice, and a good level of life in terms of well-being, in their broader meanings for people and societies. More precisely, within the consideration of a good society, whereby economic growth and social change are usually targeted as end states, development ethics argues that both concepts should be perceived as means to advance human values as mentioned. By penetrating social and economic matters, namely economic growth and social change, ethical justifications should evaluate not only the ends of any particular course of social action but also the means, economic choices, and technical methods, for instance, that have been used to attain those ends. Only in this way can ethics enter into the value context and meaning of any social action, as development ethics alleges. Otherwise, "[i]n rich and poor societies alike, only those having power can apply normative prescriptions" (Goulet, 2006a, p. 24).

Economic development depends, largely, on the rate of capital accumulation. In turn, capital accumulation is based on resources (capital, land, labour, and technology). As development economists argue, economic growth results in the expansion of productive resources and an increase in the efficiency of their use (Clark, 2002b, p. 10; Syrquin, 1988, p. 224). However, "when resources are scarce, human needs great, and existing economic distributive mechanisms ineffective or skewed, the moral weight of decisions can be particularly acute" (Schwenke, 2011, p. 320). In the normative-ethical discussion, along with resource productivity, the allocation of resources is an important parameter in the means and ends of development. Therefore, resource allocation decisions in international development should resolve the basic tension between the need of people to have enough and their desire to be more fully human. In a globalised market environment, developing countries are often forced to choose between producing a decent amount of essential goods for developed countries and underdevelopment. Even worse, internal inequality in developing countries allows a few to have more while the masses are poor. Thus, "to provide wise normative guidance in making this option is, indeed, the central task of development ethics" (Goulet, 2006a, p. 140). Therefore, productivity and resource allocation, as well as capital accumulation and economic growth, should be accepted as the means subjected to very human ends. Finally, in Goulet's words (2006a, p. 147), the normative-ethical relationship between the means and the ends of international development should subordinate:

> [T]he societal provision of essential goods to all; a mode of production which creates 'right livelihoods' for all; the use of material goods as a springboard to qualitatively enriching human riches of a spiritual nature; the pursuit of material goods in function of their capacities to nurture life and enhance the being rather than the having of people; and a primacy given to public wealth which fosters, more than do personal riches, the common good.

This normative-ethical relationship relies on the discussion of the development of ethical goals and strategies that follow.

3.3 *The Normative-Ethical Goals and Strategies of Development Ethics in International Development*

Mainstream economics, particularly in the form of neoclassical economics, proposes a bundle of policy instruments in international development in the direction of a globalised market economy. Development is viewed as a straightforward economic problem. "Growth targets would be planned, resources mobilized to reach them, and the institutional apparatus for financing, investing, managing, and producing activated. This array of organized activities would yield 'development'" (Goulet, 2001, p. 29). In the case of international development, this set of policy reforms is commonly expressed by the Washington Consensus as a neoliberal manifesto. The Washington Consensus specifies the normative-ethical relationship between the ends and the means in the principles of economic rationalism and the ideology of neoliberalism. The suggested policy instruments are the normative means for accomplishing the predetermined goals.

Jameson (2010), in his work *Ethics and Contemporary Macroeconomic Policy*, criticises contemporary neoliberalism in the form of Reaganomics,

Bushonomics, and the Washington Consensus from the angle of political economy and development ethics. After a critique on economic rationalism and neoliberalism and their applied policies in international development, he concludes that "their greatest failure was in not satisfying the ethical canons for a well-functioning economy and society that were the concern of Denis Goulet" (Jameson, 2010, p. 421), referring to Goulet's (1975a) ethical goals for development.

To our knowledge, this is the only study in the development ethics literature that approaches the theme in such a manner. Challenging the Washington Consensus as a neoliberal manifesto, however, the present analysis argues that development ethics can be seen as an alternative normative-ethical proposal in the value-based context of a good society via a set of normative-ethical goals and strategies. The development ethics proposal, however, does not comprise a policy guide. It begins a normative-ethical debate on the larger human values and how these human values can be normatively approached. In this respect, it is intended as a set of normative-ethical goals and strategies in the direction of a good life and a good global society, beyond neoclassical economics' welfarism, economic rationalism, and neoliberalism. The discussion is kept close to the development ethics normative-ethical identification and particularly to Goulet's formulation of the normative-ethical goals and strategies. As argued elsewhere (Astroulakis, 2011), even though there are always alternative ways of approaching the theme, Goulet's formulation of the normative-ethical goals and strategies offers better grounds for arguments within the development ethics community.

3.3.1 Normative-Ethical Goals

At the level of the ends, development ethicists have argued that there are three commonly accepted universal goals that societies and people ought to investigate within the value-based and ethically based contexts of a good life and a good society. These are: 1. life sustenance; 2. esteem; and 3. freedom.

1. **Life sustenance:** This concept refers to the provision of life and well-being. Goulet (1975a, p. 88) points out that "one of development's most important goals is to prolong men's lives and render those men less 'stunted' by disease, extreme exposure to nature's elements, and defenselessness against enemies." The importance of life-sustaining goods (e.g. food, shelter, healing, and medicine) is

generally acknowledged by all societies (Goulet, 1975a, pp. 87–88; 1995, pp. 41–43). Because life sustenance is a value of universal significance, life-sustaining indices are also used as a measurement of development (see, for example, the Human Development Indicators employed by the United Nations). However, life-sustaining indices should not only be viewed as a quantitative measurement of development but mostly as a qualitative assessment of a good life and a good society. On this topic, the work of Sen is influential to the qualitative and ethical evaluation of well-being, as he argues for the normative ideas of functioning, capability, and freedom in relation to living standards (see, for example, Sen, 1998, pp. 293–296).

2. **Esteem:** All human beings in all societies feel the need for respect, dignity, honour, and recognition. For development ethics, the discussion involves esteem values and material prosperity and, in particular, how esteem contends with the conventional notion of development (in the sense of economic growth and technological advances). Accordingly, the more material prosperity becomes the central task of the development of a society, the greater is the subordination of esteem to material affluence. People are enculturated in the values of consumption: "'being all they can be,' enhancing their capabilities, climbing up the ladder of success and esteem" (O'Hara, 2006, p. 34; see also Brown, 2004). The reaction of a society to development and its need for esteem can lead societies in opposite directions, either towards development or towards resistance to it. In the first case, the society tries to gain esteem via development, while in the latter case it tries to protect its profound esteem from inward development. Both acts seek to gain esteem. Therefore, esteem is a universal goal, whether development is accepted or not (Goulet, 1975a, pp. 89–90).
3. **Freedom:** Freedom is valued by both developed and traditional types of societies as one of the components of a "good life" (Goulet, 1995, pp. 44–45). Development ought to free humans from all servitudes. In Goulet's (1995, p. 45) words, "development is perceived as one way to emancipate oneself from the structural servitudes of ignorance, misery, perhaps even of exploitation by others." Even though there is a vast philosophical discussion (regarding positive and negative freedom, for instance) about the term, and some theorists claim that whether freedom is enhanced by economic development is not self-evident, the development ethics

notion of freedom is widely accepted as something beneficial and desirable. The debate lies again between freedom and material affluence. Usually, in Westernised societies, it can be accepted that the degree of freedom rises with material expansion, which increases material welfare. On the other hand, in some traditional societies, the value system may adopt a completely different view to needs and wants. For instance, freedom can be derived from the minimisation of people's desires. Usually, these societies avoid development in terms of material expansion. In any case, "the point is that freedom is valued both by those who pursue development and by those who reject it" (Goulet, 1995, p. 47). Furthermore, in the discussion of freedom, a significant distinction should be made between freedom 'from' wants and freedom 'for' wants. The former refers to the situation where human needs are adequately met, while the latter to the case where the gestations of new wants are controlled and individuals possess multiplied wants (Goulet, 1995, p. 50).

3.3.2 Normative-Ethical Strategies

In the development ethics literature, normative-ethical strategies are normative judgements that provide both the notional and practical frameworks within which ethical development goals should be discussed and policy recommendations over those goals ought to be formulated. Over the years, Goulet and other development ethicists have evaluated several normative principles, three of which are prominent, here named as normative-ethical strategies: 1. "decent sufficiency" of basic goods for all; 2. solidarity; and 3. non-elite participation in decision-making (Crocker, 2006, p. xxi). Accordingly, the normative-ethical strategies are targeted in Goulet's (1975a; 1995; 2006a) codification. In Goulet's (2006a, p. 22) words:

> The very refusal by rulers to accept as normative a development ethic based on the need for all men to have enough in order to be fully human, on universally expanding solidarity, and on maximum popular decision making is a powerful force accelerating the growth of consciousness in a hitherto culturally passive populace.

1. **Abundance of goods:** The abundance of goods refers to people's need to have "enough" in order to "be more" (Goulet, 1975a,

p. 123). In order to understand the notion of this strategy, it is necessary to take into account the ontological nature of human beings. In an ontological sense, almost all organisms must go outside of themselves in order to be perfect. Only fully perfect beings would have no needs at all. Totally imperfect beings, on the other hand, would be incapable of needing certain goods. Humans are perfect or imperfect to such a degree that:

> "[M]en have needs because their existence is rich enough to be capable of development, but poor to realize all potentialities at one time or with their resources... At any given time man is less than he can become and what he can become depends largely on what he can have" (Goulet, 1975a, pp. 129–130).

Hence, people need to have enough goods and amenities in order to be human. This must be investigated under the notion of a humanistic approach to how much is enough for people in order to have a good life. There is no unique answer to the above issue. The response to the aforementioned inquiry can be found in the historical relations among peoples and societies. Nevertheless, it is widely accepted that underdevelopment (poverty, misery, disease, mass famine, etc.) diminishes humanity. Hence, 'enough' should be, at the minimum, all the goods and amenities required to cover biological needs and to free part of the human energy in order for it to be allocated to a wider range of life aspects, beyond covering first-order needs.

In addition to the concept of enough goods, there is also the concept of superfluous wealth. Whereas underdevelopment affects two-thirds of the globe, rich classes and nations consume in a superfluous way by exploiting natural resources. This can be characterised as inhuman in two ways. First, the maintenance of superfluous wealth alongside underdevelopment conditions is unjust; the better redistribution of wealth among societies and within societies would be necessary. Second, the hyper-consumption manner of life in economically developed societies has distorted the way that a good life is perceived: 'having more' (material goods and wealth) leads to the notion of 'being more' (successful, attractive, and valuable). "The notion of 'more is better' is a basic tenet of consumerism. What drives this system in many respects is the ready acceptance that the good life is the goods life" (Brown, 2004, p. 212). With regard to the normative-ethical strategy of the abundance of goods, three distinctive points are noteworthy. First, all individuals need to have enough goods in order to realise themselves as human beings. Second, enough is not an absolutely relative measure but it can be defined in an objective way. Third, both underdevelopment situations and superfluous wealth lead to the dehumanisation of life.

Development ethics analysis on the abundance of goods can be perceived as an originator of new developments in happiness studies that suggest that overabundance does not increase happiness beyond a certain level (Dutt and Radcliff, 2009, especially Chapter 6 by Dutt). More recently, Dutt and Wilber (2010b, p. 11) have claimed that, in subjective well-being research, it has been proven that "beyond a certain level of income and consumption, further increase do not add significantly, or not at all, to a person's happiness". The authors directly connect this approach to the development ethics normative-ethical strategy of the abundance of goods.

2. **Universal solidarity**: For development ethics, universal solidarity can be distinctive in three ways (Goulet, 1975a, pp. 138–143). First, all people agree that, beyond certain differences (nationality, race, culture, status, etc.), a common 'human-ness' is present. Second, the earth as a cosmic body is governed by identical laws (physical roles), to which all people on this planet are subjected. Humans share a common occupation of the planet. In spite of differences in geography or climate, humans are linked directly or indirectly with other people, due to their cohabitation of this cosmic body. The third component of universal solidarity is derived by the unity of all humans regarding a shared destiny. Furthermore, advocating universal solidarity, development ethics accepts Perroux's notion that "no single nation, if left to its own resources and habitual economic procedures, possesses the means to create a human economy on the basis of greater need" (Goulet, 1975a, p. 34; Perroux, 1964, p. 358). In contrast, the existing state of affairs in the notion of economic globalisation is in the opposite direction. Humans have not yet realised the need for solidarity. Controversial perspectives of development focus on narrow mercantile, strategic, and ideological interests. Under present worldwide conditions, solidarity can be achieved only through conflict against present rules and redefinition of the relations of power. Conflict

is a prerequisite for solidarity. Here, it is appropriate to state the importance of class struggle and the rebuilding of institutions. Development ethicists assert that no universal solidarity exists to consolidate unfair social relations. Thus, the rebuilding of social relations and institutions on the basis of equality is more than necessary (Goulet, 1975a; 1995; Dower, 1998b; Schwenke, 2009).

3. **Participation**: Theories of participation represent an important issue in the normative-ethical study of development. In general, elite theory (Burnham, 1960; Putnam, 1977; Bottomore, 1993) claims that decision-making in a society is a 'job' for specialists in each particular field of life. Elite theory is built on the basis of the 'competence' that leads to an alleged efficiency within a society. Elite problem-solvers (the political elite, government officials, policy makers, specialists, executives of intergovernmental organisations, and so on) usually view development as a matter of competence. In contradiction to the conventional approach to issues of decision-making, development ethics offers a pluralistic alternative. In Goulet's (1995, p. 97) words, "[p]articipation is best conceptualised as a kind of moral incentive enabling hitherto excluded non-elites to negotiate new packages of material incentives benefiting them". However, participation and inclusion of everyone in moral and social life does not imply universality in the sense of the adoption of a general point of view that leaves behind particular affiliations, feelings, commitments, and desires (Harvey, 1993, pp. 107–108). Thus, development ethicists (Crocker, 2008; 2010; Drydyk, 2010; Gasper, 2012; McNeil and St. Chair, 2009; Penz et al., 2011) argue that different kinds of development require different forms of participation, in accordance with the ethical deliberation of participation at the level of value change and cultural diversity. In spite of this, in the normative-ethical discussion, it is important that non-elite participation in decision-making can enable people to mobilise and have control over their social destinies. Non-elite participation is perceived in the sense that common people are involved not only as receivers of the privileges of development but also as agents of their destinies, building their model of development. To what extent popular participation should take place is a matter for discussion. What is certain is that, via participation, at least three vital actions are performed (Goulet, 1995, pp. 91–101):

1. Participation offers to non-elites the ability to state goals independently of their social positions.
2. Participation abolishes political patron, in the sense that ordinary people themselves become problem-solvers in their social environment.
3. Participation allows individuals and social formations to escape from the rationale of the 'do-it-yourself' problems at the micro level by gaining access to the macro arena of decision-making.

4 Conclusion

The main purpose of the preceding normative-ethical analysis is to evaluate the relationship between the means and the ends of international development. As already mentioned, the dominant form of economic analysis within the perception of international development as a globalised market economy can be found in neoclassical economics. In neoclassical economic analysis, the theoretical tools of the normative evaluation of institutions, policies, and outcomes are public choice theory and welfare economics. The ends of international development are economic growth in the sense of wealth creation, economic well-being, and the establishment of a Western type of consumerist society in a globalised market economy. The means of achieving the above ends are based on economic growth theories, particularly on capital accumulation, free capital flows and trade, technological advancement, and the transformation of the institutional fabric of the economic, political, and societal structures in the direction of competitiveness and a globalised market economy. "It [neoclassical economics] combines a deep suspicion about any policy initiative that seeks greater national competitiveness with a resolute defense of free trade" (DeMartino, 2000, p. 22). As the analysis has shown, the normative-ethical background of these changes is based on neoclassical economics' welfarism, economic rationalism, and neoliberal ideology. Furthermore, the normative-ethical evaluation of the Washington Consensus policy reforms in international development evidently finds that the means (namely the institutions and policies) are subjected to the predetermined ends (the objectives and outcomes), as well as to the principles of neoclassical economics' welfarism, economic rationalism, and neoliberal ideology. Economic development is viewed as value-neutral and ethically neutral, either at the level of the means or at the level of the ends. The normative relationship between the objectives and policy is also approached as an instrumental process that reflects the above premises. However, the normative-ethical nature of neoclassical economics and the present international development as a globalised market economy embraces development change as an aid or obstacle, without evaluating the ethical meaning of such change for people and societies.

Development ethics adds the elements of the dynamic of value change, the discussion of ethical rationality, and the normative role of ethics to the discussion of the normative-ethical evaluations of international development. The normative-ethical examination of development ethics aims at eliminating the political, technological, and economic problems that development change usually brings to the institutional fabric of societies. Value change is an important ethical parameter that economic development usually approaches as a matter of interest in the direction that we have analysed. Development ethics argues for the normative-ethical investigation of value change in the mode of a triple rationality: technological, political, and ethical rationality. Regarding human well-being in the dominant form of contemporary international development, the Western model of consumption in the notion of 'more is better' is proposed to the rest of the world. For development ethicists, the normative-ethical assessment of a good life is a subjective matter related to the notion of 'enough'. 'Enough' can be defined as (at least) the elimination of poverty and hunger for all people in the world and the qualitative enrichment of all humans towards achieving their own spiritual goals.

The element of universal solidarity among people and societies is also an important ethical issue in the normative-ethical discussion of development ethics. People and nations should realise their shared habitation of Earth as a cosmic body. However, universal solidarity requires conflict at the level of class struggle and the rebuilding of social relations and institutions, along with the foundation of equality at the local, national, and international levels.

The participation of ordinary people in public decision-making enables people and societies to facilitate their own models of development. This is crucial if we desire to bring about a good society. Development ethicists (Goulet, in particular) codify the aforementioned elements as normative-ethical strategies that lead people and societies to larger human values. These larger human values are normatively involved in a set of universally accepted ethical goals under the terms 'life sustenance', 'esteem', and 'freedom', as has been discussed. To this end, normative-ethical analysis is concerned with the evaluation of international development from an ethical standpoint.

In the next chapter, the ethical investigation of the applied-ethical aspects of international development, based on the preceding analyses of the meta-ethical, and the normative-ethical nature of international development are discussed.

References

Alvey, J. E. (2000). An introduction to economics as a moral science. *International Journal of Social Economics, 27*(12), 1231–1251.

Archibald, G. C. (1959). Welfare economics, ethics, and essentialism. *Economica, 26*(104), 316–327.

Aristotle. (2000). *ARISTOTLE: Nicomachean ethics.* (R. Crisp, Ed., & R. Crisp, Trans.) Cambridge, UK: Cambridge University Press.

Arrébola-Rodríguez, C. A. (2011). From Washington consensus to post-washington consensus consensus: Consequences in transition economies. *European Perspectives, 1*(4), 19–34.

Arrow, K. J. (1951). *Social choice and individual values.* Wiley.

Arrow, K. J., Sen, A., & Suzumura, K. (Eds.). (2002). *Handbook of social choice and welfare* (Vol. I–II). Amsterdam: Elsevier.

Astroulakis, N. (2011). The development ethics approach to international development. *International Journal of Development Issues, 10*(3), 214–232.

Astroulakis, N. (2013a). Ethics and international development: The development ethics paradigm. *EAST-WEST Journal of Economics and Business, XVI*(1), 99–117.

Astroulakis, N. (2013b). Challenging conventional economics: An ethical development paradigm. *Revista Problemas del Desarrollo, 175*(44), 33–53.

Atkinson, A. B. (2009). Economics as a moral science. *Economica, 76*(s1), 791–804.

Blackorby, C., Bossert, W., & Donaldson, D. (2002). Utilitarianism and the theory of justice. In K. J. Arrow, S. Amartya, & K. Susumura (Eds.), *Handbook of social choice and welfare* (Vol. 1, pp. 543–596). London: Elsevier.

Bottomore, T. (1993). *Elites and society* (2nd ed.). Routledge.

Brown, D. (2004). Conspicuous consumption, fashion and style in the global marketplace. In P. A. O'Hara (Ed.), *Global political economy and the wealth of nations: Performance, institutions, problems and policies* (pp. 208–221). Routledge.

Buchanan, J. M. (1959). Positive economics, welfare economics, and political economy. *Journal of Law and Economics, 2*, 124–138.

Burk, A. (1938). A reformulation of certain aspects of welfare economics. *Quarterly Journal of Economics, 52*(2), 310–334.
Burnham, J. (1960). *The managerial revolution*. Indiana University Press.
Clark, D. A. (2002). Development ethics: A research agenda. *International Journal of Social Economics, 29*(11), 830–848.
Clark, D. A. (2002). *Visions of development: A study of human values*. Edward Elgar.
Crocker, D. (2006). Sen and deliberative democracy. In A. Kaufman (Ed.), *Capabilities equality: Basic issues and problems* (pp. 155–197). Routledge.
Crocker, D. (2008). *Ethics of global development*. Cambridge University Press.
Crocker, D. (2010). Participation in local development: Goulet and deliberative democracy. In C. K. Wilber & A. K. Dutt (Eds.), *New directions in development ethics: Essays in Honor of Denis Goulet* (pp. 308–332). Notre Dame University Press.
Cypher, J. M. (1998). The slow death of the Washington consensus on Latin America. *Latin American Perspectives, 25*(6), 47–51.
DeMartino, G. (2000). *Global economy, global justice: Theoretical and policy alternatives to neoliberalism*. Routledge.
Dower, N. (1988). *What is development? A philosopher's answer*. Centre for Development Studies Occasional Paper Series, 3. Glasgow: University of Glasgow.
Dower, N. (1998). *World ethics: The new agenda*. Edinburgh University Press.
Dower, N. (1998). Development ethics. In R. Chadwick (Ed.), *Encyclopedia of applied ethics* (pp. 755–766). Academic Press.
Dower, N. (2005). The nature and scope of global ethics and the relevance of the earth charter. *Journal of Global Ethics, 1*(1), 25–43.
Dower, N. (2010). Development and the ethics of the means. In C. K. Wilber & A. K. Dutt (Eds.), *Development ethics new directions: Essays in honor of Denis Goulet* (pp. 29–37). University of Notre Dame.
Drakopoulos, S. (1997). Origins and development of the trend towards value-free economics. *Journal of the History of Economic Thought, 19*(2), 286–300.
Drydyk, J. (2010). Participation, empowerment, and democracy: Three fickle friends. In C. K. Wilber & A. K. Dutt (Eds.), *New directions in development ethics: Essays in honor of Denis Goulet* (pp. 333–356). Notre Dame University Press.
Dutt, A. K., & Radciliff, B. (Eds.). (2009). *Happiness, economics and politics: Towards a multi-disciplinary approach*. Edward Elgar.
Dutt, A. K., & Wilber, C. K. (2010). Introduction: Development ethics and development economics. In C. K. Wilber & A. K. Dutt (Eds.), *New directions in development ethics—Essays in Honor of Denis Goulet* (pp. 1–26). University of Notre Dame Press.

Dutt, A. K., & Wilber, C. K. (2010). *Economics and ethics: An introduction*. Palgrave Macmillan.
Feldman, A. M., & Serrano, R. (2006). *Welfare economics and social choice theory* (2nd ed.). Springer.
Fine, B. (2003). Neither the Washington nor the post-Washington consensus: An introduction. In B. Fine, C. Lapavitsas, & J. Pincus (Eds.), *Development policy in the twenty-first century: Beyond the post-Washington consensus* (pp. 1–27). Routledge.
Fine, B., & Milonakis, D. (2009). *From economics imperialism to Freakonomics: The shifting boundaries between economics and other social sciences economics as social theory*. Routledge.
Friedman, M. (1953). *Essays in positive economics*. Chicago University Press.
Galbraith, J. K. (1991). Economics in the century ahead. *The Economic Journal, 101*(404), 41–46.
Gasper, D. (2004). *The ethics of development*. Edinburgh University Press.
Gasper, D. (2012). Development ethics—Why? What? How? A formulation of the field. *Journal of Global Ethics, 8*(1), 117–135.
Gewirth, A. (1960). Meta-ethics and normative ethics. *Mind (New Series), 69*(274), 187–205.
Gintis, H. (1972). A radical analysis of welfare economics and individual development. *The Quarterly Journal of Economics, 86*(4), 572–599.
Gore, C. (2000). The rise and fall of the Washington consensus as a paradigm for developing countries. *World Development, 28*(5), 789–804.
Goulet, D. (1968). Development for what? *Comparative Political Studies, 1*(2), 295–312.
Goulet, D. (1975). *The cruel choice: A new concept in the theory of development*. Atheneum.
Goulet, D. (1975). Pyramids of sacrifice: The high price of social change. *Christianity and Crisis, 35*(16), 231–236.
Goulet, D. (1986). Three rationalities in development decision-making. *World Development, 14*(2), 301–317.
Goulet, D. (1989). Participation in development: New avenues. *World Development, 17*(2), 165–178.
Goulet, D. (1995). *Development ethics: A guide to theory and practice*. The Apex Press.
Goulet, D. (1997). Development ethics: A new discipline. *International Journal of Social Economics, 24*(11), 1160–1171.
Goulet, D. (2001). Ethical analysis in development economics. In A. K. Dutt & K. P. Jameson (Eds.), *Crossing the mainstream: Ethical and methodological issues in economics* (pp. 29–51). University of Notre Dame Press.
Goulet, D. (2006). *Development ethics at work: Explorations 1960–2002*. Routledge.

Graafland, J. (2007). *Economics, ethics and the market: Introduction and applications*. Routledge.

Gravel, N., & Moyes, P. (2013). Utilitarianism or Welfarism: Does it make a difference? *Soc Choice Welf, 40*, 529–551.

Harvey, D. (1993). Class relations, social justice and the politics of difference. In J. Squires (Ed.), *Principled positions: Postmodernism and the rediscovery of value* (pp. 85–120). Lawrence & Wishart Ltd.

Hausman, D. M., & McPherson, M. S. (1993). Taking ethics seriously: Economics and contemporary moral philosophy. *Journal of Economic Literature, 31*(2), 671–731.

Hausman, D. M., & McPherson, M. S. (2006). *Economic analysis, moral philosophy, and public policy* (2nd ed.). Cambridge University Press.

Hodgson, G. M. (1999). *Economics and Utopia: Why the learning economy is not the end of history*. Routledge.

Hodgson, G. M. (2001). *How economics forgot history: The problem of historical specificity in social science*. Routledge.

Jameson, K. P. (2010). Ethics and contemporary macroeconomic policy. In C. K. Wilber & A. K. Dutt (Eds.), *New directions in development ethics: Essays in honor of Denis Goulet* (pp. 400–425). Notre Dame University Press.

Knoedler, J. T. (1997). Veblen and technical efficiency. *Journal of Economic Issues, 31*(4), 1011–1026.

Kuczynski, P. P., & Williamson, J. (Eds.). (2003). *After the Washington consensus*. Institute for International Studies.

Little, I. (2004). *Ethics, economics, and politics*. Oxford University Press.

Marangos, J. (2007). Was shock therapy consistent with the Washington consensus? *Comparative Economic Studies, 49*, 32–58.

Marangos, J. (2008). The evolution of the anti-Washington consensus debate: From 'Post-Washington consensus' to 'after the Washington consensus.' *Competition and Change, 12*(3), 227–244.

Marangos, J. (2009a). What happened to the Washington consensus? The evolution of international development policy. *The Journal of Socio-Economics, 38*(1), 197–208.

Marangos, J. (2009b). The evolution of the term 'Washington consensus.' *Journal of Economic Surveys, 23*(2), 350–384.

Marangos, J., & Astroulakis, N. (2009). The institutional foundation of development ethics. *Journal of Economic Issues, XLIII*(2), 381–388.

Marangos, J., & Astroulakis, N. (2012). The development ethics perspective of a good society. In J. Marangos (Ed.), *Alternative perspectives of a good society* (pp. 79–98). Palgrave Macmillan.

McNeill, D., & St. Clair, A. L. (2009). *Global poverty, ethics and human rights: The role of multilateral organisations*. Abingdon: Routledge.

Milonakis, D., & Fine, B. (2009). *From political economy to economics: Method, the social and the historical in the evolution of economic theory*. Routledge.
O'Hara, P. A. (2006). *Growth and development in the global political economy: Social structures of accumulation and modes of regulation*. Routledge.
Pareto, V. (1927). *Manual of political economy.* (A. S. Schwier, Trans.) London: Macmillan.
Parfitt, T. (2012). Development ethics: Means of the means? *Review of African Political Economy, 39*(134), 672–681.
Penz, P., Drydyk, J., & Bose, P. S. (2011). *Displacement by development: Ethics, rights and responsibilities*. Cambridge University Press.
Perroux, F. (1964). *L économie du XXème siècle*. Presses Universitaires de France.
Pigou, A. C. (1920). *The economics of welfare*. Macmillan.
Pusey, M. (1991). *Economic rationalism in Canberra: A nation-building state changes its mind*. Cambridge University Press.
Putnam, R. D. (1977). Elite transformation in advance industrial societies: An empirical assessment of the theory of technocracy. *Comparative Political Studies, 10*(3), 383–411.
Robbins, L. (1945 [1932]). *An essay on the nature and significance of economic science* (second ed.). London: Macmillan.
Samuelson, P. (1947). *Foundations of economic analysis*. Harvard University.
Schwenke, C. (2009). *Reclaiming value in international development: The moral dimensions of development policy and practice in poor countries*. Praeger Publishers.
Schwenke, C. (2011). Development ethics: The audacious agenda. In R. S. Fortner & P. M. Fackler (Eds.), *The handbook of global communication and media ethics* (Vol. I–II, pp. 317–341). Oxford: Wiley-Blackwell.
Sen, A. (1977). Rational fools: A critique of the behavioral foundations of economic theory. *Philosophy and Public Affairs, 6*(4), 317–344.
Sen, A. (1979a). Utilitarianism and welfarism. *The Journal of Philosophy, 76*(9), 463–489.
Sen, A. (1979b). Personal utilities and public judgements: Or what's wrong with welfare economics. *The Economic Journal, 89*, 537–558.
Sen, A. (1987). *On ethics and economics*. Blackwell.
Sen, A. (1998). The living standard. In D. Crocker & T. Linden (Eds.), *Ethics of consumption* (pp. 287–311). Rowman & Littlefield Publishers Inc.
Serra, N., & Stiglitz, J. (Eds.). (2008). *The Washington consensus reconsidered*. Oxford University Press.
Slim, H. (1995). What is development? *Development in Practice, 5*(2), 143–148.
Solow, R. M. (1956). A contribution to the theory of economic growth. *The Quarterly Journal of Economics, 70*(1), 65–94.
Solow, R. M. (1957). Technical change and the aggregate production function. *Review of Economics and Statistics, 39*(3), 312–320.

Stewart, F. (1997). John Williamson and the Washington consensus revisited. In L. Emmerij (Ed.), *Economic and social development in the XXI century* (pp. 62–69). Inter-American Development Bank.

Stiglitz, J. (2002a). *Globalization and its discontents*. W. W. Norton.

Stiglitz, J. (2002b). Participation and development: Perspectives from the comprehensive development paradigm. *Review of Development Economics, 6*(2), 163–182.

Street, J. H. (2001). The institutionalist theory of economic development. *Journal of Economic Issues, 21*(4), 1861–1887.

Suzumura, K. (2002). Introduction. In K. J. Arrow, A. Sen, & K. Suzumura (Eds.), *Handbook of Social choice and welfare* (Vol. 1, pp. 1–32). London: Elsevier.

Swan, T. W. (1956). Economic growth and capital accumulation. *Economic Record, 32*(2), 334–361.

Syrquin, M. (1988). Patterns of structural change. In H. Chenery & T. N. Srinivasan (Eds.), *Handbook of development economics* (Vol. 1, pp. 203–273). London: Elsevier.

Vickers, D. (1997). *Economics and ethics: An introduction to theory, institutions, and policy*. Greenwood Publishing Group.

von Neumann, J., & Morgenstern, O. (1947). *Theory of games and economic behavior* (2nd ed.). Princeton University Press.

Wilber, C. K. (2010). Economics and ethics. In C. K. Wilber & A. K. Dutt (Eds.), *New directions in development ethics: Essays in honor of Denis Goulet* (pp. 157–176). University of Notre Dame.

Williamson, J. (1990a). What Washington means by policy reform. In J. Williamson (Ed.), *Latin American adjustment: How much has happened? (Chapter 2)*. Washington, DC: Institute for International Economics. Republished online (November, 2002). http://www.iie.com/publications/papers/paper.cfm?researchid=486

Williamson, J. (Ed.). (1990b). *Latin American adjustment: How much has happened?* Institute for International Economics.

Williamson, J. (1993). Democracy and the 'Washington consensus.' *World Development, 21*(8), 1329–1336.

Williamson, J. (2000). What should the World Bank think about the Washington Consensus? *The World Bank Research Observer, 15*(2), 251–264.

Wright, J. (2003). *The ethics of economic rationalism*. University of New South Wales.

CHAPTER 6

The Applied-Ethical Basis of International Development and the Development Ethics Alternative

1 Introduction

So far, the analysis has concentrated on the meta-ethical and normative-ethical basis of international development. Both fields determine international development to be in the philosophical grounds of the ethical reflection of moral meanings. However, a critique of the philosophical discussion of the ethical reflection on development can be found through the intellectual manner in which philosophers approach the theme, scrutinising the meaning of ethical arguments while neglecting policy implications (Clark, 2002a, p. 830). In the present analysis, the ethical argument is associated with the conditionality of a good life and a good society in international development. Usually, neoclassical economics confronts ethical issues in the discussion of development, either at the level of the ends or at the level of the means, in a straightforward, 'engineering' manner. To this end, Sen (1987, p. 50) argues that the "'engineering' aspect of economics has tended to go hand in hand with sticking to a very narrow view of ethics." This narrow view of ethics can arguably be interpreted as the value-neutral and ethically neutral stance adopted by neoclassical economics in the field of international development policy. Up to now, the analysis has shown that economics, as both an analytical and policy-oriented discipline, cannot be value-neutral as its neoclassical proponents claim (see also Vickers, 1997, p. 72; van Staveren, 2001, p. 202). Neoclassical economists are

N. Astroulakis and N. Karagiannis, *Development Ethics*,
https://doi.org/10.1007/978-3-031-75476-0_6

quite outspoken about the ethical character of the two main issues on which free-market economics is based: "efficiency (the Pareto principle) and freedom or liberty (including free choice, free exchange, individual autonomy, independence, individual will and self-creation)" (Graafland, 2007, p. 9, brackets in the original). One can easily argue that freedom is an ethical concept (Sen, 1999). Likewise, as van Stavaren (2009, pp. 107–108) maintains, "Pareto efficiency is not a morally neutral criterion but expresses a strong liberal—even libertarian—ethics through the application of a strict no-harm principle towards redistribution."

In addition, neoclassical economics has emerged as a universal science. Particularly in development policy, neoclassical economists consider that the development models based on the principles of economics as a positive science are applicable to all times and places (Davidson and Davidson, 1988, p. 55; Gilpin, 2001, p. 64; Milonakis and Fine, 2009, p. 46). Even further, regarding the relationship between politics and economics, Bowles et al. (1999, p. 2) argue that, in the political science, there is little understanding of the applied functioning of the economy; simultaneously, neoclassical economics is rarely deployed to understand politics and state policy. Moreover, the ethical treatise of a good society is largely absent from the economists' development policy discussions, even the heterodox ones (Sotiropoulos et al., 2012, p. 100).

All the instances mentioned above result in analytic distortions and faulty policy prescriptions in the discussion of development. The problem of the ethical exploration of international development in the fields of philosophy and economics remains to some extent unresolved, particularly in accordance with development policy and moral issues. In order to provide a viable response to the underlying challenges, following our elucidation of the meta-ethical and normative-ethical concerns of international development (Chapters 4 and 5), in the present chapter we approach the theme in terms of its applied-ethical aspects within the contexts of political economy and moral philosophy.

The question that is primarily posed is what applied ethics is or, rather, how applied ethics is perceived in this study and how applied-ethical analysis, in the contexts of political economy and moral philosophy, approaches international development policy. Responding to this, three initial but fundamental definitional issues should be noted. First, the present analysis accepts the position that ethics has empirical, practical, and applied aspects. Endorsing this view, Moore (1960 [1903], Sec. 25), in *Principia Ethica*, states that "ethics is an empirical or positive science:

its conclusions could all be established by means of empirical observation and induction." Singer (2011, p. vii) argues that the most relevant applied-ethical issues are those that confront us in daily life. Foucault (1984, p. 377) points out that "ethics is a practice; ethos is a manner of being." Second, applied ethics is acknowledged in its broader cognizance as one of the three branches of knowledge in moral philosophy. The other two are meta-ethics and normative ethics (Kagan, 1998; Williams, 2006). In this categorisation, applied ethics can be considered as the branch of ethical knowledge that examines contentious moral, social, legal, and political issues on the grounds of ethical debates and popular attributes (Hayry, 1994, p. 46). Third, applied ethics in international development and political economy is interwoven with global ethics. In turn, global ethics involves four interrelated levels of ethical analysis: the individual level, the corporate or organisational level, the national or societal level, and the global level (Buller et al., 1991, p. 768; Owen, 1983). However, the societal and organisational levels mainly influence global ethics. "Global ethics emerge from the degree of agreement among societies, corporations, and other organizations regarding the appropriate ethical frameworks and behaviors in a given situation" (Buller et al., 1991, p. 768).

This approach of applied ethics and applied-ethical analysis contributes to the holistic exploration of development policy in international development. It investigates the ethical aspects of development policy without neglecting economic and political aspects as the main factors of development policy in international development, as moral philosophers frequently do. Moreover, the suggested analysis views applied ethics and economic policy in their broader senses. Applied ethics is not limited to the narrow aspects of the microeconomic foundations of business ethics and individual ethical behaviour under the belief of self-interest, as mainstream economists usually consider. "Moral theories are not cookbooks for good behavior" (Hausman and McPherson, 2006, p. 3). A brief critical review of the mainstream approach follows.

The mainstream literature usually approaches applied ethics as a kind of deontological ethics interwoven with the rules, duties, and obligations of moral agents in an individualistic manner. In this regard, applied ethics is specified in several sub-fields, such as environmental ethics, medical ethics, bioethics, and business ethics (Cohen and Wellman (eds.), 2005; Chadwick (ed.), 2012; LaFollette, 2002). In accordance with this, applied ethics is commonly perceived as professional ethics in any specific field of individual or corporate life (Abbott, 1983, p. 880). The vast majority of neoclassical economists accept applied ethics at the level of business ethics. In the literature on business ethics, the notion of applied ethics mainly describes the relations between firms/organisations and the internal or external economic environment. Such relations largely involve human resource management, the decision-making process, corporate responsibility, producers' and consumers' ethics, and similar deontological concepts and policy issues. At the core of business ethics are the individual preferences, decisions, and actions and the entrepreneurial economic and social activity in the predetermined economic environment of free-market economics. In almost all of the prescriptions of neoclassical economics, the sum of individuals equals the society, and the sum of private businesses makes the economy. In business ethics, the society and the economy mainly consist of producers (business corporations) and consumers (individuals or households); the society and the economy are usually analysed with the tools of microeconomic analysis. A common prescription in business ethics in the realm of neoclassical economics is the will of consumers to maximise their utility[1] and the will of producers to maximise their profits. Ethical issues are involved in these fundamental, narrow perceptions. Within this framework, applied ethics (i.e., business ethics) focuses on individual ethics based on self-interest and microeconomic foundations.

The present investigation proposes a rather different manner of analysis. It moves from the microeconomic level of business ethics to the macroeconomic level of global ethics. As mentioned, in the holistic-ethical examination of international development, applied ethics better corresponds to global ethics. In order to describe applied ethics, we borrow a metaphor from Davidson and Davidson (1988, p. 61): "[a]lthough there is an obvious relationship between a tree and a forest, nevertheless the microbiology of a tree is different from the macrobiology of forests." In a similar manner, business ethics is related to, but different from global ethics when we examine applied-ethical issues at the national or international levels. Therefore, with consideration of the aforementioned deontological nature of applied ethics, given that global ethics involves business ethics, in the present analysis, applied ethics is considered holistically as the brand of moral philosophy that responds to the

[1] Consumers' utility is explained as satisfaction and/or leisure time.

ethical guidelines regarding the ethical argument of a good life and a good society in international development.

The applied-ethical basis of international development might touch upon the key ethical issue of what form of applied ethics is the most appropriate to policy in international development. For the investigation of this issue, the analysis of the applied-ethical basis of international development manifestly focuses on global ethics and the existing economic, political, and institutional structure of international development in the era of economic globalisation and the dominance of neoliberalism.

More precisely, in the framework described, global ethics consists of the applied-ethical policies of national and multinational businesses, nation-states, and international development institutions [e.g. the World Bank, the International Monetary Fund (IMF), and the World Trade Organization (WTO)]. Almost all types of economic analysis of applied policy are associated with the relations among individuals, firms, and the state. In addition, a common characteristic of almost all interpretations is the element of policy assimilation in the framework of free-market relations, as "markets have become nationwide and worldwide" (North, 1991, p. 101).

In this light, we assume that free-market relations overlap with applied-ethical policy in contemporary international development. Ultimately, in a globalised market economy, to what extent individuals, firms, and state authorities are associated with one another is subject to elements such as market relations, public or state policy, and international development institutions' orders. Consequently, the leading applied-ethical structural factors in international development can be seen in the examination of free-market relations, nation-state policy, and the rules, canons, and policies established by international development institutions. On the latter issue, the Washington Consensus policy in Latin America and internationally is examined as an applied-ethical example of the dominant international development institutions' policies in the developing world.

We portray development ethics as an alternative applied-ethical perspective to neoclassical economics and neoliberalism in international development. As Goulet (1992b, p. 138) puts it, "[t]he failure of reductionist economic approaches to development opens the door to ethics to find its place in development debates and practices." As the particular form of neoliberal globalisation changes the real scope and meaning of international development, "[d]evelopment ethics overlaps increasingly with concerns for global ethics" (St. Clair, 2010, p. 265). At the applied policy level, we perceive development ethics as a kind of appropriate global ethics, here referred to as 'applied development ethics'. From the angle of applied development ethics, Wilber (2010, p. 173) argues that national and international economic policies need to implement ambitious programmes with good intentions, clear analyses of the issues, and sustained thought. To this end, the applied-ethical analysis of development ethics in international development plays a significant role in the determination of value issues in development policy. Schwenke (2009, p. 6) points out that "[e]thics is the ordering of moral value systems, and through ethics, moral concepts can be systematically considered, evaluated, and applied." In this way, applied development ethics contributes to the investigation of the ethical guidelines within the ethical argument of a good life and a good society. Following the structural synthesis of market relations, nation-state policy, and international development institutions' policies in international development, applied development ethics offers an alternative applied-ethical policy view beyond the neoclassical economics applied-ethical policy standpoints in international development. Subsequently, at the level of policy, development ethics states that "[e]thically based development is inclusive development: it offers and protects at least a minimally adequate level of development benefits for everyone in a society" (Crocker, 2008, pp. 42–43).

2 The Applied-Ethical Basis of Contemporary International Development

2.1 *Applied Ethics and Free Markets in International Development*

Market relations are associated with the framework of applying economic policy in the real world. For instance, the productive relationships (the way of production, the manner to distribute products, and the use of resources) and, more broadly, the established economic, political, and institutional rules can be seen as the subject matters of applied-ethical analysis of existing market relations.

To approach the theme in line with its historical roots, twentieth-century perspectives of the study of international economics have established the general division between a free-market economy and a centralised planning economy (Cohen, 2009; Gilpin, 2001; Waltz, 1979). The traditional framework developed for the structural analysis of international development in the twentieth century reflected the Cold

War and the ideological division between the two opposing economic systems. The initial commitment to this approach was the product of conflicting economic, political, and social policies: a conflict that dates as far back as the late nineteenth century, when the systems of a free-market economy and a centralised planning economy were debated and contrasted, primarily on the relative merits of their social, economic, and political foundations. To this end, late in the nineteenth century, Marshall (1920 [1890], Book V.I.19) argued:

> Thus at one extreme are world markets in which competition acts directly from all parts of the globe; and at the other those secluded markets in which all direct competition from afar is shut out, though indirect and transmitted competition may make itself felt even in these; and about midway between these extremes lie the great majority of the markets which the economist and the business man have to study.

In the years after, philosophers and economists were called to serve "as rearguard defences of one intellectual status quo or the other" (Bowles and Gintis, 1986, p. 18). Since the collapse of the Soviet Union and the end of the Cold War era, there has been the spread of the supposition of the convergence of the entire world on the Western free-market model and the end of any significant competition between alternative forms of economic policy. Many contemporary neoclassical economists would agree with Fukuyama's (1992, p. xiii) view that "liberal principles in economics—the 'free market'—have spread and have succeeded in producing unprecedented levels of material prosperity." Fukuyama (1992) also expresses the view that the free market is the only adequate economic and institutional framework in international development in which the ethical argument of a good life and a good society can be appraised. In the modern capitalist world, "[t]he celebrated ability of markets to reconcile individual interests and collective rationality—or at least to substantially attenuate the contradiction between the two—was always viewed as conditional on a kind of morality and moral action" (Bowles and Gintis, 1986, p. 149). In this respect, free-market relations could be received as an applied-ethical framework for investigating development policy in contemporary international development.

Analysis of the applied ethics model of the free-market relations in real-world conditions and development policies may be useful in specifying the role of free-market relations in the existing form of productive relationships, namely the capitalist relations of production. It is important to mention that the analysis of the applied-ethical aspects of the free-market relations in the existing economic reality embodies the dominant ideological and theoretical prescriptions of neoclassical economics. Mainly based on Fine's (1980) radical scrutiny of economic theory and the ideology of capitalist relations and the free-market mechanism, a couple of explicit implications for the applied-ethical analysis of free-market relations are explored, with the belief that ideology and theory are interwoven with real policy implementations in international development.

In the neoclassical model, the applied-ethical character of free-market relations results in the policies applied for production and distribution. At the level of production, free-market relations as reflected in the capitalist relations of production determine the applicable control of the production. For instance, employees and workers are unable to control production because of the assumption of their lack of managerial skills. In line with this, neoclassical economics usually argues that "those with managerial skills or potential will be assigned through the market to their appropriate place and rewarded for their scarce abilities accordingly" (Fine, 1980, p. 5). This assumption functions as an ethical argument to the applied-ethical issue of why the control of production is under a specific class in the consolidated production relations. At the level of distribution, free-market relations incorporate the rate of profit as the price of capital and the rate of wages as the price of labour. Furthermore, exchange relations as they are principally applied in the free-market mechanism determined by supply and demand curves are examined in terms of the relationship between the prices of inputs and the prices of outputs. In this respect, it is argued that the neoclassical applied-ethical analysis of the free market becomes preoccupied with the analysis of market exchange relations and the formation of prices by solely using supply and demand curves. In addition, free-market relations encompass an individualistic manner of approaching decision-making in the economy, as "each individual is integrated into the economy by exchanges through the market, so the economy is conceived of as the aggregation of the atomized behaviour of individuals combined and coordinated through the market" (Fine, 1980, p. 26). However, the applied-ethical individualism of neoclassical economics leaves unexplained the social relations between capital and labour. It seems that the free market as the imperative mechanism regulates the use of the resources (capital and labour) in the economy in an ethically neutral manner.

In neoclassical economics, by reducing the Adam Smith's notion of the invisible hand to the applied practices of the free-market relations, the ultimate criterion of the free-market function is consumption, not profit. In this light, the applied-ethical policy decisions in the free-market mechanism are anticipated on behalf of consumers' prosperity, not the gains of capital. Of equivalent importance is the assumption of the maximisation of consumption via free-market equilibrium conditions in the long run. In addition, Say's law states that supply creates its own demand. At the applied level of analysis, this implies that excess supply will foster demand. Nevertheless, even if we accept that supply creates its own demand, there is no evidence that this happens in the market at the national level. On the contrary, disequilibrium conditions in national economies offer space for the argument that "the equality of aggregate notional supply and demand becomes transformed into the equality of aggregate effective supply and effective demand" (Fine, 1980, pp. 33–34) at the abstract level of the worldwide economy. Otherwise, excess supply in some markets could hypothetically create excess demand in others, without specifying when, where, and for whom. Based on this, the applied policy decisions (based on neoclassical economics) formulated in free-market relations seem to be ethically 'right', as they improve the efficiency of economic outcomes and, as a consequence, individual and societal prosperity. The imperative applied-ethical posture of neoclassical economics can be seen in the equilibrium condition in the ethically neutral space of free-market relations, either nationally or internationally. Regarding the applied-ethical nature of free-market relations, "if a supply meets a demand and vice-versa, all is well and good" (Fine, 1980, p. 33).

Beyond the applied-ethical issues of equilibrium economics, free-market relations guarantee economic freedom and promote political freedom. Political freedom is perceived as a mirror image of the economic freedom derived from the established free-market relations. Friedman (2002, p. 8), in *Capitalism and Freedom*, first published in 1962, argues:

> On the one hand, freedom in economic arrangements is itself a component of freedom broadly understood, so economic freedom is an end in itself. In the second place, economic freedom is also an indispensable means towards the achievement of political freedom.

In this view, the established free-market relations in competitive capitalism separate economic power from political power.[2] Free-market relations provide economic freedom; in turn, economic freedom advances and protects political freedom. Capitalism in general, and the established free-market relations in particular, are accepted as prerequisites for political freedom (Friedman, 2002, p. 10).

The discussion of freedom, either political or economic, is mainly based on the grounds of individual choices and actions. A free-market system can be described as a system under which individuals make their own choices and bear the consequences of their choices based on the general individualistic-ethical premise that a society is solely comprised by the sum of its individuals acting under free-market relations and satisfying their own preferences. In addition, free-market relations and cooperation in the market are voluntarily exchanged by individuals. Based on these fundamental principles, "[i]ndividuals co-operate with others because they can in this way satisfy their own wants more effectively" (Friedman, 2002, p. 166). Finally, the evidence of the acceptance of free-market relations, as neoclassical economists argue, is that this system has prevailed for most of human history (Friedman and Friedman, 1980, p. 138). It has prevailed due to its superiority, even with market failures, to another economic system: the centralised planning economy (Roemer, 1994, p. 20; Friedman and Friedman, 1980, p. 138; Hayek, 1948, pp. 107–108).

These views are predominantly associated not only with liberalism but also with neoliberalism. "The assumption that individual freedoms are guaranteed by freedom of the market… is a cardinal feature of neoliberal thinking" (Harvey, 2005, p. 7). As far as this happens, free-market relations are based on private property rights and protected private contracts. Private property rights are the cornerstone of the applied economic system of competitive capitalism. "In its economic manifestation, liberalism [as neoliberalism] is the recognition of the right of free economic activity and economic exchange based on private property and markets" (Fukuyama, 1992, p. 44). In addition to this, individuals are the ultimate owners of property in society (Friedman, 2002, p. 135). Nevertheless, because of the legal and social matters of property rights, state policy guarantees private property rights, as their definition and enforcement are

[2] The ideas on political power and market power, and the applied-ethical relationship between them, are also discussed in the following section.

among the primary functions of the applied policy. Even the distribution of income and wealth is a matter of property rights relations:

> "The ethical principle that would directly justify the distribution of income in a free market society is, 'To each according to what he and the instruments he owns produces'"; thus, "[t]he final distribution of income and wealth under the full operation of this principle may well depend markedly on the rules of property adopted (Friedman, 2002, pp. 161–162)."

In a capitalist economy, free-market relations are enforced by strong private property rights as the imperative that guarantees the efficient use of resources and the efficient operation of the market. Most neoclassical economists associate the end state of development (a good society) with the establishment of free-market-relations, in which the majority of property is private. Private poverty is founded on free-market relations, and vice versa. In this premise, effective property rights are respected and enforced by free-market relations (Marangos, 2004, p. 105). Private property rights and free-market relations are strongly protected by the law. In addition, in answer to the ethical question of what constitutes a good life, neoclassical economists reply that individuals derive satisfaction from owning private property not only for the needs that such property satisfies but because other individuals recognise this. Fukuyama (1992, p. 195) acknowledges property rights as a stage or aspect of the historical struggle for recognition, as something that satisfies not only needs but also desires. In this way, private property rights, and the strong protection of them, are a legitimate end for a civil society. Consequently, free-market relations are capable of acting as a guide for all human action, substituting all previously held ethical beliefs. As far as market relations are valued as "an ethic in itself" in this way, the significance of contractual relations in the marketplace is emphasised (Harvey, 2005, p. 3), both at the national and international levels.

In accordance with some empirical studies in neoclassical economics, free-market relations (assisted by private property rights and political freedom) result in more efficient outcomes in terms of economic prosperity and growth in emerging, transitional, and developing economies. For instance, Goldsmith (1995) unswervingly associates the elements of political freedom and property rights with economic growth in international development. By testing a wide range of emerging, transitional, and developing economies, using data from the 1980s and the early 1990s,

Goldsmith's empirical study utilises institutional forced political freedom along with established property rights as dependent variable, "suggesting that national income in poor countries stands to gain from recent efforts to implant these institutions" (Goldsmith, 1995, p. 157). Similar empirical results in support of the positive association of free-market relations, political freedom, and property rights with economic growth and prosperity in international development have been mentioned in the studies of Bilson (1982), Vorhies and Glahe (1988), and Pourgerami and Assane (1992), among others.

At the same time, while several mainstream thinkers argue in favour of the notion of free-market relations, political freedom, and democratic regimes as promoting growth and prosperity in international development, some others distinguish political freedom from economic development. For instance, Huntington and Nelson (1976) state that, particularly in developing countries, there is an exchange between political participation (namely democracy or political freedom) and economic development. This result has been associated with the efficiency of free-market relations. Democracy demands public spending and a welfare state; nevertheless, public spending deprives social saving and the accumulation of capital necessary for economic growth, particularly at the early stage of economic development. Thus, the applied policy in developing countries should not necessarily consist of political freedom and economic development. From this perspective, free-market relations and economic efficiency are preferable to political freedom, if it is to be chosen. A similar argument has been posed by Olson (1993; 1982). Olson's analysis is based on Banfield's conservative ethical view of politics. For Banfield (1958, p. 26), "[m]onarchy is the best kind of government because the King is then owner of the country. Like the owner of a house, when the wiring is wrong, he fixes it." Based on this applied-ethical premise, Olsen (1993) argues that dictatorship leads to better development outcomes than anarchy. The intent of his analysis, however, is to defend free-market relations and private property rights, as "[t]he conditions necessary for a lasting democracy are the same necessary for the security of property and contract rights that generates economic growth" (Olson, 1993, p. 567). Similarly, Hayek (1979, p. 35) poses that:

> Although there is good reason for preferring limited democratic government to a non-democratic one, I must confess to preferring non-democratic government under the law to unlimited (and therefore essentially lawless) democratic government. Government under the law seems to me to be the higher value.

Therefore, it seems that, for mainstream thinkers, whether with democracy and political freedom or with a non-democratic government, the fundamental applied-ethical policy is the establishment of free-market relations and private property rights. Hence, the road to a good society is through economic growth and prosperity. In the economic history of international development, the role of governmental and nation-state policy has been valued in this manner in a variety of national trajectories. The next section analyses this role in its applied-ethical policy dimensions.

2.2 *Applied Ethics and Nation-State Policy in International Development*

The role of nation-state policy remains significant in the globalised market framework of international development. Nation-state policy refers to public or state policies, taking under consideration the whole spectrum of these policies at the national level. Even though economic globalisation shifts policy-making to the worldwide level of the global market and international institutions, nation-states continue to be the key applied policy players in international development. "This is still a world where national policies and domestic economies are the principal determinants of economic affairs" (Giplin, 2001, p. 3). Nation-states determine to a smaller or larger extent their policies regarding economic, political, and social actions and choices. In spite of the scale of nation-state policy-making in the globalised market framework, policies are typically imposed on the grounds of national confines by state authorities. In light of this, the applied-ethical context of the good lives of people and the good society in the sense of a common good for a nation, country, or society rests upon nation-state policy. Thus, nation-state policy is explored as one of the applied-ethical mainstays of international development.

How is a nation-state concerned with the applied-ethical neoclassical posture regarding applied policy? The reply to this question necessitates the discussion of the applied economic and political matters, as well as the relationship between methodological individualism and political individualism. The ethical notion of the free individual is central to both concepts. More accurately, political individualism—the idea of a political structure in which the preservation of individual liberty is made the touchstone of nation-state policy—is a mirror image or the expression of the methodological individualism applied in the political structure (Blaug, 1992 [1980], p. 45; Machlup, 1978, p. 472). In this regard, nation-state policy is approached from the individualistic-ethical idea of the free individual, in which individual preferences are at the core of the nation-state policy discussion. "[T]he country is the collection of individuals who compose it, not something over and above them" (Friedman, 2002, pp. 1–2). The scope of nation-state policy must be limited due to the ethical belief that individual freedom is always geared towards the diminishment of government or state power. Nation-state policy intervention is critically viewed, even in the spheres of social activities (such as education and health) and the failures of market institutions. Consequently, "[t]he preservation of freedom is the protective reason for limiting and decentralizing governmental power" (Friedman, 2002, p. 3). Voluntary individual cooperation and private enterprise, in both economic and political activities, ensure that "the private sector is a check on the powers of the governmental sector and an effective protection of freedom of speech, of religion, and of thought" (Friedman, 2002, p. 3).

Nation-state policy rests on the political regime and the prevailing ideology. Regarding the applied political regime of a nation-state, neoclassical theory formally suggests that the ideal type of liberal democracy leads to better societal and political outcomes:

> As mankind approaches the end of the millennium, the twin crises of authoritarianism and socialist central planning have left only one competitor standing in the ring as an ideology of potentially universal validity: liberal democracy, the doctrine of individual freedom and popular sovereignty (Fukuyama, 1992, p. 42).

With respect to ideology, neoclassical economists support a liberal ideology that emphasises and encourages self-interest based on Adam Smith's perspective. In accordance with the self-interest ideological perspective, individuals are allowed (within defined limits, including rights and obligations) to follow their own values and convictions (Smith, 1986

[1776], p. 119). Hence, individuals are not subjected to coercion. Coordination among individuals is spontaneous. Individuals participate in the market as it is guided by the 'invisible hand' and self-interest.

On the other hand, nation-state policy guarantees the individual or business contracts necessary for a civil society. This is implied in the ethical bearing in the words of Adam Smith in *The Theory of Moral Sentiments*:

> As the violation of justice is what men will never submit to from one another, the public magistrate is under a necessity of employing the power of the commonwealth to enforce the practice of this virtue. Without this precaution, civil society would become a scene of bloodshed and disorder, every man revenging himself at his own hand whenever he fancied he was injured (Smith, 2004 [1759], pp. 402–403).

At the applied-ethical level of policy-making, individuals as electoral voters join the decision-making process in a liberal democratic political structure. The reflections of the individuals' political views on the distinct political parties compose the political and liberal ideological structure of the society and affect the nation-state's policy decisions and actions. In turn, the element of power, particular market power over the political authority and individuals, is limited, under the assumptions of the public choice theory. In this respect, neoclassical economists assume that individuals' equal rights to vote ensure equal participation in decision-making. Furthermore, there is the assumption that the individual rationality that always or almost always leads to better economic choices also leads to better political choices. In spite of this, the law system as a pillar of liberal democracy maintains the performance of equal rights of individuals in the spheres of political, social, and economic life. Consequently, altogether, the neoclassical applied-ethical premises lead to the liberalisation of political structure and nation-state policy, as "the liberalization of political 'markets' is often as important as the liberalization of economic markets" (Parish and Michelson, 1996, p. 1043).

In addition, the debate on nation-state policy mainly involves the public versus private questions in the applied policy dialogue. The private question is seen in relation to free-market results, while the public question relates to state or government intervention. Regarding the discussion of private and public applied policies, decisions and actions, neoclassical economists argue that, even in the case of market-based policy failures,[3] "private solutions should be sought first" (Marangos, 2004, p. 35). Realising the enormity of neoclassical economics in favour of the private sector of the economy, more than thirty years after the economic crisis of 1929, Friedman (2002 [1962], p. 38) continued to argue that "[t]he fact is that the Great Depression, like most other periods of severe unemployment, was produced by government mismanagement rather than by inherent instability of the private economy." This is because, by definition or applied-ethical posture,[4] government failure results in worse outcomes than market failure. In such a way, private hands are always preferable. Even on the grounds of the redistribution of economic outcome, income, and wealth, nation-state policy is better not being involved due to the applied-ethical argument that the market outcome is the just outcome. Therefore, there is no need for discretionary income and wealth redistribution policies derived from nation-state policy intervention in the free-market functions. According to the neoclassical economic premises, nation-state policy intervention is limited to the applied economic decisions and actions. Free-market relations and the market mechanism lead to the efficient production and allocation of products. If this is true, however, what is the necessity of nation-state policy?

In order to appraise the above inquiry, it is necessary to review the current ideological and applied-ethical economic doctrine of neoliberalism.[5] "The doctrine is that all, or virtually all, economic and social problems have a market solution, with the corollary that state failure is typically worse than market failure" (Howard and King, 2004, p. 40; see also Harvey, 2005, p. 2; DeMartino, 2000, p. 4; and Chang, 2002, among others, for similar definitions). The main idea of neoliberals is that every policy, decision, and action, whether at the societal or individual

[3] According to the neoclassical theory of economics, market failures occur when the market mechanism fails to produce or allocate products efficiently. The reasons for such failures can be seen in imperfect competition, externalities, public goods, and the 'free rider' problem.

[4] In neoclassical economics, the private market efficiency argument is viewed as an applied-ethical posture, as neoclassical economics has specific assumptions and empirical results that support this argument.

[5] In this book (Chapters 3 and 4), it has been arguably claimed that neoliberalism, as an ideology and applied-ethical doctrine in international development, is scientifically sustained by neoclassical economic theory.

level, should advance the economic outcome through private market relations. Nation-state policy is imposed in this view. Specifically, the role of nation-state policy is to generate and protect the institutional framework in which free-market relations run. For instance, in a globalised market environment, one of the main purposes of nation-state policy is not to restrict or tax trade but to use all the nation-state's authority to extend the freedom of trade within and beyond its national boundaries. Therefore, "[i]n the neo-liberal framework, the ideal market is equated with the 'perfectly competitive market' of neoclassical economics" (Chang, 2002, p. 544). To this end, nation-state policy develops and controls the monitoring and suppression mechanisms and institutions, such as military defence, police, and other legal functions and structures formed as state institutions. By controlling monitoring and suppression mechanisms and institutions, nation-state policy forces the 'right' functioning of the economy and politics in the direction of free-market relations and capitalist democracy functions. In this regard, liberal thinkers such as Nozick (1974) and Buchanan (1986) have argued that "the state has emerged as a 'contractual' solution to the collective action problem of providing the public good of law and order, especially the security of private property, which is seen as necessary (and often sufficient) for markets to function" (Chang, 2002, p. 547, brackets in the original). In this framework, nation-state policy secures the established private property rights and capitalist productive relationships. In addition, nation-state policy sets up (mainly through privatising public ownership) free-market relations in fields where free-market conditions have not traditionally been employed, such as education, health, social provision, and water supply. Thus, for Howard and King (2004, p. 40):

> The practice is the continuing and increasingly intensive application of this doctrine [neoliberalism] to an ever-expanding area of life in the real world, via the privatization of state industries and public services, the elimination of 'dependency cultures' and the introduction of market-mimicking arrangements to those areas of government activity that remain unprivatized.

Furthermore, nation-state policy diminishes the role of labour unions and social movements by trying to eliminate any form of class struggle. Such neoliberal practices were activated by Thatcher in the United Kingdom and by Reagan in the United States in the 1980s and have generally been applied in almost all development programmes in the developing world. However, nation-state policy against collective institutions such as labour unions and other forms of social coordination on the ground level of the society raises a contradiction "between a seductive but alienating possessive individualism on the one hand and the desire for a meaningful collective life on the other" (Harvey, 2005, p. 69). This, also, fashions a paradox of the nation-state policy intervention regarding individuals' choices between collective action and political freedom. The intention of nation-state policy interventionism in the direction that has been discussed is derived from elites and political authorities in a world in which it is supposed that the state should not be interventionist. According to this line of reasoning, nation-state policy considers the solvency of market institutions, the integrity of the financial system, and the domestic economy's results or outcomes like the reduction of public deficit, for example. In this regard, the nation-state applies its policy, financial, monetary, and public economic orders by following the dominant perspectives among international development institutions, intergovernmental organisations, and inter-regional political structures. The role of the international development institutions' policies in the applied-ethical basis of international development is specified in the following section.

2.3 Applied Ethics and Institutional Policy in International Development

Globalisation and the role of international parameters are not new phenomena in worldwide economic history, international relations, and international development. Nevertheless, the role of international development institutions' policies as it is discussed here is relatively new in global affairs. More analytically, prior to the Great Depression of 1929, US President Roosevelt's New Deal in 1933, and World War II [1939–1945], international political and economic orders were based exclusively on the relations structured as the clear political and military power of the nations in the conception of Hans Morgenthau's *Politics among Nations* (Morgenthau, 1948), following traditional political realism in international politics. Accordingly, political power refers mainly to the international political and military power of each nation and the interplay between nations at the international level. In recent times, explanations of political realism have remained powerful in international relations theory and international political economy studies (Waltz, 1979; Gilpin, 2001; 2001; Cohen, 2008).

However, since the end of the Cold War until now (1990 and beyond), we can evidently argue for a different face of political realism, moving power from the politics of nations to international development institutions' policies, usually referred to as neoliberal institutionalism. According to Gilpin (2001, p. 379), neoliberal institutionalism advocates that formal international regimes such as international development institutions are necessary and have become sufficiently strong to meet the challenges of a globalised market economy for developing economies. As political economists and international relations theorists point out, nation-states continue to be at the centre of analysis; nevertheless, they are not by any means the sole actors in international development. Nation-states and their interplay are perhaps the foremost ideas in international relations; however, this does not mean that traditional political realism is "the billiard ball model of rational, unitary states, conceived as closed 'black boxes' driven solely by calculations of national interest and power" (Cohen, 2008, p. 14). After the end of World War II, from the side of free-market economies, international development institutions [e.g., the World Bank, the International Monetary Fund (IMF), and the World Trade Organization (WTO)], were established to expand and protect the global free-market relations system and to promote prosperity (economic growth) to the developing world. As Gilpin (2001, p. 42) mentions, "during the Cold War, the Western international economic system, under American leadership, was intended to strengthen security ties against the Soviet Union." After the economic depression of the 1970s, the intense influence of neoliberalism in the 1980s, and the closing moments of the Cold War at the end of the 1980s, international development institutions have shifted their policies in the direction of the applied neoliberal policies in international development.

This fact also describes the passage from classical liberalism to neoliberal institutionalism. While classical liberalism shifts the emphasis of policy action to accelerate and secure the progress of liberalisation at the national level, "[n]eoliberal institutionalism places heavy emphasis on mechanisms of intergovernmental policy cooperation to achieve liberal outcomes consonant with the maintenance of order in the international system" (Sally, 1998, p. 177). In the case of classical liberalism, we can briefly express it as 'liberalism from below', where 'below' is the decision-making and the applied policy at the level of the nation-state. Neoliberal institutionalism can be shortly described as 'liberalism from above', in which 'above' means the imposed international development institutions' policies for nations and internationally.

Nevertheless, at either of the two levels, in contemporary international development, the main applied-ethical idea of the dominant development policy remains faithful to the core principles and liberal background of neoclassical economics. What has changed is the historical epoch. The term 'neoliberal institutionalism' better describes the intention and magnitude of the liberalisation of the international development institutions' policies around the globe in the absence of alternative forms of applied policy in international development. In a similar way, Craig and Porter (2006, p. 13, capitalisation as per original) depict neoliberal institutionalism as a "historical high point of Liberal hegemony in Development". What is worth mentioning is that the liberalisation of the applied policies of international development institutions is a matter of power (political and economic) and an issue of dominant economics and international politics. The international development institutions' policies reflect such economic and political issues.

Now let us illustrate some points regarding the applied-ethical scope of the international development institutions' policies in recent times. According to their official declarations, the applied-ethical role of the international institutions' policies is to bring about and secure prosperity for international development. The IMF's monetary and financial policies, as well as the structural reforms assistance it provides to developing countries, have had a leading position among the international development institutions' policies. So, taking as a suitable example the IMF's official "about us"[6] demonstration, at the level of scope, the IMF is "working to foster global monetary cooperation, secure financial stability, facilitate international trade, promote high employment and sustainable economic growth, and reduce poverty around the world." Similar announcements can be found in the aims and scopes of other international institutions (e.g., the World Bank and the World Trade Organization). Their official declarations ideally define the ethical means and ends of development as well as the framework for achieving a good society. In practice, however, the dominant international development institutions' policies have been challenged. The results of the applied policies on economics, societal

[6] http://www.imf.org/external/about.htm.

aspects, and (in some cases) political structures are not consistent with the demonstrated ethical image of a good society.

2.3.1 *The Washington Consensus as a Policy for International Development*

The Washington Consensus policy applied in Latin America is perhaps the most explicit intervention of international development institutions' policies in international development in the years since 1980. The Washington Consensus is described as the lowest common denominator of the applied policy advice being addressed by the following Washington-based institutions and think tanks: the International Monetary Fund (IMF), the World Bank, the US Executive Branch, the Federal Reserve Board, the Inter-American Development Bank, and those members of Congress concerned with economic policy in Latin American countries (Williamson, 1990).

The term 'Washington Consensus' has, however, overcome the initial connotations established by its conceptual father, Williamson, and its exclusive relevance to Latin American countries. The term is commonly used in a political economy context in order to describe the applied neoliberal policies in international development. Therefore, the Washington Consensus has a dual explanation. In the first explanation, the Washington Consensus is a mixture of applied economic policies imposed on Latin American countries in the 1980s and 1990s. In this view, the Washington Consensus can be perceived as a set of applied policies that are geographically and historically specific. In the second definition, the Washington Consensus can be seen as a counterpart of the worldwide neoliberal policies or, rather, as a manifesto of the neoliberal policies applied in a wide range of geographical situations in international development: Africa, Latin America, Central and Eastern Europe, and East Asia.

In recent literature, the Washington Consensus has been examined as an international development policy doctrine and as a neoliberal manifesto or similar, either in Latin America or internationally. As well as being discussed in works by the Institute of International Economics and works based on Williamson's orthodox views (Williamson, 2007; Bergsten and Henning (eds.), 2012; Kuczynski and Williamson (eds.), 2003), the Washington Consensus is explored in the works of Arrébola-Rodríguez (2011), Broad and Cavanagh (1999), Cross and Strachan (2001), Rodrik (2006), Gore (2000), Kolodko (2000), Levinson (2000),

Marangos (2007; 2009a; 2009b), Naim (1994), Srinivasan (2000), Stiglitz (1998b; 2000a; 2002b), Fine et al. (eds.) (2003), and Serra and Stiglitz (eds.) (2008), among others. In regard to this literature, the Washington Consensus has been analysed in its historical evolutionary context (Rodrik, 2006; Marangos, 2009a; 2009b), in terms of the impact it has had on the transitional economies of Eastern and Central Europe (Arrébola-Rodríguez, 2011; Kolodko, 2000; Marangos, 2007), in terms of its contradictions with methodology and ideology (Gore, 2000; Naim, 1994; Marangos 2009a), in terms of the mainstream critique or defence (Serra and Stiglitz (eds.), 2008), and in reference to radical political economy appraisals (Fine et al. (eds.), 2003). A common view of almost all the aforementioned studies is the association of the applied Washington Consensus policies with the dominance of international development institutions' policies in international development.

The Washington Consensus despite its evolutionary changes, its impact on transitional economies, the alternative economic and political explanations, and the criticism it has received (orthodox or heterodox)—remains persistent regarding its meta-ethical orientation and normative-ethical evaluation of the means and ends of international development. At the meta-ethical level, the Washington Consensus policy goals are those of a globalised market economy and Western-type material influence through economic growth in the developing world. These concepts are commonly referred to collectively as prosperity. Regarding the normative-ethical issue, as already argued, the Washington Consensus is consistent with the normative-ethical evaluation of neoclassical welfarism, economic rationalism, and neoliberal ideology.[7] From this perspective, all views of the Washington Consensus and the orthodox Post-Washington Consensus are consistent with the neoclassical ethical image of a good international society as a globalised market economy.

The applied Washington Consensus proves that, after the end of the Cold War, the dominant international institutions' policies have essentially remained unchanging in their ethical orientations. From the angle of the dominant applied policy, Williamson (1993, p. 1331) claims that "[t]he hope that we can now develop far more consensus than would have been conceivable or appropriate in the 1950s is based ultimately on the

[7] This has already been discussed in Chapter 5. The normative-ethical evaluation of the Washington Consensus, as a neoliberal manifesto in international development, is mainly based on its original or initial design.

fact that we now know much more about what types of economic policy work." Williamson directly implies the free-market economics policy. On this issue, Rodrik (2006, p. 974) argues that:

> With the fall of the Berlin Wall and the collapse of the Soviet Union, former socialist countries similarly made a bold leap toward markets. There was more privatization, deregulation, and trade liberalization in Latin America and Eastern Europe than probably anywhere else at any point in economic history.

Thus, the term 'Washington Consensus' refers to the specific policies and practices in Williamson's (1990) original conception applied in Latin American countries or a neoliberal manifesto applied in the rest of the transitional economies and the developing world.

More precisely, in the following paragraphs, the Washington Consensus is analysed as an applied-ethical policy guide to contemporary international development. What is meant by this? First, the applied-ethical analysis accepts the meta-ethical and normative-ethical appraisal of the Washington Consensus, as applied ethics reflects the meta-ethical meanings of the ethical argument[8] and the normative-ethical relationship between the ends and the means of achieving a good life and a good society in international development. Second, the applied-ethical analysis validates the consistency of the Washington Consensus as an applied policy instrument within the previous discussion of the free-market relations and the role of nation-state policy in developing countries.

However, it is important to underline that the Washington Consensus policy guide is imposed on nation-states by orthodox international development institutions. This directly reveals the dominance of the applied-ethical international development policy in developing countries, either at the level of decision-making or at the level of applied policies. At the applied-ethical level of analysis, the Washington Consensus can be seen as an applied policy guide that international development institutions and groups of power (along with the dominant views of worldwide policy-making, based on neoclassical economic analysis and neoliberal ideology

[8] The ethical argument in the present analysis, as has already been defined, is based on the concepts of a good life and a good society. The Washington Consensus has been viewed as an end (policy objectives) and as a mean (policy instruments) to achieve the previously mentioned ethical argument in the field of international development.

and practices) have applied in real-world situations in international development, as in the case of Latin American countries. Finally, derived from the application of the Washington Consensus in Latin American countries, the analysis reveals the applied-ethical role of international intuitions' policies in the whole spectrum of international development.

Historically, the Washington Consensus can be seen as an evolutionary experience of the international development institutions' policies in international development, as "the evolution of the term mirrors the evolution of economic thought on economic development for nearly the last two decades" (Marangos, 2009b, p. 350). The Washington Consensus, as the applied scheme of the dominant international development institutions' policies, operates (1) institutional and structural reform policies; (2) fiscal policies; and (3) monetary policies in the developing world. The original Washington Consensus policies and the applied policies in international development that perceive the Washington Consensus as a neoliberal manifesto are revealed in the following table (Table 1).

In the first column, the applied policies are ranked; in the second and third columns, the original versions of the Washington Consensus policies and the applied Washington Consensus policies in international development are briefly mentioned, respectively. The original Washington Consensus policies were applied in Latin American countries, whereas the latter are applied to the whole range of international development. The codification of the applied policies between the original version of the Washington Consensus and its expansion as a neoliberal manifesto is useful for understanding the conceptual evolution of the Washington Consensus. Furthermore, it principally indicates the differences between the specific policies applied in Latin America and the development policies applied in the rest of the developing world. As the table shows, the chief features of the Washington Consensus as a manifesto of the neoliberal development policy in international development are: (1) mass privatisation; (2) extreme price liberalisation; and (3) unregulated openness to the market forces of the global market. As it seems, the mixture of these development policies assimilates the fundamental applied-ethical premise of neoliberalism: that free-market economics and government policy interference in this direction would solve the existing market inefficiencies in developing economies. In this regard, the applied-ethical analysis of international development institutions' policies in international development remains unchanged, as the core of the meta-ethical vision and

Table 1 International development institutions' policies based on the Washington consensus

Policy	*Original Washington consensus policy*	*Applied policy in international development: the Washington consensus as a neoliberal manifesto*
1. Fiscal discipline	Small budget deficit financed without recourse to inflation tax	Balanced budget
2. Public expenditure priorities	Redirect expenditure from politically sensitive areas to fields with the potential to improve income distribution, such as primary education, healthcare, and infrastructure	Reduce government expenditure
3. Tax reform	Broadening tax base and cutting marginal tax rates	Overall tax cuts and eliminate taxes that redistribute income
4. Financial liberalisation	Market-determined interest rates	As per the original Washington Consensus
5. Exchange rates	A unified competitive exchange rate	Convertible, freely floating exchange rates
6. Trade liberalisation	Replace quantitative trade restrictions with tariffs of around 10–20%	Free trade and the elimination of protection and capital controls
7. Foreign direct investment	Abolish barriers to entry for foreign firms	As per the original Washington Consensus
8. Privatisation	State enterprises should be privatised	As per the original Washington Consensus
9. Deregulation	Abolition of regulations that impede the entry of new firms or restrict competition	Deregulation of entry and exit barriers and the suppression of regulations designed to protect the environment
10. Property rights	Secure property rights, which are also available to the informal sector	Not a concern
11. Institution building	Not a concern	Independent central bank and money supply should grow at a fixed rate consistent with monetarism
12. Price liberalisation	No consensus. Price and wage freezes and fixed exchange rate vs. free prices	Immediate price liberalisation

Source Modified from Marangos (2009a, p. 201). Marangos (2009a) codifies the Washington Consensus as a neoliberal manifesto, mainly based on the works of Broad and Cavanagh (1999), Cross and Strachan (2001), Gore (2000), Kolodko (2000), Levinson (2000), Naim (1994), Srinivasan (2000), Stiglitz (1998; 2000a; 2002b) and Williamson's (1990) original version

the normative-ethical evaluation of the Washington Consensus remains unaffected.

Beyond the nature of the economic policies, the applied consequences of the Washington Consensus reforms in the labour market and on inequality as a major indicator of social and economic development are crucially important issues in the applied-ethical analysis. Regarding the first issue, Saavedra (2003), in his study of what happened to the labour markets in Latin America during the 1990s, acknowledges that the neoliberal reforms had a negative impact on employment, particularly on job positions relating to the public sector, state-owned enterprises, and protected manufacturing industries. At the same time, in the private sector, employment creation occurred but with low-quality jobs. Commenting on the second issue, Behrman et al. (2003) apply an index combining a set of policy changes in six fields according to the Washington Consensus neoliberal reforms for 18 Latin American countries for the period 1977–1998. These fields were trade policy, financial policy, tax policy, external capital transactions policy, privatisation policy, and labour policy. The authors questioned if these policy changes had increased wage differentials and income inequality. Their evident answer is precisely 'yes'. However, they relate the profound inequality to educational level and other inefficiencies of the market structure.

It is important to mention that both of the aforementioned studies are based on neoclassical economic analysis. Consequently, the application of the Washington Consensus in Latin America has evidently shown that the applied neoliberal policies and practices failed in terms of economic and social development. Thus, more than a decade later, Williamson (2002) criticised the way that neoliberal reforms had been applied in Latin American countries and somewhat accepted the failure of the initial Washington Consensus by mentioning "it is important to analyze why growth and employment and poverty reduction were disappointing in countries that attempted to implement the sort of policies that I intended to cover under the term" (Williamson, 2002, p. 3). To this end, the failure of the Washington Consensus in Latin American countries, particularly in the field of social development, can be viewed as evidence of the applied-ethical consequences of the dominant international development institutional policy in international development.

As has been already claimed, the applied-ethical basis of international development in the era of globalisation and neoliberalism is composed of a framework of free-market relations, nation-state policy, and international development institutions' directives. Within this framework, neoclassical economics tends to believe that the principles that govern development policy are universal in character; thus, the policies applied to international development are essentially similar everywhere. In fact, the view that free-market policies can promote worldwide prosperity, good lives for individuals, and a good global society is an applied-ethical premise of neoclassical economics and neoliberalism. Taken as a whole, the applied international development policy can be explained as an ethics in itself: as a global ethics derived from the meta-ethical orientation and normative-ethical evaluation of the present form of international development as a globalised market economy.

3 The Development Ethics Applied-Ethical Alternative to International Development

3.1 Applied Development Ethics

There is a strong position among development ethicists of accepting applied development ethics as identical to global ethics served as the ethics of global development (Croker, 1991; 2008) or as world ethics (Dower, 1998a) and as a criticism of the economic globalisation and Westernised modernisation in the real-world situation of international development (Goulet, 1983; 2006a; Stiglitz, 1998; 2002c; St. Clair, 2007). In this approach, applied development ethics is perceived as many things together or separately, including international relations and the divisions between the North and the South; national trajectories and public policies; and institutional/organisational contact, and personal relations/individual contact (Gasper, 2012, p. 122). In the development ethics literature, there is also a body of knowledge, sometimes coming from the same scholars of development ethics, that approaches applied development ethics as a kind of professional ethics in its broader definition. In this approach, applied development ethics contributes to different areas of the profession in an eclectic manner. For instance, Gasper and Truong (2005) call for an agenda of debates between development ethics and human security; Murithi (2009) synthesises applied moral philosophy with international relations, involving issues such as the ethics of negotiation, mediation, forgiveness, and reconciliation; Crocker and Linden (eds.) (1998) investigate various issues of the ethics of consumption in the principles of development ethics (a good life, justice, and global stewardship); Camacho (2008) explores agricultural intensification from the perspective of development ethics; Goulet (1992c) discusses international ethics and human rights; Pogge (2008; 2005) scrutinises the moral and economic reasoning of global poverty and how economic policy and ethical considerations affect human rights; McNeill and St. Clair (2009) also analyse global poverty and human rights in reference to the role of multilateral institutions, from the angle of development ethics; Dower (1983; 2005) examines the role of global ethics in environmental responsibility; and Harry (2010) explores applied issues related to world ethics, climate change, and social justice. Subsequently, the editors of the volume titled *Development Ethics*, Gasper and St. Clair (2010a, 2010b, p. xv), point out that applied development ethics is comparable to other fields of professional ethics. The relevance of development ethics to global ethics can be better seen as "a forum for serious reflection (including feeling), on a broader scale than implied in the traditional model of professional ethics" (Gasper, 2004, p. 21).

In the framework of global ethics, development ethics serves not only for theoretical reflection but also for application and practice. According to the International Development Ethics Association (IDEA)[9], 'application' means that development ethicists from different affiliations (e.g., social scientists, technologists, and agriculturists) can assimilate their expertise with properly articulated values, while 'practice' denotes that policy-makers in the development process can gain from ethical reflections and hold ethical thinking firmly rooted in, and informed by development practice (see also Dutt and Wilber, 2010b, p. 15).

At the applied-ethical level of the present analysis, applied development ethics is conceived both as global ethics and as an ethical reflection on the field of professional ethics regarding local, national, and international development. The novel exploration of the current analysis is that it embodies applied development ethics as a form of global ethics in the context of political economy. In this light, applied development ethics stands as an alternative to the applied form of economic development and the policies imposed either by nation-states or by international development institutions in the applied-ethical framework of free-market relations and neoliberalism. In this attempt, the discussion of the applied

[9] http://developmentethics.org/about-2/what-is-development-ethics/.

development ethics alternative follows the structure of the aforementioned analysis of the applied-ethical basis of contemporary international development.

3.2 *Applied Development Ethics and Free Markets in International Development*

According to neoclassical economics, a free market is efficient in terms of economics because the established free-market relations lead to the efficient allocation of resources and equilibrium conditions in the economy, either nationally or internationally. In neoclassical economic modelling, an equilibrium condition in the demand and supply curves is the ideal economic situation. Neoclassical economists assume that free-market relations maximise consumers' consumption as the excess of supply leads to the excess of demand. Moreover, free-market relations with private property rights rest on political freedom. In turn, political freedom, namely democratic capitalism, promotes prosperity. However, in many cases, particularly in developing countries, when neoclassical economists have to choose between political freedom and economic efficiency, they favour the latter. The imperative ethical idea of neoclassical economics is that free-market relations are consistent with free individual right preferences, decisions, and actions; thus, free-market relations imply the ethically 'right' manner of approaching any form of applied economic policy. Finally, for neoclassical economics, the establishment of free-market relations in international economics, in terms of open trade and free capital flows, leads to worldwide prosperity.

Are free-market relations, however, an appropriate ethical framework for applied policy in international development? To respond adequately to this question, we firstly need to understand what an appropriate applied-ethical policy is. For development ethics, an applied-ethical policy is a means and an end in itself. A good society is not only defined as an end state but also in terms of how this end state is achieved and who is benefited. In this principal development ethics idea, the existing market relations in international development ought to be tested not only at the level of demonstrational objectives but also at the level of actual social policy results, either for persons and societies or for international development as a whole. In addition, what constitutes the applied development policy as a means "will tend to vary in relation to a political community's history and stage of social change as well as to regional and global forces, such as globalization and international institutions" (Crocker, 2008, p. 42). Applied development policy as a means to larger goals cannot be universal in character as any nation or society has its own historical heritage and societal, economic, and cultural structure. Furthermore, "when the rules for states and the particular actions of states are up for evaluation, it must be with reference to the impacts on human beings" (Dower, 1998a, p. 64).

In this framework, the first set of applied development ethics queries is formed in the applied-ethical issue of who benefits from economic efficiency. The argument for economic efficiency is perhaps the main applied-ethical position of neoclassical economics resulting in the applied development policy. In addition, the ethical premise of development as economic growth through free-market relations, preached as universal values for all, may seem to many in the South as an ethical manner of promoting the values important to the leading players in the global market (Dower, 1998a, p. 32). Neoclassical economists, under the argument of economic efficiency, can straightforwardly decide among alternative development policies. Economic efficiency gives neoclassical economics a very significant advantage in the context of economic development as it directly provides a simple and powerful linkage between the theory and the specific challenges confronting applied development policy:

> If preferences and utilities constitute the human good and if free exchanges within a competitive market lead to efficient equilibria in the allocation of resources, then we can conclude that social welfare is maximized by efficient markets (Little, 2003, p. 6).

In this regard, free-market relations are an efficient manner of organising economic activity based on the preferences, actions, and choices of individuals and businesses. This view underlies the current applied-ethical framework for the free-market-relations ideal of the global economy and the imposed policies in international development, following the beliefs of neoclassical economics and neoliberalism.

Development ethics critically stands against the market-efficiency policy of neoclassical economics and how it has been employed in international development. "When it comes to evaluating economic policies, efficiency needs to be supplemented with ethical judgments" (Wilber, 2010, p. 168). Development ethics follows a specific ethical manner of approaching free markets and economic efficiency in relation to poor people and societies in developing countries. With reference to the poor peoples of the developing world, Goulet (2006a, p. 46) points out that the "existing structures are biassed in favour of elitist conceptions of efficiency." Development ethics relates the existing free-market relations and economic efficiency to the notion of structural vulnerability, where structural vulnerability is defined as the case in which poor people do not have access to the decision-making process. In this way, market relations are biassed by professional elites and business specialists.

Similarly, economic efficiency is approached as an ethically vacant term if it cannot exist alongside the populace's participation in the market functions. Thus:

> The difficult elaboration of a suitable ethics and wisdom of development requires an unending effort to redefine efficiency, to contrast culturally multiple images of development, and to create new forms of power-sharing among specialists and populace (Goulet, 2006a, p. 48).

Nevertheless, in neoclassical economics, individual preferences are based on rational choices among alternative options, derived from self-interested behaviour. This ethical idea involves an instrumental conceptualisation of rationality in the sense that individual choices and actions are carried out in a rational manner to realise economic-efficiency goals. In the writings of Peter Sedgwick, the instrumental conceptualisation of rationality "says nothing about how goals are decided, or what they might be"; thus, ethical concepts such as "'the good' are discounted" (Sedgwick, 2004, p. 36). Utilising this approach, development ethicists denote that, within the market mechanism, it is difficult to define individual preferences in the ethical concept of a good life, in the sense of meeting actual human needs, because markets usually force the effective purchasing power of those individuals or groups who already have more than enough, while poor people and socially excluded groups lack participation in economic and political decision-making. In addition, markets can strengthen the power of producers to control the preferences of potential consumers.

In spite of this, neoclassical economists, in the tradition of utilitarianism, set down the concept of the simple aggregation and maximisation of individual utilities (Crocker, 2008, p. 46). Many neoclassical economists use individual preference satisfaction as a criterion for measuring the success of a development policy. In applied-ethical terms, this can be labelled as a case of consequentialism. It can be explained in the tradition of utilitarianism: the ethical premise that the morally relevant features of a policy result from the outcomes. "Neoclassical economics is a special case of consequentialism because it restricts its attention to one particular set of consequences: effects on the utility of agents" (Wilber, 2010, p. 169). For individual preferences satisfaction, "[t]here is no mechanism for collective decisions or for critical analysis of desires to determine if they meet genuine needs or alienate human satisfactions" (Goulet, 2006a, p. 58). Thus, the neoclassical position of the economic efficiency of the free market is deficient in terms of applied ethics in most real-world situations. Usually, poor people in the developing world do not have access to decision-making in the framework of free-market relations in which policy decisions are taken and economically efficient applied policies are formulated. "Markets as masters of society enrich the rich and pauperize the poor" (Ward, 1976, p. xii; see also Goulet, 2006a, p. 180). In light of this, free-market relations and economic efficiency are ethically deficient for development policy, if we accept that a good development policy ought to work as an adequate means to a good society.

The participation of poor peoples in decision-making in either the market or other social institutions can be seen as an applied development ethics alternative to the proposed neoclassical economics formulation of free-market relations and economic efficiency. As development ethicists assert, "[t]his ethical stance clearly differs from an ethic of pure efficiency in societal problem-solving, or an ethic of elitist interest rationalization and protection" (Goulet, 2006a, p. 42). In addition, applied development ethics recognises that markets are embedded as a subsystem in a larger societal system. This societal system mainly involves social and institutional structures that adequately support ethical goals and civic values such as social justice, the elimination of poverty, environmental sustainability, and economic, political, and spiritual sufficiency for all people. Free-market relations (or, put it differently, free-market competitive functions and economic efficiency) cannot adequately work as the basic organising principle for broad societal and ethical aims, such as equity, sufficient goods for all people, ecological integrity, and the elimination of large-scale systematic violence of human life. "It is this larger societal system which must provide the organizing principle of economic activity and the rules of governance for making market competition function as a social mechanism at the service of that organizing principle" (Goulet, 2006a, p. 181).

A second set of arguments in the applied-ethical neoclassical economic discourse is based on the conception that the establishment of a free-market economy results in the promotion of political freedom. In this way, many neoclassical economists perceive political freedom as an extension of the economic freedom derived from the liberalisation of the economy. For this reason, structural reform in the direction of the liberalisation of market functions and the institutional fabric of developing societies is believed to promote liberal democracy, as has been occurring in developed societies. Neoclassical economics is very much premised on the conceptions of development policy on the values of the free market and individual freedom. For development ethicists, there are more general, rather than materialist and individualist, conceptions of a good life and a good society. The approach of free markets (along with economic and political freedom through liberalisation) constitutes a flawed developmental and socio-political order to the ethical exploration of a good life and a good society.[10] This stance, "in being presented as a global ethic, may well be guilty of a kind of 'cultural imperialism' if it is seen as something to be imposed on societies which do not share these values" (Dower, 1998a, p. 144). Economic, political, and (as a consequence) cultural imperialism are central concepts in the applied development ethics debates on freedom. To this end, Goulet (2006a, p. 139) points out that "[t]his approach also leads to undue destruction of cultural values because it is uncritically biassed in favour of modernity, which it treats in all important respects as superior to tradition." Freedom means respecting differences, rather than promoting a Western-type free-market development policy. An ethical development policy has to accept the principles of cultural relativism, in which each separate nation or community "does and should devise its own ethical code for guiding and assessing its own behavior" (DeMartino, 2000, p. 22). In this way, applied development ethics defends a cross-cultural notion of freedom.

Beyond the criticism of the Westernised modernisation of free-market relations in international development, development ethics offers an ethical alternative. The debates on the ethical alternative in accordance with freedom and development policy are long in the development ethics literature. "Freedom is a powerful term, but fuzzy and unclear" (St. Clair, 2010, p. 264). Freedom is one of the core ideas and an ethical

[10] This point also reveals major limitations and failings of the *a*historical, *a*political, context-free neoclassical and neoliberal analyses.

goal of development ethics. “Any ethics whose goal is to make humans ‘be more’ ought to lead people to freedom” (Goulet, 2006a, p. 35). If we look for agreement within development ethicists’ discussions of freedom and development policy, this might be found in the writings of Goulet and his general premise that “[t]his defence of freedom, in the face of the seductive flattery of the myth of happiness, is the fundamental task of any development ethics which is realistic and effective” (Goulet, 2006a, p. 35; see also Goulet, 1976) and Sen’s notion of ‘development as freedom’ in relation to the ethical criticism of the rationality implications of the neoclassical economics development policy (Sen, 2004; 1999; 1987; 1977).

In the discussion of freedom and market relations, development ethicists such as Sen are not generally opposed to the concept of freedom of exchanges and transactions within the market. Commenting on the classical political economy conception of market exchanges, Sen (1999, p. 6) argues that “freedom of exchange and transactions is itself part and parcel of the basic liberties that people have reason to value.” Nonetheless, freedom and free-market relations as they are implied in the neoclassical economics development policy need further applied-ethical examination in relation to ethical values, as economics has tended to study utilities, income, and wealth, rather than focusing on the value of freedom (Sen, 1999, p. 27). Usually, the term ‘freedom’ is posed as an end state of the applied development policy, without deeper ethical incorporation. If we have to accept freedom only as an abstract demonstrational objective of development policy, then there is the issue that “even tyrants profess to cherish freedom and warmongers peace” (Goulet, 2006a, p. 42). By contrast, “[t]he objective of development relates to the valuation of actual freedom enjoyed by the people involved” (Sen, 1999, p. 53). The development ethics discussion of freedom and development policy can mainly be positioned on the grounds of values, equity, participation, capabilities, and the concept of development as freedom. Furthermore, other development ethicists (Crocker, 2008; Goulet, 2006a; Gasper, 2002) agree with Sen’s (1999, p. 53) ethical position that:

> The ends and means of development call for placing the perspective of freedom at the center of the stage. The people have to be seen, in this perspective, as being actively involved—given the opportunity—in shaping their own destiny, and not just as passive recipients of the fruits of cunning development programs.

Crocker (2008, pp. 157–158), based on Sen's development policy views and his own view of the notion of freedom as development, argues for an agent-oriented approach in development policy, which is built on the applied-ethical general premise that "with adequate social opportunities, individuals can effectively shape their own destiny and help each other".

A third set of arguments of neoclassical economics is that free-market relations within a globalised economy provide worldwide economic prosperity. Adherents of free-market economics put this clearly: "trade enhances growth, and that growth reduces poverty" (Bhagwati, 2004, p. 3). In the discussion of globalisation and prosperity, St. Clair (2010, p. 253) gives an applied development ethics interpretation: "'[g]lobalisation friendly' policies are held to lend to more 'development', defenders argue, and the proof is often presented in the guise of poverty data, showing decreases in poverty over time as evidence of this fairness." Globalisation and the current model of economic growth bring benefits and gains to a small part of the world, to either producers or consumers. However, do global free-market relations increase, even steadily, the prosperity of extremely poor people in the developing world? In such societies, extremely poor people are often neither producers nor consumers (St. Clair, 2010, p. 253). They live and act outside of the sphere of the usual applied market functions. Thus, the ethical framework applied for free-market relations and a globalised market economy is inappropriate for addressing development policies towards poverty reduction. In contrast, globalisation forces involve worldwide policies that increase extreme poverty, particularly for those people and societies excluded by free-market functions. In other words, the applied-ethical framework of free-market relations negatively affects international development and poor people's lives.

In the conventional framework of a globalised economy, free-market relations are assisted by a system of individual property rights and businesses. This is necessary to lay the groundwork for business enterprise, either nationally or internationally: "[a] system of contract, accounting, and private rules and guidelines provides the basis for a spirit of enterprise" (O'Hara, 2006, p. 51). These rules and guidelines are driven by the meta-ethical orientation of a free-market economy as a profit economy. Business expansion and profits, not poverty reduction, are the 'metric system' of globalisation, according to the policy discussion we have explored.

This can be further explained with an adequate and concise example from the commodities and food sector, as these fields directly influence consumption and poor people's lives. During the years 2007–2008, the field of commodities and particularly the food sector confronted a crisis. The prices of the food bought and sold in international stock markets increased dramatically. According to the International Monetary Fund (IMF), "in commodities generally, speculative activity responded to price movements rather than the other way round… A large part of the reason, it decided, was financial buying" (*Financial Times*, cited in Lines, 2010, p. 1). In addition, therefore (particularly after the credit crisis of 2007), international investors found that the prices of shares, commercial property, and financial derivatives had stopped increasing. On the other hand, there had been upward movement in commodity and food prices. Thus, international stock market buyers invested in this sector. Some of the fastest moving prices were for corn, wheat, and rice, which started to rise rapidly in price. In the beginning of 2008, more and more capital flows were diverted into commodities, and commodity prices started to increase faster and faster. International funds turned their financial attention to commodities and, largely, to the food sector. When the banks cut back their financial liquidness in the middle of 2008, prices for commodities and food fell back by up to 20 per cent (Lines, 2010, p. 2). Afterwards, the U.S. launched the first of its schemes to save the banks' finances; credit flowed and commodity prices took off once more. It is noteworthy that, when loans were used to finance grain price speculation, ordinary people's savings were used, without their knowledge or choice, to make poorer people go hungry. Hence, "[i]t is such speculation that turned a food price problem into a world crisis" (Lines, 2010, p. 2). The reason is simple. Global financial investors do not mind where or how they make profits as long as they make them. In the aforementioned example, speculation—not food shortages or scarcity—was responsible for the food crisis and the increase in prices that resulted. The food crisis was based on speculation, on business and financial profits contrary to the neoclassical economics demonstrations of prosperity within a global framework of free-market relations. Inspired by this example, an applied-ethical question needs to be investigated: 'is the goal of making profits an immoral economic behaviour in free-market economic relations?' The above example of the speculation in the food commodity market is mentioned because it principally shows that the existing free-market relations and its applied-ethical orientation affected economic and social choices, which in turn negatively affected poor people's lives, specifically extremely poor people.

3.3 Applied Development Ethics and Nation-State Policy

In this section, we deploy a further investigation of the applied-ethical role of nation-state policy in times of neoliberalism and illustrate possible agreement on the applied development ethics alternative. It is maintained as a possible agreement because, to our knowledge, the literature on development ethics has so far not included a specific discussion against neoliberal policies on the grounds of the implemented nation-state policies.

In the considerations of neoclassical economics regarding nation-state policy in the direction of good lives for people and a good society, there is an apparent contradiction. In theory, neoclassical economics suggests no governmental interventions in the market functions and the elimination of state power in the economy. On the other hand, by adopting the principles of neoliberalism, nation-state policy results in the privatisation of the economy by fostering free-market relations in almost any field of the economy, such as education, health services, and social protection. To this effect, Harvey (2005, p. 21) points out that "[w]e have to pay careful attention, therefore, to the tension between the theory of neoliberalism [related with neoclassical economic theory] and the actual pragmatics of neoliberalization." Furthermore, in many international development economic crises, for instance the debt crisis of Mexico in 1982, nation-state policy protected the financial sector by socialising its loss. Such nation-state policy is based on the neoliberal practice in which profits are privatised while risks are socialised. Neoliberals favour nation-state policies that "privatize profits and socialize risks; save the banks and put the screws on the people" (Harvey, 2010, p. 10).

In terms of ethical analysis, this apparent contradiction between neoclassical theory and neoliberal practice has been explained in the 'outcome' principle of utilitarianism. Neoclassical economics and the applied neoliberal policies in international development focus on outcomes. Applied policies are formulated in accordance with the meta-ethical principles and the normative-ethical evaluation of the means and ends of international development as a globalised market economy. Within this framework, a desirable applied policy leads to the best outcome, interwoven with the meta-ethical orientation and normative-ethical appraisal of what the best outcome is. There is no objection that nation-state policy influences market outcomes (Gilpin, 2001, p. 129). However, within the discussed framework, nation-state policy avails the interests of those who gain benefits from free-market capitalism. Therefore, as mentioned, the applied nation-state policies mirror the prevailing ideology of neoliberalism in international development. Furthermore, this might be viewed as an applied ethic in the direction of economic efficiency and the materialisation of all human actions (Harvey, 2005, p. 165).

If we accept the premise that neoliberalism as a guide for nation-state policy adopts the applied-ethical position that the best policies are those based on free-market relations and the materialisation of almost all human actions in accomplishing economic efficiency, we can then argue that applied development ethics involves an alternative ethical stance against the adopted neoliberal principles in the field of nation-state policy. In existing international development, for instance, in the Washington Consensus development policies adopted by the nation-states of Latin America, neoliberals tend to impose nation-state policies towards decreasing citizens' freedoms in favour of market outcomes. By contrast, most development ethicists are moving towards the general viewpoint that any authentic form of applied development ethics must reject the notion that personal freedoms have to be shattered if economic problems are to be solved. As Goulet (2006a, p. 12, capitals in the original) underscores, "[w]e must say YES to discipline, to collective responsibility, and to limits, while saying NO to the suppression of freedom or to the reductionist 'materialization' of humans." As historical evidence has shown, the enforcement of free-market relations for almost all human actions is not always the case of providing freedom from servitudes (ignorance, misery, and exploitation by others) to all people in society. A good society frequently needs an institutional arrangement beyond free-market functions. This institutional arrangement can be found in the collective responsibility mainly derived from an appropriate applied-ethical nation-state policy regarding capability equality for all people in society. However, solidarity among the people in a particular society is a prerequisite ethical condition for any good applied-ethical policy. In addition, a nation-state policy ought to provide all the necessary goods and services (such as food, healthcare, and education) to poor people and vulnerable groups and eliminate any form of social exclusion. The abundance of goods in the ethical sense of 'enough', the solidarity among people, and the capability of the people of the nation or society to participate in the process of policy-making can be considered as an appropriate applied-ethical guide for a good nation-state policy. In this light, a good nation-state policy should remain faithful to the normative-ethical goals and strategies of development ethics, as has been previously discussed (Chapter 5). This describes an ethical framework of a good nation-state policy within applied development ethics.

In this framework and in accordance with the discussion of democracy and other forms of political governance in reference to the implementation of applied-ethical development policy in the direction of a good society, development ethicists are lucidly in favour of popular governance that functions on the principles of various modes of participation for elites and non-elites in policy-making (Drydyk, 2005; 2010; Clark, 2005; Gasper, 2002; Goulet, 1975a; 1989; Sen, 1999). A leading applied policy concept within the aforementioned analysis is that of 'a deliberative democracy' (Crocker, 2006b; 2007; 2008 [Chap. 10]; 2010). In a deliberative democracy, decision-making is perceived as non-elites' participation in local and national applied policy. Crocker (2010, p. 314) argues that, in a deliberative democracy, "[n]onelites (sometimes among themselves and sometimes with elites) deliberate together, sifting proposals and reasons to forge agreements that at least a majority can accept." In a similar vein, Drydyk (2005; 2010) asserts that a deliberative democracy (or, in his words, 'participatory development') serves both empowerment and democratic functioning. Empowerment is perceived as the process in which people become the agents of their own development (Drydyk, 2010, p. 336). Democratic functioning suggests that popular governance cannot be exercised only by those who have been chosen by elections; instead, all people's capabilities regarding decision-making should be enhanced. "Political life functions more democratically when political influence on decision-making affecting valuable capabilities is better shared" (Drydyk, 2010, p. 339). Meanwhile, as nation-state policy is related to the control of resources and the institutional fabric of a nation, a deliberative democracy means that non-elite participation results in people's decision-making in the control of resources and institutions towards a good society (Crocker, 2010, p. 312). Thus, in the existing democracies, even if nation-state policy is upstream oriented by political and economic elites, ordinary people's participation in decision-making, at multiple levels of the societal structure, "guarantees government's non-instrumental treatment of powerless people by bringing them dignity as beings of worth, independent of their productivity, utility, or importance to state goals" (Goulet, 1989, p. 175). To this end, for development ethicists, the right kind of participation in decision-making, whether it is in a pure form of deliberative democracy or in the direction of the aforementioned type of decision-making, "is likely to have good consequences in reducing poverty, expanding solidarity, and strengthening self-reliance" (Crocker, 2010, p. 311). Consequently, a good nation-state policy is based on popular governance with the highest number of people participating in the decision-making towards a deliberative democracy and popular governance functioning.

Regarding applied-ethical policy and the debate between the private sector and the public sector, development ethicists address a space for convergence. This convergence holds the general position that, within a nation or society, the applied development policy needs both a good private sector and a good public sector. Neither of the two can work in the direction of a good life and a good society without the adequate response of the other. Stiglitz (1998) addresses the aforementioned idea on the grounds of applied policy towards a new development paradigm after the failure of the Washington Consensus as the dominant applied policy guide in international development.[11] More precisely, in the debate between the private and public sectors, Stiglitz (1998, p. 18) argues that a good applied development policy should involve both sectors, as well as the community, the family, and the individual. Stiglitz (1998) begins his analysis by proposing a couple of institutional policies for the efficiency of the private sector. "A key objective is the creation of a strong, competitive, stable and efficient private sector" (Stiglitz, 1998, p. 18). He also presents a set of policies for community, family, and individual actions. What is most important for our analysis at this point is his proposed strategy for the nation-state policy. Accordingly:

> Central ingredients to the public sector strategy are (i) a focus of the public sector on the unique functions that it must perform, such as: creating the enabling environment for the private sector... ensuring that health

[11] Stiglitz is mentioned in the recent development ethics literature as a contributor to development ethics. For his particular contribution to the subject matter of democracy and globalisation, see Crocker's (2006a) paper "Development Ethics, Globalization, and Stiglitz".

> and education are widely available; and spearheading the drive to eliminate poverty; (ii) a strengthening of the capabilities of the public sector, including the development of an effective civil service, and a restructuring of the public sector, to make more effective use of incentives and of market and market-like mechanisms; and (iii) a matching both of responsibilities and modes of operation to the capabilities of the State (Stiglitz, 1998, pp. 19–20).

Development ethicists agree with the general viewpoint that the crucial question of applied policy is "how the two [the private and public sectors] can best complement each other, acting as partners in the development effort" (Stiglitz, 1998, p. 19). However, applied development ethics rejects the neoclassical economics argument of private market efficiency without state involvement. Economic efficiency is beneficial if it leads people and society to better lives, eliminates poverty, and reduces inequality. Meanwhile, as development ethicists observe, the formation of efficiency in neoclassical economics omits interpersonal equity (Gasper, 2004, p. 80; Wilber, 2010, p. 168). Thus, if economic efficiency is to be achieved in the private market, an alternative institutional framework for eliminating the negative impacts of free-market relations on social policy should be invented. These negative consequences of the free market for poor people and vulnerable groups in society call for an alternative role of nation-state policy beyond the applied neoclassical economic premises and applied neoliberal policy. For instance, Jameson (2010) relates post-Keynesian state policy to development ethics as an alternative to neoliberalism. Specifically, in the field of income distribution and poverty policy, Jameson (2010, p. 418–420) underscores that neoliberal applied policies seem to tighten the relationship between the private business sector and state policy, in which political power or intervention is used for the benefits of the private sector. Jameson (2010, p. 420) concludes by mentioning that, even though the dominance of neoliberalism in state policies makes the task of bringing nation-state policies back into the economic equation much more difficult, policy recommendations should aid in this effort.[12]

As it seems, "mainstream economics requires considerable reconstruction" (Brown, cited in Gasper, 2004, p. 81). In relation to nation-state

[12] Post-Keynesian and heterodox authors recommend genuine state policy interventions to addressing various social problems and developmental challenges.

policy, development ethics seeks this reconstruction in the various forms of deliberative democracy; such democracy enables people to have the capabilities to be involved in policy-making. Stiglitz and the other development ethicists mentioned here, such as Crocker and Gasper, are advocators of applied development ethics. Regarding nation-state policy, they have argued that economic efficiency and popular governance take place in nation-states in which democracy is more robust (Crocker, 2006a, p. 23). Thus, a nation-state policy should work in the direction of the enforcement of democratic popular governance. In turn, economic efficiency has been viewed as a means to the larger societal goals of life sustenance, esteem, and freedom. Nation-state policy should remain faithful to the aforementioned goals throughout an applied policy based on the development ethics ethical strategies of the abundance of goods, solidarity among people, and the participation of ordinary people at some levels of decision-making.[13] These ethical goals and strategies have policy implications not only at the level of nation-state policy but also at the level of international development institutions' policies.

3.4 *Applied Development Ethics and International Institutions*

International development institutions adopt the neoliberal ideology and the policy tools of neoclassical economics. As has already been mentioned, neoliberal institutionalism dominates modern globalisation while its practice is justified by a set of theoretical claims rooted in neoclassical economic theory. In historical retrospect, the neoliberal dominance in worldwide capitalism and development policy was addressed during the second half of the 1970s. However, the worst excesses of neoliberalism, especially within international development institutions, came to the fore in the 1980s and 1990s. In most of the applied development programmes in international development, such as the Washington Consensus applied policy reforms in Latin America and elsewhere, neoliberal economic and social policies have been imposed by international development institutions on many developing economies. From the angle of development ethics, St. Clair (2010, p. 253) mentions that, within the Washington Consensus framework, development policy means something very specific: "to follow the call for increasingly globalised markets and

[13] For the development ethics normative-ethical goals and strategies, see Chapter 5.

the privatisation of social services; to prioritise economic concerns above anything else; [and] to measure every aspect of social life with a monetary metric." In such a way, neoliberal institutionalism (the emergence of the influence of international development institutions on national and global applied development policies), as the dominant policy doctrine in the present form of international development, espouses the applied-ethical policy instruments and objectives of neoclassical economics and neoliberalism.

One of the basic ethical assumptions of neoclassical economics that is adopted by international development institutions' applied policies is that the proposed economic policies are universal in character and applicable in every time.[14] By contrast, the applied development ethics critique of this approach argues that the development policies provided by the neoclassical model cannot have universal application in all times. Furthermore, criticising the existing applied development policy in international development, Bowles and Gintis (2000, pp. 1427–1428) point out that the neoclassical model is wrong not in its details but in its basic abstractions and, especially, in its inability to cast light on such fundamental questions as the recent contrasting growth trajectories of Latin America in the 1980s and 1990s. These basic abstractions can be briefly described in the framework of the free-market relations and the adoption of open-trade policies and free capital flows. This has led international development to a new kind of colonialism of the developing world by way of the global market and international development/financial institutions.[15] This kind of colonialism usually embodies an economic dualism between the North and the South, developed and developing economies, capital and labour, and rich and poor classes. Thus, development ethics undoubtedly stands against any kind of applied development policy that leads to such divisions.

Regarding the applied-ethical issues and the role of international development institutions, the Washington Consensus policy applied in Latin America and in the rest of the developing world is ethically criticised under the applied development ethics alternative policy perspective. The applied Washington Consensus policy mainly refers to the means of development policy (the policy instruments), which represents the manner in

[14] See again footnote 11.

[15] We have referred to this as the meta-ethical nature of international development as a globalised market economy (Chapter 4).

which development as economic growth is being accomplished. Developing economies are usually subjected to international development institutions' orders on a range of economic and structural reforms in the direction of free-market economies. Mentioning the reasons for the Washington Consensus policy's failure in international development, Stiglitz (1998, p. 4) stresses "[t]hat consensus [Washington Consensus] all too often confused means with ends: it took privatisation and trade liberalisation as ends in themselves, rather than as means to more sustainable, equitable, and democratic growth."

The criticism of development ethics of the applied international development policies of the Washington Consensus is not only of the meta-ethical level of the ends or, differently, the vision of good international development but also at the applied-ethical level of the means (i.e., the policy instruments used). In the dominant applied models of international development (like the Washington Consensus), "[t]hese means range from economic planning to propaganda campaigns, from comprehensive social engineering to sectoral interventions of all sorts, with a view to altering values, behaviors, and social structures" (Goulet, 2004, p. 9). Furthermore, as Table 1 shows, we can ascertain that the Washington Consensus policies as means are interwoven with neoclassical economics policy recommendations. In this manner, Stiglitz perhaps erred in his argument that there is an inversion between the means and the ends of the Washington Consensus. The Washington Consensus applied policies as means of achieving economic development and prosperity in the developing world are tightly bound to neoclassical economics and neoliberal policy prescriptions as necessary, appropriate, and applicable in almost all applied situations.

To this end, Cortina (2010, p. 67), from the perspective of development ethics, questioned: "[i]s the economic model of the Washington Consensus, even with is corrective adjustments, the only economic model possible?" In response to this question, a couple of ethical objections to the dominant international development applied policy are offered by Cortina (2003; 2010) regarding development policy as the road to a good life and a good society. Cortina argues that the patterns or models of a good life and a good society cannot be forced by external agents, either universally or particularly, as in the case of the Washington Consensus. Development ethicists share the belief that development policy has to be socially demanded by ordinary people and the societies in which the specific development policy is formulated. In relation to this, it is socially and morally undesirable to generalise or universalise a particular development policy for everyone, individual or society, as any person or society realises their own conception of a good life. For Cortina, development policy and, as a consequence, a good life and a good society are based, to some extent, on the notion of justice. Development policy results "from the establishment of the conditions of justice that enable people to make use of their freedom" (Cortina, 2010, pp. 67–68).

More broadly, the discussion of justice and development policy takes various forms in the literature on ethical development and applied development ethics. For instance, Rawls (1971) talks about the influence of primary goods on development theory and policy; Streeten et al. (1981) and Gasper (2004) adopt the basic human needs approach; Pogge (2008) underlines the protection of human rights; and Nussbaum (2000) and Crocker (2008), among many other development ethicists, share the views of Sen regarding the empowerment of human capabilities (Sen, 1999). Despite the emphasis of each development scholar on a particular form of development policy, a common idea shared among development ethicists is that the change that development policy usually brings to people and societies should not be imposed by alien interests and forces. A good development policy gives people and societies the ability to choose their development paths. In this light, in most of the cases, the policies that have been imposed by international development institutions on developing societies and people are ethically undesirable. Therefore, other forms beyond the interventionism of international development institutions should be invented, either in the direction of avoiding such types of intervention or in the reconsideration of the applied policies of international development institutions, enabling developing nations to follow their own development policy patterns.

In terms of global poverty and social justice conditions in international development, Eskelinen's (2011) ethical analysis[16] of the "global basic structure", including the international development institutions' relevance in distributing the benefits of the social cooperation of international development, arguably proves that "the problems of global poverty cannot be located exclusively, or even primarily, to the injustices or misfunctionings of the global institutions" (Eskelinen, 2011, p. 48).

[16] Eskelinen's ethical analysis has been influenced by the perspectives of development ethicists, particularly Pogge (2002; 2008).

Moreover, apart from the international development institutions' demonstrational aims, the applied policy in international development is far from being fair and just. Eskelinen's (2011, p. 48) ethical critique of international development institutions' policies argues that "the problems of global poverty and radical injustice can be explained by reference to the existing basic structure practically means calling for a reform of the institutions key to the functioning of this basic structure."

Eskelinen's (2011) critique of the global institutional structure is of considerable policy importance. In the present analysis, however, it is argued that the ethical issues of poverty and injustice conditions in international development should not be merely seen as 'functioning problems' of the international development institutions' organisational structures. The international development institutions' structures consolidate longsighted dealings with political and economic power, either at the level of national conflicts or at the level of international coalitions. The Cold War division between free-market economies and centralised planning economies reflects such a conflict of power. Nonetheless, in recent times, we cannot argue for a balance of power in international development. The dominant worldwide economic framework and ideology are those of free-market relations and neoliberalism. In this framework, international development institutions' policies replicate the dominant positions at the level of the scopes and applied policies in international development.

For the present analysis, perhaps a more appropriate way of approaching the theme is by investigating the element of 'power', namely economic and political power, in development policy. Conceptually, power can be seen as the effective influence of an individual or group to adjust the conduct of others in some desired way (Goulet, 1975a, p. 335). In the international policy arena, "unleashing market and other economic forces has caused an intense struggle among individual nations, economic classes, and powerful groups" (Gilpin, 2001, p. 9). In this manner, international relations and, as a consequence, the applied development policy are generally determined by the calculations of power in the national or international interest (Dower, 1998a, p. 18). Throughout worldwide coalitions and politics—a game of power—international development institutions manipulate international development policy towards the dominant economic and political doctrine. In the case of the Washington Consensus, the policy instruments implicitly reflect the dominance of Western institutions and politics: a free-market economy and democratic capitalism. Crocker (2006, p. xx) underlines that "the development ethicist must draw on recent current analyses of asymmetries of social and economic power in order to take into account the ways in which elites can capture the most progressive institutions." Put it differently, even if international institutions have been designed under progressive principles, the political and economic power of elites can affect their policy objectives and applied policy. In spite of this, but relevant to the discussion of power, international development institutions can impose, mainly through economic and political power, their policy guides on the policy-making of developing nations in the direction that has been outlined. If we accept that power is one of the key issues of applied-ethical policy, either at the international scale or locally, we can quote the remarks of Goulet:

> Where power is badly used within underdeveloped countries, the blame does not rest primarily on the personal deficiencies of rulers. In most cases the problem is structural: society is so organized that only the representatives of certain interests enjoy access to the wealth, culture, contracts, information, and influence without which decisions cannot be made. Consequently, meaningful policy changes cannot be brought about simply by 'throwing the rascals out' because those who replace them may emerge from the same structures and represent identical interests (Goulet 1975a, p. 336; see also Goulet, 2006a, pp. 19–20).

Finally, as Crocker (2008, pp. 49–51) mentions, development ethicists debate which agents and structures are responsible for the failures of the existing development policy, which involves the discussion of power and applied ethics. Beitz's view (cited in Crocker, 2008, p. 49) is more elucidating: "[t]here is a large, complex, and unresolved empirical question about the relative contributions of local and global factors to the wealth and poverty of societies." For instance, Pogge (2005) discusses the development ethicists who blame international dominance, the advanced nations, and international institutions' regimes as the main factors of global economic dualism, poverty, and the exploitation of vulnerable nations and societies. By contrast, other development ethicists "ascribe development failure much less to global and foreign sources and much more to national and local causes—such as elite capture of power, widespread corruption, and the lack of democratic institutions"

(Crocker, 2008, p. 50). In our analysis, there are no grounds for such disagreement. In most of the cases in the applied development policy, international development institutions' policies and nation-state policy are entwined regarding the meta-ethical vision of a globalised market economy governed by the dominant laws of free-market economics and neoliberalism. In light of this, national elites and dominant classes adopt the international development institutions' policy instruments and applied development policy objectives.

4 Conclusion

The preceding analysis has discussed the applied-ethical basis of international development and the development ethics alternative. Beyond the meta-ethical concern of what a good society is, and the normative-ethical evaluation of how this good society should be achieved, there is an ethical manner by which the ethical judgement of a good life and a good society is formulated in real-world situations. In this chapter, we have argued that applied ethics in international development is interwoven with global ethics, which affects actual policy issues. The applied-ethical analysis is innately related to applied development policy, wherein applied development policy is interlaced with economic, political, institutional, and moral factors. Taken as a whole, applied ethics and applied-ethical analysis interpret the ethical argument of a good life and a good society at the level of the examination of applied development policy reasoning in the real-world situations of international development.

In the mainstream literature, applied ethics is usually accepted as business ethics. In turn, business ethics typically incorporates applied ethics by investigating deontological and professional issues. This is a microeconomic formation of applied ethics, which is based on individual ethics and the self-interest perspective of seeing the world reality. The present chapter contributes to a holistic applied-ethical interpretation of international development. Thus, applied ethics as a form of global ethics is positioned in a political economy context. In this context, applied-ethical policy issues in international development have been investigated in three aspects:

1. The framework of market relations;
2. The role of nation-state policy; and
3. The role of international development institutions' policies

The results of the analysis reveal that the existing reality in international development policy is dominated by the development policy of free-market economics and neoliberalism. In this chapter and elsewhere, we have argued that the applied policy cannot be detached from its meta-ethical orientation—the ends—and its normative-ethical evaluation—the relationship between the ends and the means. The analysis is also assisted by the findings on the application of the Washington Consensus in Latin America and in the rest of the developing world. Consequently, the development policy in international development is applied in the framework of free-market relations. Briefly, free-market relations can be interpreted as the linearisation of the economic and political environment in almost all its functions. As per Harvey (2005; 2010), DeMartino (2000), and others, we maintain that neoliberalism is a policy doctrine that is assisted by many neoclassical economists and the scientific or analytical tools of neoclassical economic positivism. Even if there are contradictions in theory and practice, the theoretical objectives of neoclassical economics and the applied neoliberal policy, as in the case of government intervention in economic matters within and beyond the market, the present analysis is very close to Albo et al.'s (2010, p. 28) position that neoliberalism is not about the extent of deregulation as opposed to regulation. Neoliberals use nation-state power for their own purposes. What is noteworthy is that nation-state domestic policy and international development institutions' policy orders follow a similar applied-ethical policy that is compatible with free-market economics and the image of international development as a globalised market economy.

The analysis argues that applied development ethics could serve as an alternative policy perspective to neoclassical economics and neoliberalism in international development. Development ethics in its applied dimension is accepted as appropriate global ethics towards good international development, here labelled as applied development ethics. The analysis has followed the aforementioned structure of inquiry by putting applied development ethics in a political economy context. In this respect, applied development ethics revokes free-market relations as an appropriate applied-ethical framework for policy in international development, particularly as it has been argued that the dominant free-market relations are ethically deficient. Therefore, applied development ethics puts forward the idea that a good development policy results in 1. a decent sufficiency of basic goods for all; 2. solidarity among people and societies; and 3. non-elites' participation in policy-making. The existing development policy in international development does not seem to involve the aforementioned policy aims. For instance, the applied Washington Consensus policies appear to have opposite results. Nevertheless, applied development ethics is not against policies that are formulated with the view that the market institution and exchanges, as well as the private sector of the economy, are the means to a good society. Applied development ethics recognises that a good private sector must coexist with a good public sector. Some implications for the role of the public sector which can be suitable for the private sector have been mentioned. The real lesson derived from this illustration is that an appropriable applied-ethical policy can boost economic efficiency and civic values. As has already been pointed out, economic efficiency is beneficial if it leads people and societies to better lives, eliminates poverty, and reduces inequality. Sufficiency in terms of civic values means establishing a good society based on the development ethics principles of life sustenance, esteem, and freedom for all people and nations in the world.

References

Abbott, A. (1983). Professional ethics. *American Journal of Sociology, 88*(5), 855–885.

Albo, G., Gindin, S., & Panitch, L. (2010). *In and out of crisis: The global financial meltdown and left alternatives*. PM Press.

Arrébola-Rodríguez, C. A. (2011). From Washington consensus to post-washington consensus consensus: Consequences in transition economies. *European Perspectives, 1*(4), 19–34.

Banfield, E. (1958). *The moral basis of a backward society*. Free Press.

Behrman, J., Birdsall, N., & Szekely, M. (2003). *Economic policy and wage differentials in Latin America*. Center for Global Development: Working Paper, No. 29.

Bergsten, C., & Henning, C. R. (Eds.). (2012). *Global economics in extraordinary times: Essays in honor of John Williamson*. Peterson Institute for International Economics.

Bhaqwati, J. (2004). *In Defence of Globalization*. Oxford University Press.

Bilson, J. F. (1982). Civil liberty—An econometric investigation. *Kyklos, 35*, 94–114.

Blaug, M. (1992 [1980]). *The methodology of economics or how economics explain*. Cambridge University Press.

Bowels, S., Franzini, M., & Pagano, U. (1999). Introduction: Trespassing the boundaries of politics and economics. In S. Bowels, M. Franzini, & U. Pagano (Eds.), *The politics and economics of power* (pp. 2–8). Routledge.

Bowles, S., & Gintis, H. (1986). *Democracy and capitalism*. Basic Books.

Bowles, S., & Gintis, H. (2000). Walrasian economics in retrospect. *Quarterly Journal of Economics, 115*(4), 1411–1439.

Broad, R., & Cavanagh, L. (1999). The death of the Washington consensus. *World Policy Journal, 16*(3), 79–88.

Buchanan, J. M. (1986). Contractarianism and democracy. In J. Buchanan (Ed.), *Liberty, market and state*. Brighton: Wheatsheat Books.

Buller, P. F., Kohls, J. J., & Anderson, K. S. (1991). The challenge of global ethics. *Journal of Business Ethics, 10*(10), 767–775.

Camacho, L. (2008). Agriculture intensification from the perspective of development ethics. In P. B. Thompson (Ed.), *The ethics of intensification* (pp. 97–110). London: Springer.

Chadwick, R. (Ed.). (2012). *Encyclopedia of applied ethics* (2nd ed.). Academic Press-Elsevier.

Chang, H.-J. (2002). Breaking the mould: An institutionalist political economy alternative to the neoliberal theory of the market and the state. *Cambridge Journal of Economics, 26*(5), 539–559.

Clark, D. A. (2002). Development ethics: A research agenda. *International Journal of Social Economics, 29*(11), 830–848.

Clark, D. A. (2005). Sen's capability approach and the many spaces of human well-being. *The Journal of Development Studies, 41*(8), 1339–1368.

Cohen, A. I., & Wellman, C. H. (Eds.). (2005). *Contemporary debates in applied ethics*. Blackwell Publishing.

Cohen, B. J. (2008). *International political economy: An intellectual history*. Princeton University Press.

Cohen, S. I. (2009). *Economic systems analysis and policies: Explaining global differences, transitions and developments*. Palgrave Macmillan.

Cortina, A. (2003). *Covenant and contact: Politics, ethics and religion*. Peeters.

Cortina, A. (2010). Development ethics: A road to peace. In C. K. Wilber & A. K. Dutt (Eds.), *New directions in development ethics: Essays in honor of Denis Goulet* (pp. 59–78). University of Notre Dame Press.

Craig, D., & Porter, D. (2006). *Development beyond neoliberalism? Governance, poverty reduction, and political economy*. Routledge.

Crocker, D. (1991). Toward development ethics. *World Development, 19*(5), 457–483.

Crocker, D. (2006a). Development ethics, globalization, and Stiglitz. pp. 1–47. Working paper to appear in M. Krausz and D. Chottergee (Eds.), *Globalization, development, and democracy: Philosophical perspectives*. Retrieved

from http://terpconnect.umd.edu/~dcrocker/Courses/Docs/PUAF698Q-Dev%20Ethics,%20Globalization%20and%20Stiglitz.pdf
Crocker, D. (2006b). Sen and deliberative democracy. In A. Kaufman (Ed.), *Capabilities equality: Basic issues and problems* (pp. 155–197). Routledge.
Crocker, D. (2007). Deliberative participation in local development. *Journal of Human Development, 8*(3), 431–455.
Crocker, D. (2008). *Ethics of global development*. Cambridge University Press.
Crocker, D. (2010). Participation in local development: Goulet and deliberative democracy. In C. K. Wilber & A. K. Dutt (Eds.), *New directions in development ethics: Essays in Honor of Denis Goulet* (pp. 308–332). Notre Dame University Press.
Crocker, D., & Linden, T. (Eds.). (1998). *Ethics of consumptions: The good life, justice, and global stewardship*. Lanham, Maryland: Rownan & Littlefield.
Cross, R., & Strachan, D. (2001). Three pillars of conventional wisdom. *Review of Political Economy, 13*(2), 181–200.
Davidson, G., & Davidson, P. (1988). *Economics for a civilised society*. W.W. Norton & Company.
DeMartino, G. (2000). *Global economy, global justice: Theoretical and policy alternatives to neoliberalism*. Routledge.
Dower, N. (1983). Ethics and environmental futures. *International Journal of Environmental Studies, 21*(1), 29–44.
Dower, N. (1998). *World ethics: The new agenda*. Edinburgh University Press.
Dower, N. (1998). Development ethics. In R. Chadwick (Ed.), *Encyclopedia of applied ethics* (pp. 755–766). Academic Press.
Dower, N. (2005). The nature and scope of global ethics and the relevance of the earth charter. *Journal of Global Ethics, 1*(1), 25–43.
Drydyk, J. (2005). When is development more democratic? *Journal of Human Development, 6*(2), 247–267.
Drydyk, J. (2010). Participation, empowerment, and democracy: Three fickle friends. In C. K. Wilber & A. K. Dutt (Eds.), *New directions in development ethics: Essays in honor of Denis Goulet* (pp. 333–356). Notre Dame University Press.
Dutt, A. K., & Wilber, C. K. (2010). *Economics and ethics: An introduction*. Palgrave Macmillan.
Eskelinen, T. (2011). Global basis structure and institutions: The WTO as a practical example. *Journal of Global Ethics, 7*(1), 47–58.
Fine, B. (1980). *Economic theory and ideology*. Edward Arnold.
Fine, B. (2003). Neither the Washington nor the post-Washington consensus: An introduction. In B. Fine, C. Lapavitsas, & J. Pincus (Eds.), *Development policy in the twenty-first century: Beyond the post-Washington consensus* (pp. 1–27). Routledge.

Fine, B., Lapavitsas, C., & Pincus, J. (Eds.). (2003). *Development policy in the twenty-first century: Beyond the post-Washington consensus*. Routledge.
Foucault, M. (1984). Politics and ethics: An interview. In P. Rabinow (Ed.), *The Foucault reader* (pp. 373–380). Pantheon Books.
Friedman, M. (2002 [1962]). *Capitalism and freedom*. Chicago: University of Chicago Press.
Friedman, M., & Friedman, R. (1980). *Free to choose: A personal statement*. New York: Harcourt Brace Jovanovich.
Fukuyama, F. (1992). *The end of history and the last man*. New York: The Free Press: A Division of Macmillan, Inc.
Gasper, D. (2002). Is Sen's capability approach an adequate basis for considering human development? *Review of Political Economy, 14*(2), 435–461.
Gasper, D. (2004). *The ethics of development*. Edinburgh University Press.
Gasper, D. (2012). Development ethics—Why? What? How? A formulation of the field. *Journal of Global Ethics, 8*(1), 117–135.
Gasper, D., & St. Clair, A. L. (Eds.). (2010). *Development ethics*. London: Ashgate.
Gasper, D., & St. Clair, A. L. (2010). The field of development ethics—An introduction. In D. Gasper & A. L. St. Clair (Eds.), *Development ethics* (pp. 13–33). London: Ashgate.
Gasper, D., & Truong, T.-D. (2005). Deepening development ethics: From economism to human development to human security. *The European Journal of Development Research, 17*(3), 372–384.
Gilpin, R. (2001). *Global political economy: Understanding the international economic order*. Princeton University Press.
Goldsmith, A. A. (1995). Democracy, property rights and economic growth. *Journal of Development Studies, 32*(2), 157–174.
Gore, C. (2000). The rise and fall of the Washington consensus as a paradigm for developing countries. *World Development, 28*(5), 789–804.
Goulet, D. (1975). *The cruel choice: A new concept in the theory of development*. Atheneum.
Goulet, D. (1976). On the ethics of development planning. *Studies in Comparative International Development, 11*(1), 25–43.
Goulet, D. (1983). Obstacles to world development: An ethical reflection. *World Development, 11*(7), 609–624.
Goulet, D. (1989). Participation in development: New avenues. *World Development, 17*(2), 165–178.
Goulet, D. (1992). Ethics and development: A development ethicist at work. *Research and Explorations, 8*(2), 138–147.
Goulet, D. (1992). International ethics and human rights. *Alternatives, 17*(2), 231–246.

Goulet, D. (2004). Changing development debates under globalization: The evolving nature of development in the light of globalization. *Journal of Law and Social Challenges, 6*(1), 1–17.

Goulet, D. (2006). *Development ethics at work: Explorations 1960–2002*. Routledge.

Graafland, J. (2007). *Economics, ethics and the market: Introduction and applications*. Routledge.

Guillén, M. F. (2001). Is globalization civilizing, destructive, or feeble? A critique of five key debates in the social science literature. *Annual Review of Sociology, 27*, 235–260.

Harry, P. (2010). *World ethics and climate change: From international to global justice*. Edinburgh University Press.

Harvey, D. (2005). *A brief history of neoliberalism*. Oxford University Press.

Harvey, D. (2010). *The enigma of capital, and the crises of capitalism*. Oxford University Press.

Hausman, D. M., & McPherson, M. S. (2006). *Economic analysis, moral philosophy, and public policy* (2nd ed.). Cambridge University Press.

Hayek, F. A. (1948). *Individualism and economic order*. University of Chicago.

Hayek, F. A. (1979). *Social justice, socialism and democracy: Three Australian lectures*. Centre of Independent Studies.

Häyry, M. (1994). *Liberal utilitarianism and applied ethics*. Routledge.

Howard, M. C., & King, J. E. (2004). The rise of neo-liberalism in advanced capitalist economies: Towards a materialist explanation. In P. Arestis & M. Sawyer (Eds.), *The rise of the market: Critical essays on the political economy of neo-liberalism* (pp. 38–73). Edward Elgar.

Huntington, S., & Nelson, J. (1976). *No easy choice: Political participation in developing countries*. Harvard University Press.

Jameson, K. P. (2010). Ethics and contemporary macroeconomic policy. In C. K. Wilber & A. K. Dutt (Eds.), *New directions in development ethics: Essays in honor of Denis Goulet* (pp. 400–425). Notre Dame University Press.

Kagan, S. (1998). *Normative ethics*. Westview Press.

Kolodko, G. W. (2000). Transition to a market and entrepreneurship: The systemic factors and policy options. *Communist and Post-Communist Studies, 33*(3), 271–293.

Kuczynski, P. P., & Williamson, J. (Eds.). (2003). *After the Washington consensus*. Institute for International Studies.

LaFollette, H. (2002). *Ethics in practice: An anthology* (2nd ed.). Blackwell Publishing.

Levinson, M. (2000). The cracking Washington consensus. *Dissent, 47*(4), 11–14.

Lines, T. (2010). Speculation in food commodity markets. *A report commissioned by the World Development Movement* (pp. 1–18).

Little, D. (2003). *The paradox of wealth and poverty*. Westview Press.
Machlup, F. (1978). *Methodology of economics and other social sciences*. Academic Press.
Marangos, J. (2004). *Alternative economic models of transition*. Ashgate.
Marangos, J. (2007). Was shock therapy consistent with the Washington consensus? *Comparative Economic Studies, 49*, 32–58.
Marangos, J. (2009a). What happened to the Washington consensus? The evolution of international development policy. *The Journal of Socio-Economics, 38*(1), 197–208.
Marangos, J. (2009b). The evolution of the term 'Washington consensus.' *Journal of Economic Surveys, 23*(2), 350–384.
Marshall, A. (1920 [1890]). *Principles of economics* (Eight ed.). London: Macmillan and Co., Ltd (Retrieved by Library of Economics and Liberty: http://www.econlib.org/library/Marshall/marP28.html).
McNeill, D., & St. Clair, A. L. (2009). *Global poverty, ethics and human rights: The role of multilateral organisations*. Abingdon: Routledge.
Milonakis, D., & Fine, B. (2009). *From political economy to economics: Method, the social and the historical in the evolution of economic theory*. Routledge.
Moore, G. E. (1960 [1903]). *Principia ethica (1903)*. Cambridge: Cambridge University Press.
Morgenthau, H. (1948). *Politics among nations*. Alfred A. Knopf.
Murithi, T. (2009). *The ethics of peace building*. Edinburgh University Press.
Naim, M. (1994). Latin America: The second stage of reforms. *Journal of Democracy, 5*(4), 32–48.
North, D. (1991). Institutions. *Journal of Economic Perspectives, 5*(1), 97–112.
Nozick, R. (1974). *Anarchy, state, and utopia*. Blackwell.
Nussbaum, M. (2000). *Women and human development: The capabilities approach*. Cambridge University Press.
O'Hara, P. A. (2006). *Growth and development in the global political economy: Social structures of accumulation and modes of regulation*. Routledge.
Olson, M. (1982). *The rise and decline of nations*. Yale University Press.
Olson, M. (1993). Dictatorship, democracy, and development. *The American Political Science Review, 87*(3), 567–576.
Owens, J. (1983). Business ethics in the college classroom. *Journal of Business Education, 58*(7), 258–262.
Parish, W. L., & Michelson, E. (1996). Politics and markets: Dual transformations. *American Journal of Sociology, 101*(4), 1042–1059.
Pogge, T. (2002). *World poverty and human rights: Cosmopolitan responsibilities and reforms*. Polity Press.
Pogge, T. (2005). World poverty and human rights. *Ethics & International Affairs, 19*(1), 1–7.
Pogge, T. (2008). *World, poverty, and human rights*. Polity press.

Pourgerami, A., & Assane, D. (1992). Macroeconomic determinants of growth: New measurement and evidence on the effect of political freedom. *Applied Economics, 24*(1), 129–136.

Rawls, J. (1971). *A theory of justice*. Oxford University Press.

Rodrik, D. (2006). Goodbye Washington consensus, hello Washington confusion? A review of the world bank's economic growth in the 1990s: Learning from a decade of reform. *Journal of Economic Literature, 44*(4), 973–987.

Roemer, J. E. (1994). *A future for socialism*. Harvard University Press.

Saavedra, J. (2003). Labor Markets during the 1990s. In P. P. Kuczynski & J. Williamson (Eds.), *After the Washington consensus: Restarting growth and reform in Latin America* (pp. 213–263). Institute for International Economics.

Sally, R. (1998). *Classical liberalism and international economic order: Studies in theory and intellectual history*. Routledge.

Schwenke, C. (2009). *Reclaiming value in international development: The moral dimensions of development policy and practice in poor countries*. Praeger Publishers.

Sedgwick, P. H. (2004). *The market economy and Christian ethics*. Cambridge University Press.

Sen, A. (1977). Rational fools: A critique of the behavioral foundations of economic theory. *Philosophy and Public Affairs, 6*(4), 317–344.

Sen, A. (1987). *On ethics and economics*. Blackwell.

Sen, A. (1999). *Development as freedom*. Oxford University Press.

Sen, A. (2004). *Rationality and freedom*. Harvard University Press.

Serra, N., & Stiglitz, J. (Eds.). (2008). *The Washington consensus reconsidered*. Oxford University Press.

Singer, P. (2011). *Practical ethics*. Cambridge University Press.

Smith, A. (1986 [1776]). *The wealth of nations*. London: Penguin.

Smith, A. (2004 [1759]). *The theory of moral sentiments*. (K. Haakonssen, Ed.) Cambridge: Cambridge University Press.

Sotiropoulos, D. P., Milios, J., & Lapatsioras, S. (2012). Demystifying finance: How to understand financialization and think of strategies for a good society. In J. Marangos (Ed.), *Alternative perspectives of a good society* (pp. 99–120). Palgrave-Macmillan.

Srinivasan, T. N. (2000). The Washington consensus a decade later: Ideology and the art and science of policy advice. *The World Bank Research Observer, 15*(2), 265–270.

St Clair, A. L. (2007). A methodologically pragmatist approach to development ethics. *Journal of Global Ethics, 3*(2), 143–164.

St Clair, A. L. (2010). Global poverty: Development ethics meet global justice. In C. K. Wilber & A. K. Dutt (Eds.), *New directions in development ethics:*

Essays in honor of Denis Goulet (pp. 249–278). Notre Dame, IN: University of Notre Dame Press.

Stiglitz, J. (1998). Towards a new paradigm for development: Strategies, policies and processes. In *9th Raúl Prebisch lecture, October 19* (pp. 1–33). Geneva: United Nations Conference on Trade and Development.

Stiglitz, J. (2000a). Unraveling the Washington consensus. *Multinational Monitor, 21*(4), 13–21.

Stiglitz, J. (2002b). *Globalization and its discontents*. W. W. Norton.

Stiglitz, J. (2002c). Participation and development: Perspectives from the comprehensive development paradigm. *Review of Development Economics, 6*(2), 163–182.

Streeten, P., Burki, S. J., Haq, M. U., Hicks, N., & Stewart, F. (1981). *First things first: Meeting basic human needs in development countries*. New York: Oxford University Press (Published for the World Bank).

van Staveren, I. (2001). *The values of economics: An Aristotelian perspective*. Routledge.

van Staveren, I. (2009). Efficiency. In J. Peil & I. van Staveren (Eds.), *Handbook of economics and ethics* (pp. 107–114). Edward Elgar.

Vickers, D. (1997). *Economics and ethics: An introduction to theory, institutions, and policy*. Greenwood Publishing Group.

Vorhies, F., & Glahe, F. (1988). Political liberty and development: An empirical investigation. *Public Choice, 58*(1), 45–71.

Waltz, K. N. (1979). *Theory of international politics*. McGraw-Hill.

Ward, B. (1976). Foreword. In M. U. Haq (Ed.), *The poverty curtain, choice for the third world*. New York: Columbia University Press.

Wilber, C. K. (2010). Economics and ethics. In C. K. Wilber & A. K. Dutt (Eds.), *New directions in development ethics: Essays in honor of Denis Goulet* (pp. 157–176). University of Notre Dame.

Williams, B. (2006). *Ethics and the limits of philosophy*. Routledge.

Williamson, J. (1990). What Washington means by policy reform. In J. Williamson (Ed.), *Latin American adjustment: How much has happened? (Chapter 2)*. Washington, DC: Institute for International Economics. Republished online (November, 2002). http://www.iie.com/publications/papers/paper.cfm?researchid=486

Williamson, J. (1993). Democracy and the 'Washington consensus.' *World Development, 21*(8), 1329–1336.

Williamson, J. (2007). Shock therapy and the Washington consensus: A comment. *Comparative Economic Studies, 49*(1), 59–60.

Williamson, J. (2002). *Did the Washington consensus fail?* Outline of remarks at the Center for Strategic & International Studies, November 6 (pp. 1–4).

CHAPTER 7

Conclusion: Neoliberalism in International Development and the Comprehensive Development Ethics Alternative

The preceding analysis is based on the general perspective that the study of international development within economics in the political economy context has an ethical dimension, posed by the ethical question of 'what is a good society?' The main aim of the book has been to develop an ethical framework for the holistic investigation of international development theory and policy, without neglecting the existing world reality. As has been demonstrated, international development is dominated by neoclassical economics and neoliberalism. Thus, every alternative approach or paradigm has to respond sufficiently to the basic theoretical premises of neoclassical economic analysis and the applied neoliberal policies in international development. So far, in the development ethics literature, a solid methodological framework has not been established for investigating international development in such a manner. The development ethics alternative to the dominant theory and policy of international development has been developed in the previous analysis. At the final section of each chapter of the book, the results of the analysis have been stated in accordance with the particular chapter's topic. In this closing chapter, we recap the main remarks of the analysis by focusing on the neoliberal ascendancy in international development, the neoclassical economics postures on the formulation of contemporary international development, and the development ethics alternative to neoliberalism and neoclassical economics. In this way, this final chapter entails an inclusive analysis of

N. Astroulakis and N. Karagiannis, *Development Ethics*,
https://doi.org/10.1007/978-3-031-75476-0_7

international development from the angle of development ethics, without ignoring the existing reality of neoliberalism in international development.

In constructing a social science paradigm, however, there is always the danger to avoid in its method the "historical specificity": different socioeconomic phenomena and different historical periods may require different explanatory theories (Hodgson, 2001). We have attempted to integrate in all forms of our methodology a historical specific manner of analysis. First, the analysis has focused on contemporary international development, from the 1970s and beyond. In these times, we highlight the dominance of neoclassical economic thinking and neoliberalism in international development theory and policy. Second, the key term 'development' describes a process between the means and the ends of a good society. Nevertheless, the term has a different meaning when it refers to its dominant usage by neoclassical economists and their neoliberal counterparts, and it has another connotation when it is mentioned by development ethicists. For the former group, development directly implies economic development that includes social choice in a predetermined manner: Westernised material affluence. For development ethicists, development is seen as a question of the values and requirements of a new civilisation, where "development is the ascent of all men and societies in their total humanity" (Goulet, 1975, p. x). Third, in the political economy approach, a model or paradigm does not always predict equilibrium conditions among factors of production but instead analyses and predicts broad socioeconomic and ethical relationships.

Development ethics is, by definition, the field of questioning the values and ethical issues in development, at the local, national, and international levels (Goulet, 2006; Crocker; 2008; Gasper, 2012). In his presidential speech at the nineteenth International Conference of the International Development Ethics Association in 2011, Drydyk addresses seven value areas of a good society, which comprise "worthwhile development", in his words. Concisely: first, development must enhance people's well-being; second, it ought to be equitable in the sense of "well-being freedom"[1]; third, ordinary people have to be the agents of their own development; fourth, development should be environmentally sustainable; fifth, development must strengthen human rights; sixth, development should

[1] This concept was first introduced by Sen, who mentions the dependency of well-being on agent-oriented factors (Sen, 1987).

enhance cultural freedom and, in this manner, also reduce social exclusion; and seventh, development should not utilise corrupt means and ends (Drydyk, 2013, p. 6). All these valuable issues have been extensively analysed by development ethicists and scholars in the field of development ethics. Likewise, much work has been carried out by recent development ethicists on specific issues such as the basic needs approach, human rights, social justice, and the integration of Sen's capability approach and similar perspectives into development (Crocker, 2008; 2010; Drydyk, 2010; Gasper, 2002; 2007; Clark, 2005). However, these approaches enlist important but frequently micro insights into the ethical analysis of international development. Where such insights are offered, there are warnings against focusing on the superficial aspects of ethical development and neglecting the core values and inclusive ethical image of international development theory and policy.

In the present analysis, these values and ethical issues have been uncovered in the determination of a holistic-ethical viewpoint of international development. In this regard, we have approached international development on the meta-ethical grounds of the moral reasoning and ends of development, the normative-ethical level of the evaluation of the relationship between the means and the ends of development, and the applied-ethical analysis of the role of the dominant applied policy. In doing so, we have built our analysis on the basis that, to investigate international development ethically, the existing world reality and ethics have to coexist. The conjunction of the fields of political economy and moral philosophy fits with this premise. Political economy appraises international development's economic, social, and political nature, while moral philosophy endows the analysis with suitable ethical inquiries, deeper moral meanings, and explanations.

We have exposed an overall image of the dominant doctrine in international development in recent times. According to the aforementioned analysis, international development has been dominated by economic neoliberalism virtually since the 1970s. Historically, the neoliberal influence emerged during the 1970s, when recessions became deeper, growth became lower, and unemployment and inflation became higher (O'Hara, 2004, p. 328). The analysis has evaluated neoliberalism in international development as a theory and policy doctrine of extreme free-market economics applied at the national and international levels. As previously stated, Howard and King (2004, p. 40) approach neoliberalism "as a doctrine and a related social practice. The doctrine is that all, or virtually all, economic and social problems have a market solution, with the corollary that state failure is typically worse than market failure." More than this, neoliberalism is a philosophical pattern that functions as an ethic in itself in the formation of international development theory and policy. Harvey (2005, p. 165) argues for the "commodification of everything", under the dominant premise that "[t]he market is presumed to work as an appropriate guide—an ethic—for all human action." Based on this, we further claim that neoliberal dominance mirrors the prevailing influence of neoclassical economics on development economics. Particularly after the 1970s, neoclassical economics positivism emerged in the social sciences, including international development studies. In this framework, even in ethical perspectives within development economics, an individualistic notion of ethics is predominant.

In contrast to the apparent presence of neoclassical economics as an ethically neutral and positive science—the general premise that "positive economics is in principle independent of any particular ethical position or normative judgments" (Friedman, 1966, p. 4)—we have shown that neoclassical economics follows a specific notion of ethics: individual ethics. Individual ethics employ ethical analysis at the level of economic agents. In neoclassical economic analysis, these agents are mainly business organisations and consumers. Theoretically, the economy operates effectively without the element of power (whether state or market power). For the typical modelling of neoclassical economics, "there is nothing for power to be about" (Bowles and Gintis, 2000, p. 1413). In this simplified rhetoric, society is perceived as the sum of its individual agents (firms and consumers). Accordingly, economic and societal choices are based solely on the preferences of the individual agents. Dominant perspectives in welfare economics also underline the level of individual preferences. "By so absorbing morality into subjective and incomparable individual preferences, neoclassical economics has effectively removed [actual] ethical evaluation from welfare analysis" (van Staveren, 2007, pp. 22–23). In neoclassical social choice theory, "individuals are self-interested, having no regard whatsoever to notions such as public duty, the common good, or social commitment" (Gill, 1996, p. 140). In this respect, the good ethical stances of individual agents, in terms of motivation, are more or less sufficient for a good society. The society and its market most effectively function when the people make the best choices for themselves without any form of interference from the state or market power. In this approach, the notion of individual ethics reflects the core principles of neoclassical economics. The individual agents' behaviour, "based on self-interested, exogenous preferences and complete and costless contracting, underpin the distinctive analytical results of what came to be known as neoclassical economics" (Bowels and Gintis, 2000, p. 1411). The view of ethics exclusively as individual ethics—the morality of individual agents in a self-interested manner—detaches the analysis of international development from broad social and economic relationships. Social values and conflicts of power are reluctant in the ethical meanings and explanations of neoclassical economics. However, even under these weaknesses, neoclassical economics is the imperative form of theory and policy within the social sciences. On this issue, Fine and Milonakis (2009, p. 14) provide a concise explanation:

> What gives economics its imperialistic invasive power is that our analytical categories—scarcity, cost, preferences, opportunities, etc.—are truly universal in application. Even more important is our structured organization of these concepts into the distinct yet intertwined processes of optimization on the individual decision level.

We have challenged, in particular, the individualistic-ethical perspective of neoclassical economics. In contrast, we incorporate ethics as social ethics. In this view, ethics refers to social interactions as a whole that involves social norms, values, institutions, and the element of power. Thus, social ethics better explores the ethical meaning of a good life; how society ought to be ethically structured; and the requirements for a good life within society. The overall premise for assimilating social ethics into our analysis is that society is something much more than individual preferences interacting in a value-neutral way in the market. The value-based and ethical exploration of society and economy is a matter of broad social and political relationships, while "politics and economics are not reducible to one another" (Marangos, 2003, p. 198; see also Caparaso and Levine, 1993, p. 225; Arestis and Sawyer, 1993, p. 9). We have claimed that, in order to understand international development, the aspects of institutions, values, and the relationships of power within the economy and society should be unified in the analysis. Therefore, we have argued for a political economy perspective on ethics. In this manner, social ethics can be seen as a matter of political economy analysis. The concepts of right or wrong, good or bad, morality or immorality, which ethics usually incorporate into its examinations, are viewed as both individual and social constructions in historically specific environments. International development is a historical and dynamic process; thus, we have employed social ethics in the same attributes within the political economy approach.

One of the main components of a good society is the good lives of the people. At the level of ethical analysis, the Ancient Greek philosopher Aristotle argues that the end and purpose of the state (*polis* in Greek) is the good lives of its citizens. Aristotle could be considered as one of the pioneers in elaborating the ethical concepts of a good life and a good society within a political and social context. "[F]or Aristotle, ethics is a part and aspect of politics… the human good is to be achieved in and through participation in the lives of political communities" (MacIntyre, 2006, p. vii). Aristotle explores ethics not only on a narrow, individual level but also in relation to society. According to Aristotle's ethical philosophy, ethics examines and determines the rules of human behaviour within society. In his works *Nicomachean Ethics* and *Politics*, Aristotle postulates his view of human ethical behaviour, the stance of citizens on political affairs, and his proposal for a good society. Moreover, Aristotle incorporates the concept of a good life not only in his ethical work but also in his work concerning politics. In his view, politics is associated not only with the political affairs of a state but also with the state's social and ethical affairs. The individual, as a citizen, is placed at the centre of the discussion of politics, and the state is placed at the centre of ethics. In *Politics*, Aristotle describes a good life as a virtuous life for every individual who, at the same time, is an integral part of the social structure of the state. In Aristotelian ethics, the good of the state (*polis*) in its totality is perceived as superior to the aim of a good life of any individual separately. This can also broadly describe the notion of the common good in inquiries regarding a good society within our proposal.

So far, we have retrieved some of the key ideas and specific concepts from which the line of reasoning was developed. Accordingly, the inquiry is conceptually heterodox. We have shared the position that, in the ethical study of international development, development ethics is an important alternative to neoclassical economics, which is often neglected in the literature on heterodox economics. The present analysis attempts to fill this gap in the heterodox economics literature. In doing so, we have delivered a specific approach to a paradigm for the ethical study of international development. This approach has placed development ethics in the agenda of political economy and social ethics. However, as we have noted in previous sections, it is fruitless to offer an alternative position without adequately elucidating the precise framework and for whom this alternative position stands. In this vein, we have constructed a comprehensive paradigm for development ethics in international development. This means that the framework responds to the dominant theory and policy of international development. This book has confronted this challenge by focusing on neoliberalism and neoclassical economic analysis in international development theory and policy.

International development theory and policy are dominated by neoliberalism in the intellectual appraisals of neoclassical economics (Chang, 2002; DeMartino, 2000; Lapavitsas, 2005). Examining international development in deeper economic and ethical terms, the question that firstly arises is 'what is the nature of the existing international development?' If it is accepted that the leading worldwide economic system is that of capitalism, the question can instead be posed as 'what is going wrong with the worldwide capitalist economy?'.

To answer this question, we have explored the root functions of market-driven capitalism in the era of neoliberalism. Since the 1970s, applied neoliberal economic policies and strategies have been accelerated in the global economy. In 1979, it was Margaret Thatcher in the United Kingdom that inaugurated neoliberal economic reforms. In the U.S., neoliberalism in the economy became dominant mainly during the years of Reagan's presidency (1981–1989). The reforms of Thatcher and Reagan led the worldwide economy and international development policy towards the Washington Consensus. With the dominance of the Washington Consensus under the support of Reagan and Thatcher's "less state, more market" policies, a neoliberal counter-revolution emerged in developing economies (Toye, 2004, p. 30), mainly focusing on international development theory and policy. This neoliberal shift "insisted on the universal relevance of its presumed notion of economic rationality, and, hence, of laws of supply and demand based on the optimizing behaviour of individuals" (Jomo and Fine, 2006, p. viii).

At this point, it is perhaps appropriate to mention that the worldwide capitalist economy has always been a market-oriented economy, in which the production and distribution of goods and services are regulated by the market mechanism. Nevertheless, "[h]istorically, markets have in fact been embedded in social relations—limited by social customs, constrained by social demands for fairness and, at least in part, directed towards social goals" (MacEwan, 2005, p. 171). In the period following World War

II, along with the market functions, social welfare states (in the cases of the capitalist developed economies) adjusted for market failures. In developing economies, protectionist policies (for example, import-substituted industrialisation) were established. In this era of neoliberalism, the private market functions replaced almost all economic and social activities and penetrated into every sphere of human action. In summary, "neoliberalism refers to new rules of functioning of capitalism, which affect the centre, the periphery, and the relationship between the two" (Duménil and Levy, 2005, p. 10).

The analysis has examined the impact of neoliberalism (in the form of the Washington Consensus policies) on the international economy. Neoliberalism has been imposed around the world by powerful financial institutions and interest groups based in North America, particularly in the United States. This is a kind of Western-exported neoliberalism. The application of neoliberal policies has taken place in many Latin American countries. Williamson (1990) called the imposed neoliberalism in Latin American countries the 'Washington Consensus'. Specifically, Williamson describes the Washington Consensus as an umbrella of interests and institutions, such as the International Monetary Fund (IMF), the World Bank, the U.S. Executive Branch, the Federal Reserve Board, the Inter-American Development Bank, those members of Congress interested in Latin America, and the think tanks concerned with economic policy. Essentially, the Washington Consensus imposed neoliberal economic and social policies on Latin Americans. For Williamson (1990), these policies can be typified around ten axes: (1) fiscal discipline; (2) reordering public expenditure priorities; (3) tax reform; (4) liberalising interest rates; (5) a competitive exchange rate; (6) trade liberalisation; (7) the liberalisation of inward foreign direct investment; (8) privatisation; (9) deregulation; and (10) property rights. We have evaluated the normative-ethical and applied-ethical nature of the Washington consensus policies in Chapters 5 and 6. These policies were intellectually forced by dominant international development institutions, prevailing academic institutes and universities, and worldwide and national economic elites and groups of powers. The Washington Consensus as a neoliberal manifesto (Marangos, 2009; 2007) constitutes a dominant ideology in international development that is mainly applied in the principles and tools of neoclassical economics.

Turning to the theoretical background, we have argued that neoliberalism is conceptually supported by neoclassical economic analysis. In other words, neoliberalism can be perceived as the applied type of neoclassical economic theory in its most positive form. As is mentioned elsewhere in this book, "[t]he most forceful and coherent defence of neoliberalism appears in mainstream economic theory, or 'neoclassical theory'" (DeMartino, 2000, p. 4; see also Chang, 2002). The questions that have been posed include 'what are the fundamentals of neoclassical economic analysis in relation to the ends and means of development?' To answer this, for neoclassical economic analysis, the end state of an economic process (what we have called a good society) is an affluent society in terms of Westernised well-being. At the centre of this discussion is the consumption of goods and services. Regarding the question 'how can a good society be achieved?', the neoclassical answer is through economic development, specifically economic growth. Based on the dominant neoclassical economics conception of economic growth, a good society is determined by the amount of savings that lead to investments, and the growth of gross domestic product (GDP). Economic growth leads to an increase in material consumption in terms of economic well-being; finally, it maximises individual utility through consumption, as can be measured by neoclassical welfare theory. Welfare theory, by using the utility function, measures individual satisfaction, which is mainly determined by the consumption of goods and services and the possession of leisure time and wealth. For neoclassical economists, higher GDP reflects higher economic growth, and higher economic growth implies greater human well-being. Therefore, according to neoclassical economics, the higher the GDP of an economy is, the higher the level of economic well-being and the better off the society will be. In the end, from the neoclassical perspective of a good life, the key element is individuals' consumption. Furthermore, neoclassical economists do not pay significant attention to the notion of equality, precisely because they embrace economics as a value-free science. For example, the neoclassical economists Kaplow and Shavell (2002, xvii) argue that social decision-making should be based exclusively on welfare theory and should not depend on fairness, justice, and/or "cognate concepts". In this manner, neoclassical welfare economics, as analytically discussed in Chapter 5, evaluates economic development as value-neutral and ethically neutral, either at the level of the means or at the level of the ends.

Among the fundamentals of neoclassical economic analysis in the policy format of neoliberalism are individual and entrepreneurial self-interest, property rights, and market efficiency through free markets and open trade. According to Harvey (2005, p. 2):

> Neoliberalism is in the first instance a theory of political economic practices that proposes that human well-being can best be advanced by liberating individual entrepreneurial freedoms and skills within an institutional framework characterized by strong private property rights, free markets, and free trade.

Even according to this brief definition of neoliberalism, individuality overlaps social structures. At the centre of the discussion is the individual self-interest as it is expressed by private property rights and a free-market framework. "The market is an extraordinary mechanism that allows a society—any society, no matter how small or large, simple or complex—to organize the production and distribution of goods and services efficiently" (DeMartino, 2000, p. 4). In neoliberalism, this premise not only refers to market-oriented transactions (such as the production and distribution of goods and services) but also to almost all human and social structures (such as social policy and social relations). Thus, the market is seen as a mechanism capable of acting as an efficient guide for almost all human actions.

To enhance our understanding of neoliberal imperialism's penetration of a wide range of human actions beyond distribution and production, we have perceived neoliberalism not only as an economic doctrine but also as a philosophical pattern. As stated by Harvey, "[n]eoliberalism has, in short, become hegemonic as a mode of discourse" (Harvey, 2005, p. 3). Market efficiency, consumer choice, and transactional thinking extend this kind of neoliberal market logic into the realm of social and personal relationships. As a philosophical pattern, neoliberalism provides answers to questions such as 'why are we here?' and 'what should we do?' In response to these questions, neoliberals answer 'we are here for the market' and 'to compete', respectively. In this respect, neoliberals tend to believe that people exist for the market. The general neoliberal ethical vision is that every human being is an 'entrepreneur'. Individuals should manage their own lives as business units, taking into account the market logic, as previously mentioned. Such social behaviour represents an extension of the market relations into non-economic areas of life. The dominance of market efficiency in all spheres of human actions reflects the ethical imperialism of self-interest. The neoclassical argument is based on the position that a society is simply composed of the sum of its individual agents. Thus, as in the case of neoclassical economics as already discussed, at the centre of the ethical discussion of neoliberalism is individual ethics based on self-interest.

Inspired by the political economy of social ethics and Aristotle's philosophy of examining ethics and politics in combined analysis, we have developed an ethical model for evaluating neoliberalism and neoclassical economics. With reference to ethical theory, there are three commonly accepted moral philosophy sub-categories: meta-ethics, normative ethics, and applied ethics (Kagan, 1998, p. 2). Meta-ethics is defined as the branch of ethical theory that explores, from a higher order, the nature of ethical views, assumptions, and commitments. If we accept that the ethical argument centres on the concept of a good society, meta-ethics answers the question 'what is a good society?' In our analysis, the question has been posed as 'what is the nature of international development?', by expressing the vision of a good society. Normative ethics has been described as an attempt to determine the principles that can be used to evaluate and justify ethical views, assumptions, and commitments within the vision of meta-ethics. At the level of normative-ethical analysis, we have explored the question 'what should the relationship be between the means and the ends of international development?' Finally, we have defined applied ethics as the branch of moral philosophy that investigates ethical issues in private and public life in an applied manner. Applied ethics aspires to solve world problems in the vision of meta-ethics and under the evolution of normative ethics. From a political economy perspective, we have explored the question 'what form of applied ethics could be the most appropriate to policy in international development?'

None of the aforementioned sub-categories of moral philosophy can be characterised as independent. Ethical views, statements, and actions cannot be interpreted specifically under one of the three aforementioned areas; such views, statements, and actions can only be interpreted in view of the ethical interconnections among them. We have used this categorisation in our analysis.

At this stage, we summarise some of the results in accordance with neoliberalism in international development and neoclassical economics. According to the meta-ethical question 'what is the nature of international development?', neoclassical economics interprets the objective of development as being the maximisation of economic well-being on an individual basis through the consumption of goods and services. The consumerist model is based on the notion of a private market. However, in neoliberalism, the private market has a significant role not only in the production or distribution of goods and services but for all human activities. The meta-ethical basis of neoliberalism is economic well-being through a neoliberal market-oriented economy, in which all or almost all human preferences and actions can be expressed in market transactional relations.

Regarding the normative-ethical question 'what should the relationship be between the means and the ends of international development?', in neoclassical theory, the maximisation of consumption comes from the accelerated production of goods and services. In other words, economic growth assures the material prosperity of individuals within society. In neoliberalism, economic growth is private investment-oriented. The minimisation of state intervention in the economy is also important. By definition, a private market failure is better accepted than a government failure. Thus, private solutions are always preferable, even in the case of non-market goods and services (such as social assistance). The normative basis of neoliberalism in international development is economic growth under private market relations or, in other words, a profit economy with a private, free-market structure. In neoliberalism, applied ethics, responding to the question 'what form of applied ethics could be the most appropriate to policy in international development?', takes the form of individual and business ethics. At the core of neoclassical economic analysis is the individual and, by extension, the business unit. It is important to mention that neoliberals usually explain macroeconomics by using microeconomic tools. In neoclassical macroeconomic analysis, the state or nation is usually understood as another form of corporation or household and can therefore be examined as a micro unit. At the level of ethics, neoliberals focus on individual ethics based on self-interest, as well as business ethics based on corporate responsibility. Again, the assumption is the same: the sum of individuals and business units comprises the economy and society.

Development ethics is commonly approached as the ethical reflection on the means and ends of the local, national, and international dimensions of development (Goulet, 1975; Crocker, 1991; 2008). In the holistic-ethical investigation of international development, development ethics has been integrated in the political economy agenda. Furthermore, we have explored the relation of development ethics with Aristotle's philosophy and have shown that development ethics has a strong Aristotelian influence in the manner that it perceives the association of politics and ethics and the notion of the good society. As we have noted in Chapter 2, development ethics implicitly espouses ***eudaimonia*** as the end state of human actions and advances this concept to the macro level of the global world. Thus, development ethics is consistent with the conception of examining ethics and politics in combined analysis, namely social ethics. In the effort towards constructing a comprehensive paradigm for development ethics in international development, a summary of the development ethics alternative to the meta-ethical, normative-ethical, and applied-ethical aspects of neoliberalism and neoclassical economics has been presented.

Challenging worldwide neoliberalism, development ethics precisely defines that a good society is viewed not as growth in the narrow sense of the material expansion of well-being but as the qualitative enrichment of human beings in all relevant aspects of human life. However, are economic growth and material prosperity essential aspects of a good life? Arguably, yes, they are. Nevertheless, they are not the only aspects. At the centre of development ethics analysis is covering people's needs at the material, cultural, and spiritual levels; ensuring social justice; and maintaining ecological balance. Any social construction or institution should service the aforementioned aims. In addition, development ethics focuses on the microeconomic as well as the macroeconomic environment. In other words, development ethics considers ordinary people to be the smallest societal units, considering them as members of local communities and nation-states within intergovernmental surroundings.

Development ethics directly responds to the aforementioned ethical discourse as follows. At the level of meta-ethics, development ethics approaches the notion of development as a multifaceted matter involving economic, political, cultural, and spiritual features, as well as much more too. In the development ethics literature, this is usually referred to as human ascent:

> This total of development can perhaps best be expressed as the 'human ascent'—the ascent of all men in their integral humanity, including the economic, biological, psychological, social, cultural, ideological, spiritual, mystical, and transcendental dimensions (Goulet, 1971, pp. 206–207).

In the development ethics discourse, development is a synonym of a good society. The ingredients of a good society are as follows. First, there must be good lives for all people in all relevant aspects of life, including material and spiritual well-being. People need to cover their biological needs before they can fulfil their cultural and spiritual ones. Nevertheless, a good life is perceived as 'being more' instead of 'having more'. This means that value issues (such as esteem or dignity) play a significant role beyond covering material needs or 'illusionary' wants. Second, a good society is fundamentally based on the notion of social justice. Development ethics mainly relates social justice (in its global or local dimensions) with theories of people's participation, as part of the capability approach in general, and as part of capability equality in particular. The capability approach implies the broad ethical idea that the good lives of people are principally based on the capabilities of the people to act freely in their societies, in terms of transforming available commodities and resources into actions (in the sense of the options of 'doing' and 'being'). Capability equality specifies this concept in the discussion of social justice.

Because inequality is usually derived from economic and political factors with social reflections (such as the free-market economy, in the case of neoliberalism), social policy intrusions are therefore needed to rectify the wrongs of inequality across the spectrum of capabilities within the established free-market relations (DeMartino, 2000, p. 120). In relation to this, the abolishment of vulnerability—the forces that a person or society cannot control—can be seen as a key element of social justice. The third component of a good society in the development ethics discourse is environmental sustainability. As we have previously noted in Chapter 5, development ethicists state that "[t]he ecological imperative is clear and cruel: nature must be saved or we humans will die" (Goulet, 2006, p. 151). For development ethics, sustainability with nature is not only a technical matter but also a mostly political and ethical issue. The analysis is clear: the globalised market economy in the mode of free-market economics and neoliberalism destroys the environmental relations of people with nature. Thus, sustainability with nature can mean "moving away from the self-interested, consumer-oriented values that characterize the modern capitalist societies" (Brennan, 2004, p. 261). For instance, technological advances give the means of attaining sustainability; the decision to attain sustainable development is a matter of an alternative vision of development through ethics and politics.

In the normative-ethical evaluation of international development, development ethics offers a different appraisal to the dominant perspective. Neoclassical economics, as formerly claimed, evaluates the relationship between the ends and the means of development in an instrumental manner. The ends of development are predetermined and the tools for attaining those ends (economic choices and actions) are also predetermined in the framework of a globalised market economy. We have shown that the market mechanism, which supposedly leads to efficient outcomes, is the principal apparatus in the normative analysis of neoclassical welfare economics. For development ethics, either the ends or the means of development are subjected to normative evaluations within ethics. In this manner, ethics becomes 'the means of the means'. In this book, this has been explained as follows. Ethics should work as a device for evaluating not only the vision of a good society but also the very means of attaining this vision.[2] Normative-ethical evaluation of the means of development (policy decisions and instruments, for example) is equally important because, in real-world conditions, development functions at this level. This has implications for the meaning and practice of development. Development should not be upstream oriented by international and national elites and groups of power but by societies and people themselves. Profoundly, this pre-exists a conflict of power at the political level, as politics is the expression of social relations and interests. The normative role of ethics "should not be regarded by developers as mere velleities born of moral passion over the indignities wrought on mankind's poor by heartless wielders of power" (Goulet, 1975, p. 337). Instead, ethics should be regarded as helping politics to become the 'art of redefining the possible', rather than being the 'art of the possible'. Based on these normative premises, development ethics determines a set of normative-ethical goals and strategies for a good international society. In Chapter 5, we have arranged and examined the development ethics normative-ethical goals (life sustenance, esteem, and freedom) and ethical strategies (the abundance of goods, universal solidarity, and participation) as alternative normative-ethical standpoints to neoclassical economics and neoliberalism in international development.

Finally, we have presented a novel exploration of applied ethics in international development policy. In the political economy context, applied ethics has been interwoven with global ethics. In this framework, we examine applied development ethics as an appropriate global ethics, as

[2] Development ethics identifies different approaches to outcomes evaluation, allowing scholars to assess whether a development situation has improved or deteriorated. Furthermore, development ethics provides appropriate means for normative evaluations in development policy. It is therefore both a necessary and a useful area of inquiry in development policy.

opposed to individualistic perspectives of mainstream business ethics. Particularly in the mainstream literature, applied ethics is viewed as professional or deontological ethics in any field of life (e.g., environmental ethics, medical ethics, business ethics, etc.). In neoclassical economics, business ethics explores the moral issues in economics and business mainly from a microeconomic and an individualistic perspective. To investigate international development from the angle of applied ethics as global ethics, we have structured the analysis in the framework of: 1. market relations; 2. the role of nation-state policy; and 3. the role of international development institutions' policies in international development. Neoclassical economics endorses a free-market relations framework in the formation of development policy. Accordingly, neoclassical economists generally allege that free-market economics leads to economic efficiency. Applied development ethics challenges this posture by questioning economic efficiency in terms of 'who it is for' and 'whether it is an adequate framework for all people in the world'. We have argued for the applied-ethical inappropriateness of free-market relations in international development.

At the level of nation-state policy, neoclassical economists are typically against any public policy interventions into market functions. Nevertheless, their neoliberal counterparts use state power to establish free-market conditions, even in the fields of social policy, health services, and education, for instance. In neoliberalism, the main aim of nation-state interventionism is to shift any form of social policy to private hands and to diminish the power of workers' unions (Albo et al., 2010; Duménil and Levy, 2005; Harvey, 2005).

Despite the general critique of the existing reality of public policy in international development, there is no specific discussion within the development ethics literature against the particular nation-state policy in times of neoliberalism. Thus, we have argued for the potential agreement among development ethicists. As it seems from the writings of Stiglitz (1998; 2002) and of Crocker (2008), who discusses development ethics and Stiglitz's development paradigm, a good nation-state policy should involve the private and public sectors. Nation-state policy should be formulated in consideration of the meta-ethical and normative-ethical appraisal of development ethics. In international development institutions' policies, the fundamental development ethics aspect is that the neoliberal policy guide (the Washington Consensus) imposed on the developing world has distorted the real meaning of development policy in many ways, as already discussed. An ethical international development policy should be based on people's solidarity, national independence, resource control, and a nation-state policy involving the participation of the whole society. All of the above should be motivated by the ethical goals of life sustenance, esteem, and freedom for all people and societies in the world.

In this manner, the overall analysis has contributed to the discussions of contemporary neoliberalism and neoclassical economics in international development and has offered an ethical pattern for policy in the direction of good lives for people and good societies for nations. This pattern can be used in nations' future economic strategies and policies based on development ethics viewpoints. In the pluralistic view of political economy, there are always many alternative perspectives. Development ethics offers a pathway towards an alternative ethical paradigm in international development theory.

References

Albo, G., Gindin, S., & Panitch, L. (2010). *In and out of crisis: The global financial meltdown and left alternatives*. PM Press.

Arestis, P., & Sawyer, M. (1993). Political economy: An editorial manifesto. *International Papers in Political Economy, 1*(1), 1–38.

Bowles, S., & Gintis, H. (2000). Walrasian economics in retrospect. *Quarterly Journal of Economics, 115*(4), 1411–1439.

Brennan, A. J. (2004). Environmental problems of the world: Global warming and biodiversity. In P. A. O'Hara (Ed.), *Global political economy and the wealth of nations: Performance, institutions, problems and policies* (pp. 245–266). Routledge.

Caporaso, A., & Levine, D. P. (1993). *Theories of political economy*. Cambridge University Press.

Chang, H.-J. (2002). Breaking the mould: An institutionalist political economy alternative to the neoliberal theory of the market and the state. *Cambridge Journal of Economics, 26*(5), 539–559.

Clark, D. A. (2005). Sen's capability approach and the many spaces of human well-being. *The Journal of Development Studies, 41*(8), 1339–1368.

Crocker, D. (1991). Toward development ethics. *World Development, 19*(5), 457–483.

Crocker, D. (1996). Hunger, capability, and development. In W. Aiken & H. LaFollette (Eds.), *World hunger and morality* (2nd ed., pp. 211–230). Prentice Hall.

Crocker, D. (2008). *Ethics of global development*. Cambridge University Press.

Crocker, D. (2010). Participation in local development: Goulet and deliberative democracy. In C. K. Wilber & A. K. Dutt (Eds.), *New directions in development ethics: Essays in honor of Denis Goulet* (pp. 308–332). Notre Dame University Press.

DeMartino, G. (2000). *Global economy, global justice: Theoretical and policy alternatives to neoliberalism*. Routledge.

Drydyk, J. (2010). Participation, empowerment, and democracy: Three fickle friends. In C. K. Wilber & A. K. Dutt (Eds.), *New directions in development ethics: Essays in honor of Denis Goulet* (pp. 333–356). Notre Dame University Press.

Drydyk, J. (2013). Development ethics and gender justice. *Éthique et économique/Ethics and Economics, 10*(2), 4–10.

Duménil, G., & Levy, D. (2005). The neoliberal (counter-) revolution. In A. Saad-Filho & J. Johnston (Eds.), *Neoliberalism: A critical reader* (pp. 9–19). Pluto Press.

Fine, B., & Milonakis, D. (2009). *From economics imperialism to Freakonomics: The shifting boundaries between economics and other social sciences economics as social theory*. Routledge.

Friedman, M. (1966). The methodology of positive economics. In M. Friedman (Ed.), *Essays in positive economics* (pp. 1–16). University of Chicago Press.

Gasper, D. (2002). Is Sen's capability approach an adequate basis for considering human development? *Review of Political Economy, 14*(2), 435–461.

Gasper, D. (2007). What is the capability approach? Its core, rationale, partners and dangers. *The Journal of Socio-Economics, 36*(3), 335–359.

Gasper, D. (2012). Development ethics—Why? What? How? A formulation of the field. *Journal of Global Ethics, 8*(1), 117–135.

Gill, F. (1996). On ethics and economic science. In P. Groenewegen (Ed.), *Economics and ethics?* (pp. 138–156). Routledge.

Goulet, D. (1971). An ethical model for the study of values. *Harvard Educational Review, 41*(2), 205–227.

Goulet, D. (1975). *The cruel choice: A new concept in the theory of development*. Atheneum.

Goulet, D. (2006). *Development ethics at work: Explorations 1960–2002*. Routledge.

Harvey, D. (2005). *A brief history of neoliberalism*. Oxford University Press.

Hodgson, G. M. (2001). *How economics forgot history: The problem of historical specificity in social science*. Routledge.

Howard, M. C., & King, J. E. (2004). The rise of neo-liberalism in advanced capitalist economies: Towards a materialist explanation. In P. Arestis & M. Sawyer (Eds.), *The rise of the market: Critical essays on the political economy of neo-liberalism* (pp. 38–73). Edward Elgar.

Jomo, K. S., & Fine, B. (2006). Preface. In K. S. Jomo & B. Fine (Eds.), *The new development economics: After the Washington consensus* (pp. vii–xii). Tulika Books.

Kagan, S. (1998). *Normative ethics*. Westview Press.

Kaplow, L., & Shavel, S. (2002). *Fairness versus welfare*. Harvard University Press.

Lapavitsas, C. (2005). Mainstream economics in the neoliberal era. In A. Saad-Filho & D. Johnston (Eds.), *Neoliberalism: A critical reader* (pp. 30–40). Pluto Press.

MacEwan, A. (2005). Neoliberalism and democracy: Market power versus democratic power. In A. Saad-Filho & D. Johnston (Eds.), *Neoliberalism: A critical reader* (pp. 170–176). Pluto Press.

MacIntyre, A. (2006). *Ethics and politics: Selected essays* (Vol. 2). Cambridge University Press.

Marangos, J. (2003). A political economy methodology of modelling the transition process. *Global Business & Economics Review, 5*(2), 197–225.

Marangos, J. (2007). Was shock therapy consistent with the Washington consensus? *Comparative Economic Studies, 49*, 32–58.

Marangos, J. (2009). What happened to the Washington consensus? The evolution of international development policy. *The Journal of Socio-Economics, 38*(1), 197–208.

O'Hara, P. A. (2004). Viability of national government policies in a global political economy. In P. A. O'Hara (Ed.), *Global political economy and the wealth of nations performance, institutions, problems and policies* (pp. 327–346). Routledge.

Sen, A. (1987). *On ethics and economics*. Blackwell.

Stiglitz, J. (1998). Towards a new paradigm for development: Strategies, policies and processes. In *9th Raúl Prebisch Lecture, October 19* (pp. 1–33). United Nations Conference on Trade and Development.

Stiglitz, J. (2002). Participation and development: Perspectives from the comprehensive development paradigm. *Review of Development Economics, 6*(2), 163–182.

Toye, J. & Richard, T., (2004). *The UN and Global Political Economy: Trade, Finance, and Development*, Bloomington and Indianapolis: Indiana University Press.

van Staveren, I. (2007). Beyond utilitarianism and deontology: Ethics in economics. *Review of Political Economy, 19*(1), 21–35.

Williamson, J. (1990). What Washington means by policy reform. In J. Williamson (Ed.), *Latin American adjustment: How much has happened?* (*Chapter 2*). Institute for International Economics. Republished Online (November, 2002). http://www.iie.com/publications/papers/paper.cfm?researchid=486

References

Abbott, A. (1983). Professional ethics. *American Journal of Sociology, 88*(5), 855–885.

Albo, G., Gindin, S., & Panitch, L. (2010). *In and out of crisis: The global financial meltdown and left alternatives*. PM Press.

Alvey, J. E. (1999). A short history of economics as a moral science. *Journal of Markets and Morality, 2*(1), 53–73.

Alvey, J. E. (2000). An introduction to economics as a moral science. *International Journal of Social Economics, 27*(12), 1231–1251.

Anderson, T. L., & Leal, D. R. (1991). *Free market environmentalism*. Westview Press.

Appleby, S., & Bindenagel, C. (2010). The economy of the spirit: Religion, ethics, and development in the thought of denis goulet and in contemporary practice. In C. K. Wilber & A. K. Dutt (Eds.), *New directions in development ethics: Essays in honor of Denis Goulet* (pp. 281–307). University of Notre Dame Press.

Archibald, G. C. (1959). Welfare economics, ethics, and essentialism. *Economica, 26*(104), 316–327.

Arestis, P., & Sawyer, M. (1993). Political economy: An editorial manifesto. *International Papers in Political Economy, 1*(1), 1–38.

Aristotle. (1959 [1932]). *Aristotle politics*. (T. Page, E. Capps, W. Rouse, L. Post, E. Warmington, Eds., & H. Rackham, Trans.) London: William Heinemann Ltd.

Aristotle. (2000). *ARISTOTLE: Nicomachean ethics*. (R. Crisp, Ed., & R. Crisp, Trans.) Cambridge, UK: Cambridge University Press.

N. Astroulakis and N. Karagiannis, *Development Ethics*,
https://doi.org/10.1007/978-3-031-75476-0

Arndt, H. W. (1989). *Economic development: The history of an idea*. University of Chicago Press.

Arrébola-Rodríguez, C. A. (2011). From Washington consensus to post-washington consensus consensus: Consequences in transition economies. *European Perspectives, 1*(4), 19–34.

Arrow, K. J. (1951). *Social choice and individual values*. Wiley.

Arrow, K. J. (1974). *The limits of organization*. Norton.

Arrow, K. J., Sen, A., & Suzumura, K. (Eds.). (2002). *Handbook of social choice and welfare* (Vol. I–II). Amsterdam: Elsevier.

Astroulakis, N. (2011). The development ethics approach to international development. *International Journal of Development Issues, 10*(3), 214–232.

Astroulakis, N. (2013a). Ethics and international development: The development ethics paradigm. *EAST-WEST Journal of Economics and Business, XVI*(1), 99–117.

Astroulakis, N. (2013b). Challenging conventional economics: An ethical development paradigm. *Revista Problemas del Desarrollo, 175*(44), 33–53.

Atkinson, A. B. (2009). Economics as a moral science. *Economica, 76*(s1), 791–804.

Banfield, E. (1958). *The moral basis of a backward society*. Free Press.

Barratt-Brown, M. (1994). *The economics of imperialism*. Penguin Books.

Barratt-Brown, M. (1995). *Models in political economy* (2nd ed.). Penguin Books.

Behrman, J., Birdsall, N., & Szekely, M. (2003). *Economic policy and wage differentials in Latin America*. Center for Global Development: Working Paper, No. 29.

Bentham, J. (2000 [1781]). *An introduction to the principles of morals and legislation*. Kitchener: Batoche Books.

Berger, P. (1974). *Pyramids of sacrifice*. Basic Books.

Berger, P. (1987). *The capitalist revolution*. Aldershot: Wildwood House.

Bergsten, C., & Henning, C. R. (Eds.). (2012). *Global economics in extraordinary times: Essays in honor of John Williamson*. Peterson Institute for International Economics.

Bertin, A. L., & Sirven, N. (2006). Social capital and the capability approach: A social economic theory. In B. J. Clary, W. Dolfsma, & D. M. Figart (Eds.), *Ethics and the market: Insights from social economics* (pp. 191–203). Routledge.

Bhagwati, J. (1993). The case of free trade. *Scientific American, 269*(November), 42–49.

Bhaqwati, J. (2004). *In Defence of Globalization*. Oxford University Press.

Bilson, J. F. (1982). Civil liberty—An econometric investigation. *Kyklos, 35*, 94–114.

Blackorby, C., Bossert, W., & Donaldson, D. (2002). Utilitarianism and the theory of justice. In K. J. Arrow, S. Amartya, & K. Susumura (Eds.), *Handbook of social choice and welfare* (Vol. 1, pp. 543–596). London: Elsevier.

Blaug, M. (1992 [1980]). *The methodology of economics or how economics explain*. Cambridge University Press.

Bottomore, T. (1993). *Elites and society* (2nd ed.). Routledge.

Boulding, K. E. (1969). Economics as a moral science. *The American Economic Review, 59*(1), 1–12.

Bowels, S., Franzini, M., & Pagano, U. (1999). Introduction: Trespassing the boundaries of politics and economics. In S. Bowels, M. Franzini, & U. Pagano (Eds.), *The politics and economics of power* (pp. 2–8). Routledge.

Bowles, S. (2004). *Microeconomics: Behavior, institutions, and evolution*. Princeton University Press.

Bowles, S., & Gintis, H. (1986). *Democracy and capitalism*. Basic Books.

Bowles, S., & Gintis, H. (2000). Walrasian economics in retrospect. *Quarterly Journal of Economics, 115*(4), 1411–1439.

Boylan, T., & Gekker, R. (Eds.). (2009). *Economics, rational choice and normative philosophy*. Routledge.

Bozyk, P. (2006). *Globalization and the transformation of foreign economic policy*. Ashgate.

Brennan, A. J. (2004). Environmental problems of the world: Global warming and biodiversity. In P. A. O'Hara (Ed.), *Global political economy and the wealth of nations: Performance, institutions, problems and policies* (pp. 245–266). Routledge.

Brennan, G., & Eusepi, G. (Eds.). (2009). *The economics of ethics and the ethics of economics: Values, markets and the state*. Edward Elgar.

Broad, R., & Cavanagh, L. (1999). The death of the Washington consensus. *World Policy Journal, 16*(3), 79–88.

Brown, D. (2004). Conspicuous consumption, fashion and style in the global marketplace. In P. A. O'Hara (Ed.), *Global political economy and the wealth of nations: Performance, institutions, problems and policies* (pp. 208–221). Routledge.

Buchanan, A. (1985). *Ethics, efficiency, and the market*. Clarendon Press.

Buchanan, J. M. (1959). Positive economics, welfare economics, and political economy. *Journal of Law and Economics, 2*, 124–138.

Buchanan, J. M. (1986). Contractarianism and democracy. In J. Buchanan (Ed.), *Liberty, market and state*. Brighton: Wheatsheat Books.

Buller, P. F., Kohls, J. J., & Anderson, K. S. (1991). The challenge of global ethics. *Journal of Business Ethics, 10*(10), 767–775.

Bunyard, P. (2002). Deforest the Amazon—Destroy the world. *The Ecologist, 32*(6), 32–33.

Burk, A. (1938). A reformulation of certain aspects of welfare economics. *Quarterly Journal of Economics, 52*(2), 310–334.

Burnham, J. (1960). *The managerial revolution*. Indiana University Press.

Caldwell, B. J. (1988). Hayek's transformation. *History of Political Economy, 20*(4), 513–541.

Caldwell, B. J. (1994 [1982]). *Beyond positivism: Economic methodology in the twentieth century* (Revised ed.). London: Routledge.

Callinicos, A. (2009). *Imperialism and global economy*. Polity Press.

Camacho, L. (2008). Agriculture intensification from the perspective of development ethics. In P. B. Thompson (Ed.), *The ethics of intensification* (pp. 97–110). London: Springer.

Camacho, L. (2010). Goulet on vulnerability as a key concept in development ethics. In C. K. Wilber & A. K. Dutt (Eds.), *New directions in development ethics: Essays in honor of Denis Goulet* (pp. 142–154). Notre Dame University.

Campbell, A. (2012). Marx and Engels's vision of building a good society. In A. P. Society, & J. Marangos (Ed.). New York: Palgrave Macmillan.

Caporaso, A., & Levine, D. P. (1993). *Theories of political economy*. Cambridge University Press.

Carvalho, G. (2001). Sustainable development: Is it achievable within the existing international political economy context? *Sustainable Development, 9*(2), 61–73.

Chadwick, R. (Ed.). (2012). *Encyclopedia of applied ethics* (2nd ed.). Academic Press-Elsevier.

Chang, H.-J. (2002). Breaking the mould: An institutionalist political economy alternative to the neoliberal theory of the market and the state. *Cambridge Journal of Economics, 26*(5), 539–559.

Chomsky, N. (1999). *Profit over people: Neoliberalism and global order*. Seven Story Press.

Clark, D. A. (2002). Development ethics: A research agenda. *International Journal of Social Economics, 29*(11), 830–848.

Clark, D. A. (2002). *Visions of development: A study of human values*. Edward Elgar.

Clark, D. A. (2005). Sen's capability approach and the many spaces of human well-being. *The Journal of Development Studies, 41*(8), 1339–1368.

Clark, D. A. (2006). Capability approach. In D. A. Clark (Ed.), *The Elgar companion to development studies* (pp. 32–45). Edward Elgar.

Clary, B. J., Dolfsma, W., & Figart, D. M. (2006). Introduction. In B. J. Clary, W. Dolfsma, & D. M. Figart (Eds.), *Ethics and the market: Insights from social economics* (pp. 1–8). Routledge.

Clary, B., Dolfsma, W., & Figart, D. (Eds.). (2006). *Ethics and the market: Insights from social economics*. Routledge.

Coats, A. W. (1969). Is there a 'structure of scientific revolutions' in economics? *Kyklos, 22*(2), 289–296.

Cochran, K. P. (1974). Economics as a moral science. *Review of Social Economy, 32*(2), 186–195.

Cohen, A. I., & Wellman, C. H. (Eds.). (2005). *Contemporary debates in applied ethics*. Blackwell Publishing.

Cohen, B. J. (2008). *International political economy: An intellectual history*. Princeton University Press.

Cohen, S. I. (2009). *Economic systems analysis and policies: Explaining global differences, transitions and developments*. Palgrave Macmillan.

Copp, D. (2007). *Morality in a natural world: Selected essays in metaethics*. Cambridge University Press.

Cortina, A. (2003). *Covenant and contact: Politics, ethics and religion*. Peeters.

Cortina, A. (2010). Development ethics: A road to peace. In C. K. Wilber & A. K. Dutt (Eds.), *New directions in development ethics: Essays in honor of Denis Goulet* (pp. 59–78). University of Notre Dame Press.

Costanza, R. (1999). The ecological, economic, and social importance of the oceans. *Ecological Economics, 31*(2), 199–213.

Craig, D., & Porter, D. (2006). *Development beyond neoliberalism? Governance, poverty reduction, and political economy*. Routledge.

Crocker, D. (2001). Globalization and human development: Ethical approaches. In E. Malinvaud, & L. Sabourin (Eds.), *Globalization ethical and institutional concerns, proceedings of the seventh plenary session of the pontifical academy of social sciences, 25–28 April 2001*. Vatican City: The Pontifical Academy of Social Sciences.

Crocker, D. (1991). Toward development ethics. *World Development, 19*(5), 457–483.

Crocker, D. (1996). Hunger, capability, and development. In W. Aiken & H. LaFollette (Eds.), *World hunger and morality* (2nd ed., pp. 211–230). Prentice Hall.

Crocker, D. (1998). Development ethics. In C. Edward (Ed.), *Routledge encyclopedia of philosophy* (Vol. 3, pp. 39–44). Routledge.

Crocker, D. (2006a). Foreword. In D. Goulet (Ed.), *Development ethics at work: Explorations—1960–2002* (pp. v–xxix). London: Routledge.

Crocker, D. (2006b). Development ethics, globalization, and Stiglitz. pp. 1–47. Working paper to appear in M. Krausz and D. Chottergee (Eds.), *Globalization, development, and democracy: Philosophical perspectives*. Retrieved from http://terpconnect.umd.edu/~dcrocker/Courses/Docs/PUAF698Q-Dev%20Ethics,%20Globalization%20and%20Stiglitz.pdf

Crocker, D. (2006c). Sen and deliberative democracy. In A. Kaufman (Ed.), *Capabilities equality: Basic issues and problems* (pp. 155–197). Routledge.

Crocker, D. (2007). Deliberative participation in local development. *Journal of Human Development, 8*(3), 431–455.
Crocker, D. (2008). *Ethics of global development*. Cambridge University Press.
Crocker, D. (2010). Participation in local development: Goulet and deliberative democracy. In C. K. Wilber & A. K. Dutt (Eds.), *New directions in development ethics: Essays in Honor of Denis Goulet* (pp. 308–332). Notre Dame University Press.
Crocker, D., & Linden, T. (Eds.). (1998). *Ethics of consumptions: The good life, justice, and global stewardship*. Lanham, Maryland: Rownan & Littlefield.
Cross, R., & Strachan, D. (2001). Three pillars of conventional wisdom. *Review of Political Economy, 13*(2), 181–200.
Cypher, J. M. (1998). The slow death of the Washington consensus on Latin America. *Latin American Perspectives, 25*(6), 47–51.
Das, A. (1979). *Foundations of gandhian economics*. St Martin's Press.
Davidson, G., & Davidson, P. (1988). *Economics for a civilised society*. W.W. Norton & Company.
DeMartino, G. (2000). *Global economy, global justice: Theoretical and policy alternatives to neoliberalism*. Routledge.
Dobb, M. (1973). *Theories of value and distribution since Adam Smith*. Cambridge University Press.
Dobson, A. (1996). Environment sustainabilities: An analysis and a typology. *Environmental Politics, 5*(3), 401–428.
Dobson, A. (1998). *Justice and the environment: Conceptions of environmental sustainability and dimensions of social justice*. Oxford University Press.
Dolfsma, W., Finch, J., & McMaster, R. (2005). Market and society: (How) do they relate, and contribute to welfare? *Journal of Economic Issues, 39*(2), 347–356.
Dow, S. C. (2000). Prospects for the progress of heterodox economics. *Journal of the History of Economic Thought, 22*(2), 157–170.
Dow, S. C. (2002). *Economic methodology: An inquiry*. Oxford University Press.
Dower, N. (1988). *What is development? A philosopher's answer*. Centre for Development Studies Occasional Paper Series, 3. Glasgow: University of Glasgow.
Dower, N. (1983). Ethics and environmental futures. *International Journal of Environmental Studies, 21*(1), 29–44.
Dower, N. (1998). *World ethics: The new agenda*. Edinburgh University Press.
Dower, N. (1998). Development ethics. In R. Chadwick (Ed.), *Encyclopedia of applied ethics* (pp. 755–766). Academic Press.
Dower, N. (2005). The nature and scope of global ethics and the relevance of the earth charter. *Journal of Global Ethics, 1*(1), 25–43.

Dower, N. (2010). Development and the ethics of the means. In C. K. Wilber & A. K. Dutt (Eds.), *Development ethics new directions: Essays in honor of Denis Goulet* (pp. 29–37). University of Notre Dame.

Drakopoulos, S. (1997). Origins and development of the trend towards value-free economics. *Journal of the History of Economic Thought, 19*(2), 286–300.

Drakopoulos, S., & Karayiannis, A. (2005). A review of Kuhnian and Lakatosian "explanations" in economics. *History of Economic Ideas, XIII*(2), 51–73.

Drydyk, J. (2005). When is development more democratic? *Journal of Human Development, 6*(2), 247–267.

Drydyk, J. (2010). Participation, empowerment, and democracy: Three fickle friends. In C. K. Wilber & A. K. Dutt (Eds.), *New directions in development ethics: Essays in honor of Denis Goulet* (pp. 333–356). Notre Dame University Press.

Drydyk, J. (2013). Development ethics and gender justice. *Éthique et économique/Ethics and Economics, 10*(2), 4–10.

Dugger, W. M. (1977). Social economics: One perspective. *Review of Social Economy, 35*(3), 299–310.

Duménil, G., & Levy, D. (2005). The neoliberal (counter-) revolution. In A. Saad-Filho & J. Johnston (Eds.), *Neoliberalism: A critical reader* (pp. 9–19). Pluto Press.

Dunleavy, P. (2003). *Authoring a Ph.D.: How to plan, draft, write and finish a doctoral thesis or dissertation*. Palgrave Macmillan.

Dutt, A. K. (2004). Uneven development, convergence and north-south Interaction. In P. A. O'Hara (Ed.), *Global political economy and the wealth of nations: Performance, institutions, problems and policies* (pp. 63–83). Routledge.

Dutt, A. K. (2004). Foreword. In P. A. O'Hara (Ed.), *Global political economy and the wealth of nations: Performance, institutions, problems*. London: Routledge.

Dutt, A. K., & Radciliff, B. (Eds.). (2009). *Happiness, economics and politics: Towards a multi-disciplinary approach*. Edward Elgar.

Dutt, A. K., & Wilber, C. K. (2010). Introduction: Development ethics and development economics. In C. K. Wilber & A. K. Dutt (Eds.), *New directions in development ethics—Essays in Honor of Denis Goulet* (pp. 1–26). University of Notre Dame Press.

Dutt, A. K., & Wilber, C. K. (2010). *Economics and ethics: An introduction*. Palgrave Macmillan.

Enderle, G. (1999). An introduction to international business ethics. In G. Enderle (Ed.), *International business ethics: Challenges and approaches*. Notre Dame, IN: University of Notre Dame Press.

Enderle, G. (2000). Business ethics in the intercultural and global context: A conceptual framework. *Zeitschrift für Wirtschafts und Unternehmensethik (ZfWU)[Journal for Business, Economics & Ethics], 1*(3), 263–285.

Enderle, G. (2009). A rich concept of wealth creation beyond profit maximization and adding value. *Journal of Business Ethics, 84*(3), 281–295.
Eskelinen, T. (2009). *Putting global poverty in context: A philosophical essay on power, justice and economy*. University of Jyväskylä.
Eskelinen, T. (2011). Global basis structure and institutions: The WTO as a practical example. *Journal of Global Ethics, 7*(1), 47–58.
Etzioni, A. (1987). Toward a Kantian socio-economics. *Review of Social Economics, 45*(1), 37–47.
Feldman, A. M., & Serrano, R. (2006). *Welfare economics and social choice theory* (2nd ed.). Springer.
Fine, B. (1980). *Economic theory and ideology*. Edward Arnold.
Fine, B. (2003). Neither the Washington nor the post-Washington consensus: An introduction. In B. Fine, C. Lapavitsas, & J. Pincus (Eds.), *Development policy in the twenty-first century: Beyond the post-Washington consensus* (pp. 1–27). Routledge.
Fine, B. (2004). Economics and ethics: Amartya Sen as point of departure. *New School Economic Review, 1*(1), 95–103.
Fine, B. (2004). Examining the ideas of globalisation and development critically: What role for political economy? *New Political Economy, 9*(2), 213–231.
Fine, B., Lapavitsas, C., & Pincus, J. (Eds.). (2003). *Development policy in the twenty-first century: Beyond the post-Washington consensus*. Routledge.
Fine, B., & Milonakis, D. (2009). *From economics imperialism to Freakonomics: The shifting boundaries between economics and other social sciences economics as social theory*. Routledge.
Firebauht, G. (2006). *The new geography of global income inequality*. Harvard University Press.
Foucault, M. (1984). Politics and ethics: An interview. In P. Rabinow (Ed.), *The Foucault reader* (pp. 373–380). Pantheon Books.
Frankena, W. (1951). Moral philosophy at mid-century. *The Philosophical Review, 60*(1), 44–55.
Friedman, M. (1953). *Essays in positive economics*. Chicago University Press.
Friedman, M. (2002 [1962]). *Capitalism and freedom*. Chicago: University of Chicago Press.
Friedman, M. (1966). The methodology of positive economics. In M. Friedman (Ed.), *Essays in positive economics* (pp. 1–16). University of Chicago Press.
Friedman, M., & Friedman, R. (1980). *Free to choose: A personal statement*. New York: Harcourt Brace Jovanovich.
Fromm, E. (1999). *Man for himself*. Routledge.
Fromm, E. (2005). *To have or to be*. Continuum International Publishing Group.
Fukuyama, F. (1992). *The end of history and the last man*. New York: The Free Press: A Division of Macmillan, Inc.

Galbraith, J. K. (1991). Economics in the century ahead. *The Economic Journal, 101*(404), 41–46.
Gasper, D. (2002). Is Sen's capability approach an adequate basis for considering human development? *Review of Political Economy, 14*(2), 435–461.
Gasper, D. (2004). *The ethics of development*. Edinburgh University Press.
Gasper, D. (2006). Introduction: Working in development ethics—A tribute to Denis Goulet. *Éthique et économique/Ethics and Economics, 4*(2), 1–24.
Gasper, D. (2007). What is the capability approach? Its core, rationale, partners and dangers. *The Journal of Socio-Economics, 36*(3), 335–359.
Gasper, D. (2008). Denis Goulet and the project of development ethics: Choices in methodology, focus and organization. *Journal of Human Development, 9*(3), 453–474.
Gasper, D. (2012). Development ethics—Why? What? How? A formulation of the field. *Journal of Global Ethics, 8*(1), 117–135.
Gasper, D., & St. Clair, A. L. (Eds.). (2010). *Development ethics*. London: Ashgate.
Gasper, D., & St. Clair, A. L. (2010). The field of development ethics—An introduction. In D. Gasper & A. L. St. Clair (Eds.), *Development ethics* (pp. 13–33). London: Ashgate.
Gasper, D., & Truong, T.-D. (2005). Deepening development ethics: From economism to human development to human security. *The European Journal of Development Research, 17*(3), 372–384.
Gassler, R. S. (2007). Political and social economics: Beyond orthodoxy and heterodoxy. *Forum for Social Economics, 36*(2), 109–125.
Geivett, D. R. (2005). Metaethics. In K. J. Roth (Ed.), *Ethic-encyclopedias* (pp. 943–944). Salem Press.
Gewirth, A. (1960). Meta-ethics and normative ethics. *Mind (New Series), 69*(274), 187–205.
Gill, F. (1996). On ethics and economic science. In P. Groenewegen (Ed.), *Economics and ethics?* (pp. 138–156). Routledge.
Gill, R. T. (1973). Reviewed work(s): The cruel choice: A new concept in the theory of development by Denis Goulet. *Political Science Quarterly, 88*(1), 116–117.
Gilpin, R. (2001). *Global political economy: Understanding the international economic order*. Princeton University Press.
Gintis, H. (1972). A radical analysis of welfare economics and individual development. *The Quarterly Journal of Economics, 86*(4), 572–599.
Goldsmith, A. A. (1995). Democracy, property rights and economic growth. *Journal of Development Studies, 32*(2), 157–174.
Gore, C. (2000). The rise and fall of the Washington consensus as a paradigm for developing countries. *World Development, 28*(5), 789–804.

Goulet, D. (1968). Development for what? *Comparative Political Studies, 1*(2), 295–312.
Goulet, D. (1971). An ethical model for the study of values. *Harvard Educational Review, 41*(2), 205–227.
Goulet, D. (1975). *The cruel choice: A new concept in the theory of development.* Atheneum.
Goulet, D. (1975). Pyramids of sacrifice: The high price of social change. *Christianity and Crisis, 35*(16), 231–236.
Goulet, D. (1976). On the ethics of development planning. *Studies in Comparative International Development, 11*(1), 25–43.
Goulet, D. (1983). Obstacles to world development: An ethical reflection. *World Development, 11*(7), 609–624.
Goulet, D. (1986). Three rationalities in development decision-making. *World Development, 14*(2), 301–317.
Goulet, D. (1989). Participation in development: New avenues. *World Development, 17*(2), 165–178.
Goulet, D. (1992). Development indicators: A research problem, a policy problem. *The Journal of Socio-Economics, 21*(3), 245–260.
Goulet, D. (1992). Ethics and development: A development ethicist at work. *Research and Explorations, 8*(2), 138–147.
Goulet, D. (1992). International ethics and human rights. *Alternatives, 17*(2), 231–246.
Goulet, D. (1995). *Development ethics: A guide to theory and practice.* The Apex Press.
Goulet, D. (1996). Authentic development: Is it sustainable? In D. C. Pirages (Ed.), *Building sustainable societies: A blueprint for a post-industrial world* (pp. 189–205). Armonk, NY: M.E. Sharpe.
Goulet, D. (1997). Development ethics: A new discipline. *International Journal of Social Economics, 24*(11), 1160–1171.
Goulet, D. (2001). Ethical analysis in development economics. In A. K. Dutt & K. P. Jameson (Eds.), *Crossing the mainstream: Ethical and methodological issues in economics* (pp. 29–51). University of Notre Dame Press.
Goulet, D. (2004). Changing development debates under globalization: The evolving nature of development in the light of globalization. *Journal of Law and Social Challenges, 6*(1), 1–17.
Goulet, D. (2006). *Development ethics at work: Explorations 1960–2002.* Routledge.
Goulet, D. (2006). Development ethics. In D. Clark (Ed.), *The Elgar companion to development studies* (pp. 115–120). Cheltenham: Edward Elgar Publishing.
Goulet, D., & Hudson, M. (1971). *The myth of aid: The hidden agenda of the development reports.* IDOC.

Graafland, J. (2007). *Economics, ethics and the market: Introduction and applications*. Routledge.

Gravel, N., & Moyes, P. (2013). Utilitarianism or Welfarism: Does it make a difference? *Soc Choice Welf, 40*, 529–551.

Griffin, J. (1986). *Well-being; Its meaning, measurements and moral importance*. Oxford University Press.

Groenewegen, P. (Ed.). (1996). *Economics and ethics?* Routledge.

Guillén, M. F. (2001). Is globalization civilizing, destructive, or feeble? A critique of five key debates in the social science literature. *Annual Review of Sociology, 27*, 235–260.

Haq, K., & Ponzio, R. (Eds.). (2008). *Pioneering the human development revolution: An intellectual biography of Mahbub ul Haq*. Oxford University Press.

Hardison, F., & Myers, C. A. (1964). *Education, manpower, and economic growth*. McGraw-Hill.

Harman, G. (1977). *The nature of morality: An introduction to ethics*. Oxford University Press.

Harry, P. (2010). *World ethics and climate change: From international to global justice*. Edinburgh University Press.

Harvey, D. (1993). Class relations, social justice and the politics of difference. In J. Squires (Ed.), *Principled positions: Postmodernism and the rediscovery of value* (pp. 85–120). Lawrence & Wishart Ltd.

Harvey, D. (2005). *A brief history of neoliberalism*. Oxford University Press.

Harvey, D. (2010). *The enigma of capital, and the crises of capitalism*. Oxford University Press.

Hausman, D. M. (1989). Economic methodology in a nutshell. *The Journal of Economic Perspectives, 3*(2), 115–127.

Hausman, D. M., & McPherson, M. S. (1993). Taking ethics seriously: Economics and contemporary moral philosophy. *Journal of Economic Literature, 31*(2), 671–731.

Hausman, D. M., & McPherson, M. S. (2006). *Economic analysis, moral philosophy, and public policy* (2nd ed.). Cambridge University Press.

Hayek, F. A. (1948). *Individualism and economic order*. University of Chicago.

Hayek, F. A. (1979). *Social justice, socialism and democracy: Three Australian lectures*. Centre of Independent Studies.

Häyry, M. (1994). *Liberal utilitarianism and applied ethics*. Routledge.

Hicks, J. (1939). *Value and capital*. Oxford University Press.

Hicks, J. (1959). *Essays in world economy*. Oxford University Press.

Hirsch, F. (1976). *Social limits to growth*. Harvard University Press.

Hirschman, A. O. (1988 [1958]). *The strategy of economic development*. Boulder: Westview Press.

Hirschman, A. O. (1985). Against parsimony: Three easy ways of complicating some categories of economic discourse. *Economics and Philosophy, 1*(1), 7–21.
Hirshleifer, J. (1985). The expanding domain of economics. *The American Economic Review, 75*(6), 53–68.
Hodgson, G. M. (1999). *Economics and Utopia: Why the learning economy is not the end of history*. Routledge.
Hodgson, G. M. (2001). *How economics forgot history: The problem of historical specificity in social science*. Routledge.
Honderich, T. (1995). *The Oxford companion to philosophy*. Oxford University Press.
Howard, M. C., & King, J. E. (2004). The rise of neo-liberalism in advanced capitalist economies: Towards a materialist explanation. In P. Arestis & M. Sawyer (Eds.), *The rise of the market: Critical essays on the political economy of neo-liberalism* (pp. 38–73). Edward Elgar.
Human Development Report. (2013). *The rise of the south: Human progress in a diverse world*. New York, NY: The United Nations Development Programme.
Hunter, J. D., & Yates, J. (2002). In the vanguard of globalization. In P. L. Berger & S. P. Huntington (Eds.), *Many globalizations: Cultural diversity in the contemporary world* (pp. 323–357). Oxford University Press.
Huntington, S., & Nelson, J. (1976). *No easy choice: Political participation in developing countries*. Harvard University Press.
Hutchison, T. W. (1938). *The significance and basic postures of economic theory*. Macmillan.
Jameson, K. P. (2010). Ethics and contemporary macroeconomic policy. In C. K. Wilber & A. K. Dutt (Eds.), *New directions in development ethics: Essays in honor of Denis Goulet* (pp. 400–425). Notre Dame University Press.
Jevons, S. (1911 [1871]). *The theory of political economy*. London: Macmillan.
Jomo, K. S. (2005). Introduction. In K. S. Jomo (Ed.), *The pioneers of development economics: Great economists on development* (pp. 7–8). London: Zed Books.
Jomo, K. S., & Fine, B. (2006). Preface. In K. S. Jomo & B. Fine (Eds.), *The new development economics: After the Washington consensus* (pp. vii–xii). Tulika Books.
Jomo, K. S., & Reinert, E. S. (Eds.). (2005). *Origins of development economics: How schools of economic thought addressed development*. Zed Books.
Kagan, S. (1998). *Normative ethics*. Westview Press.
Kaplow, L., & Shavel, S. (2002). *Fairness versus welfare*. Harvard University Press.
Keynes, J. M. (1972 [1926]). The end of laissez-faire [1926]. In D. Moggridge (Ed.), *The collected writings of John Maynard Keynes* (Vol. 9). London: Macmillan.

Knoedler, J. T. (1997). Veblen and technical efficiency. *Journal of Economic Issues, 31*(4), 1011–1026.
Kolodko, G. W. (2000). Transition to a market and entrepreneurship: The systemic factors and policy options. *Communist and Post-Communist Studies, 33*(3), 271–293.
Kraut, R. (2022). Aristotle's ethics. In E. N. Zalta and U. Nodelman (Eds.) *The Stanford encyclopedia of philosophy* (Fall). Stanford, CA: Stanford University. https://plato.stanford.edu/archives/fall2022/entries/aristotle-ethics/
Kuczynski, P. P., & Williamson, J. (Eds.). (2003). *After the Washington consensus*. Institute for International Studies.
Kuhn, T. S. (1970 [1962]). *The structure of scientific revolutions* (Second ed.). Chicago: The University of Chicago Press.
Kuznets, S. (1955). Economic growth and income inequality. *The American Economic Review, 45*(1), 1–28.
Kuznets, S. (1971). *Economic growth of nations: Total output and production structure*. Belknap Press of Harvard University Press.
LaFollette, H. (2002). *Ethics in practice: An anthology* (2nd ed.). Blackwell Publishing.
Lapavitsas, C. (2005). Mainstream economics in the neoliberal era. In A. Saad-Filho & D. Johnston (Eds.), *Neoliberalism: A critical reader* (pp. 30–40). Pluto Press.
Lawson, T. (2006). The nature of heterodox economics. *Cambridge Journal of Economics, 30*(4), 483–505.
Lee, F. S. (2008). Heterodox economics. *The Long Term View, 7*(1), 23–30.
Levinson, M. (2000). The cracking Washington consensus. *Dissent, 47*(4), 11–14.
Lines, T. (2010). Speculation in food commodity markets. *A report commissioned by the World Development Movement* (pp. 1–18).
Little, D. (1995). *On the reliability of economic models: Essays in the philosophy of economics*. Kluwer Academic Publishers.
Little, D. (2003). *The paradox of wealth and poverty*. Westview Press.
Little, I. (2004). *Ethics, economics, and politics*. Oxford University Press.
Lucas, R. E. (2000). Some macroeconomics for the 21st century. *Journal of Economic Perspectives, 14*(1), 159–168.
Lutz, M. A. (1999). *Economics for the common good*. Routledge.
MacEwan, A. (2005). Neoliberalism and democracy: Market power versus democratic power. In A. Saad-Filho & D. Johnston (Eds.), *Neoliberalism: A critical reader* (pp. 170–176). Pluto Press.
Machlup, F. (1978). *Methodology of economics and other social sciences*. Academic Press.
MacIntyre, A. (2006). *Ethics and politics: Selected essays* (Vol. 2). Cambridge University Press.

Madjd-Sadjadi, Z., & Karagiannis, N. (2013). Why is neoliberalism dangerous? Criticism, alternative perspectives, and government policy implications. In N. Karagiannis, Z. Madjd-Sadjadi, & S. Sen (Eds.), *The US economy and neoliberalism: Alternative strategies and policies* (pp. 11–31). Routledge.

Malthus, T. R. (1798). *An essay on the principle of population*. London: J. Johnson.

Marangos, J. (2003). A political economy methodology of modelling the transition process. *Global Business and Economics Review, 5*(2), 197–225.

Marangos, J. (2004). *Alternative economic models of transition*. Ashgate.

Marangos, J. (2007). Was shock therapy consistent with the Washington consensus? *Comparative Economic Studies, 49*, 32–58.

Marangos, J. (2008). The evolution of the anti-Washington consensus debate: From 'Post-Washington consensus' to 'after the Washington consensus.' *Competition and Change, 12*(3), 227–244.

Marangos, J. (2009a). What happened to the Washington consensus? The evolution of international development policy. *The Journal of Socio-Economics, 38*(1), 197–208.

Marangos, J. (2009b). The evolution of the term 'Washington consensus.' *Journal of Economic Surveys, 23*(2), 350–384.

Marangos, J., & Astroulakis, N. (2009). The institutional foundation of development ethics. *Journal of Economic Issues, XLIII*(2), 381–388.

Marangos, J., & Astroulakis, N. (2012). The development ethics perspective of a good society. In J. Marangos (Ed.), *Alternative perspectives of a good society* (pp. 79–98). Palgrave Macmillan.

Marshall, A. (1920 [1890]). *Principles of economics* (Eight ed.). London: Macmillan and Co., Ltd (Retrieved by Library of Economics and Liberty: http://www.econlib.org/library/Marshall/marP28.html).

Max-Neef, M. A. (1992). *From the outside looking in: Experiences in 'Barefoot Economics.'* London: Zed Books.

McNeill, D., & St. Clair, A. L. (2009). *Global poverty, ethics and human rights: The role of multilateral organisations*. Abingdon: Routledge.

Milios, J., & Sotiropoulos, D. P. (2009). *Rethinking imperialism: A study of capitalist rule*. Palgrave Macmillan.

Mill, J. S. (2004 [1879]). Utilitarianism by John Stuart Mill. (Reprinted from FRASER'S MAGAZINE (Seventh Ed.) London Longmans, Green, and Co.[1879]). A Penn state electronic classics series publication: Pennsylvania State University. http://www2.hn.psu.edu/faculty/jmanis/jsmill/Utilitarianism.pdf

Milonakis, D., & Fine, B. (2009). *From political economy to economics: Method, the social and the historical in the evolution of economic theory*. Routledge.

Moore, G. E. (1960 [1903]). *Principia ethica (1903)*. Cambridge: Cambridge University Press.

Morgenthau, H. (1948). *Politics among nations*. Alfred A. Knopf.
Muradian, R., & Martinez-Alier, J. (2001). Trade and the environment: From a 'Southern' perspective. *Ecological Economics, 36*(2), 281–297.
Murithi, T. (2009). *The ethics of peace building*. Edinburgh University Press.
Myrdal, G. (1969). *Objectivity in social research*. Pantheon Books.
Myrdal, G. (1974). What is development? *Journal of Economic Issues, III*(4), 729–736.
Myrdal, G. (1977 [1968]). *Asian drama: An inquiry into the poverty of nations*. London: Pelican books.
Naim, M. (1994). Latin America: The second stage of reforms. *Journal of Democracy, 5*(4), 32–48.
North, D. C. (1990). *Institutions, institutional change and economic performance*. Cambridge University Press.
North, D. (1991). Institutions. *Journal of Economic Perspectives, 5*(1), 97–112.
Nozick, R. (1974). *Anarchy, state, and utopia*. Blackwell.
Nussbaum, M. (2000). *Women and human development: The capabilities approach*. Cambridge University Press.
Nussbaum, M. (2003). Capabilities as fundamental entitlements: Sen and social justice. *Feminist Economics, 9*(2–3), 33–60.
O'Neil, J. (1998). *The market: Ethics, knowledge and politics*. Routledge.
O'Boyle, E. J. (1994). Homo socio-economicus: Foundational to social economics and the social economy. *Review of Social Economy, 52*(3), 286–313.
O'Hara, P. A. (Ed.). (2004). *Global political economy and the wealth of nations: Performance, institutions, problems and policies*. Routledge.
O'Hara, P. A. (2004). Viability of national government policies in a global political economy. In P. A. O'Hara (Ed.), *Global political economy and the wealth of nations performance, institutions, problems and policies* (pp. 327–346). Routledge.
O'Hara, P. A. (2006). *Growth and development in the global political economy: Social structures of accumulation and modes of regulation*. Routledge.
Okereke, C. (2008). *Global justice and neoliberal environmental governance*. Routledge.
Olson, M. (1982). *The rise and decline of nations*. Yale University Press.
Olson, M. (1993). Dictatorship, democracy, and development. *The American Political Science Review, 87*(3), 567–576.
Owens, J. (1983). Business ethics in the college classroom. *Journal of Business Education, 58*(7), 258–262.
Pareto, V. (1927). *Manual of political economy*. (A. S. Schwier, Trans.) London: Macmillan.
Parfitt, T. (2012). Development ethics: Means of the means? *Review of African Political Economy, 39*(134), 672–681.

Parish, W. L., & Michelson, E. (1996). Politics and markets: Dual transformations. *American Journal of Sociology, 101*(4), 1042–1059.
Penz, P., Drydyk, J., & Bose, P. S. (2011). *Displacement by development: Ethics, rights and responsibilities*. Cambridge University Press.
Perroux, F. (1950). Economic space: Theory and applications. *The Quarterly Journal of Economics, 64*(1), 89–104.
Perroux, F. (1955). Note sur la notion de pôle de croissance. *Economie appliquée, 8*(1–2), 307–320.
Perroux, F. (1964). *L économie du XXème siècle*. Presses Universitaires de France.
Perroux, F. (1981). *Pour une philosophie du nouveau développement* (Vol. 4). Presses de l'UNESCO.
Petter, D. (1996). *Modern environmentalism: An introduction*. London: Routledge.
Pigou, A. C. (1920). *The economics of welfare*. Macmillan.
Pogge, T. (2002). *World poverty and human rights: Cosmopolitan responsibilities and reforms*. Polity Press.
Pogge, T. (2005). World poverty and human rights. *Ethics & International Affairs, 19*(1), 1–7.
Pogge, T. (2008). *World, poverty, and human rights*. Polity press.
Polanyi, K. (2001 [1944]). *The great transformation*. Boston, MA: Beacon Press.
Posner, R. A. (1977). *The economic analysis of law* (2nd ed.). Little, Brown and Co.
Pourgerami, A., & Assane, D. (1992). Macroeconomic determinants of growth: New measurement and evidence on the effect of political freedom. *Applied Economics, 24*(1), 129–136.
Pusey, M. (1991). *Economic rationalism in Canberra: A nation-building state changes its mind*. Cambridge University Press.
Putnam, R. D. (1977). Elite transformation in advance industrial societies: An empirical assessment of the theory of technocracy. *Comparative Political Studies, 10*(3), 383–411.
Qizilbash, M. (1996). Ethical development. *World Development, 24*(7), 1209–1221.
Radice, H. (2005). Neoliberal globalisation: Imperialism without empires? In A. Saad-Filho & D. Johnston (Eds.), *Neoliberalism: A critical reader* (pp. 91–98). Pluto Press.
Rassekh, F., & Speir, J. (2010). Can economic globalization lead to a more just society? *Journal of Global Ethics, 6*(1), 27–43.
Rawls, J. (1951). Outline of a decision procedure for ethics. *The Philosophical Review, 60*(2), 177–197.
Rawls, J. (1971). *A theory of justice*. Oxford University Press.
Rifkin, J. (2000). *The age of access*. Tarcher/Putnam.

Robbins, L. (1945 [1932]). *An essay on the nature and significance of economic science* (second ed.). London: Macmillan.
Rodrik, D. (2006). Goodbye Washington consensus, hello Washington confusion? A review of the world bank's economic growth in the 1990s: Learning from a decade of reform. *Journal of Economic Literature, 44*(4), 973–987.
Roemer, J. E. (1994). *A future for socialism.* Harvard University Press.
Røpke, I. (1999). The dynamics of willingness to consume. *Ecological Economics, 28*(3), 399–420.
Ross, D. (1995 [1923]). *ARISTOTLE* (Sixth ed.). Routledge.
Rosser, B. J., & Rosser, M. V. (2004). *Comparative economics in a transforming world economy.* The MIT Press.
Rothschild, K. W. (1993). *Ethics and economic theory: Ideas, models, dilemmas.* Edward Elgar.
Rowthorn, R. (1996). Ethics and economics: An economist's view. In P. Groenewegen (Ed.), *Economics and ethics?* (pp. 15–33). Routledge.
Saad-Filho, A., & Johnston, D. (2005). Introduction. In A. Saad-Filho & D. Johnston (Eds.), *Neoliberalism: A critical reader* (pp. 1–6). Pluto Press.
Saad-Filho, A., & Johnston, D. (Eds.). (2005). *Neoliberalism: A critical reader.* Pluto Press.
Saavedra, J. (2003). Labor Markets during the 1990s. In P. P. Kuczynski & J. Williamson (Eds.), *After the Washington consensus: Restarting growth and reform in Latin America* (pp. 213–263). Institute for International Economics.
Sachs, I. (1984). *Dıvelopper, les Champs de Planification.* Universitı Coopırative.
Sally, R. (1998). *Classical liberalism and international economic order: Studies in theory and intellectual history.* Routledge.
Samuelson, P. (1947). *Foundations of economic analysis.* Harvard University.
Schumpeter, S. A. (2006 [1954]). *History of economic analysis. Edited from manuscript by E.B. Schumpeter, with an introduction by M. Perlman.* Taylor & Francis e-Library, Routledge. (First published in Great Britain in 1954 by Allen & Unwin (Publishers) Ltd.)
Schwenke, C. (2009). *Reclaiming value in international development: The moral dimensions of development policy and practice in poor countries.* Praeger Publishers.
Schwenke, C. (2011). Development ethics: The audacious agenda. In R. S. Fortner & P. M. Fackler (Eds.), *The handbook of global communication and media ethics* (Vol. I–II, pp. 317–341). Oxford: Wiley-Blackwell.
Sedgwick, P. H. (2004). *The market economy and Christian ethics.* Cambridge University Press.
Seer, D. (1972). The meaning of development. *Journal of Development Studies, 8*(3), 21–36.

Sen, A. (1977). Rational fools: A critique of the behavioral foundations of economic theory. *Philosophy and Public Affairs, 6*(4), 317–344.

Sen, A. (1979a). Utilitarianism and welfarism. *The Journal of Philosophy, 76*(9), 463–489.

Sen, A. (1979b). Personal utilities and public judgements: Or what's wrong with welfare economics. *The Economic Journal, 89*, 537–558.

Sen, A. (1980). Description as choice. *Oxford Economic Paper, 32*(3), 353–369.

Sen, A. (1981). *Poverty and famines: An essay on entitlements and deprivation*. Oxford University Press.

Sen, A. (1984). *Resources, values and development*. Blackwell.

Sen, A. (1987). *On ethics and economics*. Blackwell.

Sen, A. (1997). *Resources, values, and development* (Expanded). Harvard University Press.

Sen, A. (1998). The living standard. In D. Crocker & T. Linden (Eds.), *Ethics of consumption* (pp. 287–311). Rowman & Littlefield Publishers Inc.

Sen, A. (1999). *Development as freedom*. Oxford University Press.

Sen, A. (2004). *Rationality and freedom*. Harvard University Press.

Serra, N., & Stiglitz, J. (Eds.). (2008). *The Washington consensus reconsidered*. Oxford University Press.

Sidgwick, H. (2005 [1897]). The Elements of Politics. *Elibron classics edition first published in 1897 by Macmillan and Co. Limited, London*. Adamant Media Corporation.

Singer, P. (2002). *One world: The ethics of globalization*. Yale University Press.

Singer, P. (2011). *Practical ethics*. Cambridge University Press.

Slim, H. (1995). What is development? *Development in Practice, 5*(2), 143–148.

Smith, A. (1776). *An inquiry into the nature and causes of the wealth of nation*. [E. Cannan, Ed. (1904), *2 vols*, London: Methuen]. Retrieved from ElecBook Classics, Book I–V.

Smith, A. (1986 [1776]). *The wealth of nations*. London: Penguin.

Smith, A. (2004 [1759]). *The theory of moral sentiments*. (K. Haakonssen, Ed.) Cambridge: Cambridge University Press.

Solow, R. M. (1956). A contribution to the theory of economic growth. *The Quarterly Journal of Economics, 70*(1), 65–94.

Solow, R. M. (1957). Technical change and the aggregate production function. *Review of Economics and Statistics, 39*(3), 312–320.

Sotiropoulos, D. P., Milios, J., & Lapatsioras, S. (2012). Demystifying finance: How to understand financialization and think of strategies for a good society. In J. Marangos (Ed.), *Alternative perspectives of a good society* (pp. 99–120). Palgrave-Macmillan.

Soubbotina, T. P. (2004). *Beyond economic growth: An introduction to sustainable development* (2nd ed.). Washington, DC: The World Bank.

Srinivasan, T. N. (2000). The Washington consensus a decade later: Ideology and the art and science of policy advice. *The World Bank Research Observer, 15*(2), 265–270.

St Clair, A. L. (2007). A methodologically pragmatist approach to development ethics. *Journal of Global Ethics, 3*(2), 143–164.

St Clair, A. L. (2010). Global poverty: Development ethics meet global justice. In C. K. Wilber & A. K. Dutt (Eds.), *New directions in development ethics: Essays in honor of Denis Goulet* (pp. 249–278). Notre Dame, IN: University of Notre Dame Press.

Steele, G. R. (2007). *The economics of Friedrich Hayek*. Palgrave Macmillan.

Stewart, F. (1997). John Williamson and the Washington consensus revisited. In L. Emmerij (Ed.), *Economic and social development in the XXI century* (pp. 62–69). Inter-American Development Bank.

Stiglitz, J. (1998). Towards a new paradigm for development: Strategies, policies and processes. In *9th Raúl Prebisch lecture, October 19* (pp. 1–33). Geneva: United Nations Conference on Trade and Development.

Stiglitz, J. (1999). More instruments and broader goals: Moving toward the post-Washington consensus. *Revista de Economia Politica, 19*(1), 94–120.

Stiglitz, J. (2000a). Unraveling the Washington consensus. *Multinational Monitor, 21*(4), 13–21.

Stiglitz, J. (2000b). Capital market liberalization, economic growth, and instability. *World Development, 28*(6), 1075–1086.

Stiglitz, J. (2002a). Information and the change in the paradigm in economics. *The American Economic Review, 92*(3), 460–501.

Stiglitz, J. (2002b). *Globalization and its discontents*. W. W. Norton.

Stiglitz, J. (2002c). Participation and development: Perspectives from the comprehensive development paradigm. *Review of Development Economics, 6*(2), 163–182.

Stiglitz, J., Ocampo, J. A., Spiegel, S., Ffrench-Davis, R., & Nayyar, D. (2006). *Stability with growth*. Oxford University Press.

Street, J. H. (2001). The institutionalist theory of economic development. *Journal of Economic Issues, 21*(4), 1861–1887.

Streeten, P. (1994). Human development: Means and ends. *The American Economic Review, 84*(2), 232–237.

Streeten, P., Burki, S. J., Haq, M. U., Hicks, N., & Stewart, F. (1981). *First things first: Meeting basic human needs in development countries*. New York: Oxford University Press (Published for the World Bank).

Suzumura, K. (2002). Introduction. In K. J. Arrow, A. Sen, & K. Suzumura (Eds.), *Handbook of Social choice and welfare* (Vol. 1, pp. 1–32). London: Elsevier.

Swan, T. W. (1956). Economic growth and capital accumulation. *Economic Record, 32*(2), 334–361.

Syrquin, M. (1988). Patterns of structural change. In H. Chenery & T. N. Srinivasan (Eds.), *Handbook of development economics* (Vol. 1, pp. 203–273). London: Elsevier.

Tomas, A. (2000). Development as practice in a liberal capitalist world. *Journal of International Development, 12*(6), 773–787.

Toy, J. (1993). *Dilemmas of development* (2nd ed.). Blackwell.

Tsakalotos, E. (2004). Social norms and endogenous preferences: The political economy of market expansion. In P. Arestis & M. Sawyer (Eds.), *The rise of the market: Critical essays on the political economy of neo-liberalism* (pp. 5–37). Edward Elgar.

Tsoufidis, L. (2010). *Competing schools of economic thought*. Springer.

van Staveren, I. (2001). *The values of economics: An Aristotelian perspective*. Routledge.

van Staveren, I. (2007). Beyond utilitarianism and deontology: Ethics in economics. *Review of Political Economy, 19*(1), 21–35.

van Staveren, I. (2009). Efficiency. In J. Peil & I. van Staveren (Eds.), *Handbook of economics and ethics* (pp. 107–114). Edward Elgar.

Vickers, D. (1997). *Economics and ethics: An introduction to theory, institutions, and policy*. Greenwood Publishing Group.

von Neumann, J., & Morgenstern, O. (1947). *Theory of games and economic behavior* (2nd ed.). Princeton University Press.

Vorhies, F., & Glahe, F. (1988). Political liberty and development: An empirical investigation. *Public Choice, 58*(1), 45–71.

Walras, L. (1954 [1874]). *Elements of pure economics*. London: George Allen and Unwin.

Waltz, K. N. (1979). *Theory of international politics*. McGraw-Hill.

Ward, B. (1976). Foreword. In M. U. Haq (Ed.), *The poverty curtain, choice for the third world*. New York: Columbia University Press.

Warnock, M. (2003). Introduction. In M. Warnock (Ed.), *Utilitarianism and on liberty (including Mill's 'Essay on Bentham' and selections from the writings of Jeremy Bentham and John Austin)* (2nd ed., pp. 1–16). Blackwell Publishing.

Waters, W. A. (1988). Social economics: A solidarist perspective. *Review of Social Economy, 46*(2), 113–143.

Weber, M. (2001[1930]). *The protestant ethic and the spirit of capitalism*. (T. Parsons, Trans.) London and New York: Routledge.

Weintraub, E. R. (2002). *How economics became a mathematical science*. Duke University Press.

Wilber, C. K. (2004). Ethics and social economics: ASE presidential address, January 2004, San Diego, California. *Review of Social Economy, 62*(4), 425–439.

Wilber, C. K. (2010). Economics and ethics. In C. K. Wilber & A. K. Dutt (Eds.), *New directions in development ethics: Essays in honor of Denis Goulet* (pp. 157–176). University of Notre Dame.

Wilber, C. K., & Dutt, A. K. (Eds.). (2010). *New directions in development ethics: Essays in honor of Denis Goulet*. University of Notre Dame.

Williams, B. (2006). *Ethics and the limits of philosophy*. Routledge.

Williamson, J. (1990a). What Washington means by policy reform. In J. Williamson (Ed.), *Latin American adjustment: How much has happened? (Chapter 2)*. Washington, DC: Institute for International Economics. Republished online (November, 2002). http://www.iie.com/publications/papers/paper.cfm?researchid=486

Williamson, J. (Ed.). (1990b). *Latin American adjustment: How much has happened?* Institute for International Economics.

Williamson, J. (1990b). *The progress of policy reform in Latin America* (Vols. Policy Analyses in International Economics, 28). Washington, DC: Institute for International Economics.

Williamson, J. (1993). Democracy and the 'Washington consensus.' *World Development, 21*(8), 1329–1336.

Williamson, J. (2000). What should the World Bank think about the Washington Consensus? *The World Bank Research Observer, 15*(2), 251–264.

Williamson, J. (2007). Shock therapy and the Washington consensus: A comment. *Comparative Economic Studies, 49*(1), 59–60.

Williamson, J. (2002). *Did the Washington consensus fail*? Outline of remarks at the Center for Strategic & International Studies, November 6 (pp. 1–4).

Wright, J. (2003). *The ethics of economic rationalism*. University of New South Wales.

Yeager, L. B. (2001). *Ethics as social science: The moral philosophy of social cooperation*. Edward Elgar.

Index

N. Astroulakis and N. Karagiannis, *Development Ethics*,
https://doi.org/10.1007/978-3-031-75476-0

SPRINGER NATURE

GPSR Compliance

The European Union's (EU) General Product Safety Regulation (GPSR) is a set of rules that requires consumer products to be safe and our obligations to ensure this.

If you have any concerns about our products, you can contact us on ProductSafety@springernature.com

In case Publisher is established outside the EU, the EU authorized representative is:

Springer Nature Customer Service Center GmbH
Europaplatz 3
69115 Heidelberg, Germany

The manufacturer's authorised representative in the EU is Springer Nature Customer Service Centre GmbH, Europaplatz 3, 69115 Heidelberg, Germany. If you have any concerns regarding our products, please contact ProductSafety@springernature.com

Printed and bound by CPI Group (UK) Ltd, Croydon, CR0 4YY
30/09/2026
02225565-0011